OUTWARD BOUND USA

OUTWARD BOUND USA

Crew Not Passengers

Joshua L. Miner

and Joe Boldt

With additional material by Madeleine Eno and Katharine Wroth
Foreword by Rev. William Sloane Coffin

Second Edition
The Mountaineers Books
Seattle

THE MOUNTAINEERS BOOKS

Published by
The Mountaineers Books
1001 SW Klickitat Way, Suite 201
Seattle, WA 98134

Printed in the United States of America

Acquiring Editor: Cassandra Conyers
Editor: Andrea Jarvela, Watershed Books
Contributing Editors: Madeleine Eno, Christian Kallen, Katharine Wroth
Front cover design: Ani Rucki
Book design: Constance Bollen, Watershed Books
Jacket composition: Constance Bollen, Watershed Books

Photographs courtesy of Chris Brown, Kim Budd, Colorado Outward Bound School, Andrew Dalrymple, Frederick Fuller, Cobi Harris, Brian Litz, Jeremy Lucke, Ty Milford, Outward Bound Archives, Pacific Crest Outward Bound School, Sanford Schulwolf, Mark Zelinski, and Michael Vladeck

Cover photograph: Photo © Mark Zelinski, www.markzelinski.com
Title page photograph: *Backpacker in silhouette amid the rock cathedrals of California's High Sierra.* (Photo © Michael Vladeck)

Library of Congress Cataloging-in-Publication Data
Miner, Joshua L.
  Outward Bound USA : crew not passengers / Joshua Miner and Joe
Boldt.—2nd ed.
    p. cm.
Rev. ed. of: Outward Bound U.S.A. 1st ed. 1981.
Includes bibliographical references and index.
  ISBN 0-89886-830-0 (hardcover)—ISBN 0-89886-874-2 (pbk.)
  1. Outward Bound, Inc.—History. 2. Outward bound schools—United
States. I. Boldt, Joseph R. II. Miner, Joshua L. Outward Bound U.S.A.
III. Title.
  GV200.53 .M56 2002
  371.3'84'0973—dc21
                                      2002013883

TO

THE MEMORY OF KURT HAHN

Kurt Hahn, founder of the Outward Bound philosophy.
(Photo by Frederick Fuller, courtesy Kurt Hahn Organization)

CONTENTS

Backpacking across Joshua Tree National Park. (Photo © PCOBS, Kim Budd)

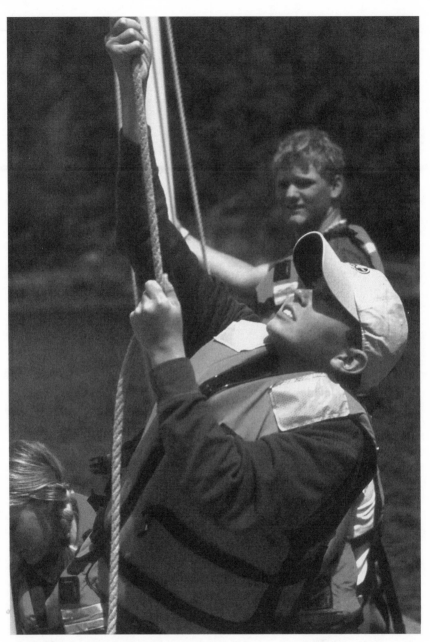

Young Outward Bound students learn the ropes on a Puget Sound longboat sailing course in Washington State. (Photo © Andrew Dalrymple)

OUTWARD BOUND:
THE PASSION OF COMPASSION

by William Sloane Coffin

I 'll never forget Kurt Hahn. We met in July 1961 in a small London office. I knew he was the founder of Outward Bound and had heard that he was seventy-five years old. What surprised me was to see him still so physically fit and to feel his powerful sense of purpose. He came straight to the point. "Mr. Coffin, you are looking at an old man in a hurry. Your educational system in America is as bad as Britain's. There, as here, individuals are being nurtured and humored regardless of the interests of the community. I consider an individual a moral cripple if he is not qualified by education to give his humanity to those who need his service."

Forty years later, his words continue to be on target. Clearly today the greatest threats to our endangered planet and fragile democracies come not from the poor and ignorant, for whom education is the answer, but rather from the well-educated, for whom self-interest is the problem.

For this reason I continue to look to Outward Bound, which, with Hahn, I consider to be essentially a moral enterprise. The journalist Nicholas von Hoffman once observed that when people get active they get the feeling they count. Outward Bound tries hard to save people from the misery of their unimportance, but wants them to count for others as well as for themselves. Outward Bound's chief passion is compassion, its strength to develop the capacity to face squarely and to overcome calmly all manner of adversity.

It is a deep belief of Outward Bound that values are more caught than taught. They are experienced concretely rather than taught abstractly. Thus, for instance, if the makeup of an Outward Bound training group crosses racial, class, and even national lines, its members by training's end will have learned to celebrate, rather than fear, their differences.

Unabashedly, Outward Bound embraces adventure. Youth hungers for it; they long to be tested, to prove their reserves. To pit them against nature makes sense, for most of them know little about nature, and in the course of their training they come to respect and cherish it. It's scary to be in a small boat among large waves, to scale a rock face somewhere between earth and sky, and to be sent alone into the wild for twenty-four hours. (Said one trainee: "I realized I would have to pay a call on myself and I was afraid no one would be at home.")

These adventures are designed for people to compete against themselves, not against each other. Kurt Hahn hoped to develop "a sense of conquest without the humiliation of the conquered." His aim was to develop people through performance, not to make expert performers out of people. And as all Outward Bound activities—with the exception of the solo expedition—are conducted with others on whom they have to depend, the trainees are caught up in the spirit of "all for one and one for all."

Inevitably, the weakest part of such a highly charged program is the follow-up, how to translate the Outward Bound excitement into the more humdrum experience of everyday life, be that life on the streets of an inner city, in offices and boardrooms, or in the corridors of political power. "By their fruits ye shall know them." How fine it would be to say of Outward Bound graduates, "They earn their livelihood by helping others."

I hope that the national board and directors of Outward Bound will be disposed to accord the follow-up the profound concern it deserves, helped perhaps by lessons learned from the exciting new urban training centers. And I have an additional hope: that one man who certainly did earn his livelihood by helping others will be remembered as long as there is an Outward Bound in America.

A "circle up" provides the opportunity for self-evaluation, team-building, and reflection on the day's activities with Outward Bound. (Photo © Cobi Harris)

After leaving Kurt Hahn and visiting the British Outward Bound schools at Aberdovey and Eskdale, I flew home to help Joshua Miner found, in a Puerto Rican rain forest, the first Outward Bound school in America. It was designed to be a capstone training experience for the volunteers of the newly formed Peace Corps, organized and led brilliantly by Sargent Shriver.

Joshua Miner was the most spirited, cheerful colleague I ever worked with. His vitality was colossal, his enthusiasm infectious. He went on to found one Outward Bound school after another, with graduates now totaling 750,000. For the last forty years he has been the standard bearer and chief inspiration of Outward Bound in America, and often well beyond our borders. A world-class visionary like his mentor, Kurt Hahn, Josh was always in a hurry to inject more life into countless other lives through the generous power of his own. I had the privilege to preside over his memorial service when he died at the age of eighty-one on January 29, 2002.

God bless you, Josh. May we not fail to further your highest hopes.

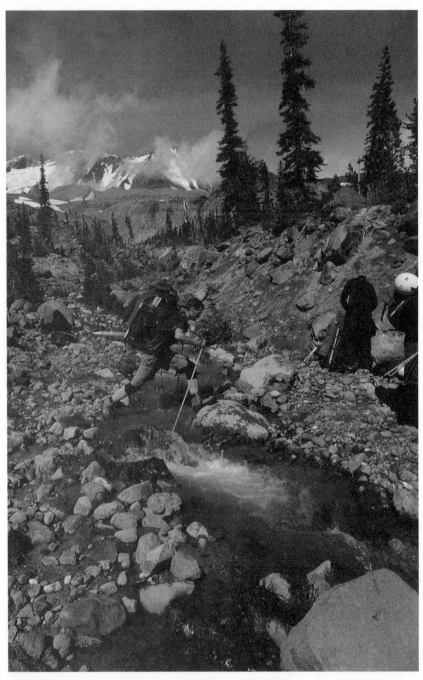

Crossing an alpine stream on the flanks of Mount Adams in Washington State. (Photo © Cobi Harris)

SCOTTISH JOURNEY

❊

My heart's in the Highlands, wherever I go . . .
The birthplace of valor, the country of worth,
Wherever I wander, wherever I rove,
The hills of the Highlands forever I love.

—Robert Burns

From Glasgow north to the Moray Firth is one hundred twenty miles "as the craw flees." By rail, it's a fair piece more. I had been warned that the train stopped in every field to see if the hay was ripe. In June 1950 the journey consumed seven hours.

The train swung around northwestward into the valley of the Tay, following the river upstream. The country grew wilder, the station names more wonderfully Scottish. Dunkeld. Pitlochry. Through the Pass of Killiecrankie, to where the headwaters of the Carry and the Spey nearly touched, the one stream flowing southward, the other north.

Some thirty hours earlier, I had taken off from New York's Idlewild Airport. Fourteen hours later—3 A.M. in Princeton, New Jersey—the prop-driven Constellation aircraft had put down at Prestwick. Then courteous, burred questioning at customs and a one-and-a-half-hour bus ride to Glasgow. The telephone call to Gordonstoun, with Mr. Hahn's puzzling instruction not to buy a ticket through to Forres, the stop closest to my destination. Instead I was to get off a full hour sooner, at Aviemore.

In league now with the Spey as it flowed to the North Sea, the train called more on brakes than power. The wild moors merged with the mountains, the ancient rugged Cairngorms.

Thirty hours out of Idlewild Airport, with little sleep, I dozed off and on. Though I no longer directly remember the reverie of that journey, I can recall its sense. Uncertain of what lay ahead, I reflected on whence I came. The day's stream of consciousness comes back, thirty years later, as a kind of internal slide show—image succeeding image on an interior screen.

We can skip lightly over the early scenes. A youngster growing toward adolescence in an American suburb amid the certainties of the 1920s; the snug family suddenly buffeted by the Great Depression, improvising its defenses, wondering where the certainties had gone. In my high school junior year I won a scholarship to a school named Exeter. I was an enthusiastic, curious kid, fooling around with radio in a time when kits did not yet exist, when I could not get the printed information I needed, when I could not get questions answered. At my new school I was told I would find people who knew an awful lot, and it was difficult to wait to have them answer my questions.

But at Exeter nobody had time for those questions. Too busy teaching me what they thought I ought to know, they paid scant attention to my own innate curiosity. My preparatory school record was not distinguished.

As a college student, I was still out of synch with the educational establishment. At Princeton I flunked out—twice. Technically, I did not flunk out that second time, at the end of my junior year, because I did not give them the chance. It was six months after Pearl Harbor, and when I was supposed to be sitting in the big examination halls, scribbling in a blue-covered book, I was on Staten Island, standing naked in line for hours, enlisting in the United States Army. At Fort Dix I heard someone say you must have an IQ of 120 to qualify for officer candidate school. IQ! Maybe that had been my trouble all along. A panic-stricken youngster in a phone booth, I called a girl I'd dated at Princeton who worked in the dean's office. "Get my folder out and see what my IQ is and call me right back."

The 696th Armored Field Artillery Battalion of Patton's Third Army, in which I served as forward observer, landed on Utah Beach on D-Day-plus-26.

A group of early Outward Bound students participate in the "run and dip" exercise at the basecamp in Marble, Colorado. (Photo courtesy COBS)

From there it was a long trek—the breakthrough at St. Lô, Coutances, and Avranches; the Battle of the Bulge, the relief of Bastogne; Holland; across the Rhine, across the Elbe. VE Day found us forty-five miles from Berlin, swapping stories with the Russians. In February 1946, I was honorably discharged.

The same classrooms, the same lecture halls, the same courses—and a whole new world. In Princeton's McCosh 10 the day's lecture ended, the huge class rose and flooded out the exits. I was elbowing my way down the center aisle against the stream to get at that silly fool on the platform gathering up his notes. I pounded on the floor at his feet: "What in the name of the Lord were you trying to tell us? If you can't do better than that, I've got to get out of this course. I'm twenty-six years old, I can't be wasting my time here!" One or two other veterans joined me. Together we nailed the poor devil to the wall, and that ten o'clock lecture was not over until midafternoon.

We were a subgeneration that had come back full of questions, hungry for meaningful answers. I was taking courses and on paths of inquiry I had never before dared. At Exeter a failure in American history had cost me my diploma, but now I found I could do history as readily as my "good" courses like math and physics. In my economics major I dug into the history of economic thought, the lives of the economists themselves. I was enjoying courses in philosophy and art and music composition. I was suddenly aware of how ignorant I was, alive with curiosity, doing academic work at a level I would not have thought possible a few years before. I did not know it yet, but I was learning the basic educational fact of life: the answers are meaningless until the questions are asked.

To eke out my GI scholarship income, I took on a job at the Hun School, a small boarding school for boys located in the town of Princeton. At first I was a sort of preserver of law and order and tutor. Mike Morgan, on the university staff, had said I could have the job on one condition: "Promise me you'll never go into education." I told him, "Couldn't be further from my mind."

The Hun students were mostly combat veterans, as anxious to get their high school diplomas as I was to get mine from the university. We were a tight group. We spoke the same language, had the same reference, had been through it together. Every night they sprawled on the floor of my room, struggling with math or physics or chemistry. These were things I could help them with. Sometimes they had no money to pay the school a bill, and I said, "Hell, you can work it off," and they paid by doing some painting or plastering or glazing that the school needed.

I had been having such fun with these guys, and working so hard at my own courses, that I had not done much thinking about a career after graduation. Bob McAllen, who had taken over as headmaster, said, "Why don't you stay on here and teach?" I said, "Great—I'd love it." I was to teach algebra and physics, do some coaching, and help with administration. In June 1947 I graduated from Princeton cum laude in my major, and I married Phebe Stevens.

In that time the Hun School was a great place for a young educator to learn about education and about operating a school. Within three years the school had four headmasters, and I was helping to break in each in turn. I was doing everything from teaching to coaching to balancing the books, hiring teachers, firing kids, dealing with trustees, dealing with accreditation authorities. We had needed a history teacher, and over at Princeton I found a graduate student named Tom Hartmann. Tom and I became partners. We swapped every job in the school. You be dean, I'll be director of studies. You be treasurer, and I'll be in charge of grounds and buildings. You be director of admissions, and I'll be director of athletics. You be varsity baseball coach, and I'll be development officer. We bought the supplies and the food. We emptied our savings accounts to pay bills to keep the merchants off our backs. And all the time we were counseling with parents who had problems with their kids, and with kids who had problems with their parents.

The school plant was a former private estate. There was not enough money for upkeep of the grounds and buildings and equipment. From the precedent of letting the veterans work off a bill came the idea of giving the kids varsity letters for doing work—cutting the lawns, painting, floor waxing, plumbing, and so on. You could not tell a football player's letter from the one a truck-engine specialist was wearing. The football players looked down their noses a little, but how envious they were of the kid driving the three-gang power mower!

One day in the spring of 1950 my father-in-law came to see me. Jack Stevens was a businessman with a lively interest in hopeful things that were happening in the world, and quite often he got involved in fund-raising for one or another cause.

He told me "Josh, some friends of mine have asked me to help raise money for the work being done by a German headmaster of a school in Scotland. One of these friends is Peggy Douglas, whose husband, Lewis Douglas, is our ambassador to Great Britain, and another is her sister Ellen McCloy, whose husband, John McCloy, is American Allied High Commissioner of Germany. They think that this man can have a helpful influence on postwar Germany. His name is Kurt Hahn. Just what he is up to I can't tell you. He seems to be involved in several different projects—his

Gordonstoun School in Scotland, some other schools on the continent, and some kind of an outdoor and rescue training school. My friends say the things he's doing are extremely worthwhile. I asked them if they've ever had an American schoolteacher look at his work, and they asked me if I knew one, and I said I might just. How would you like to go over and take a look at this, and write a report on it?"

"I'd like it," I said.

■ ■ ■

The train rolled on, following the Spey down through the mountains. Studying my map, I wondered again why Mr. Hahn had instructed me to get off at Aviemore, fifty miles short of the northern coast where the Gordonstoun School was located. The "ticket inspector" leaned into the compartment. "Aviemore!" I gathered my baggage. In another minute the train puffed to a stop, and I stepped down to the platform. I was thirty years old. I had no notion that I was keeping a rendezvous with the rest of my life.

GORDONSTOUN

❊

Plus Est en Vous.
(You've got more in you than you think.)

—The Gordonstoun school motto,
found on the wall of a Belgian church

Whoever was to meet me apparently had not arrived, for the only vehicle in sight was a London taxicab. My musing that this vehicle made no sense in the middle of the Scottish Highlands was interrupted by a man who came up and introduced himself. He was Hunter, Mr. Hahn's driver. The London taxi was Mr. Hahn's car. It was a standard black Austin model, with glass separating the driver and passenger compartments. I sat in front with Hunter, who explained that Mr. Hahn had arranged for me to proceed from Aviemore by automobile the better to see the countryside that lay between us and the coast. In particular, Mr. Hahn wanted me to experience "the evening light." Hunter was to get me out of the car at various points, the better to enjoy the vistas in the evening light.

It was a glory ride for all time—knee-high purple heather, riots of yellow broom. As we left the Cairngorms behind, the moors stretched endlessly, the sky grew bigger, the clouds more enormous. Pushing northward through Forres, we swung a bit to the east.

> *How far is't called to Forres? What are these*
> *So wither'd, and wild in their attire,*

That look not like the inhabitants of the earth,
And yet are on't?

These moors were Macbeth's blasted heath—and had Hunter called on my credulity, I could readily have believed that somewhere in this wild terrain the three witches still laid their choppy fingers upon their skinny lips.

The long twilight had only just set in when we arrived at Gordonstoun at 9:30. I had a sense of old buildings and long-tended landscaping, then the incongruity of several quonset huts. Hunter deposited me at the door of the main building where a student was awaiting my arrival. Shorts, knee-length socks, an open-necked shirt, and a wool sweater, all the same powder-blue color—I had never seen a school uniform before.

Hunter and the London taxi bore my luggage off to the guest house. My spirits drooped as I realized I was to have no chance to change. I was travel-weary, hungry, dirty, unshaved, my eyes bloodshot, my clothes rumpled. I had scarcely slept in thirty-six hours. On the forays from the car to view the evening light, my feet had got wet. I was cold, the chill of the north Scottish night cutting through the thin fabric of my summer suit.

I was led inside and up a wide, highly polished central staircase. The student informed me that this was Gordonstoun House, which had once been a castle, and that it was more than three centuries old. Creaking stairs, antiquity, and the pungent smell of floor wax. On the second floor the student knocked on a door. As it opened and I entered, Kurt Hahn shook my hand. I would learn not to be disconcerted by that trait of a silent greeting that let the smile express it all—recognition, welcome, kindliness. But in the moment of meeting I found my host a bit daunting. He was a big man of perhaps sixty years, great shoulders somewhat stooped, big hand giving a firm grip. Partial baldness called attention to the massive skull that suggested an equally massive brain. Large features and ears, the complexion startlingly soft and pink, deep-set eyes with their full, live gaze. The mouth, smiling now, that through some infinitesimal reflex could go instantly from stern to amused and back. An extraordinary face, with experience, wisdom, and goodwill in the expression.

His first words were, "But, my good man, you must be tired. You must sit down immediately."

I was quickly made aware of his omnivorous curiosity about people. Abetted by the three elderly ladies who were dining with him, he simultaneously plied me with questions and bade me eat. By the end of the meal he knew a great deal about me and my family. I remember well that I was cold—particularly that my feet were cold and damp—because of an incident during the meal. The student who had greeted me entered and spoke to Hahn. This was Humphrey Taylor, he told me, and if I would step out in the hall, Humphrey had something for me. What young Humphrey had was a pair of my dry wool socks. I had no idea how the boy had received the word to fetch those socks. Nor did I realize that the fetching had required a four-mile round trip by bicycle to go to the guest house and extract the socks from my luggage. Humphrey informed me that he was the Helper of Guests. That was his post in the student hierarchy.

That evening and my whole first week at Gordonstoun tend to blur in memory, parts coming in and out of focus. Arriving on Monday, I was kept so busy that I had no chance to write home until late Thursday night. Phebe still has that letter, and passages in it help my recall.

Breakfast at Burnside—a delightful and picturesque Scotch farm which is the guest house—9 a.m. chat with Hahn. Morning with Mr. Sime, old boy and currently farm manager and chemistry teacher. Lunch with Hahn. Afternoon spent with 15-year-old Humphrey Taylor—delightful boy-guided tour of school . . .

Why did Hahn pick Ian Sime, that first morning, to introduce me to the academic side of the school? In part, for sure, because he was a Gordonstoun old boy. Was it also because he was a very direct, outspoken young fellow, with sharp opinions of how Hahn was not running things efficiently, of colleagues who were not pulling their oar, of the shortcomings of Americans? Sime showed me his chemistry laboratories, located in one of the "naffies"—what I called a quonset hut. Gordonstoun had been taken over by the army during the war, and the school was still utilizing names the military had left behind. The labs were primitive, but sound.

Joshua L. Miner III, founder of Outward Bound USA. (Photo courtesy Outward Bound USA)

After lunch Humphrey Taylor gave me a good look at the school through a student's eyes. Humphrey told me about the Training Plan, which was the foundation of an elaborate system of student responsibility. It was a checkoff list of each student's daily routine, starting with the morning run, cold shower, and room chores, and so on through doing of assignments, promptness for class, writing home, bedtime teeth brushing. Once a student was judged ready to be responsible for himself, he made his own daily checkoff and carried out his own penalties for such infractions as being late for class. The prescribed penalty for lateness and other infractions was to get up early for an extra long run. I asked Humphrey why, since nobody checked on him, he didn't just skip doing his "lates," as he called them.

"Come on, Humphrey," I said. "I would."

Humphrey smiled. "I used to," he said. "But I got tired of lying to myself." That sold me. I didn't know if the Training Plan would work in an American school, but it was working here.

. . . Supper with Hahn + 8 foreign students—Belgian, French, Dane, Norwegian, + 4 Germans from Salem. I read Ivanhoe *out loud after supper. Followed by private talk with Hahn.*

One of Kurt Hahn's ideals for Gordonstoun was that the student body should have a strong international mix. Among his overriding concerns as an educator, and philosophically as a world citizen, was that people, retaining love of country, should rise above the constraints of nationalism. When did American schools stop reading Scott? *Ivanhoe* was new to me. Hahn, I am sure, knew it as a boy in German.

Breakfast at 7 with Hahn—then off to the Moray Sea School— a new short course school located at Burghead (see map—due west). They were taking the final expeditionary endurance test of the course. What an experience! Home at midnight. Dead to the world!

The Moray Sea School was my first exposure to Outward Bound. No one called it that, however; I had not yet heard the name. Hahn and others simply referred to it as the short-term school. They explained to me that boys ages fourteen and a half to eighteen came here for a twenty-eight-day course that was physically rugged and challenging, and in a general way I gathered that the purpose of the school was character building. Most of the boys were apprentices sent by industry, some were police cadets. A few were from correctional institutions or had been referred by social agencies.

That day, the next-to-last of the course, the boys were doing a final cross-country endurance test—roughly comparable to the final-day marathon in the U.S. Outward Bound schools today. Divided by age into groups of six, they had to travel cross country, with the aid of map and compass, through a series of checkpoints in the moor wilderness. This was a difficult test in land navigation, for it is easy to get lost in the moors. The terrain has no landmarks, and the boys had to travel around boggy areas. The distance was twenty-eight miles for the oldest group and ranged down to twenty-two for the youngest, and they were to travel as rapidly as they could without breaking up the group.

These were youngsters from more or less disadvantaged backgrounds, who had been born in the Depression years and grown while undergoing the privations of World War II. Their postwar, still-rationed diets had not enabled them to recover from a poor start. They were scrawny, undersize—and wiry. It was a real eye-opener that they could cover twenty-eight miles in a day, under pressure. I had never seen anything like it with boys in the States. Sure, I had done a fourteen-mile hike, but that was tame compared to this.

Breakfast at Burnside at 8:30 and talk with Hahn at 9:15—10:00 off to Sea School with Guggenheim to witness the final test in seamanship. Spent 3 hours in sailing cutter—delightful.

O. A. Guggenheim and his wife were fellow visitors staying at the guest house. They had a son in the school. Of Swiss extraction, the father was a textile manufacturer who had spent most of his life in India. His son, he told me, was no great shakes as a scholar, but Hahn was discovering the boy's attributes. He had been made head of the Cliff Watchers Rescue Service. Impressed by Hahn's educational ideas, Guggenheim was becoming his close friend and ally. He informed me he was a director of the new mountain rescue school. I had no idea what that was.

The students at the Moray Sea School were formed in groups of twelve, called watches. Each watch manned a two-masted sailing cutter about thirty-four feet in length. We looked on as the crews were put through a rigorous sequence of seamanship exercises. Four weeks earlier most of these lads had never been in a sailboat. Now I marveled at their deft teamwork in handling their craft.

Spent afternoon writh Hahn and the Guggenheims witnessing the Gordonstoun sea rescue group work with a breeches buoy.

A mile or so from Gordonstoun is the Firth of Moray. Running along the coast are precipitous cliffs, two hundred to four hundred feet high. The prevailing winds are northerly—this is a lee shore, strewn with rocky shoals—and at their base the cliffs have been scooped out by the sea. Above, you can lie with your head projecting over the edge and look straight down at the pounding surf. It is a gut-qualming sight.

Here, before and during the early days of World War II, the Gordonstoun Cliff Watchers, functioning as an auxiliary of His Majesty's Coastguard, stood watch for ships in distress and enemy submarine activity. After the school returned from its wartime quarters in Wales, the Watchers were reactivated. In fog and foul weather, students maintained a vigilant watch around the clock "lest," in the phrase Hahn had happily appropriated from the Coastguard manual, "a ship burn an inefficient flare."

The Cliff Watchers were organized into two rescue groups, a breeches-buoy team, and a cliff-ladder evacuation team. On the day of my visit the breeches-buoy team drove their lorry, laden with standard Coastguard equipment, to the cliff and carried out a rescue exercise. We looked on as they set up a rocket launcher and fired a line out to a small, rocky offshore island. With this line a group on the island hauled out a strong rope and secured it to a masonry ruin, perhaps the remains of an ancient lighthouse, which simulated a shipwreck. At the cliff top the rope was run over a tripod and anchored in the ground. When all was secured, the breeches buoy was suspended from a pulley that ran back and forth on the rope. The buoy consisted of a cork ring with canvas breeches attached, designed so that the person being rescued could sit in the ring with legs through the breeches. Lines attached to the buoy were used to pull it in either direction. I watched, fascinated. I had never seen anything like this either. The boys knew exactly what they were doing, and they did it with dispatch. One had no doubt that were a wreck, in fact, out there, these boys would be competently saving lives.

As we hiked back through the gorse and broom, Hahn told me how the Watchers got started. He had learned about St. Gernadius, an eighth-century Irish monk who once lived in a cave in the area and on stormy nights walked the rocky shoreline, waving a lantern to warn fishermen of rocks and shoals. Hoping to enthuse the students for coast watching, he recited the monk's story. "I had a bad reception," he said. "I saw in their eyes the look of mistrust that meant, 'The old man wants to save our souls.'" He looked at me, a smile touching the corners of his mouth. "The young, you know, are allergic to the manifest improvers."

Then the Coastguard, who had heard of Hahn's interest, sent two officers with an offer: if the school would build and man a lookout hut, the Coastguard would equip it and give the volunteers auxiliary status. Summoning the school, Hahn had the officers make their request directly to the students, who gave enthusiastic assent.

Hahn gave me another of those looks and drew the moral. "There are three ways of trying to win the young. You can preach at them, that is a hook without a worm. You can say, 'You must volunteer,' that is of the devil. And you can tell them, 'You are needed.' That appeal hardly ever fails."

. . . dinner with Mr. and Mrs. Chew, who is activities director and housemaster of Duffus House. Very attractive and competent.

As director of activities, Bobby Chew was one of the school's most important people. Hahn had a unique idea of what a school's staff structure should be. Under the headmaster were two men of equal rank—a director of studies and a director of activities. One was responsible for the curricular program, the other for everything that did not take place in the classroom, which at Gordonstoun was a broad gamut. Hahn made the two posts equal because he felt the school should pay equal attention to the academic and nonacademic sides of a youngster's development. When one program encroached on the other, the other was expected to fight back; Hahn relished that seesaw tension between his two lieutenants. Chew had taught at Salem, Hahn's school in Germany in the 1920s. In World War II he had been a colonel in the British commandos. His lovely Norwegian wife, Eva, was the widow of a Norwegian fellow commando and friend who had been killed in the line of duty.

Chew's opposite number as director of studies was Henry Brereton, a fine scholar and innovative educator who had held the post virtually from Gordonstoun's beginning. Since he and Chew had great respect for each other, and both were intensely loyal to Hahn, the school's top administrative structure was solid.

Hahn is extremely unique. What a personality. What drive! What energy! What vision! At 64 he is an excellent cricketer, tennis player, and beats all up and down stairs and hills alike. He has that amazing faculty for broad vision and the most minute detail! Astounding memory. Quite terrifying except that he always inspires anyone to his very best, at the same time somehow preventing you from saying and doing the wrong thing and in general putting your foot in your mouth. He is extremely busy. I am grateful for every 2 minutes with him and try to make the most of them. He's on the go every minute—can't sit still a second. Makes at least 4 telephone calls during any meal and the boys say he can run 3 dinner parties at a time, hopping from room to room. He is loved, admired, respected, and feared by boys and faculty alike. They never know what he will do next. He's always doing something and keeps them in same state.

How avid I was for each few minutes of Hahn's time! I was so full of questions, and each day they piled higher. The morning encounters that started my day were frustratingly short—little more than time enough for him to brief me on my always-full schedule for the day. But at night, toward bedtime, he would say, "We must go see the wonderful light of the evening." He would summon the ever-ready Hunter, and off we would go in the London taxi, perhaps along the coast, or to someplace like Cawdor Castle. Then we would get out and walk two or three miles. On these occasions I had my best chance to get him to talk about himself and his ideas.

Even that time had to be shared with his consuming desire to know about me. I was the subject of relentless questioning—and not just about myself. I was beginning to find out that Hahn learned about people by learning about their family. He would want to know where your mother was born, how she happened to meet your father, where they lived, and what your father did. Even more important, what did your mother do? "And tell me about your grandmothers—I am the world's greatest collector of grandmothers." When he was through with that generation, he would switch to one's mother-in-law—"I am president of the Benevolent Association for the Protection of Mothers-in-law"—then your brothers and sisters. I was to learn that every acquaintance Hahn made was subjected to this line of inquiry. It was the way he came to know every student, and he retained it all. Through the years, when he wrote, when he telephoned, he would ask about my mother, my wife's mother, my brothers, my sisters-in-law, our children, our dog. His power of recall was astounding.

Strangely, despite the relentless questioning one never felt under pressure. He had a way of putting you at ease so that your answers flowed. You found yourself being more articulate than at any time in your life. I would always feel he brought out the best in me.

So Hahn knew all about me long before I learned his story. But then, I had a great deal more to learn.

HAHN

✳

*Eccentric perhaps, innovator certainly, great
beyond doubt.*

—HRH The Duke of Edinburgh

*Kurt Hahn, who often appears so Victorian in
manners and language, belongs in a deep
sense to the new age of hope. Like the great
artists and scientists, like the astronauts, he is
a citizen of global mankind.*

—Henry Brereton

Rowing bareheaded on a blazing hot day in his nineteenth year, Kurt Hahn suffered a severe sunstroke. The injury, centering at the cerebellum, where the spine joins the base of the brain, threatened to cripple him. To ease his suffering he spent a year in a darkened room. Periodically thereafter—"despair stalking him like a sinister shadow," as Henry Brereton has written—the affliction returned in full force, casting him back into the dark. Even after a great London neurosurgeon performed a series of brain-decompressing operations that helped him greatly, light and heat remained his lifelong torment.

In those lonely ordeals of his young manhood he was working out a life principle that years later a remarkable physical educator would articulate and

Hahn would make his leitmotiv: "Your disability is your opportunity." To make his confinement productive, he devised regimens of physical activity and disciplined thought. He practiced the standing high jump—scarcely to the delight of the Oxford students living beneath him—and the legend is that he broke records in that event. With the study of Plato's *Republic* fresh in his mind he conceived a new kind of school, where the worlds of thought and action would no longer be divided into hostile camps. Later he wrote out the concept and put it away for future reference.

Hahn was born into a cultured Jewish family in Berlin in 1886. His father was a successful industrialist. His mother was a beautiful woman of artistic temperament and powerful faith in the innate goodness of man. One of her forebears was Jecheskiel Landau, Chief Rabbi of Prague in the eighteenth century, whose writings on the Talmud are still taught at academies of Jewish studies. His grandmother on his mother's side was his adored "Anschulka," whose wise and droll sayings he noted down in a book. ("Anschulka, which of your eight children is the best?" "A mother is like a shopkeeper—she has various kinds of goods.") The home in which he grew up, radiating human warmth, was a gathering place for the city's intelligentsia and artists.

His father, enamored of England, built the family summer residence, Wannsee, in English country-house style. Kurt, the eldest of three sons, was a born teacher. In the summers at Wannsee he would gather the young people in the pavilion and read them tales of heroic adventure. Often he led them on long hikes over rough terrain. At Gottingen, one of several German universities he attended, his Greek professor told him, "If you are interested in the old in order to help the new, it is not the German universities that can help you, but Oxford." He studied at Oxford from 1910 to 1914. On August 1, 1914, he took leave of his English friends to return home. Two days later Great Britain declared war on Germany.

In the war Hahn held a succession of minor Foreign Office posts from which he nevertheless emerged as a person of influence. He worked with the moderates—against unrestricted submarine warfare, for a negotiated peace—and became one of their spokesmen. Although his counsel did not prevail, the quality of his work won the attention of persons in high places. He was made adviser to Colonel von Haeften, who was in turn political adviser to General von Ludendorff.

At the war's end Hahn was assistant to Prince Max of Baden, Germany's last imperial chancellor. The prince was a scholarly, humane man who in a speech in 1917 dared to say, "To love your enemy is the sign of those who remain loyal to the Lord even in time of war." The two men shared an enthusiasm for Plato's educational ideas, and in 1920 Prince Max founded a coeducational boarding school with Hahn as headmaster. This was the Salem (shalom, salaam, peace) Schule; it was the school Hahn had conceived seven years before.

The times were, quite literally, fearful. Defeated Germany was on the edge of anarchy. The school thwarted two plots, one by Communists to kidnap Prince Max, another by nationalists to murder Hahn. (Typically, Hahn was more concerned over his would-be assassins' despair for the nation's plight than he was to see them punished.) Guerrilla bands were setting fire to farms. Salem boys joined the night patrols guarding the lonely countryside. It was in that time that William Butler Yeats wrote the lines, so prophetic of the coming European tragedy, that Hahn would come to quote often, a statement of his lifelong concern:

> The best lack all conviction, while the worst
> Are full of passionate intensity.

Yeats was defining the very condition that Prince Max and Hahn had set out to deal with. Through Salem, and by spreading the Salem gospel to other educators, they sought to nurture a German youth with convictions rooted in personal responsibility, kindness, and justice. The intent, in Hahn's words, was to equip young people "to effect what they have recognized to be right, despite hardships, despite dangers, despite inner skepticism, despite boredom, despite mockery from the world, despite emotion of the moment." The school's report to parents, developed at Salem and later used at Gordonstoun, evaluated the degree to which the students displayed these traits.

Hahn was at once a champion and hard taskmaster of youth in its conflicts with the elder generation. If young people were to play an influential

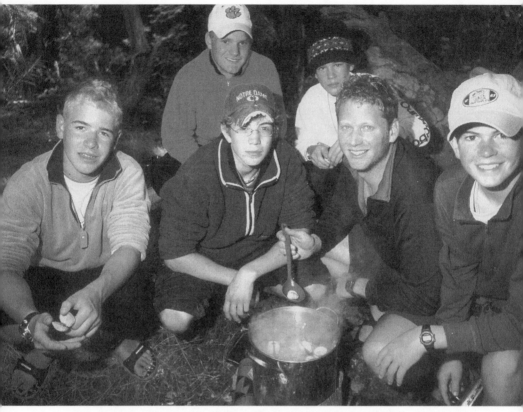

A sailboat crew enjoys fresh camp chowder after a day on the waters of Puget
Sound with Pacific Crest Outward Bound School. (Photo © Andrew Dalrymple)

role in society, he insisted, they must earn the right. Even as he welcomed the
German youth movement of that time, he took sharp issue with indulgent
adult attitudes. Long after I first knew him, in the time of the youth revolt in
England and the United States in the 1960s, it was uncanny to discover that
in Germany in 1928 he had said: "With phrases such as 'Youth Culture' these
people besmear the souls of the young with the ointment of flattery—as
though the young no longer had to become anything, but were everything
already. They rob them of their joy of development and do violence to the
natural process of spiritual growth."

Inevitably, the ideals of Salem clashed with the spirit of Nazism. Apprehensive of the growing strength of Hitler's movement, Hahn stepped up his efforts to win the German educational community over to Salem principles. But the Nazi tide continued to rise. In 1932 five storm troopers trampled a young Communist to death in front of his mother. They were arrested, tried, and condemned to death. In his notorious "Beuthen telegram," Hitler hailed them as comrades and demanded their release. "Your freedom," he said, "is our honor." For Hahn this was in fact the hour when men of honor must declare themselves. He sent a letter to all Salem alumni: "Hitler's telegram has brought on a crisis that goes beyond politics. Germany is at stake, her Christian civilization, her good name, her soldiers' honor. Salem cannot remain neutral. I ask the members of the Salem Union who are active in a S.A. or S.S. to break with Salem or with Hitler." It was, said a Briton who was teaching at Salem at the time, "the bravest deed in cold blood that I have witnessed."

Sir Robert Birley, who was Hahn's contemporary as headmaster of Eton, has given us a record of his courage in the German crisis. Discussing the education provided under Hahn at Salem, Birley wrote:

> But there was a second element quite as important. It was impressively expressed in an address Kurt Hahn gave in Hamburg on 16 February 1933. (The significance of the date, seventeen days after the Nazis gained power, will be obvious.) It began with a study of the Fascist state and educational ideals, and an account of Fascism which seems to make inevitable the uncomfortable statement which is to be found in the address, that, if one looked at the educational principles of the Italian youth organizations, "you find that you might be quoting the whole Salem Certificate of Maturity with its capacity to endure hardships, to face dangers, a talent for organization, prudence, a fighting spirit, presence of mind, success in dealing with unexpected difficulties"—and then come the words, "Only one item is and must be missing: The power of carrying out what is recognized to be just." And a little later, "Sacro egoismo, sacred egoism. There is also sacred lying, sacred killing, sacred perjury, sacred breaking of promises." To speak in

this way of Fascist principles at that moment was indeed coura-
geous, but Kurt Hahn went on to turn to his own country, and it
was with continual references to the state of things in Germany
that he gave his reasons why Salem rejected Fascist education.
Among these was to be found this one: "We need to be able to feel
that as a people we are just and kindly. On this consciousness
depends our inner strength."

Hahn became a marked man. In the mass arrests following the Reichstag fire in February 1933, he was jailed. The shock waves swiftly reached Britain, where his friends—some from the Oxford days, others gained as Salem's fame had spread—took up his cause. When Prime Minister Ramsay MacDonald made official representations, Hahn was let go. In July he left for England.

In those first months of exile he was profoundly depressed. At forty-seven he had lost his homeland, his school, the battle for German youth. A man of means, overnight he had become a nearly penniless refugee. Worse, his spiritual resources were depleted. When he was asked to found a new school along Salem lines, he lacked the will. When he was offered an established school to work with, he said, "I do not have time to overcome the inertia of tradition." Then he returned to Moray, the north of Scotland country where he had spent the convalescent summers of his Oxford years. He met old friends among the fishermen and crofters of the district. On the wharf in Hopeman Harbor, he listened to Captain Danny Main tell tales of men of simple courage against the forces of the sea. With another friend, Lord Malcolm Douglas-Hamilton, he inspected the empty castle at Gordonstoun, badly in need of repair, as a possible site for a school. Its vistas seized his spirit, and he knew again the truth that he would summon so often in guiding others: "Your disability is your opportunity."

Gordonstoun opened as a school for boys in April 1934; by September there were twenty-one students (among them a Greek prince of Danish blood named Philip, who one day would marry the future queen of England). The board of governors included the Archbishop of York, later of Canterbury, the headmaster of Eton, the master of Trinity College at Cambridge, a distinguished British historian, and the future governor-general of Canada. The school's enrollment grew steadily.

In 1938 Hahn became a naturalized British subject. It was in character that even as he struggled to cope with the acute money problems of an expanding, unendowed school, he poured part of his energies into national concerns—alerting the British people to the dimensions of the Hitlerian threat, calling on them to hear the muffled cries from the concentration camps, campaigning at the War Office for a system of training that in months, he declared, could make British infantrymen the equal in stamina, hardihood, and self-confidence of German soldiers whose training had started years before in the Hitler Youth.

War broke out. The British Army commandeered Gordonstoun, and the school had to trek to wartime quarters in Wales. The move was a major disability. In it Hahn found a new opportunity—and brought forth Outward Bound.

Opportunity's name was Lawrence Holt. Hahn had been trying to launch a "County Badge scheme," an ambitious national plan for fostering physical fitness, enterprise, tenacity, and compassion among British youth. But in the wartime climate his prestigious County Badge Experimental Committee—scientist Julian Huxley, historian George Trevelyan, and others—had made small headway. At that same time Holt, a Gordonstoun father and Hahn admirer who was partner in Alfred Holt & Company, a large merchant-shipping enterprise, was gravely concerned about the human toll in the Battle of the Atlantic. He was convinced that due to faulty training, many seamen on torpedoed merchant ships were dying unnecessarily. Unlike sail-trained old-timers, he maintained, the younger men and youths had not acquired a sense of wind and weather, a reliance on their own resources, and a selfless bond with their fellows. "I would rather," he told Hahn, "entrust the lowering of a lifeboat in mid-Atlantic to a sail-trained octogenarian than to a young sea technician who is competently trained in the modern way but has never been sprayed by salt water."

Hahn proposed they join forces to start a new kind of school offering young people one-month courses that would use Hahn's County Badge scheme to implement Holt's quest for training to turn attitudes around. Holt agreed, his company providing funds and the maritime staff members. The school, called Outward Bound at Holt's insistence, opened at Aberdovey, Wales, in 1941. It was not, as the mythologized version has it, a school for young merchant seamen. While many of the students were youngsters sponsored by Holt's Blue Funnel Line and other shipping companies and from the government training ship HMS *Conway*, others were apprentices sent by industry, or police, fire, and other cadets, or boys on leave from their regular schools or about to go into the armed services. It was Holt himself who articulated a Hahnian concept in words Hahn never forgot. "The training at Aberdovey," Holt said, "must be less a training *for* the sea than *through* the sea, and so benefit all walks of life." The month-long course was, in fact, a mix of small-boat training, athletic endeavor to reach standards of competence, cross-country route-finding by map and compass, rescue training, an expedition at sea, a land expedition across three mountain ranges, and service to the local people. The school was fortunate from the outset in two key staff members. Jim Hogan, a resourceful young school-master whom Hahn had recruited from the national educational system to be secretary of his County Badge Experimental Committee, was warden. His assistant in charge of athletic activity was Captain B. Zimmerman, who had been a great innovative physical educator in Germany until he fled his country to avoid Nazi imprisonment. Hahn had brought him from Switzerland to Gordonstoun. It was "Zim" who first exhorted his charges that their liability was their opportunity, who—seizing on Holt's phrase—talked of "training through the body, not of the body," and worked on each student until he could proclaim, "The bug has bit!"

Although beset by a prodigious series of start-up difficulties, Outward Bound worked from the first. The youths who came were the products of Britain's dozen years of depression and dole. Invariably, when they were told what they were expected to achieve in thirty days, murmurs of incredulity and derision ran through the group. But they were soon caught up by "the magic of the puzzle," Hahn's odd phrase for the phenomenon he knew so well—that when a young person "defeats his defeatism" to meet a challenge, it primes him to try for still more difficult achievement. There was a half-concealed pride of accomplishment in the assertion of the Cockney boy, exhausted and footsore after his first cross-country effort: "Cor blimey, if this had been Larndon, they'd shift them bleedin' hills." A moving human story underlay the statement of the half-caste lad from Liverpool, warmed by his watchmates' acclaim for his self-improvement: "This is the first time in my life I have seemed to matter." Wise old Alec Fraser, the former missionary who served as the school chaplain, saw what was happening: "They come for the wrong reasons, and they leave sorry for the right ones that it's over."

Holt's prepositional distinction—training *through* rather than *for*—was always to be the essence of the Outward Bound dynamic. Life-enhancing experience is obtained through the sea, the mountains, the wild lake country, the desert. Outward Bound has evolved since those early Aberdovey days. But it has not departed from Hahn and Holt's essential concept of an intense experience surmounting challenges in a natural setting, through which the individual builds his sense of self-worth, the group comes to a heightened awareness of human interdependence, and all grow in concern for those in danger and in need.

OUTWARD BOUND AND SALEM

Give children the chance to discover themselves.
See to it that children experience both success and defeat.
See to it that there are periods of silence.
Train the imagination, the ability to anticipate and to plan.
Take sports and games seriously,
    but only as a part of the whole.
Free the children of rich and influential parents from the
    paralyzing influence of wealth and privilege.

—Kurt Hahn's prescription for German education, circa 1930

Aﬅer a week at Gordonstoun, Hahn sent me traveling, first to visit a new Outward Bound school.

Monday. Am at the moment bumping my way to the short term 'Outward Bound Mountain School' at Eskdale, near Whitehaven, near Carlisle, on a very jouncy train. Had breakfast at 6:30 this A.M. with Hahn. On top of a 15-mile bird walk yesterday ending at 8 P.M., followed by supper with Hahn and a rehearsal of Macbeth with bed finally at 12:30. The day finds me somewhat physically bushed, but as always (in this atmosphere) ready for more. The guy certainly has something. More ideas working, and more to be worked than you can imagine . . .

The school at Eskdale brought my first awareness of the name "Outward Bound." Hahn, who had not cared for the name when Lawrence Holt insisted on it at Aberdovey, still referred to "short-term schools." (In later years he would enjoy telling audiences how right Holt—and how wrong he—had been.) What I did not then realize was how significant a development Eskdale and the manner of its founding was for what would become a worldwide Outward Bound movement. A few years before, a group of prominent British men and women, strong believers in the concept that had proved itself at Aberdovey, had formed the Outward Bound Trust. The intent was to free the Aberdovey School of the insecurity of depending on the goodwill and magnanimity of a commercial firm, and to foster growth of Outward Bound on a national basis. Alfred Holt & Company (its head, now Sir Lawrence Holt) generously deeded the school to the Trust. By 1949 there were funds in hand to enable the purchase at auction of "Gatehouse," the ancestral home of Lord Rea at Eskdale, as a base for a new school.

England's Lake District, in which Eskdale is located, is in the northwest corner of the country. Its lakes are produced by the runoff of water from the Cumbrian Mountains, which rise to Scaffell Pike, the country's highest peak. Gatehouse was a large baronial structure in a splendid setting that looked out across a tarn, as the Scots call a small lake, to the higher fells of the Scafell group. On arrival I was immediately swept into the school's activity. The warden, Adam Arnold-Brown—a Gordonstoun old boy and one of its first Guardians—was about my age. The students were doing the five-mile walk, a stressful heel-and-toe exercise that consumed, it seemed to me, more energy than would jogging over the same rugged terrain. "Come along, old chap," Arnold-Brown called out, fitting our pace to that of the student pack. Accepting an invitation I could not refuse, I was soon reduced to a state of heaving lungs, aching legs, and thorough lather.

That evening, as Arnold-Brown explained the recruiting procedure for the school, I learned about the English educational scheme. At that time all British eleven-year-olds took an examination, the "Eleven Plus," which separated those who would go on to try for the universities from those who would join a vocational stream and whose formal education would end at fourteen. Most of the latter went into industry as apprentices. It was from this apprentice group that Eskdale and the other Outward Bound schools (the Gordonstoun-affiliated Moray Sea School was soon to be taken under the Outward Bound Trust's wing) drew most of their student body. Their employers paid their way—selecting them either because they showed leadership potential or problem potential, sometimes both. Other students came as cadets in such services as the police and coastguard, or as ordinary schoolboys, and a few were boys in trouble with the law referred by juvenile authorities.

> Two voices are there; one is of the Sea,
> One the Mountains: each a mighty voice.

The Eskdale course, like that at Moray, had been designed on the Aberdovey model, except that at Eskdale mountaineering and rock climbing replaced seamanship, and training for mountain rescue replaced that for rescue at sea. But again the training was *through* rather than *for*. On a rocky promontory overlooking fields green with young crops I watched the students practice first aid and lowering a litter-borne injured person down a cliff. A highlight of the first course, Arnold-Brown told me, had been an emergency "call-out" on a dark, blustery night, the boys joining in the search for a lost mountaineering party. This was Eskdale's second course, and Arnold-Brown and his attractive wife were profoundly excited by the daily revelations of the school's potential. There had been enough in the way of dramatic incident and human interplay to convince them they were committed to an enterprise capable of producing dramatic change in young people.

■ ■ ■

Back at Gordonstoun four days later, Hahn informed me at breakfast that the leader of the visiting group from the Carnegie Foundation was "a codfish-eyed Englishman of a type I cannot handle." I got the assignment. The next day I was given another, this one putting me through a Saturday's misery of preparing a talk to the Cliff Watchers at their final Sunday chapel service.

Sunday night I was off again, this time to visit the Outward Bound Sea School at Aberdovey. On the station platform at Crewe at 4 A.M., Guggenheim

Writing in a journal at day's end is encouraged at Outward Bound as a way to process the day's activities and personal insights. (Photo © Cobi Harris)

was waiting with his Bentley. The sleek car's long shafts of light swept the blackness, picking out the new curve that seemed always to lie ahead. Gugg had scant respect for curves. Before Wales, another stop. I had said to Hahn: "I would like to meet a prominent British educator who disagrees strongly with your ideas." Those remarkable eyes had flashed, a note almost of glee in his voice: "Capital! You will meet the enemy!"

The enemy was the headmaster of the Shrewsbury School. "A very stiff and proper Englishman," I wrote home. He greeted us cordially, clearly relishing this chance to disabuse the young American of any faulty notions of British education he might have picked up. His school was an academic powerhouse—all stress on preparation for the university examinations. A great rowing school. Character was developed in the rowing shell and on the cricket pitch. No reference to service, no concern with matters of social conscience, with deriving education from experience as well as in the class-room. Of its kind, Shrewsbury was one of England's best. Its very quality qualified its headmaster as "the enemy."

Over morning tea and biscuit the headmaster expatiated on what was wrong with the Hahn philosophy. I perceived he did not even know—did not want to know—what Hahn was doing. He said things like, "You know, at Gordonstoun they have boys who can't read or write." This was a half-truth. He had no comprehension of Hahn's stern principle that a boy must not be penalized for something he could not help—his IQ, for example, or a child-hood bombing trauma that had blighted his early schooling.

I did not have to defend Hahn in order to disagree with my host. He stood for the very emphases in education that more and more I had been coming to doubt. We got into a pretty heavy argument. Gugg kept silent. Back on the highway, he shifted the Bentley into high. "I say, old boy, I've never heard anyone speak to a headmaster as you did."

I said, "How about the parents who are paying the bill? Haven't they the right to object?"

"Of course not. They'd be terrified. They'd lose their child's place in the school immediately."

It had helped that I had not known better. Later, on hearing my report, Hahn would laugh. Then frown. "But you see what our problem is. He speaks well for his position. This is the inertia of tradition."

The Bentley purred on, across the Welsh border, toward Aberdovey, where we were welcomed by Captain J. F. "Freddy" Fuller, the warden of the Aberdovey School. From fifteen years of age, the sea had been the only life Freddy Fuller knew until, in 1943, the experience of surviving the successive torpedoing of two ships and commanding a lifeboat in the open sea for thirty-five days had brought him a landlubber assignment.

"Perhaps it was as well," he has written, "that I came to Aberdovey with no preconceived ideas of the School and the work it was intended that I should serve with my seaman's craft and skill, but I knew that I came with an added self-confidence and new-found humility, born of the trial and experi-ence of long days in an open boat, scantily equipped for the battle with the elements, with hunger and thirst, with self!"

I was impressed by the versatility of the Aberdovey School's terrain, which included both the sea and the hills. In contrast to the pioneer ambiance at Eskdale, one sensed immediately the established quality that eight years of operation had given Aberdovey. The routine was smooth, professional, knowing. The staff, thoroughly imbued with an understanding of the Outward Bound undertaking, was in control of the process. I was struck by the active allegiance to Hahnian ideas; the evolving school remained strongly conscious of its founder and his philosophy. The rescue ethic was pervasive, and the school had built a strong tradition of service to the area.

From Aberdovey I went to London to fly to Zurich. I was going to the fount—the Salem Schule. The ferry crossed Lake Constance, the Alps at our backs. An hour's drive brought us to the extraordinary sight of Schloss Salem, the Margrave of Baden's great castle, a portion of which housed the school. At the entrance a servant led me inside. Broad, seemingly endless corridors, the walls crowded with paintings and prints—or again, with thousands of antlers, tokens of centuries of hunting in ancient forests. Finally the doorway to my room, where an attractive young woman welcomed me. What with the language difficulties and the culture shock, I was slow in realizing that this was Princess Sophia, my hostess, wife of Prince George of Hanover, headmaster of Salem. Writing home as I awaited the call to dinner, I set down:

It's all too unbelievable. This main building is 4 floors high and forms a complete courtyard, with entrance through an archway. Each floor must have at least an 18-foot ceiling and the court must measure 130 by 75 feet anyway. So you get an idea of the size of this centuries old castle. My room opens on the court, in which there are two large Douglas fir trees that tower out of the court, taking up all the space. They must be 6 feet in diameter.

At Salem I was indeed at the source. I saw it all happening in the German environment as I had already seen it in the Scottish, except that this school was coeducational. The early morning running, the midmorning Break in the sedentary hours. The student government hierarchy—Guardian, Color Bearers, and Helpers. The Fire Service answering a call. The practical work, the crafts, and the individual projects. The great student orchestra and chorus rehearsing Handel's "Alexander's Feast." The school was a scant five years out of Nazism. Apparently Prince George was succeeding in his vigorous effort to win back its prewar eminence, for the school was getting more applicants than it could accommodate.

One day I lunched with three of the Helpers—those in charge of practical work, dormitory proctors, and athletics. In the afternoon a boy whose title was "assistant supervisor of practical work" gave me a tour. The work the students were doing reflected the postwar poverty. Groups were gathering huge quantities of wood for the winter fires. Others were working in the field; in this time of severe shortages, the school produced most of its own food. Still others were grooming the athletic fields, working in the carpentry and blacksmith shops, as electricians, in the laundry, wherever work was needed to keep the school going. I wrote home: "The student government is the most amazing system and operating under the most adverse conditions both here and at Gordonstoun (but especially here)—no money, no equipment . . . and until recently inadequate food, so much so, in fact, that athletics had to be suspended as too tiring."

Twenty-four hours of continuous travel brought me back to a 5 A.M. rendezvous at Inverness with Hunter and the London taxi, and a long breakfast with Hahn to report on my trip. That afternoon was the *Macbeth* production, which Hahn had directed. It was performed outdoors on an extremely simple stage built up against the old Gordonstoun castle, in a foggy "fair is foul, and foul still fouler" kind of weather. The casting was extraordinarily good, the authentic Scots accents wonderful. It was the most enjoyable Shakespeare I had ever seen.

My pilgrimage—it had become that—was almost at an end. On my last day I had long talks with Henry Brereton and Bobby Chew. These were salutary meetings, for those two were among the most understanding and staunchly loyal of Hahn's staff. They did not make light of the difficulties that attached to their loyalty. Hahn's very certitude that all things in his philosophy were doable could create extremely trying conditions for those charged with devising and executing the practical details. But concerning the merits and values of the headmaster's philosophy, neither had doubts.

On the flight home I studied and reflected on the Gordonstoun School Final Report to Parents. This was virtually a duplicate of the form Hahn had long ago developed at Salem. Better than any other document, it encapsulated his educational concerns. The student was rated on his public spirit, sense of justice, and ability to follow out what he believed to be the right course in the face of various physical and psychological obstacles; on ability to state facts precisely, and to plan; on ability to organize—both as shown in the doing of his work and his direction of younger boys; on ability to deal with the unexpected; and on his conscientiousness—both in everyday affairs and in tasks with which he was especially entrusted. His imagination and manners were evaluated, as were his manual dexterity, the quality of his handicraft and other practical work, and the quality of his work in music, drawing, and other artistic endeavors. Then came the report on his academic performance and, if he were a member of the Cliff Watchers, the Fire Service, or the Army or Sea Cadets, a service report by his command officer.

It was like no report card I had ever seen. For three decades, I reflected, this man had been doing things in education that I had merely dreamed of in a theoretical way, and had carried them far beyond the blurred limits of my wishful speculations. More than any other educator of whom I was aware, Hahn practiced the philosophy that education had a twin objective: to enable the student to make intelligent judgments and to develop the inherent strengths of his selfhood (to build character, in the old-fashioned phrase too likely to touch off the allergy of the young to "manifest improvers"). The report to parents was the frame of reference that defined the goal Hahn had stated so stirringly years before: "To produce young people able to effect what they see to be right, despite hardships, despite dangers, despite inner skepticism, despite boredom, despite mockery from the world, despite emotion of the moment."

REPORT AND DECISION

✳

Report me and my cause aright.

—Hamlet

Back at Hun I tried to tell people where I had been, what I had learned. Few were more than politely interested. In that day nobody saw a need to question what we were doing in education. Actually, "nobody" was a goodly number, scattered across the land, but we did not know each other. We were little islands. I had no one who wanted to listen to me except Tom Hartmann. Tom caught on fast. We talked a lot about how Gordonstoun concepts might be adapted to American schools.

I learned something about the group of Americans who had banded together to support Hahn's work abroad. When the war ended, Hahn had been the first former German national in private life permitted to enter defeated Germany. Soon he was at odds with the Allied Military Government policy for "reeducation" of the German people. "Restoration," he held, was the proper term. In 1948 he visited the United States to win support for his ideas. That visit led to six prominent Americans forming the American-British Foundation for European Education as a vehicle for helping him. The six made a formidable roster: Thomas McKittrick, a senior vice-president of the Chase National Bank, who was chairman of the group; Allen Dulles, ex-president of Johns Hopkins University and soon to become director of the Central Intelligence Agency; Abraham Flexner, director emeritus of the Institute of Advanced Study at Princeton; Congressman Christian Herter, soon to be

46

Rock climbing requires intense concentration for a student's first ascent.
(Photo © Ty Milford)

elected governor of Massachusetts, and a future U.S. Secretary of State; Henry Pitney Van Dusen, president of Union Theological Seminary; and Eric Warburg, international financier and senior partner in Kuhn, Loeb and Company, whose sister Lola was married to Rudolf Hahn, Kurt's brother. Despite their bond of public distinction, they were a disparate group. But somewhere, sometime, each had come under Hahn's spell. Each had come to believe in Hahn's ideas for creating "islands of healing" in a war-torn world, especially for restoring health to democratic forces in his corrupted, defeated, demoralized native land.

A three-year program was adopted for which the foundation undertook to raise funds. It called for scholarships to four German schools—Salem, Lietz, the Odenwaldschule, and Luisenlund, a new school being founded on Hahnian principles—and the creation in Germany of three short-term schools (*kurzschulen*) modeled on Britain's Outward Bound. A "German Seminary" was to be established at Gordonstoun to train the *kurzschulen* instructors. A "German Department" was also to be created there, to enable thirty outstanding German boys to spend a year at Gordonstoun on a basis that would not handicap them in the fiercely competitive examinations to German universities. In addition, some help was to be given to equipping the Gordonstoun Cliff Watchers and the Moray Sea School.

In support of the plan for Outward Bound Schools in Germany, Thomas McKittrick arranged for Hahn to meet the newly appointed American High Commissioner in Germany, John McCloy, who was immediately sympathetic. (So was his wife, Ellen, who later would join and then become chairman of the board of the American-British Foundation for European Education. So was her sister, Peggy Douglas, wife of Lewis Douglas, U.S. ambassador to Great Britain.) McCloy provided friends to help finance a *kurzschule*, but all kinds of practical and people difficulties continued to hold back the project. A major inhibiting element was the German educational establishment, an old *bête noire* of Hahn's, which was opposed to spending energy and funds on this kind of school when normal instruction had not yet been adequately implemented. Hahn dealt with this opposition by boring from within, winning adherents among leading professional educators. He was also conducting the standard skirmishes with governmental bureaucrats. He even tangled with the Quakers, whose work in the defeated country he greatly admired. To their sensitive, but in this instance not discriminating, ears the Outward Bound concept of adventure education was too programmatically reminiscent of the regimen of the Nazi youth whose moral ravages they were working to repair. Hahn, fired by a response that he found automatic rather than empathetic, replied, "You care more about pacifism than you do about peace!"

I made my report to the foundation. Reading it years later brings vividly to mind how my exposure to Hahn, Gordonstoun, Salem, and Outward Bound had influenced me. I was sold on the short-term school concept, impressed by the British Ministry of Education's endorsement of it, and by the depth of satisfaction with the results that was motivating British companies to continue to invest in the experience for their employees. I was completely taken with Hahn's own schools, describing the Gordonstoun program in considerable detail. "The headmaster is certainly a genius and a most inspiring person," I reported. "I have never seen his equal at handling people, especially young people. His ideas of education are, however, so fundamental and so essentially sound that personnel trained by him or by his system are perfectly capable of carrying on."

I had been impressed by the Gordonstoun boys. "Naive socially perhaps, according to American standards, they are a collection of individuals, manly, confident, healthy, and enthusiastic. Above all, they are honest. I was surprised at the lack of off-color humor, obscene language, and petty vulgarities that one expects in a boys' school. This factor, however, does not place them above healthy mischief, practical jokes, and a normal amount of boy troubles."

Toward the end of the document I wrote: "A boy who respects the rights and privileges of an individual will never become a part of an organization or state that disregards those rights and privileges. There is no question in my mind that Hahn's boys are proof against these powers."

My firsthand report must have given added assurance to the directors of the American-British Foundation, none of whom had had my exposure. Their interests, however, were entirely oriented to what was happening overseas. They had no thought of trying to bring any aspect of Hahn's work to this country.

Talking with Hartmann, I realized how ill-prepared I would be to implement any American version of the Hahn philosophy. At Gordonstoun and Salem, Aberdovey and Eskdale, the visitor who ran could read, and I had indeed been running. A mere passing observer of the product of three decades of educational thought, experimentation, and energy, I had served no apprenticeship.

In October 1950 I wrote Hahn that I would like to return to Gordonstoun as a staff member the following year. Characteristically he replied by cable: "Your suggestion thrills me. I know of no man whose help would be more fruitful at this juncture. I only hope it can start soon. You can easily bring the daughters. Warmest greetings to you both. Writing."

On February 15, 1951, the entire family—Phebe, our two infant daughters, and I—sailed on the *Parthia* for Liverpool.

RETURN TO GORDONSTOUN

✳

*The schools absorb so much nervous strength through mere
bookwork that there is not much spirit left in the young to
fashion for themselves soul-restoring activities. I do not wish to
be misunderstood; I do not advocate the lowering of the intellectual standards. On the contrary, I would like to see the mind
trained by a sterner exercise of the thinking faculty. I do,
however, advocate less memory work. May the young, to quote
Wordsworth, "not purchase knowledge at the price of power."*

—Kurt Hahn

*What avail is it to win prescribed amounts of information
about geography and history, to win the ability to read and
write, if in the process the individual loses his own soul;
loses his appreciation of things worthwhile, of the values to
which these are related; if he loses the desire to apply what
he learned, and above all, loses the ability to extract
meaning from his future experiences as they occur?*

—John Dewey

M y first teaching assignments at Gordonstoun included general science,
current events, and what we would call a "remedial class" in arithmetic. The latter group was my first hands-on exposure to Hahn's working
principle that a boy was not to be penalized for a deficiency over which he

had no control. Two factors that should not prevail in denying admission to the school were a family's inability to pay and a boy's low IQ. The important question was: What is the boy doing with his endowment? Many Gordonstoun students did splendidly in the university examinations. We also had some interesting youngsters who were far from what would be considered academically qualified at most British or American schools. Those boys in my special class were just about mathematically illiterate. Many of these lads had endured the bombing in the Battle of Britain, and undoubtedly some had suffered traumas. Emotional disturbances, manifested in such aberrations as bedwetting, were then common among young Britishers. But in that arithmetic class was a socially powerful youngster who would win a place of leadership among the students. Another would become a master farmer, the greatest grower of tomatoes under glass in Great Britain; academia did not come easily for him, but he had fine common sense. A third was an artist, a genius in stained-glass design.

There were sons of bricklayers in the school who had aspirations different from their fathers', and there were others who intended also to be bricklayers. Both were equally honored. Hahn hoped the latter would go back into their world better bricklayers because they were better citizens. There were boys who were going to sea; their careers in the merchant service had already been chosen for them. They were honored at the same level as somebody destined for a university to become a doctor. It was a part of Hahn's greatness as a headmaster that he gave youngsters a sense of being members of a community in which all had the same opportunity to earn the same kind of respect from their peers. At the same time he was on the alert for any kind of lateral shift an individual might develop. Here comes, say, a youngster who has a genius for working in stained glass but whose academic tickets are subpar. He is exposed to poetry and drama and music, and perhaps he will be enthused by one of these. Also he is exposed to competing with others from other streams in a political sense, in the school governing structure. That could hardly happen to him under the Eleven Plus system, which might only divert him into a vocational stream.

The core of Hahn's educational purpose was to conserve and strengthen the attributes of childhood into manhood. "What happens in adolescence," he asked, "to your children who in the nursery are so self-confident and happy?" Too often youngsters who were joyous, zestful, and enterprisingly curious, with the gift of wonder and an inborn compassion, grew "dimmed and diluted." Adolescence became "the loutish years," a shallow pre-maturing while strengths remained undiscovered and untrained. Hahn pledged himself "to unseat the dogma that puberty need deform." To this end he sought to create an educational environment where "healthy passions"—craving for adventure, joy of exploration, zest for building, devotion to a skill demanding patience and care, love of music, painting, or writing—would flourish as "guardian angels of adolescence."

Another of my early responsibilities was The Break. It was essential, in Hahn's thinking, that a healthy youngster "have his powers of resilience, coordination, acceleration, and endurance purposefully developed." The Break was his unique contribution to physical education. He had invented it in the early Salem days, and from the beginning had made it an imperative part of the Gordonstoun scheme. Four mornings a week, during a fifty-minute break in what Hahn called "the sedentary hours," each boy took part in two of a half-dozen events—sprinting or distance running, long or high jumping, and discus or javelin throwing. He competed only against himself, trying to better his previous best performance. The frail youngster who broke ten feet in the long jump for the first time in his life got as big a cheer as the track team star beating his previous mark at close to twenty. Every boy had to do every event. That same star jumper might be a dud at throwing the discus. It was as important to overcome a weakness as to develop a strength.

When I was put in charge of The Break, I became a fascinated witness to its remarkable results. It was not just that the average performance would have put the average American schoolboy to shame. The great satisfaction lay in seeing the physical duffer discover that through trying from day to day he could do much better than he would have dared to dream. He had learned, in Hahn's phrase, to "defeat his defeatism." You could see him shed—Hahn again—"the misery of his unimportance." His new-found confidence would carry over into his peer relationships, his classroom performance, the quality of work on his project. It was not unusual for a timid or sensitive boy with an undeveloped physique to emerge from the chrysalis of his underconfidence a competent athlete, surprised to find himself confirming what the headmaster had so often told the school: "Your disability is your opportunity."

Sometimes Hahn stood with me, the big hat with the wide, turned-down brim angled over his ears, a pleased observer of Break activity all around us. Perhaps at the high jump a boy would start his run toward the bar, then shy off, and Hahn would smile. "The high jumpers," he told me, "love to dwell in the valley of indecision." And then, "But they must commit themselves!" The high jump, he claimed, had cured stammerers. Distance running had cured asthmatics. There was a whole Hahnian folklore based on The Break. At least, I tended then to regard it as folklore. I have since become a believer. Medical people now tell us about stammerers being cured by a wilderness experience—why doubt high-jump therapy? Every Outward Bound school can cite cases of asthmatic students whose two-mile early morning run, perhaps undertaken in the face of a physician's concern that the boy should attempt it at all, did much to ease their affliction.

When we first arrived at Gordonstoun, there were no quarters for us at the school; we lived in Elgin, five miles away. In August we moved into Windmill Lodge, a residence on the school grounds. Nearby, some former kennels had just been converted to a dormitory, and I was master of this new "house." At that time Bobby Chew went as headmaster to Altyre, a new Gordonstoun satellite school, and I was given his post as director of activities. I taught physics and still had my class of "mathematical illiterates." My responsibilities as director of activities included all those considerable parts of the school program that took place outside the classroom.

As housemaster I learned firsthand about the Training Plan and the whole Gordonstoun scheme of student self-government. When Jones was a new boy at the school, an older student came to him each night and checked off his Training Plan. This was a list of questions that covered the gamut of Jones's daily duties, from taking his morning shower and doing his before-breakfast household chores, through completing his lessons and getting to classes on time, to brushing his teeth at night. To each query Jones would answer yes or no, and for any shortcomings the older boy would mete out the prescribed penalties. In time, perhaps after three or four months, the older boy would decide that Jones had reached a stage of responsibility where he could be entrusted with his own Training Plan and his own punishments. He would so report to McDonald, who as Helper of the House was Windmill Lodge's number-one boy. McDonald would come to me and say, "I think it's time for Jones to take on his own Training Plan."

I would say, "What's the evidence? What makes you think Jones is ready?" and McDonald would say something like "Well, sir, I'm satisfied that he is answering Williams honestly every night. And the other day something happened, and when I asked how it happened, he immediately popped up with all the facts, even though it involved him in some of the blame." So I would call Jones down and talk with him. If I was convinced, I would take the recommendation to the headmaster, who would give me a thorough grilling. I would have to have my facts and make a really good case for Jones.

Then, a month or so after he had been given his own Training Plan, I would say to Jones, "Get your Training Plan, I want to see it." Perhaps a look of horror would come over his face. He would jog over to the house and come back with his plan, on which he had made no entries for the past ten days. So he would have to go back down the line, and Williams would take over again. Then after a while McDonald would come once more and say it was time for Jones, and I would say, "Now look, don't get me in trouble again. Are you sure?" I would go to the headmaster and he would say, "Are you sure?" I would be on trial, not Jones. So Jones would get his Training Plan back, and this time when I checked up on him, it would be in good order, and Jones was well on his way to being a self-responsible member of the school community.

Eventually he might show enough leadership talent that I would say, "It's time for Jones to become a Color Bearer candidate." All the Helpers, the students in charge of the school, were Color Bearers. The Color Bearer candidates were the ones you went to when something needed doing, and you needed someone to see that it got done. They were the ones who checked the newcomers' Training Plans, ran the study halls, did the inspections, supervised all the dirty work. They were the Helpers' noncommissioned officers. During their candidacy they were paragons of exemplary behavior. Hahn maintained that once in a youngster's life he should go through a period of being a paragon, but he should not be expected to keep it up too long. The Color Bearer competition lasted three months. At the end of that time one of three things happened. A candidate was elected by the Color Bearers to their society. He was rejected and went back to his status as a Training Plan holder. Or in rare cases, he was given three more months as a candidate.

When a boy was elected a Color Bearer, he was given a highly responsible job—as the Helper of the House, or the Helper of Guests, or the Helper in charge of The Break, or of the practical work program or athletic program, or of one of the Samaritan services or whatever. The whole school was turned over to the Color Bearers. Their leader, the Guardian, was head boy of the school. But the cement of the entire structure was the Training Plan, whereby every individual in the school was given responsibility for himself.

Hahn was then sixty-five. He was running the school, making frequent trips to London to raise money for it and advance other projects, and shuttling across the English Channel in his campaigns to influence the postwar education of German youth. "I am," he told me, "an old man in a hurry." I wondered how many obstacles he had hurdled with that trumpet cry of his determination. The hurry part was literally true. He climbed stairs two at a time, took an entire downflight in a single *r-r-r-p-p!* His day marched. Frequently it began with three separate breakfast meetings. In theory they were staggered, but usually he wound up circulating from one to the other. On a not-untypical morning, staff members, school governors, and the sheriff of Elgin might be breakfasting at a table in his study as they made plans for the forthcoming visit of Princess Elizabeth and Prince Philip. In an adjoining room the warden of the Moray Outward Bound School might be meeting with a high official of the Schleswig-Holstein Ministry of Education and an emissary of Count von Platen Haller-Mund, principal sponsor of a proposed new German *kurzschule.* In the school dining hall perhaps some of the *Hamlet* cast, the director of studies, and the headmaster, who was also directing the play, would be inquiring into Shakespeare's intentions in Act IV. The telephoning would have started, Hahn's refrain of "We will call him [or her] immediately" running through the day. Employing the telephone as a means of persuasion, he seemed more to play it than simply to use it. He would speak straight to the point— he had no small talk, ever—and somehow there would be no way for the person at the other end to say no.

However tight the day's schedule, he found time to reconnoiter about the school. "A headmaster's job," he said, "is to walk around." His antennae were always out, fine-tuned and waving, probing for each lad's potential strengths that they might be developed, for his innate weaknesses that they might be overcome. Repeatedly he homed in on some shielded aspect of a boy's ego that others had missed and that cast a sudden light on deviant behavior. He was his own psychologist, drawing on a vast bank of observations.

The day's end was signaled at that hour of the evening when Hunter brought the London taxicab around to Gordonstoun House. Hunter would drive him across the moors to the sea cliffs. Then Hahn would get out and jog along the line of the cliffs, his way illuminated by the headlights of the cab following behind.

But the days did not always end so routinely. Periodically, roused from slumber by his call, four or five of us—housemaster, teachers, activity leader—would make our way through the night to his study. The call would have but one meaning—some boy was in trouble. Perhaps a student had been caught stealing. Hahn would have spent a long evening getting the report, talking with the boy and with the student leaders who knew him best. Conscious of the contrast between our disheveled aspects and his neat daytime attire, we would wait for him to stop pacing the floor and tell us why we were there. Finally, when he had given us the facts, came the inevitable, dreaded question, the blue eyes boring in: "Josh! When did you first notice this boy was in difficulty, and what did you do about it?"—dreaded because one had sensed and done nothing. When a boy was in danger of expulsion at Gordonstoun, it was not he but the adult community who was on trial. A boy steals because he has some deeper trouble. If one is sensitive enough, if one cares enough, one can detect symptoms of the trouble early, when there may still be time for remedy.

The following day, Hahn would decide the penalty, posting the facts on the bulletin board to prevent the rumor-mongering he detested: "Put it on my tombstone, 'Here lies Kurt Hahn. He scotched a rumor every day.'"

He ran the school in tensile fashion. It began with his hiring strong people who would stand up to him. Offering Henry Brereton the post of director of studies in 1935, he said, "You must defend your department. If I want to send

A student confronts big rapids in the kayak portion of a multi-element course with Voyageur Outward Bound School. (Photo © Mark Zelinski, www.markzelinski.com)

a boy into the hills for his health just before examinations, you must resist me." He staffed the school's nautical department with a Royal Navy officer and a Merchant Navy officer, in the belief that the inevitable conflict of two traditions would be a creative force—as it proved to be. When I became director of activities, I found that Brereton and I were duty bound to maintain a rival stance, lest either poach on the other's share of school time. If Hahn thought we were not being wary enough, he took some subtle action, created some threat of encroachment, to put us on guard.

The same tensilizing principle infused his way with the young. His core tenet, stated a thousand times as though it were cut in bronze, was: "It is the sin of the soul to force young people into opinions—indoctrination is of the devil—but it is culpable neglect not to impel them into health-giving experiences."[1] The indoor type was to be chased outdoors, the introvert turned inside out, the extrovert outside in. The tough were to be gentled, the timid emboldened. Above all, the complacent were to be disturbed. "It is my mission in life to molest the contentedly unfit."

He had powerful ideas about which experiences were "health-giving." We did not play soccer (football, they called it) at Gordonstoun even though it was the Scottish national game, because Hahn felt the professional players, with their tactics of going for the man instead of the ball, had brutalized the sport. It was, in fact, another of his declared missions in life to "dethrone games," i.e., team sports. Games were good when they taught a lesson of "the good ally" and teamwork, modesty in winning, resolution in defeat. They did harm when they glorified individual performance, or brute power, and when they stifled other interests. And they did nothing for the physical development of the boys who did not take part.

Once when I was coaching the track team, we had gotten off to a good start and built a lead in a meet at Gordonstoun with another school. At first I had been troubled that the other team was competing barefoot and that our boys, all wearing proper footgear, had an unfair advantage. However, the competent showing the visitors made in the opening events had diluted my concern. After all, I reasoned, the meet was taking place on grass, not the cinder runways I was used to, and those unshod youngsters seemed at home on the thick turf. Suddenly Hahn was on the scene, talking with the visitors. He came over to me and said, "Those boys can't afford track shoes. Have our lads take off theirs and start the meet over." "But—." The decision in his eyes stopped me. We started again, the meet now more closely contested. It took a long time for me to absorb fully the meaning of that incident. The lesson of fairness was clear enough. Still, no one would have thought it unfair if the headmaster had decided the only expedient was for our team to go barefoot in the remaining events. But in matters of fairness it was not Hahn's habit to consider expedience. In time I came to realize

[1] Years later, when Bill Coffin and I were working on the Outward Bound program for the Peace Corps, we came up with a variation of this precept, better suited to our then needs, in which "value-forming" was substituted for "health-giving." Hahn endorsed the change. It is the later version that has become familiar in the United States.

that the heart of the incident was his instant, uncompromising doing of what he knew to be right.

Not so many years before, Hahn himself had played on the Gordonstoun cricket and field hockey teams. "Mad as a boy to win," Henry Brereton said, recalling with a chuckle Hahn's running downfield, hockey stick at the ready, exhorting his teammates: "Always say to yourself, when you are up against a more formidable opponent than yourself, Homer's memorable words, 'You have suffered worse than this and triumphed at last!'" Perhaps there was an element of self-discipline in his game-dethroning policy. It was a policy of moderation. We played competitive cricket, field hockey, and rugby, and competed in track, but the school teams practiced only two afternoons a week. The headmaster's dethroning technique was to create competition for games, finding other ways to feed the "healthy passions." The Break, offering each an opportunity to build a base for his self-esteem, was a strong antidote to the campus sports-hero syndrome. So were the Samaritan services—the Cliff Watchers, the Fire Service, and, a little later, the Mountain Rescue team—and the school's mountain and sea expeditions. So were the Saturday mornings devoted to crafts; likewise the project. Every student had a long-term project. It might involve a craft, but it could be in nature, science, the arts, or some other area of student interest. The chief requirement was that it demand a sustained effort.

Hahn's zeal for the educational value of the crafts is especially memorable. He was himself "mechanically illiterate," as he put it; he would have been incapable of the simplest task in a wood or metal-working shop. While his own sense of deficiency was probably a factor in prompting him to encourage others to gain some kind of creative manual competence, his chief motivation was a deep respect for craftsmanship as a social force. The decline in skill and care, a major count in his indictment of the times, was "due to the weakened tradition of craftsmanship."

Perhaps the finest of his education stratagems was his use of the sea as a classroom. In nearby Hopeman Harbor, all Gordonstoun boys mastered small-boat seamanship and qualified to crew the *Prince Louis,* the school's seagoing sailing vessel. Again this was training not *for,* but *through,* the sea. Hahn said, "My best schoolmaster is the Moray Firth." Henry Brereton, scholar, historian, striver for academic excellence, perceived that in that challenging body of water, with its strong tides, frequent high winds, and rocky shore, the elements were strict teachers of the values of discipline, order, skill, and of mathematics, learned as a tool of navigation. At the end of one holiday time the *Prince Louis* came back from a harrowing sea voyage around the Orkney and Shetland Islands having weathered three gales. Hahn asked a boy, "How did you enjoy yourself?" The boy said, "Magnificently, sir—except at the time." That became one of the headmaster's favorite stories, for it so beautifully supported his thesis that young people should be impelled into experience.

"Hahn's educational actions," noted an admiring German educator, "seems always to stem from two poles—justice and love. Should these ever be in conflict, then love conquers." He could, however, be very stern. The finer the boy being judged, the sterner the judgment.[2] He was most demanding of the school's leaders; a leader had not only to earn his way to leadership but also his right to stay there. We had a youngster at Gordonstoun whose antisocial behavior—due apparently to a severe childhood trauma suffered during the war—became so bad that the school could not keep him. After much effort, Hahn found another school willing to take this boy. In a fury of spite on the day he was to leave, the boy made a shambles of his dormitory. When his housemates discovered the havoc, a group grabbed him arm and leg and started for the pond at the far end of the south lawn. The pond underlay the school's ropes course, and there was a rule that if you fell into its stagnant water, you had to be dosed with castor oil to purge tadpoles and other organisms you might have swallowed.

The Guardian, the school's student leader, was at some distance talking with companions when he saw what was happening. He watched as he continued talking. When, in a burst of decision, he raced to break up the kangaroo court, he was too late. By the time he reached the group, the boy had got his dunking and was suffering, if not a fit, a severe reaction. Under the Gordonstoun code, if a punishable offense took place in the Guardian's presence, only he was punished. I was astonished at the severity of Hahn's penalty. He not only relieved the Guardian of his post of leadership, he took

[2] From Hahn's (at the time) confidential report to the Royal Navy on Prince Philip's student career at Gordonstoun: "Prince Philip is a born leader, but he will need the exacting demands of a great service to do justice to himself. His best is outstanding, his second best is not good enough."

away his Training Plan. What was most arresting was the reason for the penalty. The boy was not punished for his failure to prevent the dunking. His offense, said the bulletin board notice, was that he had hesitated before acting.

I used to tell that story but had to stop because I found it angered people. There would be murmurings: "Why, of course he hesitated. Any normal person would." Not in Hahn's book. In any moral crisis, he believed, a leader could hardly fail more grievously than not to know immediately what he should do, and promptly do it.

He had least patience with overprotective and overpermissive parents. "I know parents," he said, "who negotiate with their children as though they were a foreign power." Once when I was in his office with a student's mother, I saw his tune-out mask drop into place as she pleaded with him on behalf of a son in trouble for chronic tardiness. The boy's difficulty, she argued, was congenital—he had a faulty interior clock. "You just don't understand him, Headmaster," she said. "Madame," said Hahn, "how many vacation trains has he missed?"

It may have been another mother, the one who packed her son off to school with pills for when he was homesick, that caused him to explode to me on the subject of pill-popping adults. The growing dependence on quiet-downers and pep-uppers, he maintained, was bound to produce a youth blighted by narcotics addiction. This was years before the drug problem emerged. It was one more time when I did not know what he was talking about—not the first or last time that someone mistook as gross exaggeration his accurate sense of what was happening beneath the societal surface.

He was an intrepid traveler; a journey with him was exhilarating. To see him cope with the usual frustrations of getting from one place to the next was to observe in microcosm ways in which he advanced his grand designs. Policemen, taxi drivers, ticket agents were his instant confidants. No matter how negative an agent's initial response, the ensuing friendship almost surely produced the needed overnight train accommodation or pair of plane tickets. Henry Brereton, who accompanied him on trips to Germany in the difficult travel years right after the war, has provided a lovely reminiscence: "Timetables seem to adjust to his whim, engine-drivers are in league with him and hold up the start of the express whilst he conducts an excited invalid infinitely slowly to her reserved compartment, saying with irritating assurance as guards blow whistles and porters shout and safely seated travelers stare from the windows, 'We have plenty of time, my dear. Don't hurry. There's plenty of time.'"

Brereton's vignette catches Hahn in a moment that, in its small but touching way, reflects the very heart of his personal philosophy. This was his profound commitment to the Samaritan ethic. He had one hero above all: the compassionate traveler on the road to Jericho. Again and again he called for the Parable of the Good Samaritan to be read to the school. In the years to come I was to witness the growing power of his ultimate conviction—that through help to those "in danger and in need" youth can strike the deepest chords of the human spirit. It would become a creed: "He who drills and labors, accepts hardship, boredom, and dangers, all for the sake of helping his brother in peril and distress, discovers God's purpose in his inner life."

■ ■ ■

The summer of 1952 approached, when our time at Gordonstoun would be up. The matter of what I would do on our return to the States was of growing concern. In May came a letter from John Kemper, headmaster of Phillips Academy in Andover, Massachusetts, offering a teaching post there. I had good memories of an apprenticeship summer that I had spent at Andover just before I joined the Hun faculty, and I had great respect for Kemper as an educator and a person. Andover would be a big change from Gordonstoun, but in his letter Kemper indicated that he would expect me to contribute to my new school from my Gordonstoun experience. It was an honor to be offered a place on the Andover faculty, and I decided to accept.

The day came for leave-taking. Hahn stood by the car with his gentle smile, bidding our family good-bye. "Look back over your left shoulder, but only once," he said. "Then you will surely return." When down the road we took that last look, the man who had changed my life forever was still standing with his hand raised in farewell. Turning back to the view of the road ahead, I made a promise to myself. I was resolved to help bring some aspect of his work to the United States.

ANDOVER AND THE BREAK

❈

*Let us build up physical fitness for the
sake of the soul,*

—Plato

John Kemper had written that he wanted me to bring to Andover aspects of the Hahn philosophy and method that were applicable to the Andover scene, so long as they changed none of the existing structure. I was just young enough to pay scant heed to the inherent contradiction. At Phillips Academy—best known simply as Andover—I found myself part of an institution where the faculty and administrators were secure and comfortable with the school's 175-year-old traditions, its high academic standards, its splendid record in getting graduates into leading colleges, its prestige in the educational community, its eminence on the athletic field, its Andover way of doing things. They were not in search of innovation. Most of them had never heard of Kurt Hahn, or Gordonstoun, or Salem, or Outward Bound. Had they, it would not have occurred to them that Hahn or his institutions had anything to offer them or the school.

At the same time, I was intent on maintaining a low profile. I realized that were it to get bruited about that I had an innovating mission, I would have two strikes on me at the outset. Those good low-profile intentions were abruptly shattered within a month by the arrival, on short notice, of Kurt Hahn and Prince George to visit the school. Suddenly I was consorting with these distinguished guests, one of them (Hahn's fame raced out over the

Traversing Avalanche Glacier on Mount Adams in Washington is a journey toward building self-confidence and climbing skills. (Photo © Cobi Harris)

campus grapevine) an educator of international renown, the other not only a headmaster but royalty. Put in charge of their visit, I did not even know the names of my fellow faculty members, let alone the students.

Hahn stayed at our home. He had no more than arrived when he managed to lock himself in the bathroom. We had to call on the combined competence of the town police and fire departments to free him. Touring the school, he and the prince were a colorful pair. John Kemper was much taken with them both. In those first meetings he was somewhat disconcerted by Hahn's readiness to give him fatherly (age sixty-six to forty) instruction in the arts of headmastership, but he would grow to relish that. The two were to become great friends.

I could not wait to hear Hahn's reactions to Andover. That he was instantly impressed by the physical plant was hardly surprising. He found the Cage—a big, glass-covered, dirt-floored building that housed a full athletic program indoors—a thing of wonder. He thought the library and music and art programs superb, and he quickly perceived the high academic quality in the Andover ambiance. But when, walking home after the third day of his visit, I asked him what he thought of the school, he said, "Phillips Academy is like a ship on a first-class voyage through education, but without a member of the crew in sight."

He meant that the students, always in his thinking the most visible part of the crew, were only passengers on this cruise. He missed the sight and sense of what was the essence of his own school's environment—the total involvement of the students in its operation. That every student did not have some responsibility whereby he was contributing to the functioning and well-being of the community—or some responsibility that he was being deprived of as a penalty—was for Hahn a denial of part of the education the school owed him. He was appalled to learn that the scholarship students had to work several hours each week while the full-paying students did not. (This is no longer true at Andover.) That made a shambles of his principle that a boy should not be penalized for a factor—especially his family's income—over which he had no control. At the same time, there was that nice Hahnian switch: The "underprivileged sons of the wealthy" were being deprived of a value-forming experience the scholarship students were getting.

He was impressed by the high level of performance achieved by Andover athletes. The school records in track and field, for example, were consistently superior to those at Gordonstoun. But he embarrassed us by asking for the average for the entire student body. We did not know our averages, never having measured them—but the facts would have been even more embarrassing. I was aware that whereas the average high jump for a Gordonstoun sixth former (senior) approached five feet, it would be near four for his Andover peer.

Hahn's departure left me with a depressed sense of how difficult it was going to be to weave any part of the Gordonstoun scheme into the Andover fabric. Kemper was urging me to come up with a proposal, but he made it clear I could expect no help in the form of administrative fiat. Whatever I might propose or undertake, it would be up to me to persuade the school community of its worth.

I decided that the one thing I might be able to accomplish at that juncture was the very thing that, it seemed to me, most needed doing: to set up some version of Gordonstoun's physical-education method. Andover was in the anomalous posture of having one of the finest athletic programs of any secondary school in the country, and virtually no physical education. Every student was required to put in ninety minutes four afternoons a week in some part of an extraordinary gamut of team sports. There were five levels of inter-school and intramural leagues, approximating five levels of skill, that enabled every boy to take part in a competitive sport. Altogether some five thousand youngsters from other schools were engaging Andover in one or another contest each year. These contests and the practice for them made for a fine program with many virtues, but this was athletics, not physical education.

How well I now understood Hahn's statement, "It is my mission in life to dethrone games." Competitive sports provide exercise, recreation, physical development, the social experience of team effort, the personal and social values of acquired skills, and competitive experience. Inevitably, however, the stress on competition denies to the athletically inferior youngster the chance to know authentic competitive pressure. When the contest is close, coaches are reluctant to use substitutes. Even a Class E league has its bench-sitters. Embarrassed by their poor performance, turned off by a reenforced sense of inferiority, the inept withdraw from athletic endeavor as soon as they can; yet they may well be the ones who most need to be impelled into the physical and competitive experience.

Not only was the physically subpar boy not overcoming his deficiencies and "the misery of unimportance" that they bred; neither, for the most part, was the competent athlete correcting his areas of weakness. And even if the desire to win was not permitted to dilute sportsmanship, there were other hazards for the physically gifted youngster. He could loaf—could become, in Hahn's phrase, "the prima donna athlete who is no friend of wind and weather, who takes a rest cure between rare maximum efforts." He could satisfy himself with a mediocre effort. He could gloss over his shortcomings by basking in the stardom of his specialty. He could get a distorted sense of his relative importance in the student mix.

John Kemper was aware of all this, especially of the potential of physical education for increasing the confidence of adolescent boys. Two years before he had brought in a young teacher named Reagh Wetmore, a fine athlete with first-rate physical-education competency, and charged him to set up a program. But Reagh too had his problems. The faculty, defending their territorial imperatives, refused to surrender any morning time. A strict rule forbade students to set foot in the gymnasium during study hours. The only concession the faculty had made to Reagh was to let him work with those students who were so low on the physical motor scale as to be clearly in need of special attention. But now the gymnasium was being rebuilt, and he had virtually no program at all. I told Reagh about The Break at Gordonstoun. He was not impressed. He was fresh from earning his master's degree at Springfield College in Massachusetts, the fount of conventional wisdom on physical education, and the Hahnian principles were not the ones he had been taught. He let me go to work with his collection of twenty or so physical misfits but took a dim view of what I was doing.

I dubbed them "the lame and the halt." What a great bunch of kids they were! Fat kids, frail kids whose muscles were virtually unused, kids who had never done anything physical, some of them terrified, one youngster who had been crippled by infantile paralysis (poliomyelitis). Most of them eventually gave it a good try, and these surprised themselves by what they could do. This confirmed my Gordonstoun experience. But the results obtained with a handful of boys who were physically very subpar were not going to sell the program to the faculty. They could perceive that this was useful therapy, but what did it have to do with the welfare of the student body at large? At the same time, I was aware that while my lads had certainly acquired an improved opinion of themselves, they still suffered the stigma of having been singled out as the poorest physical specimens in the school.

At this point Jack Hawes, an English teacher, came to my rescue. Jack had listened with interest to my Gordonstoun and Outward Bound stories, and now he was impressed by the improved physical prowess and heightened self-concept of the "lame and halt" kids. He was housemaster of Williams, one of the two dormitories that housed the "juniors," as Andover ninth-graders are called. Jack said, "Why don't you take my dormitory next year? Put them through the program, measure their progress, keep track of their classroom records, and compare them with the boys in Rockwell." Rockwell was the other ninth-grade dormitory. This looked like a way to gain credibility for The Break. We managed to persuade the faculty to approve the experiment of excusing the fifty boys in Williams from a one-hour study period two mornings a week. It was a reluctant approval. No one was really for the scheme except Kemper, Hawes, and myself. With Wetmore's counsel—he maintained his dim view—we settled on six events: the broad jump, high jump, shot put, discus, seventy-five-yard dash, and half-mile run. We set "Standard" and "Silver" levels of achievement for each event according to age. As always in The Break, the competition was only with oneself. I posted an improvement chart for each boy in the Cage, where I conducted the course, much as I had set it up at Gordonstoun.

Beautiful! Once again the combination of release from "the sedentary hours" and self-challenge worked its magic. In the classroom, it was easy to spot the ones who had just come in from The Break. They were more alive and alert. That kid sitting back there bright-eyed and bushy-tailed, you knew what had happened to him. He had made a quantifiable gain that day. One he could measure and send home, saying, "It is I who is gaining." That is important to a fourteen-year-old boy. I recall three youngsters in particular, each representative of a kind of experience common to The Break.

Frank was a short, chubby thirteen-year-old who, at the start, had complete disdain for the program. Fearful of revealing how subpar he actually was, he refused to extend himself and made a comical act of his poor performance. He seemed to enjoy the jeers he induced. Then, in spite of himself, he began to improve. Gradually, his attitude changed. One day he ran the dash two seconds better than his previous best time, faster than a lot of the others were doing. He forgot his act. The day he first put the shot twenty feet—nine feet better than his starting effort—the onlookers gave an acclaiming shout. You could see the new self-respect in his face. He went on to earn Silvers in both these events and a Standard in the discus. His late start cost him his Standards in the other three, but he had won a great discovery—that through trying, one can do what he thought he could not do.

Art was a slightly built, high-strung boy, sincere and studious. Physically he was poorly coordinated to the point of clumsiness, with little experience in sports. A sensitive lad, he took kindly neither to helpful nor deriding comments. But essentially there was nothing wrong with his physique except development. His improvement was startling. He bettered himself by nearly four and a half feet in the broad jump, thirteen inches in the high jump, more than twelve feet in the shot put, thirty feet in the discus, one and a half seconds in the seventy-five-yard dash, and thirty-five seconds in the half-mile run. His time for the half-mile beat the school's junior indoor record. By the end of the winter term this boy who had gone into The Break labeled a nonathlete by himself and his peers was on the school's junior relay team.

Tim was one of two boys who failed to win a single Standard. He was a pudgy, physically immature little boy who was all but helpless in physical activity. He lacked both coordination and the strength to carry his excess load of baby fat, and his performance measurements at the start were abysmal. He showed total disinterest. After about six weeks, something happened. He began to improve. By the end of the second term he had bettered the improvement average for the class in four of the six events. His classmates were regarding him with new respect, and so was he. One day he brought his mother to my office. He wanted me to tell her what The Break was all about and to explain what he had achieved. I guess the memory of that boy and his mother as they went out together, both with new pride in their eyes, is my favorite among the many rewards The Break brought to me. This boy who had failed to achieve a single Standard was one of my great successes.

I made a report at a faculty meeting in April 1954. After briefly reviewing the philosophy of the concept and the program structure, I gave the impressive statistics of the overall improvement in physical competence. Near the end I quietly dropped a bombshell—the comparative academic records for Williams Hall, the ninth-graders who had been in the Break program, and Rockwell Hall, those who had not. The data told a persuasive story. The average IQs of the two groups were virtually identical. In both terms the Break group had a higher average grade and higher average rank. They won honors in many more courses than the control group, failed in far fewer, and showed greater improvement from one term to next.

I said only, "It is apparent that the program was not detrimental to the academic interests of the boys involved," and sat down. There was a long, silent moment. Then Harper Follansbee, Rockwell's housemaster, stood up and said, "Next year I want my boys to have that program." That did it.

I won quite a few faculty adherents that afternoon, but Reagh Wetmore was my great convert. Convinced, he grabbed the ball, and thereafter we ran with it together. "Let's have something more than track events," Reagh said. That made sense to me; I bought his idea for a kind of indoor obstacle course in the gym, tests that would put a premium on agility and overcoming fear. Then Reagh said, "Okay, we've got something on the ground, something in the air, we ought to have something for the third element, the water." He was Andover's swim coach. But he was not thinking of just a pool counterpart to the track events. He wanted a water activity that would be different and valuable to the average youngster. He told me of a magazine article he had read about Fred Lanoue, the Georgia Tech swimming coach, who had developed a technique he called "drownproofing." According to Lanoue, anybody could be taught to survive in the water indefinitely.

As good luck would have it, we caught up with Lanoue shortly after that at a physical-education conference in New York, where the three of us huddled for a whole afternoon.

DROWNPROOFING: VISIT TO HAHN

✳

We try to teach youngsters that a technique in
the head is worth a million helping hands that
may be out of reach.

—Fred Lanoue

Fred Lanoue was one of the most colorful, most profane, and most Christian persons I have ever known. Of French Canadian parentage, he grew up in Worcester, Massachusetts. He earned his way through Springfield College as a daredevil high diver. The Lanoue stories at Springfield were in the folk-hero genre. They liked to tell you that he had earned a term's tuition by diving from a two-hundred-foot tower into a damp washcloth, with Roman candles sticking out of each ear and his rear end. He walked with a kind of foot-slapping limp, the consequence of an injury incurred while experimenting on a wild new dive.

Fred was a natural athlete, but as a boy swimming had been his poorest sport. Thin and bony, he was that relatively rare creature, a natural sinker. The strain of keeping his head above water sapped his energy. He discovered that he did much better swimming underwater, coming up only to breathe. It was not fast, but it got him where he wanted to go without tiring him out. That discovery provided the germ of his drownproofing theory.

He maintained there are only four good reasons for drowning. One, you are knocked unconscious. Two, the water is too cold, and you die from loss of body heat. Three, there is froth on the water, and you cannot get your head above it to breathe. Four, you starve to death. If you drown for any other reason, he said, you should get a demerit. He had developed a method for staying afloat indefinitely, even with cramps. Eschewing what he called the "cosmetic crawl," he employed a "travel stroke" for negotiating long distances with minimum energy. It was sheer absurdity, Fred argued, that a mere fifty-yard swim was considered an adequate beginner's test. If you find yourself in the water one hundred fifty yards off shore, he pointed out, being able to swim fifty yards is unlikely to help you much. His beginner's test was the ability to stay afloat one hour and swim one mile. He halved that for four-year-olds, but not for seven-year-olds.

Listening to my story of Gordonstoun and Outward Bound, Lanoue was greatly taken by the ideas of Kurt Hahn. He caught on just like that. He said, "I'm doing that with drownproofing. It's self-control under circumstances that approach panic and demand self-respect. And it leads to a respect for other people that you can express in a profound way—by saving their lives. This is what I believe in. Nobody graduates from Georgia Tech, nobody, until he passes drownproofing. I even put the president through [it]."

That fall Wetmore and I launched our new three-part version of The Break for the entire ninth grade. For an indoor obstacle course we rigged a circuit that involved vertical rope ladders, horizontal ladders twenty feet in the air, a trampoline leap to a horizontal overhead rope that then had to be traversed for twenty feet, followed by a flying swing to a cargo net, and so on. Its effectiveness as a test exceeded our fondest expectations. It was a great leveler. A football player would traverse that horizontal rope trip in an agony of effort, apprehension, and acrophobia. Right behind him a skinny little monkey of a kid would scramble through the whole exercise as though it were just a lark. The 200-pound tackle on the freshman team, who was a big shot because he had the bulk and strength to push smaller kids around, learned something about humility. Up to then he had been getting his ego-building input on the football field, which was just a congenital accident. Now he was learning the difference between the self-respect that your genes give you and the self-respect that you have earned.

Lanoue came up to help us get the drownproofing started. Fred taught me a lot, not only about water survival skills but about how to approach that kind of problem analytically. Most drownings, he pointed out, are due to some combination of panic and exhaustion. When even a reasonably good swimmer encounters a sudden crisis in the water—a fall into the water far from shore, a cramp, a strong current pulling him away from safety—his instinctive reaction is too often a fatal one. He may try to buck a current wearing heavy water-logged clothes. Or he may shuck clothes that he needs for warmth. He may use a stroke he is unable to maintain. He may exhaust himself trying to keep his head out of water—the equivalent of supporting a ten-pound brick as he swims. He may gasp for air at the instant a swell fills his mouth with water. A cramp may frighten him to greater exertion and quicker exhaustion. Or he may turn over on his back to rest—which consumes more energy than is commonly thought—and choke as a wave washes over his face.

Lanoue's drownproofing technique is based on the natural buoyancy of most human bodies when the lungs are filled with air. The victim takes a full breath and allows himself to sink to his natural float position. The body is angled forward at the waist, face in the water, the back of the neck at the surface, arms and legs hanging loosely downward. The air does the work of keeping him afloat near the surface. Every six to ten seconds, he folds his arms in front of his head, raises his head far enough out of the water to inhale, supporting this act with a scissors kick, then resumes the float position. He expends so little energy that terrifying complications like cramps, heavy clothes, a disabling injury, rough water, or long immersion do not threaten his survival. An adaptation of this basic subsurface float enables him, using the "travel stroke," to swim through the water at about one mile per hour without tiring. A few who lack natural buoyancy—only about one percent of white males (although a considerable percentage of black males) and the rare female are sinkers—must use the travel stroke to stay afloat.

To pass drownproofing, each student involved in The Break had to stay afloat for one hour, swim a mile wearing pants and shirt, and perform a sequence of maneuvers that simulated cramp conditions—first with hands tied behind back, then with legs tied Buddha-fashion. He also had to swim underwater for 150 feet, demonstrate using a pair of pants as a floating aid, and do a one-hundred-yard chest-carry of another person. Over the years Reagh Wetmore refined and added to the tests.

■ ■ ■

In 1959, during spring vacation, Wetmore and I flew to visit Hahn and his institutions. He was then living in an apartment in the castle that housed Hermannsburg, Salem's junior school. We spent a day with him, visited the Hermannsburg and Salem schools, the two new German Outward Bound schools at Weissenhaus and Baad, and went on to England for visits to Aberdovey and Gordonstoun and a final rendezvous with Hahn in London.

Hahn had retired from Gordonstoun in 1953 at the age of sixty-six, charging his co-successors, Henry Brereton and Robert Chew: "You will not permit Gordonstoun to descend to the level of a first-class traditional school!" The next year the University of Edinburgh conferred on him an honorary Doctor of Law. The university's chancellor, Prince Philip, Duke of Edinburgh, made the presentation. "It cannot be given to many," said Gordonstoun's most distinguished old boy, "to have the opportunity and the desire to heap honors upon their former headmaster." Presumably the university conceived its accolade as capping the brilliant career of a man entering retirement. But Hahn still had promises to keep, and some he had not yet even made. He carried on, more than ever, "an old man in a hurry," dividing his time largely between Hermannsburg and London, where in a suite at Brown's Hotel he maintained a kind of personal global headquarters.

We found him in great form. His work was bearing fruit literally around the world. In addition to new Outward Bound schools in England, and the two in Germany for which he was personally responsible, others had been started in Nigeria, Kenya, Malaysia, and Australia. In the preceding year his eighteen-year campaign for his County Badge plan had won the smashing success of royal sponsorship, when Prince Philip launched it as the Duke of Edinburgh's Award Scheme. In later years Philip, reflecting on how well the scheme had taken hold throughout the British Commonwealth, would remember: "It would never have started but for Hahn, certainly not. He suggested I ought to do it, and I fought against it for quite a long time.

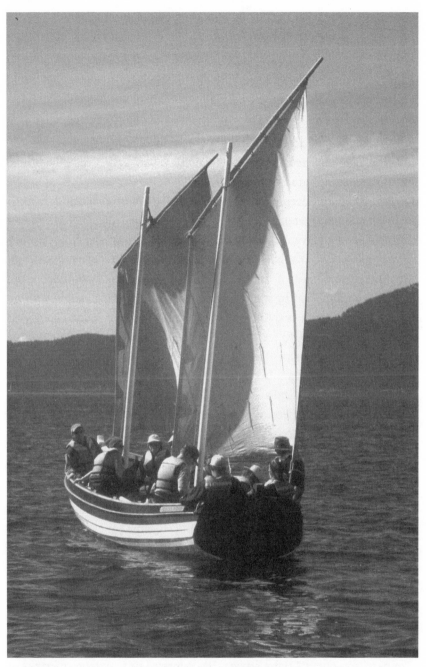

Washington State's San Juan Islands have provided excellent sailing waters for Outward Bound students for over a quarter of a century. (Photo © PCOBS, Jeremy Lucke)

Because you know what the British are like in relation to that sort of thing. And I said, well, I'm not going to stick my neck out and do anything as stupid as that, and everybody saying, 'Ah, silly ass,' you know?" Hahn's faith proved sounder than the Duke's apprehension. Nobody said, "Ah, silly ass." By 1970 the award scheme was established in twenty-eight countries. In 1980 it was established as the Congressional Award and I was asked to be one of the sixteen founding trustees.

Now Hahn was deeply involved in inventing a new institution. In 1955 Air Marshal Sir Lawrence Darvall, Commandant of the NATO Defense College in Paris, had said to him: "The conservative, nationalistic military officers attending our school are achieving a remarkable degree of international understanding in a mere six-month course. Think how much more could be accomplished by a nonmilitarist school for young people with an international student body!" Fired by Darvall's concept, Hahn had joined forces with him. The two men were recruiting committees in many countries to support their proposal for an Atlantic College—a two-year, precollege school enrolling students from all over the world. In such a school, they envisioned, Briton and Indian, Israeli and Arab, Greek and Turk, students of all colors and political persuasions would study and adventure together in a self-governing international environment.

That trip completed Wetmore's conversion to the Hahnian philosophy. He peppered Hahn with questions. How did he know this, know that? Hahn's answers were mostly grounded in homely observation. On what basis did he claim children had an innate sense of order? Ask a four-year-old to fetch you a pail of sand, Hahn said, and see how he pats and smooths the top before he hands it to you. "All the treasures of childhood come alive in the four-year-old," he told us.

Kemper had been critical of our reports on students in The Break, as being too statistical, not interpretive enough of individual development. We told Hahn about this, explaining that we were chary of trespassing into areas that were more properly the province of the housemasters and teachers. "Trespass continually," Hahn replied. He counseled us to extend the range of our reports. We should make a diagnosis like a doctor; this would help the boy's housemaster and his parents.

There was an incident on that trip that neither Wetmore nor I have forgotten. Discoursing on one of his favorite themes—"your liability is your opportunity"—Hahn had remarked that people who have surmounted a serious handicap have a "glint" in their eye. At the Hamburg Airport, intending to fly to London, we found no record of our reservations. It was close to flight time; informed that there were no places for us, we were dismayed at the prospect of losing a day of our already brief time in Britain. The clerk took our situation to a colleague, who was immediately all concern. When his initial resort to the telephone was of no avail, he literally sprinted off. Several minutes later he came running back, his expression telling us that all was well, swiftly wrote out our tickets, and gave us a hurried escort to our departure gate. As we settled breathlessly into our plane seats, deeply grateful to our rescuer, Wetmore said to me, "Did you see the glint in his eye?" The man had an artificial hand.

We returned to Andover revitalized. Following Hahn's suggestion, we made our Break evaluating format more subjective. Each boy's housemaster received a rather elaborate developmental report. As Hahn had predicted, the housemasters found these reports invaluable in their day-to-day and counseling contacts, as well as a help when they talked with parents. The reports stayed in the boys' files, and in time they were useful to the upper housemasters too.

It was interesting to observe Hahn's influence on Wetmore. He continued to improve and refine The Break. He completely changed his method of teaching chemistry, cutting down the theoretical, beefing up the experiential. In his first year as swimming coach, twelve boys had come out for the team. After the visit to Hahn, Reagh recruited vigorously. The swim squad enrollment built to more than two hundred. He had seven teams—varsity, junior varsity, four "club" teams, and juniors (freshmen)—swimming competitively outside the school. Broadening the base produced more champions; the school had one national champion after another.

The Break became an Andover institution. Reagh did a lot of speaking and writing, creating considerable interest in the physical-education community. But it has never taken hold in other schools. To sell it, to win institutional status for it, requires too much educating of the educators. I still consider it the finest physical-education program I have known.

▪ ▪ ▪

In January 1958, in cognizance of Hahn's new centering of effort on the Atlantic College undertaking, the American-British Foundation for European Education changed its name to the Atlantic Foundation for the Education of the Free. At that time John Kemper and I were elected to the board, along with Sir Lawrence Darvall and Professor H. Wentworth Eldredge of Dartmouth College, an early Atlantic College enthusiast. A year later I was made secretary. Ellen McCloy and Eric Warburg, who had become respectively president and executive vice president in 1954, continued in those posts. By 1960 it was definite that the first Atlantic College would be established in Llantwit Major, Wales, and Hahn was urging us to launch a campaign for a second college in this country. We scouted for possible sites. But the timing was not right for the task of raising the needed millions of dollars. John Kemper and Jack Stevens (who had been a director since 1953), the foundation's two best money-raising talents, were both deeply involved in a six-million-dollar campaign for Phillips Academy.

I was strongly conscious of not yet having redeemed my self-promise to play a part in bringing Kurt Hahn's work to the United States. While an American Atlantic College was then the project closest to Hahn's heart, I continued to hope we could also find the means of establishing Outward Bound in this country. As the new decade began, I was unaware of how close to feasibility that hope lay. I did not know about a schoolmaster in Colorado seeking a way "to give students a sense of purpose and involvement in something larger than themselves." Nor about a Princeton classmate turning from a life-negating cloak-and-dagger career to a search for affirmation. The separate aspirations of the three of us were destined to come together in the founding of U.S. Outward Bound.

THE BIRTH OF U.S. OUTWARD BOUND

✳

Whatever you can do, or dream you can, begin it;
Boldness has genius, power, and magic in it.

—Goethe

In March 1959, F. Charles Froelicher, headmaster of Colorado Academy, a Denver independent day school, was a guest of the British consul on a Denver radio station. A second guest was Ted Hopkins, a cadet at the Air Force Academy, who had lived in England and told about having been a student at the Eskdale Outward Bound School. The young man's description of his challenging experience fascinated Froelicher, who was unable to point to anything comparable in the States. Not long afterward, British educator Sir John Wolfenden, visiting in Denver, told him more about Outward Bound. His interest further whetted, Froelicher wrote to the Outward Bound Trust in London. He sought information about the course syllabus, in the thought that he might be able to use his school plant in the summertime for an adventure program on the British model. "The more I got into it," he said, "the more I realized that that wouldn't work—that Outward Bound was a much more significant educational undertaking than I had any notion of when I started exploring it. So the matter lay fallow for a while."

Gilbert Burnett came to Princeton the same year as I. He was from Kentucky, where he had grown up in an open country environment of horses and freedom. A war-accelerated graduate in the summer of 1943, Gil enlisted in the army and was tapped by the Office of Strategic Services. He completed

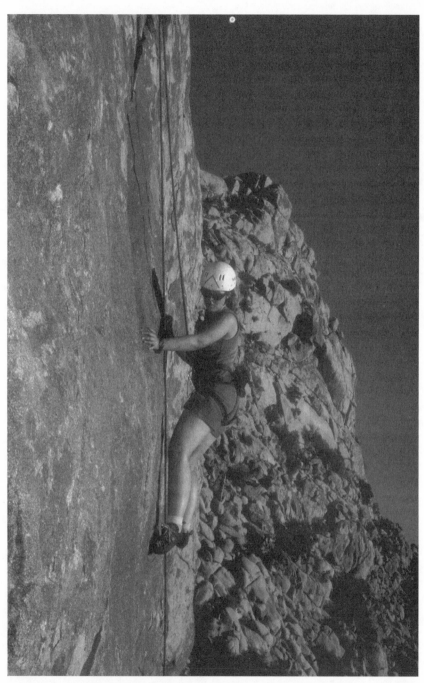

A student navigates the sheer rock walls in Joshua Tree National Park, a valuable classroom for Outward Bound climbing courses. (Photo © PCOBS, Kim Budd)

his OSS training, including proficiency in the employment of a palm-sized stiletto, in Indochina, where he became part of a joint British-American operation. For Burnett it was a "good war." When it ended and the OSS was dissolved, he continued in intelligence for the Army General Staff, then transferred to the newly formed Central Intelligence Agency.

His CIA "targets" took him to various parts of the world. As the postwar decade went by, the dirty-tricks existence palled, then soured. Gil remembers, "There came a point when I realized that as a human being I was becoming more and more kamikaze, without any roots, without any heart, without anything—a kind of smiling ego without any insides." Sometime during that period of progressive disillusionment he chatted in a Washington bistro with a British acquaintance who was a correspondent for the London *Times*. The conversation took a philosophical turn that led the Britisher to tell him about the work of a schoolmaster in England named Kurt Hahn. "The *Times* man brought up Hahn in connection with William James's concept of 'a moral equivalent of war.' He talked about the idiom of compassion, something I had entirely lost touch with. There were, I gathered, elements of adventure and derring-do in Hahn's program. I was fascinated. The conversation and this man Hahn stuck in my mind. I thought of him as a romantic, but as one who was trying to do something about the appalling negativism after the war, the arms race, the Cold War, the whole filthy business I was involved in personally."

Deciding he had to make a move, wondering what he was cut out for, Burnett thought perhaps it was teaching. Through Princeton connections he found a post at the Pounahou School in Honolulu. Arriving there, he immediately noticed that the area was wonderfully suited for involving youngsters with the sea. But the school was doing nothing of that sort. Recalling the vague information he had picked up about Hahn's work, he wrote to London for information and received some pamphlets Hahn had written. "Then I did my homework. I began to read James, and look up the words 'character' and 'compassion' and this kind of thing." He came back to the States to teach at St. George's School in Newport, Rhode Island, where he set up an adventure-based program for the students. One day early in 1960 he drove up to Andover to talk with John Kemper about an opening on the Andover faculty.

He arrived just as I was saying good-bye to the Guggenheims, who had been visiting us. After introductions, as they drove off, Gil asked, "Who's that?" I told him about meeting the Guggenheims at Gordonstoun and Gugg's supportive role in Hahn's work. Gil took fire. It blew his mind to discover that I had been at Gordonstoun and knew Hahn, had been exposed to Outward Bound and Atlantic College. He drilled me with questions.

Kemper perceived that here was an ally for the Hahnian cause. He gave Gil an appointment to teach biology the following year, with the understanding that Burnett would go to England that summer to learn all he could about Outward Bound. In London the Outward Bound Trust gave him VIP treatment. Eddie Dawson, England's great ex-cricketer who was then executive secretary of the Trust, opened up the files to him and set up visits to several schools.

Guggenheim arranged for him to meet Hahn in London. Gil recalled the large, dim figure in the darkened sitting room in Brown's Hotel, the immediate sense of being in an Old World presence, the initial impact of Hahn's gentleness, of being put immediately at ease by a pleasantry about Americans. "The philosophy that he gave me at that particular time in my own life was what I was looking for. He understood about the work I had been doing and the question that I was facing, of how to shift from being a destructive representative of the postwar period. How, instead of blowing up bridges, do you build a bridge in order to effect a rescue? That was an idea that had never before occurred to me."

Gil came back to Andover gung ho to get something started. While in London he had compiled a list of Americans, including Chuck Froelicher, who had written to the Outward Bound Trust. Sometime in the fall he called Froelicher and asked him if he was interested in the possibility of starting an Outward Bound school in Colorado. Froelicher said he was. Kemper gave us permission to fly to Denver to meet with him at the January 1961 end of term. Reagh Wetmore and Ed Williams, another Andover teacher, who were doing graduate study at the University of Colorado at Boulder, joined us for a lunch meeting at Froelicher's school.

Chuck Froelicher had grown up in Baltimore, where his grandfather had been president of Goucher College, his grandmother had taught Romance languages at Goucher for forty years, and his father had been headmaster of the Park School. After naval service in World War II and graduation from Johns Hopkins, Chuck became a teacher. In 1955 he took on the headmastership of the Colorado Military Academy, a Denver school for boys that had a declining enrollment of fifty-six and was in financial straits. He dropped the military component, persuaded a group of community leaders to become trustees, and set about the task of regenerating the school. When he left it twenty years later to become executive director of the Gates Foundation, it was one of the West's prestigious country day schools, with more than five hundred boy and girl students.

Through the meal, with mounting enthusiasm, we kicked around the idea of a Colorado Outward Bound school. Finally Froelicher said, "Let's just decide we're going to start a school, and line out what we have to do to get it started." He still bore the scars and growing pains of Colorado Academy's rebirth, and that experience helped as we drew up a battle plan: interest a group of influential Colorado sponsors, find some possible sites, bring someone over from England to advise on the site and the organizing of a school, and so on, through a long list. And raise money, of course. We dreamed up a rough budget and agreed in principle on the idea of half to be raised in Colorado, half by the Atlantic Foundation.

Two weeks later Froelicher came east for the foundation's annual meeting, and the undertaking was made official. By then we had a schedule. Acquire and develop the site and organize the school in the current year, offer the first two courses in the summer of 1962. The foundation voted to raise $60,000 to help get the school started. Jack Stevens made an immediate contribution of $10,000. We voted to ask Captain Freddy Fuller to journey from Aberdovey to Colorado in the following month, to advise on site and organization and to make presentations of the Outward Bound concept in support of fund-raising in Colorado. We were off and running.

Froelicher stayed on for an appointment Eric Warburg had made for him and me to meet the next day with Stephen Currier, the executive director at the Taconic Foundation. Currier listened to our story and said, "Go see Harris Wofford in Washington. He's one of our directors and, if he agrees, we might consider giving you some money." Kemper joined us on the trip to Washington to talk with Wofford. Congress had recently passed the Peace Corps legislation, and President John F. Kennedy had appointed Sargent Shriver, his brother-in-law, to create it. Wofford was helping him. When he had heard us out, he said, "You simply must talk with Shriver about this, because the Peace Corps has a problem." He took us to Shriver's office, and we told our story again. Shriver's response flabbergasted us. He said, "I want you to start eight Outward Bound schools for the Peace Corps. We'll pump our volunteers through them before they go overseas." We said that was out of the question. That we were struggling with the possibility of starting one school in Colorado. We could not possibly get involved in training the Peace Corps.

Shriver grew very earnest as he explained that the Peace Corps had a serious problem. They were getting a lot of flak from people who did not think it would work. These people just did not believe the government could take young people fresh from college classrooms, still wet behind the ears, and send them out in ambassadorial roles. The Corps' problem was that it just might not get a chance to prove its case. The opposition was so strong that if the Corps should have the same rate of attrition that federal agencies traditionally experienced overseas—losing one out of two—the program would die in its first year. Shriver and his colleagues needed some assurance that if they took a youngster from an air-conditioned college classroom and sent him to Tanganyika (now part of Tanzania), he would stay there long enough to find he could make a go of it. What would happen when the first bug dropped out of the thatch into his soup, or the rains came, or the mails did not come, or people would not work, or he got homesick? "I believe Outward Bound as you describe it could be the answer to our problem," Shriver said. "If you can't start eight schools for us, start one."

We realized it was going to be difficult to turn down the White House. Shriver made it clear that in the matter of the Peace Corps he spoke for the President. Also, this was an exciting challenge. It offered a dramatic way to launch the Outward Bound concept into the national consciousness. We told him we would report back with an answer.

Three weeks later, in March, Freddy Fuller arrived, and Burnett and I flew to Colorado with him. Freddy made a presentation at Colorado Academy to a group whose support Chuck Froelicher hoped to win, and we drove out to the western part of the state to look for a site in the Rockies. Our first stop was the Rocky Mountain School in Carbondale. John Holden, the school's headmaster, and Jack Snobble, his assistant, listened to Fuller's presentation and were enthusiastic. Snobble told us about a "mountain man" friend of his who he thought would be just the man to take hold of the project. "His name is Tap Tapley. He's part Indian, an extraordinary guy. There is just nothing he doesn't know about these mountains, and how to function in them." The next day we went up into the mountains where Tapley was dynamiting avalanches and stringing fence for a mining camp, and told him about Outward Bound and why we were there. He told us of a mining claim above the mountain town of Marble that belonged to friends of his named Howard and Blu Stroud. He thought it might meet the site specifications, and we decided to look at it.

The next morning we drove down to Redstone, where I transferred into an International Harvester vehicle with Tapley and his wife, Lee. Soon we were on a dirt-and-rock mountain road and climbing. Tap drove with competence and said little. We would be driving, three in front, and Lee would say to me, "He means for us to get in back," and she and I would scramble over into the back seat to put more weight on the rear wheels. We would get past that tough spot and climb back in front. Pretty soon Lee would say, "He means for us to get in back." How she got the messages I never knew because Tap had not spoken.

Howard Stroud was waiting for us at Marble, a mining ghost town with a scattering of residents. We all piled into Stroud's snowcat. The snow was deep now, and the climb even steeper. We were smack in the middle of the Rockies, twenty miles southwest of Aspen, at nine thousand feet, on a "road" where part of the track seemed to be over nothing. It was an awesome ride.

The climb leveled out. We were at the Stroud property. Under six or seven feet of snow, it formed a level bench about one thousand by two hundred feet before the mountain started to rise again. A beautiful grove of aspen roughly delineated its boundaries. In the distance, the summit of Treasury Mountain was majestic in its white mantle. We could see that the level area offered a splendid setting for a base camp.

Later we looked at another site, which had a large old residence on it. Freddy Fuller preferred this one; it was much closer to the British model. All the British Outward Bound schools have a fine residence to which, most nights, the students return to eat and sleep in comfortable quarters. It is Hahn's "dunk 'em and dry 'em" philosophy, and there is a lot of soundness in the theory. But here we were getting our first variation between British and U.S. Outward Bound.

When we got back to Denver, there was a message to call Shriver. I reached Wofford and told him, "We'll start an Outward Bound School in Colorado for the Peace Corps." Shriver called back. Colorado would not do. "Congress will never buy it," he said. "We're going to be sending people to tropical climates. It doesn't make sense to prepare them in the arctic altitudes of Colorado." It was the classic misunderstanding of the Outward Bound method—the failure to comprehend that we would be training *through* the mountains, not *for* them. But I could understand Shriver's reluctance to battle that one out with Congress—especially the politically unfriendly congressmen and the ones who were doubtful about the whole Peace Corps idea. He said, "How about starting an Outward Bound school in Puerto Rico? As long as Captain Fuller is here, why doesn't he come see us on the way home?"

Fuller went to Washington, and from there down to Puerto Rico to look for a site, and Burnett and I went back to Andover. I felt overwhelmed by the pace and mounting complications. I was working in the admissions office, teaching, and coaching, and now suddenly there were these two giant undertakings in Colorado and Puerto Rico for which I was responsible to the Atlantic Foundation. The trustees were excited that something was happening at long last, and they gave their enthusiastic backing to both ventures. Fortunately, the school year would be over in two months.

WASHINGTON, ARECIBO, AND MARBLE

❊

What we have to learn to do, we learn by doing.

—Aristotle

Early in the spring of 1961 we presented the formal Outward Bound proposal to the Peace Corps and received an official go-ahead. I began to shuttle between Andover and Washington. One day Sargent Shriver called me in and said, "I'm delighted with the reports we're getting on your progress. You're going to be the director in Puerto Rico."

I said, "I'm glad you're getting good reports, but let's get it straight that I'm not the director."

"Why not?"

"First, I feel much more responsible for Outward Bound as a private operation than I do for Outward Bound in the Peace Corps. I can't do for both. Second, for the Peace Corps you need a very charismatic kind of guy. You need somebody who can handle the press, handle Congress, handle top brass, handle ambassadors, handle the Puerto Rican government."

"Who's that guy?" Shriver asked.

I said, "I know only one—Bill Coffin, William Sloane Coffin."

"You mean Reverend Coffin, the Yale chaplain? I went to Yale; I bet I can get him." Shriver flipped his intercom. "Get me Reverend William Coffin, the chaplain at Yale University." Soon the phone rang. "Bill. This is Sarge. Sargent Shriver. No, we haven't met—I'm director of the Peace Corps. I have a friend of yours here who says you're the only guy in the world to run this doggone

Outward Bound program for us. I'd like to talk with you about it. What do you mean, it's out of the question? At least you can come down and talk about it. We'll pay your way. You're coming to Washington anyway? Friday? Where're you staying? The YMCA! Nobody stays at the YMCA! We'll put you up at the Sheraton. Meet you there for breakfast Saturday morning at seven-thirty." He finally persuaded Coffin to take the job long enough to get the Puerto Rican operation under way.

As soon as school was out I went to Washington. The Puerto Rico camp was due to open in three months, and Coffin and I had a prodigious amount of work to do designing and staffing a program. Freddy Fuller had reported that Puerto Rico had fine terrain for a school, but the site had yet to be selected. I went down to make a survey and was flown all over the island in a plastic bubble helicopter belonging to the Puerto Rico Water Resources Department. The environment, though mountainous, could hardly have been more different from the Rockies. In the helicopter I was following the map, but the pilot had to show me where we were; there were no landmarks that I could see. The pilot would point and shout, "We're going down!" and I would look down at a solid mass of rain forest. We would drop almost like a leaf and land in a clearing I had not seen at all. Before the blades stopped spinning we would be surrounded by fifty kids. Puerto Rico is one of the most densely populated areas in the world.

Later I returned with Coffin. The site search had just about narrowed down to an abandoned lumber camp in the rain forest twenty miles from Arecibo, a town on the north-central coast, and we were making a final check. The area had a small stream, some usable small buildings, good trees for a ropes course. Driving around, we found a beautiful reservoir. Coffin took off his clothes and plunged in. I was about to follow when someone told us that the water had microscopic worms that infected the liver. That was a blow; we had been told the water in the area was free of parasites. The reservoir spill ran in a lovely river to the sea that we had planned to use for white-water kayaking. In the end the reservoir's only usefulness was for rappelling on the steep face of the dam.

Coffin and I were invited to the governor's palace. Governor Muñoz quickly grasped the idea of Outward Bound. He was sympathetic and gave us

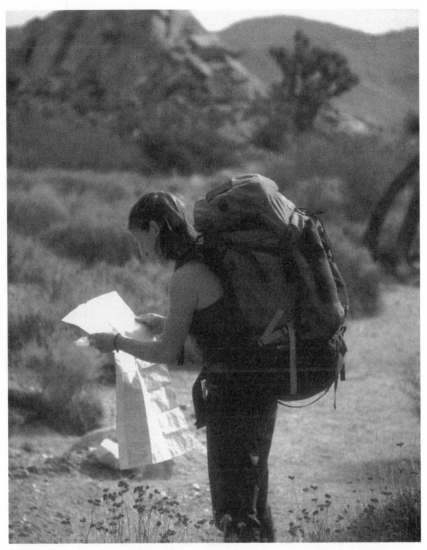

Outward Bound course curriculum includes education on navigation skills. Here, a student consults her map in Joshua Tree National Park. (Photo © PCOBS, Kim Budd)

wonderful cooperation. He hoped the Peace Corps would not just use the camp for its volunteers, but also would make it available to the young people of his country. He saw the same problems with his youth that he saw with young people elsewhere in the world.

I was distressed by the urbanization—much of it the "American-ization"—of Puerto Rico. But as soon as you were off the main arteries and into the indigenous culture, everything changed. The traffic changed, the pace changed, the people changed. They were lovely, laughing, hospitable, delightful. The country was beautiful; the people could manage cleanliness in their small *barrios*. Above all, the family ties were warm and strong. You saw poverty everywhere, but only of the pocket, not of the soul. Malnutrition was not a problem. People raised their own food, even on the handkerchief-sized plot each family lived on with its goat and chickens. You enjoyed the lighthearted ambiance, and it broke your heart to realize what a blight our urban ghettos, so far from the lovely island wildness, had worked on that blitheness of spirit.

In Washington we were immersed in the charisma of the Kennedy administration. It was an extraordinary experience for me to go from a New England classroom to a sector of the national power center. We had a great gang headed by William Haddad, a creative, dynamic, hard-bitten entrepreneur sort to whom Coffin and I reported, who became a kind of inspector general of the Peace Corps. We worked furiously, often till midnight. I worked several weeks and got no paycheck. A friend in personnel investigated. "There's some difficulty about your security clearance." Ridiculous, I told him. A couple of days later he came to see me. "What's this Atlantic Foundation for the Education of the Free you're involved in?" So this was security! I dropped the names of a few of my colleagues in the foundation—Ellen McCloy, Christian Herter, Allen Dulles, Eric Warburg.

Working and living with Bill Coffin was an experience in itself. At that time William Sloane Coffin had not yet become a controversial figure at the national level. But he had been controversial enough even at Phillips Academy when he came, fresh out of Yale Divinity School, to be acting chaplain for a year. His impact on the Andover community was the same as it was going to be everywhere else—people felt strongly for him or against him, there was nobody in the middle.

Suddenly now the chapel service before Christmas vacation floods my memory. It is snowing outside, the students are packed and dressed for the trip home, and they will take off as soon as chapel is over. They have sung the hymns and said the prayers, and Coffin steps into the pulpit to say good-bye. "I hope you all have a wonderful vacation." There is a stirring and reaching for hats. "Now, wait a minute, w-a-a-i-t a minute! You're not getting off that easy! What do I mean by 'wonderful'? Wonderful means full of wonder. I want you to go home this Christmas full of wonder. I want you to wonder about your mother. What kind of a person is she? What does life mean to her? I want you to wonder about what you mean to her life. I want you to wonder about your father. Wonder about what he is worried about. What are his concerns? What's the toll of responsibility on him? Wonder about that jerk roommate of yours. He's human too, you know. Why does he have troubles? Spend some time wondering about him. And when you're dancing around with that sweet young thing in your arms, wonder about her. Because she's worth wondering about. I hope you all have a wonderful vacation!"

He is the best preacher I have ever listened to. He can drive you crazy because he is so superb and then can get carried away and go into the detail of a rape on the cold marble floor of a Harlem drugstore. Coming from the pulpit, that upsets a lot of people, especially older people. Bill's critics say he is an egotist, that he is more interested in a spectacular performance than in the essence of what he is saying. That just is not so. He is a deeply thoughtful and concerned man, with a showman's gift. I agree with Jack Stevens, who once said, "Bill Coffin is the only practicing Christian I know."

I told Coffin we had to have drownproofing at Arecibo. I told him about Freddy Lanoue, whom we would have to shake loose from Georgia Tech. The minute I mentioned Georgia, his hackles rose. "We're going to have blacks in Puerto Rico. We can't be subjecting them to any redneck prejudices."

"Come off it, Bill," I said. "Anyway, Fred's a Canuck from Worcester, Massachusetts, and Springfield College, and everybody loves him."

Coffin was unconvinced, about Lanoue and about drownproofing. "Get him up here," he said. "I'll have to talk with him."

It was already evening when I reached Lanoue at his home in Atlanta. He greeted me with a string of affectionate expletives. I said, "Fred, what are you doing tonight?"

"What do you mean, what am I doing tonight? It's eight-thirty."

I said, "How fast can you get up here to Washington?"

He said, "I can be there at quarter to twelve. I often make that flight," and he gave me the flight number.

I called a member of our Peace Corps team, Sally Bowles, daughter of Undersecretary of State Chester Bowles, at her parents' home in Georgetown. "Sally, I need your swimming pool tomorrow morning. Can we borrow it?" "I don't think you can," Sally said. "Mother's giving a lunch party for the African envoys, and they've been invited to come early for a swim." I assured Sally we would be there early and only needed an hour. We were given permission to use the Bowleses' pool with the understanding that we would be gone before the first guest arrived.

Coffin and I were waiting for Lanoue when his plane came in. I lost track of how many people stopped us between the gate and the car. ("Coach Lanoue, you don't remember me, but—." "Sure I remember you. You're such a dumb son of a bitch you nearly drowned.") It seemed that every tenth person at National Airport was a friend of Freddy Lanoue.

In the morning, poolside at the Bowleses, Coffin was looking dubious. "All right now, Reverend," Fred said, "just put your hands behind your back and cross your wrists, that's a good boy. Let me tie 'em up tight. That's it. Now your feet. Not too tight? Okay. Usually we take twelve hours to get to this tie-up phase, but time is short." He pushed Coffin into the pool. "All right now, goddammit, Reverend, you do as I say, or I'm going to drown you. Trouble with you reverse-collar so-and-so's is you never listen to anybody else. I got you trussed up real good, so now you better listen up, hear?"

Coffin was wild. He was so mad he could not talk. Lanoue began to teach him the basics of drownproofing. Every time Coffin made a mistake, Lanoue put a foot on his head and drove him down to the bottom of the pool. Bill would float up so mad that if he could have gotten loose, I think he would have torn Lanoue apart. When he surfaced, Fred would say something like "For God's sake, Reverend, relax! I thought you were a man of faith!"

Pretty soon Coffin was getting the hang of it. "That's fine, Reverend, you got the rhythm just fine." He did the travel stroke to the shallow end, where I untied him. His wrists were bleeding; apparently he had panicked a bit in those moments on the bottom of the pool. We sat on the pool's edge while Fred gave us a fascinating discourse on the theory and practice of drownproofing. He finished just as the first of the Bowleses' guests arrived poolside. Recognizing Arthur Schlesinger, Jr., the historian and at that time a Kennedy staff member, Coffin introduced us. "Glad to meet you, Art," Lanoue said. "Put your hands behind your back." Before Schlesinger knew what was happening, he too was bobbing in the pool. In his case, however, Lanoue only tied his hands.

I spotted one of the African envoys coming out, a flowing white robe over his bathing suit. Lanoue walked up to him and held out his hand. "My name's Fred Lanoue, Ambassador, mighty pleased to meet you. Put your hands behind your back like a good boy and do exactly what I tell you." Soon he had the plenipotentiaries of a dozen African countries bobbing up and down with their hands tied.

"Goddammit, Ambassador, I'm not going to tell you four times." Pow! He would reach out a foot and push the man under. Sally's mother came out, and I could see she was beside herself with anger. I was mortified. Then, watching, she began to smile. Her guests were having the time of their lives. Afterward Mrs. Bowles said it was one of the most successful luncheon parties she had ever given. Nobody in the world but Freddy Lanoue could have pulled that off, nobody. Coffin hired him.

The summer was a primer lesson in the uses of power. For Shriver, Haddad, and the rest, anything was possible. Who's the best guy for this or that? Get him! Coffin had hired Jack Snobble to be an instructor and to help him set up the Puerto Rican operation. Then Snobble told us he could not make it; he had to go on army reserve duty. When Haddad learned we were looking for someone to replace Snobble, he gave us what-for: "When are you guys going to catch on you're working for the U.S. government? Call Adam Yarmolinsky in McNamara's office and tell him the Peace Corps wants Snobble." It was that simple.

In August Coffin took off for Arecibo to rendezvous with Freddy Fuller, who had agreed to help make the project authentically Outward Bound. They had a scant six weeks in which to transform the scorpion- and tarantula-infested remnants of a lumber camp into a habitable "advanced training" base for Peace Corps volunteers about to go abroad on their appointed missions. Coffin and Fuller were joined by Snobble, Reagh Wetmore, who had signed on to work with Lanoue, and Ray Slawson, an ex-Navy officer.

Snobble, recalling the masterful liaison-and-scrounge technique that brought the camp into being, said that while the Peace Corps may have been strictly nonmilitary, it would not have gotten off the ground in Puerto Rico without the gracious cooperation of all branches of the military service on the island, who loaned and gave to the camp vehicles, equipment, stores, and even manpower assistance. When Jack succeeded in cadging an overage bus and station wagon from Ramey Air Force Base, the motor pool there added a touch of class to the wagon by painting it with surplus off-color blue paint and emblazoning its identity in white letters. This seems to have been how the Peace Corps got its official colors, blue and white.

Coffin, happily aware of the direct power line into the White House maintained by his Washington superiors, refused to deal with anyone under the rank of general or admiral. On one occasion he went to the mat with a three-star official who was trying to withdraw a promise of four trucks. "General," he said, "if you welsh on those trucks, I'm going to wire our man in McNamara's office that you deserve a court-martial, disgrace, a firing squad, and an unmarked grave." Bill got the trucks. He made a frequent point of referring to "our man in the Pentagon." Fortunately no one ever asked for the man's name.

■ ■ ■

Meanwhile, I was combining a family-vacation pack trip in Montana with my recruiting task. We came back through Jackson Hole, Wyoming, which was headquarters for Glen Exum's climbing school in the Tetons, where I had hired two of his guides. We drove on down to visit the Outward Bound site above Marble, where Tap Tapley was directing the building of the Colorado school. Chuck Froelicher, operating on a shoestring, had moved that project resolutely forward since our exploratory visit with Captain Fuller in March. Before deciding to buy the Marble property, he had sent Tapley out in his jeep to see if he could find anything better. Tapley had reported back in favor of the Marble site: It was isolated from resort areas. It was safe from fire, flood, and landslides. The water supply was adequate. It had a southern exposure. The access was satisfactory. And it was fantastically beautiful.

Tapley and Stroud had surveyed the area, marking off 45.2 acres. Tapley mapped out a plan and gave the map to Froelicher. With Stroud's permission—there was no money for the purchase yet—Tapley and a man named Al Kirsch started cutting aspen. Froelicher, who was giving all the time he could spare to lining up a board of directors and getting pledges, would visit the site and take pictures, which he then used to help raise funds. An access road had to be built, power lines put in, ditches dug for drainage and sewer lines, a large sewer plant installed, the building foundations put down, a ropes course built. Chuck recalled: "We would okay a project and then we'd have to find the money to pay for it. That can be motivating."

Tapley hired a backhoe man and a bulldozer operator, and later carpenters and men to pour concrete for the sewer leaching beds. In June a volunteer work brigade of fourteen youngsters from Colorado Academy arrived.

We found Tap running an easy ship, yet everything was shipshape. The boys lived in tepees they had put up. Tap had built a marvelous tepee for Lee and himself. There was an excellent outdoor cooking arrangement. Running spring water was being piped in. There was an archery range and a horseshoe pitch. It was the tidiest work camp I have ever seen. The boys worked mornings, and in the afternoons Tap gave them a course in mountaineering. In midsummer they put on a rock-climbing exhibition for parents, and Froelicher used those photos to raise more money.

Tapley, I was discovering, was a contemporary mountain version of a Renaissance man. He could live in the wilderness with nothing but a knife. He was a skilled hunter, tracker, trapper, fisherman, an expert axeman, a fine outdoor cook, a virtuoso with ropes and knots. A master of all trades, he could make anything and engineer anything. He had the greatest manual intelligence I have ever seen, could do the most minute things with his hands. He was a forester, firefighter, mountaineer, canoeman, mule skinner, dogsled-team driver, navigator, meteorologist, avalanche expert, cliff evacuation expert, and survival adept. He played the violin and painted. He was a born athlete, a deadly horseshoe pitcher blindfolded. On that visit I learned his life story.

Ernest Tapley grew up in Amesbury, Massachusetts, son of the town baker, one-eighth Passamaquoddy Indian. In the winter of 1941, when he was seventeen, he had a job in North Conway, New Hampshire, as a busboy at the

Eastern Slopes Inn, which was a social center of the great skiing boom that had recently come to the country. Whenever he got off from work, Tap skied. On a day in the early spring of 1940 he was in Tuckerman's Ravine on Mount Washington when Lowell Thomas, then at the peak of his fame as an author and radio commentator, was also skiing there. At that time few skiers had the combination of courage and technique to make a successful descent of Tuckerman's famed headwall; Tapley was one.

Dining at the inn that evening, Thomas spotted him. If Tapley ever came out to Sun Valley, Idaho, Thomas told him, he would introduce him to the head of the ski patrol. A year later, without waiting to graduate from high school, Tap sold his bicycle and hitchhiked west. In Leadville, Colorado, he got a construction job, worked double shift until he had $300, and completed his journey to Idaho. In the fall he joined the Sun Valley ski patrol, one of the country's first paid patrols. In December the United States declared war on Japan and Germany. The following spring Tapley returned to Amesbury to get his diploma, so that he could join his Sun Valley buddies who were enlisting in the Tenth Mountain Division at Camp Hale, Colorado, to serve as winter skills instructors. Paul Petzoldt, a top U.S. mountaineer who was there as a civilian adviser, remembers spotting the youngster: "I thought, my gosh, he would be the guy to send to the Himalayas, because this guy had everything—strength, coordination, terrific intelligence, and ability." The war and the ensuing years would separate them, but they were destined to have a partnership.

Tapley was one of a cadre of ten who were detached and sent to the Aleutian Islands to staff the North Pacific Combat School. At one juncture he was located at an outpost near the Arctic Circle, where it was his duty to brief visiting brass on a proposed air-base site. The base was to be developed as a precautionary measure against the possibility the Russian status might change to something other than ally.

Coming back to the "Lower 48" after the war, Tap went into a partnership breaking wild horses. He helped develop the Whitefish Ski Area in Montana, operated his own ski school in Telemark, Wisconsin, then signed on as a U.S. forest ranger at Big Fork, Montana. The Forest Service was the finishing school in which he became the complete mountain man. After five years he left the service to help his mother, who was running a lodge at Redstone, Colorado; Jack Snobble, ex-Dartmouth skier and assistant headmaster of Rocky Mountain School in Carbondale, was a ski instructor at the lodge. It was Snobble, we have seen, who brought Tapley and Colorado Outward Bound together. "I'm always interested in trying something new," Tap told me.

He related the troubles he was having with Charlie Orlofsky, the sheriff of Marble. This was the beginning of a semi-epic feud between that officious gentleman and the Colorado School. In their long battle of wits Tapley usually managed to stay two steps ahead of the sheriff. One day that summer he got word that Orlofsky had lodged a complaint with the Marble Board of Health that Tap had a resident work crew and no refrigeration on the premises, which violated the code. A few days later the health inspector showed up. It was a hot day; after hiking up from his car, he was in a heavy sweat. "Have a seat," Tap said. "How about a glass of iced tea?" The inspector did a double take. "Iced tea! Up here?"

Tap went over to the aspen grove where the ropes course had been built and threw back the tarpaulin covering the camp's kerosene-operated refrigerator. He came back with two tall, moisture-beaded glasses of iced tea, cubes clinking, and handed one to the perspiring inspector. As the two men sipped their drinks, the inspector's gaze roved over the site. "Where do you put the garbage?" he asked. Tap pointed to the fire pit. The inspector walked over to the pit and poked with a stick. Nothing but clean ashes. He wandered around the camp and came back. He said, "This is the cleanest place I've inspected all summer. I don't know what the complaint is." Tap said, "I won't ask you who made the complaint. It isn't worth knowing." Charlie Orlofsky, who had not checked under the tarpaulin in the grove of aspen, never forgave that.

We went on to Denver and visited with the Froelichers. Gil Burnett was there. He was spending the summer at Marble and Denver, working on promotional material for the new Colorado Outward Bound School. The first Colorado course was still ten months away, but already that was beginning to seem close.

HECTIC YEAR

Action is eloquence.

—Coriolanus

The school year of 1961–1962 raced by. I had a full load of teaching and admissions duties and was doing my work for the Atlantic Foundation. In addition to his full-time job running Colorado Academy, Chuck Froelicher was steering the Colorado Outward Bound project and raising money for it. He had put together a strong board of trustees and been made chairman. The board hired a school director. He was William McK. Chapman, a former journalist who at that time was headmaster of a school on an Indian reservation. The construction work under Tapley went forward until winter closed in. It was a tight time. The work was barely on schedule, and there were payrolls and material and equipment costs to meet. The Atlantic Foundation was having difficulty raising the money it had pledged. The course had to be designed and staffed. The all-important task of enrolling the students had yet to be accomplished. Maybe nobody would come to the party. At the annual meeting of the National Association of Independent Schools, Froelicher, John Holden, and I made a panel presentation of the Outward Bound story. Very few of the school people there had previously heard of Outward Bound. We were encouraged by their positive response.

Through the fall the money problem hung in the balance. I began to learn about the wonderful world of foundations. People with lots of money to give away but difficult to persuade that you could put it to work worthily. On one of Froelicher's trips east I was happy to have him join me in the New York money quest. We went to see Frederick Warburg, Eric's cousin, at the offices of Kuhn, Loeb and Company. We told him about Outward Bound and the plans for the Colorado school, about the construction work in the Rocky Mountains, and the immediate critical problem of $7,000 for payroll and equipment rentals due the following week.

Warburg was a great activist in the Boy Scout movement. He was furious that we were starting a new outfit. We told him how Sir Robert Baden-Powell, the founder of the Boy Scouts, had been a strong supporter of Hahn's work. We talked some more, and I did not feel we were making progress. Suddenly he asked, "Who sent you here?" I told him it was Mrs. John McCloy. He dialed her number without having to look it up. "Ellen? Why aren't you here with these two young fellows who are asking me for money?" He kept his fierce glare on us. "Well, you should be here, because they remind me of a high-school team being sent in to play Notre Dame without a coach." That was unfair to Chuck, who had won his money-raising spurs getting his school back on its feet, but it fitted me. When Warburg hung up, he said, "Look, I won't give you one damn penny. Not until you have raised all you need except for five thousand dollars. Then come and see me, and I'll cap it off." Eventually he gave us more than that.

Friday afternoon came, and we were still scratching for that seven thousand. It was raining, and I had no raincoat. We were wet, tired, discouraged. As a last resort we called at the Taconic Foundation without an appointment. I had stayed in touch with Steve Currier after he sent us to talk with Harris Wofford in Washington the previous spring. Now, with my naive concept of how foundations functioned, I had the desperate idea that maybe we could get the Taconic Foundation to spring some money loose for us. In Currier's office the rug was ankle-deep. It was dry, warm, cozy. Currier could not have been more thoughtful. He said, "You guys sit down, you look beat! I bet you need a drink." After the drinks were served we told him our story. He said, "Look, I can't possibly get foundation money for you, but here's a personal contribution." He wrote a check for $5,000 out of his own pocket. It was one of the critical checks in Outward Bound history.

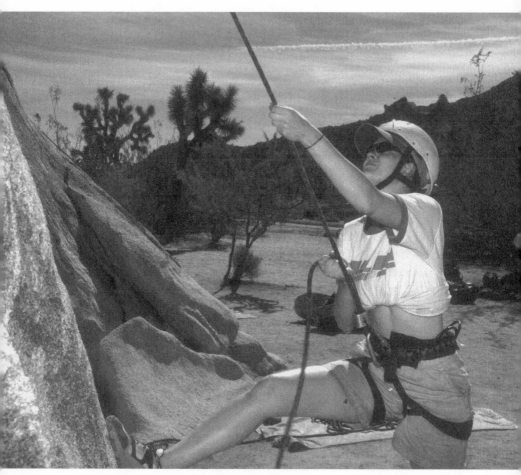

Rock climbing is not a solitary endeavor, but a partner sport, requiring a trustworthy belay. (Photo © PCOBS, Kim Budd)

The fiscal problem continued serious. In December a crisis was averted by a loan of $20,000, personally guaranteed by Jack Stevens, from Phillips Academy to the Atlantic Foundation. At the same time, John Kemper agreed to coordinate the fund-raising activity.

Bulletins came from Puerto Rico. The camp opened in early September, on schedule but not altogether propitiously. The first group of volunteers, twelve surveyors and road builders bound for Tanganyika, arrived with a collective chip on their shoulders. They had been told only two days before that they had yet to undergo a month's "capstone" training experience to qualify for Africa. At six the first morning, Coffin led them on a four-mile run along a route he personally had hacked out. Only three volunteers finished with him; the rest straggled in during the ensuing half hour. Sensing the mutinous tone of the breakfast muttering, Coffin made a kind of welcoming speech, While he could sympathize with their resentment at being there, he said, he thought they could profit by the training. In any event he and his associates could profit by their taking it, for changes were bound to be needed to make the program as helpful as possible to later volunteers. If there were some who felt they could not put themselves out for others, he would not hesitate to recommend their dismissal from the Corps.

The volunteers' grudging response gradually grew more positive toward the Outward Bound elements—morning run, ropes course, rock climbing and rappelling, drownproofing, jungle and mountain treks, overnight jungle solos—that Freddy Fuller had designed into their training regimen. But even though he earned the instant respect of instructors and students, Puerto Rico cannot have been Captain Fuller's favorite billet. The volunteers, with their mix of maturity, high motivation, and American inability to take orders without knowing the reasons why, constituted a rather different kind of human material from the younger, more respectful Britishers he was accustomed to. Jack Snobble, who with Coffin was better equipped to understand the Americans, said that ultimately "Outward Bound's inherent flexibility and ability to adapt to a variety of needs" proved its strength.

One innovation in the American program that Fuller wholly approved was drownproofing; when he returned to England, he added it to his Aberdovey curriculum. Coffin's autobiography provides a nice picture of Lanoue striding up and down in his red trunks, explaining to the volunteers the parallels between swimming underwater and dancing at the high school prom.

Lanoue told them, "You remember, you had to go to the bathroom, but the music wouldn't stop. So what did you do? You kept on dancing. It's the same principle here. The human will can postpone bodily gratifications far longer than you think. Just remember: whenever you think you have to come up for air, at that moment swim for the bottom." The rest of the afternoon he paced alongside the pool screaming, "Deeper, deeper!" till every volunteer had done what only one had originally thought he could do. That was really what we were after in all our camp training—to see how many times a day we could get volunteers to say, "I never thought I could do that."

Coffin and I had been told that Puerto Rico had one of the world's finest community-development programs. The program's codirectors, Fred Wales and his wife, Carmen, arranged for Bill to go out in the hills with one of their workers, a third-grade schoolteacher named Juan. In a pickup truck loaded with a movie projector, a gas-driven generator to power the projector, and a big screen, they drove to a tiny *barrio*, where Juan showed a film and conducted a village meeting. The villagers decided their greatest need was a deeper well and with Juan's help initiated a project to get it. That night, lying on a straw pallet in a tiny but spotless hovel, Coffin decided he had chanced on the most important part of the training program. Every volunteer spent three days in a remote barrio with one of Fred Wales's workers. Fred was so impressed by the volunteers that he came twice to the camp to spend an evening. Bill said, "I've never heard anyone speak about poverty-stricken people with more compassion and less sentimentality."

■ ■ ■

In January and March the Atlantic Foundation's financial commitment to the new Colorado school was covered by grants of $25,000 each from the Old Dominion Foundation and the Avalon Foundation. These grants proved to be a highly significant precedent. The two foundations, both Mellon family funds, were subsequently merged into the Mellon Foundation, which over the years provided $300,000 in start-up dollars for new Outward Bound schools.

Bill Chapman went to England for his Outward Bound indoctrination. Tapley, who was to be chief instructor, followed. After visiting Aberdovey,

Tap took the course at Eskdale. Toward the end they asked him to help instruct the rock climbing. Eskdale brought him into contact with the school's warden, Tom Price, one of the outstanding figures in the British Outward Bound movement. Among the instructors there, Tapley especially liked Ralph Clough, who had taught at several of the British schools and played a part in starting Outward Bound in Nigeria. He arranged for Clough to come to Colorado and help shape the course the following summer.

On his return Chapman began to make the rounds, speaking to schools and parent groups. Both the Denver group and I promoted scholarships. As the long mountain winter yielded to spring, Tapley got his construction people back at work. The staffing was completed. The enrollment applications came in, slowly but steadily. Enough were coming to assure a party.

Through April and May and into June the push to finish the school buildings—a large dining hall with a balcony library, a washhouse and a smaller facility for women who were coming in a Peace Corps group, a small administration building, an equipment house, and houses for the director and the chief instructor—was a race against the calendar. The last few days before the school opened were intense. Tapley and Clough were putting the instructors through their final training paces. The late equipment deliveries were being sorted and readied. Frank Menendez, the chef, was laying in the food supply. Tapley was riding herd on the construction wrap-up. He remembers: "Everyone was for us. The forestry people, the fish and game people, the power company people, they all liked the sound of what we were planning to do. On the day we were to open up we were putting the finishing touches on the power line and the hookup. In the morning it looked as though we would have to cook the first meal that night outdoors. But two hours before the students arrived, the power company crew cut in the electricity."

C-1

✴

*I am very glad to have taken this course, and I can think
of no substitute. My job now, and a continuing one, is to
live up to what the school has revealed to me.*

The Colorado Outward Bound School opened on June 16, 1962. C-1,[3] the first course, had thirty-five students. The three courses that summer had a total of one hundred regular students, with forty-six in C-2 and nineteen in C-3, which was primarily a contract course for seventy-six members of a Peace Corps group going to Nepal. The one hundred regular students came from twenty states. Fifty-one were on scholarships. Denver businessmen provided twenty-five scholarships for local boys, four from the jurisdiction of the Denver Juvenile Court, and the remainder came through the Eastern effort. To get as wide a social and geographical selection in each patrol of ten boys as possible, applications were examined and the students assigned before they arrived. As Bill Chapman noted in his director's report, "No one knew another's background, and the boys plunged into the strenuous course together with little time for introspection or comparison of notes. This way they frequently found out each other's worth before they learned of each other's backgrounds and, in a number of instances, boys of

---

[3] The system of designating courses by letter and number was subsequently picked up by all the U.S. schools. Hurricane Island prefixes course numbers by H-, Minnesota by M-, North Carolina by NC-, Northwest by NW-, Dartmouth by D-, Southwest by S-.

less fortunate backgrounds than others were soon able to establish their leadership on a basis of true equality."

Under Ralph Clough's guidance, the twenty-six-day course closely followed the Eskdale model. A distinctive difference was that Colorado reflected considerably less of Hahn's "dunk 'em and dry 'em" operating philosophy. Some of the contrast was between the comfortable living quarters and other indoor amenities at Eskdale and the eight-man tents the students lived in at Marble. But the marked difference lay in the Colorado plan of operating much of the course, after basic training was completed, away from the main base altogether. A base camp was established in a meadow about six miles north of Lead King Basin, at close to the ten-thousand-foot elevation. Surrounding this area were several snowcapped mountains in which major expeditions were carried out.

The initial training included physical conditioning and instruction in needed skills: "circuit training," map and compass reading (we were not yet calling it orienteering), campcraft, backpacking, first aid, axemanship, knots and rope handling, rock climbing and rappel technique, fire fighting, mountain rescue. Circuit training was a form of physical conditioning for mountaineering that British Outward Bound had devised to replace the athletic events (essentially the old Gordonstoun Break program) that were part of the original Aberdovey curriculum. On the first day, each student was put through a "circuit course"—a series of press-ups, deep-knee bends, chin-ups, and sit-ups done in rapid succession in thirty- or sixty-second spurts—and his maximum capacity was measured. Half his maximum became his "daily dose," which he did three times a day throughout the course. Near the end, maximums were tested again to measure improvement. Everybody also did a quarter-mile uphill run before the mountain climbing started. In addition to the skills instruction, the students were given an elementary review of the geology and the flora and fauna of the area.

Central to the basic training were a set of initiative tests and the aerial ropes course. The primary purpose of the initiatives was to build group cohesion and esprit. They included the wall and beam, two tests that have become virtually standard elements in the Outward Bound curriculum. The wall in particular is a highly effective means of taking a collection of individuals, strangers to each other, and transforming them into an instant group. Typically, a cadre—at Colorado a patrol—of students is led on a first-day orientation tour of the base camp area when they come to a vertical board construction, normally thirteen to fourteen feet high and eight feet wide. This wall is used to transform the casual tour into an intensive test of the raw group's ability to tackle a problem together. They are told they have so many—usually five—minutes in which to plan how they will get all their members over the wall. During that time and the ensuing effort, the group learns a lot about itself and its component strengths and weaknesses. Working out the problem becomes an exercise in group dynamics. Good and poor leader and follower qualities reveal themselves. To some in the group the problem appears impossible. Others jockey for leadership or prestige in the immediate hubbub of counsel. The more thoughtful, who may be slower to speak, may or may not succeed in carrying conviction. Some will have nothing to suggest, awaiting the group decision with varying degrees of positive or negative attitude. Carrying out the decision engages a new set of dynamics. Leadership emerges through action. As important as the effort itself is the action's effect in bringing all into close, coordinated physical contact—touching, holding, giving a lift up, clambering over bodies, seizing a down-reaching hand, in turn offering a hand down to others. The final success is a shared success; everyone senses that something significant has happened in the alchemy of the group. Usually the group will go directly from the wall to the beam, which is a log nine or so inches in diameter supported horizontally some nine feet off the ground. Again, the assignment is to get everybody over the beam. Now the group is reenforced by the experience of having solved one problem together. The second success produces a further synergistic flow.

The ropes course is a personal test, a confidence-building trial that British Outward Bound originally borrowed from the military. The course is a complex of rope and timber pathways, much of it constructed at considerable height, that must be negotiated in a series of climbing, traversing, and balancing maneuvers. In the "postman's walk," for example, the student slides feet sideways along one rope while holding on to a second. The ropes course is the part of Outward Bound experience that, except for rock climbing and rappelling, causes most students the most apprehension. The course that Tapley had built in an aspen grove called on them to start by climbing a thirty-five-foot rope ladder. They had ample occasion to look up at the course prior to the day they essayed it. As they eyed the apparently insubstantial footing and bodily support high in the air, the trial ahead grew fraught with mental hazard. Negotiating the course combined an exorcising of fears with a test of coordination, timing, balance, and arm and shoulder strength. The experience was invaluable in helping a youngster to deal with his fear of heights and to make an essential Outward Bound discovery—that with resolution one can do what one has thought or feared one could not. Success was all the more powerful when it followed on failure.

Shifting to the camp above Lead King Basin, a patrol promptly moved out on a three-day training expedition. This was a time for breaking in boots, getting used to a heavy pack, learning to cope with the exigencies of group living on the move. How to select safe, comfortable campsites. Building a fire in the wet. System and logistics of cooking, eating, cleanup, sleep, and moving on. Dealing with the wide day-and-night temperature swings and the vagaries of mountain weather. The theory of map reading, compass bearings, and route finding becoming the hard question of just where one was on a timbered trail or a naked mountainside. Getting to know one another better in group-stress situations.

A day of rest and reoutfitting back at the main base, a rock-climbing baptism, and then the major expedition, climbing one of the high peaks. Now came the full test of endurance, bodily and mental—the daylong hikes up rocky trails, traversing a great boulder-strewn terrain, moving on up into the perennial snowfields, hacking a route across treacherous blue ice; roped together to negotiate a steep pitch one step, one handhold at a time, wary of loose rock; straddling the length of a mountain ridge; confronting—or bending to—the raging power of mountain storms; blisters, hurts, fatigue. With each day's end a debriefing, a chance to articulate experiences and feelings, to share joys, to talk out tensions and irritations, the group growing in its capacity to make it together. Winning finally, having surmounted the physical and psychological obstacles, to the summits at thirteen to fourteen thousand feet, of Maroon Bells, Capitol Peak, or Snowmass, looking down

With weighted packs and steady feet, a patrol begins the journey through one of many mountain passes the students will traverse with Outward Bound. (Photo © Brian Litz)

with wonder and pride at the route traversed, looking out in elation at a sight of awesome beauty such as a young lifetime had not known till now.

Nor was the descent anticlimactic. A long traverse across a snowfield, roped together at seventy-five-foot intervals, the leader belayed lest in falling he pitch downward out of control and take others with him. Learning the art of a glissade down an incline of icy snow, picking up speed, and digging in with the ice axe to brake oneself.

Advanced rock climbing. The high rappel—the trusting lean-back off the clifftop edge, supported by two half-inch nylon lines—an act of faith to remember.

At most Outward Bound schools the marathon has come to be the final event of the course, but in the early years at Colorado it came between the major and the final expeditions. A six-mile run through mountain country from the town of Crystal, near Lead King Basin, to Marble. Few students had ever come even close to running that distance. At the start of the course, the relatively short run on rising—not quite a mile with a dip in a stream at the halfway point—had taxed most of them. For virtually all, the idea of having to go six miles later in the course had seemed an impossibility. The marathon was run as a patrol competition, counting total elapsed time of all patrol members. But as the runners spread out, often out of sight of one another, the race became very much a personal test. The decision to keep running, to try harder despite aches, pain, blisters, and shortness of breath, was one's own. Finishing, with a sense of having tried to do one's best, was another satisfaction in a time replete with successes that surprised and revealed.

The curriculum Ralph Clough brought with him included a "night alone"— one overnight when each student camped on his own, isolated from his fellows. The night alone was a successful part of C-1. For many of the youngsters it was—in retrospect, at least—a new, satisfying experience. Tapley thought it a highly valuable course element: "So many people have never been alone, completely on their own, in their whole life. Never been in a place where there was just no chance of reaching out for a telephone to say something has happened or I'm sick."

In C-2, on the day preceding the scheduled night alone, chef Frank Menendez came to Tapley in a panic. The school was running out of food, and the supplier had just called to say he could not make a delivery up the mountain for several days. Tapley perceived the crisis as opportunity. "If you have three days without having to feed anybody," he asked Frank, "will you be all right?" Frank said he would. "What we can do," Tapley said, "is something I've been wanting to try anyway. Tonight we'll get the group together, and I'll give them a talk on edible plants and berries, and what kinds of game and fish they can find to eat, and we'll tell them they're going on a three-day solo survival."

Tap remembers, "That was when we began to find out about a lot of things. First, I told the kids they didn't have to eat anything, they could get along fine on nothing but water for three days. I told them how I'd gone several days without food, just drinking water and picking plants like miner's lettuce and brook sassafras, pond-lily roots, things like that. With fire and water, they could make tea from the cambium layer of most any tree—spruce tree was especially good.[4] I told them about cattail roots, and fern fiddleheads in the spring, marmots, snakes, and frogs for meat, how to make a snare. We gave them a knife, a fishhook and a short piece of line, salt, matches, and a sleeping bag. We took them out and placed them at least a half mile apart, where they couldn't even see the smoke of another fire. We put them by a source of water and told them they were not to go more than one hundred yards in any direction. The instructors checked by day that they were all right, trying not to be seen. At night I made the rounds of the ones I was more concerned about, to be sure they had a fire and were by it.

"It was a great experience for the kids, and the greatest part of it was after they came in for the debriefing. We found they had got much more out of their solos than we had expected. They swapped confidences and learned of bad and good experiences. It was a tremendous release for a boy to learn he wasn't the only one who had been scared. I told them, 'I've been in the hills for twenty years. If I wake up and hear something like a porcupine walking right over my head, and I can't see him, it scares me. Staying by yourself out there all alone, you see how a human being just isn't equipped to take care of himself as an animal does.'"

That was how the solo, which more than any other feature of the program has brought Outward Bound its fame in the United States, came into being. The following year Colorado extended the solo's length from two nights to three, and when other American schools opened, they made the three-night solo standard to their courses as well. There has never been doubt of the high value of the solo experience. But ironically, the publicity it has received is responsible for a widespread misapprehension about Outward Bound—that it is a survival school, which it emphatically is not. Today, most students on solo simply fast. The "survival" aspects, never intended to be physically rugged, have become incidental to the solo's primary purposes, which are the

[4] Conservational proscription no longer permits this.

experience of solitude in the wilderness and an opportunity for contemplation. For most young people those experiences may well be more stressful
than being hungry or cold.

Near the end of the course the students were reorganized into four- to six-
man patrols for their final expeditions. This time they were on their own for
four days, without an instructor to turn to. The patrol planned and executed
its own undertaking as a team, each man carrying a forty-pound pack through
forty to seventy-five miles of unfamiliar mountain wilderness. The final
expedition, with its ultimate discovery by each individual that more than
anything else Outward Bound is a revelation of people's interdependence and
a challenge to their ability to work things out together, was a kind of rite of
passage.

An unscheduled event of that first summer was U.S. Outward Bound's
affirmation of the powerful rescue tradition that, deriving directly from the
consuming commitment of Kurt Hahn, Outward Bound schools had already
created around the world. Since the preceding work summer, it had become
well known in the surrounding mountain area that the school was on twenty-
four-hour rescue call. During the second course a call came in that a man was
ill at thirteen thousand feet on Snowmass Mountain. Three instructors and
eight students took off immediately, making the climb through the
snowfields and up a steep rocky trail to the ledge where the ill man lay in a
coma. They revived him, fed him hot soup, wrapped him in blankets and
secured him to a Stokes litter, and tied themselves together for the long, difficult descent. Four hours later they placed him in a truck that rushed him from
Marble to the hospital thirty miles away. The students were euphoric, on a
rescue high. One said, "Two weeks ago I couldn't have gotten myself out of
the mountains, let alone a sick man." The grateful evacuee made the school a
gift of a slide projector and screen.

The summer's health and safety record was exemplary: no broken bones; a
normal incidence of cuts, bruises, blisters, sprains; a few sore throats; two cases
of tick-bite fever, the duration of each about six days. Nurse Bonnie Condon
kept arrival and departure charts of blood pressure, weight, and pulse changes
to determine the effect of altitude (8,800 feet at the main base camp) on boys
from sea level and other parts of the country. The students apparently

acclimated more readily than had been foreseen; mountain sickness was almost unknown. The records revealed one remarkable health phenomenon, bearing out Hahn's contention that asthmatic youngsters should be encouraged to run: the students who had a history of asthma did the full normal course, including the marathon, with no symptoms of their affliction appearing.

At summer's end there was no doubt that the Colorado Outward Bound School was here to stay. Most of the students departed in various stages of outward and inward euphoria. Their journals and the evaluations they wrote on the final day attested to intense, memorable, highly valued experiences:

> I am very glad to have taken this course and I can think of no substitute. My job now, and a continuing one, is to live up to what the school has revealed to me.
>
> I learned to get along with people that I really disliked at first. Perhaps the most amazing thing to me was the different perspective with which I seemed to begin to look at things up here.
>
> The greatest single thing which helped me the most was the solo survival. Here I started to find myself.

Afterward came letters from both students and parents—the first batches of the thick testimonial accumulations now in the files of the seven U.S. Outward Bound schools. The parent letters were usually variations on the theme of "we sent you a boy and you returned us a man":

> When he returned early this month, we saw a new boy, fit, with muscles he never knew he had before. But more important than the physical changes were the self-confidence and pride that he showed. I am sure that he was not aware that he frequently used the word 'challenge' in referring to his forthcoming freshman year at college, but I think his Outward Bound experience has taught him to meet challenges with an assurance he never had before.

The school's fame was spreading. In Lander, Wyoming, Paul Petzoldt, one of the country's great pioneer mountaineers, who had directed the Petzoldt-

Group portrait of the early adapters—graduating class at C-2, the second Outward Bound course held at Marble, Colorado, in 1962. (Photo courtesy Colorado Outward Bound School)

Exum School of American Mountaineering in the Teton range, was intrigued by what he heard. During C-3 he came to see the Colorado school firsthand. A result of his visit was his appointment to be the school's mountaineering adviser the following year.

Petzoldt's visit brought him to a reunion with another great American climber, a former student and longtime mountaineering companion-in-arms, William F. "Willi" Unsoeld, who was in charge of the Peace Corps group for which C-3 had been set up. Since this group of volunteers was headed for mountainous Nepal, it had been sent to Colorado rather than Puerto Rico. Unsoeld, who was to be deputy director of the Peace Corps in Nepal, had a special interest in going there. He was one of a group of Americans planning to attempt an ascent of Mount Everest—on the Nepal-Tibet border—in the year ahead. While at the time his contact with Outward Bound seemed only a passing encounter, it proved to be the start of an important liaison.

1962–1963

❋

Not fare well
But fare forward, voyagers.

—T. S. Eliot

Among the outstanding instructors in the Colorado School's first summer was a social science teacher from the Midwest named Joe Nold. The trustees, in agreement that Joe had the qualities needed for long-term leadership, offered him the post of school director in the summer of 1963.

Joe Nold was born and grew up in Saskatchewan, Canada. When he graduated from the University of British Columbia, he had two goals—to become a teacher, and to experience the wilder and higher parts of the world. Going from one overseas teaching post to another, he spent his vacations climbing mountains, ski touring, and generally beating about remote parts of the globe. Along the way he heard about the British Outward Bound movement. His quest for more information brought him into contact with the Gordonstoun School, and in 1955 he went there to teach for a year. Immediately congenial with the Gordonstoun tradition of exposing boys to outdoor experiences, he took students on weekend backpacking trips and during the holiday periods led them on climbing expeditions in the Spanish Sierra Nevada and Morocco's Atlas range. Gordonstoun helped him get a post at a school in India, and there he trekked with youngsters in the foothills of the Himalayas.

Eventually Joe wound up teaching at the North Shore Country Day School, in the Chicago suburb of Winnetka, Illinois. Nathaniel French, the school's headmaster, was a friend of Chuck Froelicher. One day in the fall of 1961 he said to Nold, "Here's something that should interest you," and handed him a mailing piece from the new Colorado Outward Bound School. Joe promptly wrote Froelicher. One of the first instructors Chuck hired, he would become a key participant in the flowering of the U.S. Outward Bound movement.

Even with Nold's year at Gordonstoun and the enthusiasm for the Outward Bound movement that he brought with him, the effect on youngsters of the first Colorado courses was a revelation: "Before Colorado I had not experienced Outward Bound in the one-month impact kind of thing. I was deeply impressed by the whole quality of lifting a group of kids from their familiar environment and creating a new society in the mountains. There was a dynamic to it that had an impact like no other I had ever known. When Nat French asked me how the summer had gone, I told him, 'I've been teaching for you for three years, and I really think I've done more teaching in the last two months than I've done in three years in the classroom.' What excited me most was the extent to which Outward Bound spoke to the whole sense of being and meaning and values and purpose of life. That's the basic structure into which we have to fit academics. I felt that this was the most deeply educational involvement I'd ever had as a teacher with young people."

For Nold and others like him there was something else. "A penalty of teaching in one of the country's finest independent day schools in that well-to-do suburban environment was that we young teachers felt cut off from the mainstream of American life. We had come into teaching with the idea that it was a service-oriented profession. It was the early 1960s, [President John F.] Kennedy was newly in office, the national social conscience was waking, and we couldn't help feeling dissatisfied. At Colorado we not only had a chance to work with disadvantaged youngsters, we were able to mix kids from affluent families with kids from the ghetto. Part of the beauty of that was that the highly motivated, upper-mobility type of middle-class and rich kid got so much out of the social interaction. I had the feeling that Outward Bound was in the marketplace."

Nold accepted the directorship offer with a qualification. He could only be at Marble for C-4 and C-5; someone else would have to take over for C-6 in August. I was nominated. I was not keen on taking charge of a mountaineering program when I had no big mountain experience, but partly from a sense of responsibility, partly out of a realization that the experience would be valuable, I assented.

Applications were coming in slowly but steadily, and the number of scholarships mounted encouragingly. It looked like the second summer's enrollment would hit at least one hundred fifty. We were not concerned about the Colorado School's ability to survive. Froelicher had done a fine job. He had a strong, enthusiastic board, and the school was getting valuable word-of-mouth advertising as a result of the first summer's success. Our thoughts were on expansion. The Atlantic Foundation now saw its primary mission as fostering the growth of Outward Bound throughout the country. The winter and spring of 1963 brought definite indications that we had the beginnings of a national movement. One such indication was the intense interest of Peter Willauer, a former Andover colleague then on the Groton School faculty, in starting a school on the Maine coast. I encouraged Peter in his quest for a strong board chairman and board, and a site. As publicity about the Colorado Outward Bound School spread, we had a number of other inquiries from people wanting to start a second school. I wrote Sir Spencer Summers, chairman of Britain's Outward Bound Trust, requesting that the Atlantic Foundation be authorized to grant, with appropriate discretion, the use of the title "Outward Bound" in the United States. The trust's management committee instructed him to inform us that the trust would be agreeable to this arrangement as soon as the Atlantic Foundation had appointed a permanent secretary. This coincided with the foundation's thinking that the time had come to set up an office headed by a foundation officer devoting full time to Outward Bound affairs. My sabbatical year was coming up, and it was decided that I should take on the assignment for a year, starting with the coming summer of 1963.

One of the more promising letters of inquiry came to John Kemper from a fellow schoolmaster named Robert Pieh. Bob Pieh (pronounced Pay) had been running a summer camp for boys at the edge of the Superior-Quetico

Wilderness in northern Minnesota and Canada, which is great canoeing country. He had headed the department of physical education, health, and recreation at Antioch College and was currently headmaster of Anniston Academy, a boys' school in Anniston, Alabama. Pieh wrote Kemper that he had long been an admirer of Kurt Hahn and his educational philosophy and an interested follower of the British Outward Bound movement. He thought his northern Minnesota facility offered an ideal, ready-made setup for an Outward Bound school.

Pieh and his son Jerry, who was in the master of arts in teaching program at the Harvard School of Education, came to see us in Andover. They were an impressive pair. Bob was a striking physical specimen—the very image of a woodsman, articulate, a philosopher. At Antioch he had been a highly creative physical educator. We were impressed by his staunch confidence that he and Jerry could create a successful Outward Bound school in the Minnesota-Canadian wilderness. It was arranged that I would visit their camp in June. Kemper quickly perceived that Jerry had the makings of a fine teacher; the following year he put him on the Andover faculty. What he did not know was that Jerry would become his son-in-law.

Early in the spring came our first big national publicity break, an event that dramatically stepped up the pace of U.S. Outward Bound's growth. The preceding summer I had given a talk in New York. One of my listeners was Donald Watt, son of the founder of the Experiment in International Living. After hearing me tell the Colorado School story, he told Lydia Ratcliff, a writer friend, about it. Intrigued, she came to see me in Andover, and the upshot was that the March 1963 issue of the *Reader's Digest* carried her article on the Colorado school entitled "Outward Bound: Rugged Challenge for Teen-Agers."

Bonanza! The issue was hardly in the mails and on the newsstands when a torrent of letters and applications, sometimes with money enclosed, poured into the small school office that Froelicher had established at Colorado Academy. Helen Rawalt, who was operating the office, had to be given additional help just to handle the mail. Within a month all the courses were filled and had waiting lists. Applicants turned down for lack of room were offered places in a 1964 course, and most enrolled. A steady flow of mail continued through the summer and did not tail off until the new year.

School closed, and I flew to Ely, Minnesota, to see the Pieh camp and get an idea of the terrain. The camp was called Shining Trails, derived from the Ojibwa Indian word for "spirit roads." Jerry Pieh and I took off in an outboard motorboat, switched to a canoe, and paddled for hours to an overnight bivouac. I got a feel for the mode of travel, the country, and the climate. The Superior-Quetico Wilderness is a vast latticework of lakes, streams, and forest, with virtually impenetrable bush, extending well into Canada. It is wild, beautiful, dramatic country. Reporting back, I noted that the Minnesota-Canadian terrain differed greatly from that of Colorado. At that time no rocks suitable for climbing had been found. (In the end, that was not a problem; there is good rock climbing in the area.) Developing a school program based on canoeing expeditions in that unique wilderness would call for a creative new adaptation of the Outward Bound method. I gave my opinion that the Piehs had the understanding, expertise, and creativity needed to establish an Outward Bound school. Soon afterward, Jerry visited Marble, where he had a good look at the Colorado program in action. He did his first rock climbing, under Tapley's tutelage, and rappelled a 300-foot rock face. He got advice from Nold, Tapley, and others. The plan was to apply for a Minnesota Outward Bound charter in the fall.

At Colorado, C-4 had opened with more than double the 1962 enrollment and a considerably enlarged instructor staff. I arrived at Marble in July. Anxious to upgrade my qualifications for taking over the directorship from Joe Nold, I went early to participate as an observer in the C-5 course. Joe was spending much of his time in the field, giving top priority to directing the mountain program, and I assumed I would be expected to do the same. Having hiked and camped through the mountains of New England for years, I considered myself a competent outdoorsman, but the Rockies were something else. I had never been on a really big mountain, had never climbed a rock face, or rappelled, or been exposed to the risk of a precipitous fall, or scaled a high peak. I had the average person's fear of heights. I was forty-three, and not in the best shape. I went to my Marble assignment with considerable apprehension, but I was set on being a participant as well as observer with that patrol of teenagers, on having my own successful Outward Bound experience.

It was, indeed, not easy. Things like the ropes course I could handle. What I did not have was the endurance to stay with those youngsters. The morning run was agony. I very much minded the thinness of the oxygen supply at nine thousand feet. I was getting up at 5:30, a half hour before the school, to gain a head start on the run and dip. When I was partway at my own pace, the kids would pass me. I would stop behind a bush to vomit. My lungs were raw, my head ached, my teeth ached. Through the day's drive, drive, drive, I was miserable. Worst of all was the climbing. We were practicing for our first alpine expedition. The higher we went, the harder it was for me to keep up. I wondered about my ability to stay with the patrol for five days when we climbed to fourteen thousand feet. But I was determined not to appear inadequate.

The evening before the expedition was to take off, one of the instructors came into the mess hall and said, "I'm going on the alpine tomorrow. I wish I could go into town and spend the night with my family, but I have the duty." Town was Glenwood Springs, thirty miles away. I said, "What's involved in the duty?" He said, "All you have to do is be there, tend the phone, and at ten o'clock turn out the lights in the tent area." I said, "I'll take the duty for you. Show me how to turn out the lights." He took me up to the students' tent area and showed me where the switch was located on an aspen tree. When the time came, I walked the sixty yards or so from the first-aid tent, where I had been talking with Paul Petzoldt, and pulled the switch. Not having thought to bring a flashlight, I found myself in complete darkness. Feeling my way back, I stepped into a hole that had been dug that day for a new water line. As I hit bottom, pain stabbed through my left leg. Getting up on my right foot, I found I could not put weight on the other. I worked myself out of the hole and lay on the ground with the hurt leg raised, to check any internal bleeding and hold down the swelling. After a while I was able to hail someone headed for the latrine, who went for help. They carried me to the aid tent. By then the leg was considerably swollen. The consensus was that it was broken.

I lay on the tent floor with the leg propped up on a cot. Petzoldt packed it in ice and gave me a shot of morphine. He asked if I had any whiskey. To mix whiskey and an anesthetic, he said, violated every canon of first aid, but maybe it would cheer me up. I told him where I had a bottle cached. He sat and talked with me for hours, and we finished off the bottle. I was flat on my back, looking up at the ridgepole of the tent, and at about 1 A.M. the pole started to travel. It moved from right to left at a forty-mile-an-hour speed without stopping. Strangely, it never reached the side of the tent.

In the morning they took me in a jeep to the hospital at Glenwood Springs. The X-rays showed a broken tibia about eight inches above the ankle. The hospital was Amish; they took good care of me. Two days later I flew to Eugene, Oregon, where a Peace Corps group that was coming to Marble later were in training at the state university. They were gathered in an auditorium to hear me, and when I came out on the stage on crutches with my leg in a cast, they greeted me with groans. I was not the most propitious image that Outward Bound could have sent to brief those volunteers.

In the end the accident proved serendipitous. When I took over at C-6, I could not be out in the field, where I would not have been any good anyway. Except for forays on horseback, I had to stay at the base and be an administrative type, which was a useful thing for the program at that point. The rapid expansion from the year before had made for logistical, personnel, and other organizational problems, and someone was needed to run things from an overall vantage point.

That second summer the school was in the process of finding its own identity. Ralph Clough was still on hand, helping it to hold to the basic Outward Bound scheme, and it still closely resembled the British model. That was desirable as a foundation, but in the nature of things, with experience and time, U.S. Outward Bound was sure to acquire its own distinctive character. This was beginning to happen, particularly as the second-year staff members increasingly got their own feel of the Outward Bound dynamic.

Petzoldt's presence as mountaineering instructor was a valuable addition. In Petzoldt and Tapley the Colorado school had two of the country's finest outdoorsmen. While Petzoldt himself deferred to Tapley's sheer versatility, Paul brought to the school a superb expertise in his mountain expedition specialty. This was not simply because his involvement exposed instructors and students to the experience-garnered wisdom of a veteran mountaineer of the first rank. It was more due to his having massaged that experience with an analytical turn of mind that, together with his fervor for communicating

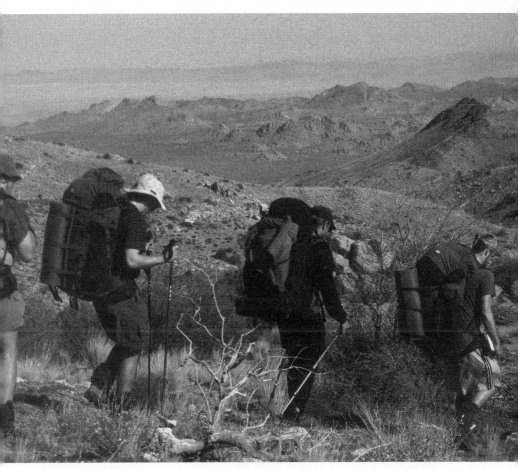

Heading off-trail during a desert backpacking course in Joshua Tree National Park is an education in ecology, navigation, and leave-no-trace camping. (Photo © PCOBS, Kim Budd)

his love of the wild outdoors and a gift of communication, made him a fine teacher of wilderness adventuring. He was then fifty-five years old, a big bear of a man in full vigor. Even when he has done his three score and ten, were I on a mountain under conditions of dire hazard, there is no one I would rather be with. As a youth Paul was the first person to climb Wyoming's Grand Teton in the winter; the mountain still often turns back efforts to duplicate that feat. Paul has never forgotten that in that successful trip of his youth he almost lost his life. At the heart of his attributes is a deep understanding, gained in a long companionship with risk, of the hard realities of safeguarding others and oneself in undertakings that are inherently dangerous. Coming out of his own particular environment, he was not wholly sympathetic to the British course model. But he had a wholehearted commitment to the Outward Bound concept of challenging young people to stretch their capabilities.

I recall a time in Lead King Basin (perhaps it was the following year) when I took a teaching lesson from Tapley. We were at supper with two patrols. It was raining, on the verge of freezing, and the students had had difficulty starting a fire. Some of the rain was coming down snow, and it was so cold and miserable that we stood to eat. Sucking on his pipe as he and I chatted, Tap took a knife from his belt. Holding the blade between thumb and forefinger, he winged it across an open space into a log by the cook-fire. At the *thk!* sound of the knife point driving into the log, the kids perked up their heads. Tap walked over, pulled the knife out, came back, went on talking and sucking on his pipe. Pretty soon he threw the knife again, stuck it in the same place in the log. This time, as he came back, one of the kids asked, "Tap, have you ever killed a deer with a knife?"

"Yes."

"How did it happen?"

"Matter of fact," he said, "it was a night pretty much like this, cold and rainy. When you camp out on a night like this, your problem is fire. How you going to start a fire? It's easier if you're prepared. You all know about snapping off the dry dead wood under the branches of the hemlock or the Engelmann spruce. That's the first thing you do." He reached into his pocket. "You get real small wood in three different sizes, like this. But if you're really prepared, you never go into the woods without a mouse's nest, like this." Out of another pocket he took a mouse's nest and blew into it. "A mouse's nest is very flammable. You puff it out, so there will be a lot of air circulation through it."

"Hey, Tap, how about that deer?"

Tap was down on the ground now. "You put the smallest wood on top of the mouse's nest. Then the next size, but you hold the third. When you light the nest, your head should be at ground level so you can blow just a little bit."

He had the fire going and was adding the larger pieces. "Just as I had my fire started, this buck walked into my camp and stood there. I moved my hand slowly and got my knife out. Slowly I raised my hand like this." Wow, he stuck that knife in the same place in the same log for the third time. Then he said, "I dropped my head to the ground and didn't move a muscle."

The kids were all questions. "Why'd you do that, Tap?" "Were you afraid to move?" "Were you afraid the deer would run and you'd have to chase it?" Tap said, "And then the deer's head sagged. Sagged. Sagged and dropped, and his legs buckled and he went down." The fire was burning briskly in the rain as he arose. "You want to remember the whole thing is one of air circulating through dry material." I doubt that any of us who were there have forgotten how to build a fire in the rain.

That summer Tapley's solo innovation had been extended to three days and three nights. When the C-6 solo was coming up, we held a staff meeting to prepare for it. Going around the circle to get ideas from each instructor, I happened to ask one if he had ever had that kind of experience. He said he had spent many hours in the woods. I asked him if he had ever spent seventy-two hours completely on his own, out of sight and sound of humanity, and he said, well, he had been in the woods all his life. I quizzed the others and got similar answers. Not one had ever had three days in the wilderness entirely by himself. I said, "I'll tell you what we're going to do," and someone said, "Oh, no!" There was a groan, and I said, "Yes," and they said, "How about you?" I said, "That means me too." On the day the solo started, Frank Menendez loaded me, my pack, and my crutches on a horse and led me on his horse up into Fravert's Basin and dumped me off to live with myself for three days and three nights.

The great discovery I got from that experience was that on a wilderness solo you become very much in tune with your environment in a way that makes you realize how out of tune you are with your everyday environment. I was picking wild currants. I would pull them off the bush with one hand and pop them into my mouth, and every now and then my head would lift up, and I would be listening to things, or for things, that I had never listened to before. Maybe a breeze stirred, or a change in the wind's direction suddenly brought tree noises or amplified brook sounds, or perhaps there was an animal or insect sound or a bird song. Whatever it might be, my head would lift up, and I would open my mouth to hear better. At the same time I would stare; with my eyes stationary, it was easier to catch sight of anything that was moving. It hit me that I was far more aware of my environment than ever before in my life, acutely tuned in to everything around me. Then I got to laughing at myself, because I realized I was behaving just the way a deer does. I would browse a bit, and my head would lift up, and turn; I would stare, then go back to browsing. At no time was I startled; I was just intensely responsive to the matrix in which I was living.

Then I remembered Bill Coffin's story of his experience on the rock face. When he visited Eskdale, he was introduced to rock climbing. Like many of us, Bill has a great fear of heights. In the OSS he had made parachute jumps with few qualms; it is when you are connected to the ground, he tells you, that heights can be psychologically formidable. He was well up the rock face, and above his companions were calling (no doubt with a dash of British glee), "Come along, old chap. Come along, Yank." Not finding a new hold to come along by, Bill said, he was in a state of terror, his face a burst of sweat. As he clung there, the granite rock suddenly jumped out in startling focus. He saw the crystalline structure, the color and composition of the individual grains, the marvelous way they interlocked. He had never looked at a rock in that way before. He found himself wondering what else he had been missing by failing to see. And then, he said, Outward Bound hit him. Because he wondered what he had been missing in the faces of the parishioners he had counseled.

Browsing like a deer on currants, my head popping up, tuned into my environment, I wondered in turn, as I recalled Bill's story, what I had been missing in my Andover environment, my family environment. It made me wonder what it takes to enhance sensitivity to that degree. As Coffin had, I got a new, revealing message. It was worth its weight in gold, for it made me realize how meaningful the solo could be. I became a persuasive advocate of incorporating the three-day solo in all Outward Bound courses.

■ ■ ■

Toward the end of the summer we had a visitor I was glad to get to know. Bill Byrd, an Oregon educator, had just finished a twenty-month stint as director of the Peace Corps training camp in Puerto Rico and was returning home. Coming away from Arecibo with a continuing interest in Outward Bound, he stopped off at Marble to learn more about what we were doing. I had pretty much lost track of what was happening in Puerto Rico after Bill Coffin, having fulfilled his commitment to see the Peace Corps undertaking through its first two training cycles, returned to Yale. Byrd's visit was my first good chance to catch up on the Arecibo story.

Soon after Coffin's departure the training center closed down for a month of breath-catching. It reopened in January 1962 under the director-ship of Grant Venn, who had been president of Western State College in Gunnison, Colorado. Byrd was a new staff member. Shriver's charge to him shows that his thinking about the purpose of the Puerto Rican operation had not changed since the day of our first meeting. He told Byrd: "Somewhere in the training program we have to do two contradictory things. We have to test them at the same time that we build them. In one and the same program you test an individual's ability to face up, and you reenforce his ability to do so. That's what I want you to go down there and do." A few months later, when Venn became ill and had to resign, Byrd was appointed director.

For a time Byrd and Fred Lanoue were roommates. The two men hit it off beautifully; Freddy was one of Bill's happy memories. Lanoue had his critics, but Byrd was not one of them: "A lot of our own staff objected to Fred's tactics as overzealous. He would pin his critics right to the wall. He'd say, 'You son of a bitch, you do that person a disservice to allow him to go away fearing the water.' And he was absolutely right. That was our obliga-tion there. If we didn't meet it, we were sentencing those people to a lifetime of fear. Lanoue's uncompromising commitment was a great lesson for the staff people who were perceptive enough to catch on. I fought the same thing on the rocks. A lot of people have the same fear of heights that they do of water, and they wouldn't rappel. I stayed out there on the rappelling cliffs for nine hours, to get them over that cliff. We got them over. There wasn't a single person who came to the Puerto Rico center who didn't rappel. You let people be conquered by their fear, and you sentence them to loss of a part of their lives they're never going to realize. You can enrich a person's life a hundredfold when he gets through with this hang-up. That's what you have to keep your sights on—not the immediate small trauma that he has to go through to get there."

Byrd made that statement much later than 1963, after years as director of an Outward Bound school. There are those in Outward Bound who would agree with it wholeheartedly; there are others who would disagree that there is no productive alternative to dealing with an individual's fears by immersing him in the feared element.[5] The issue makes for keen debate when both proponents argue from thoughtful conviction. It is perhaps one of those moot issues where personality, temperament, and subtleties of method may decisively influence the rightness or wrongness of an action principle.

---

[5] For a differing, also authentic Outward Bound view, see "A Gestalt Conundrum: Lady on the Rocks or Rockclimbing as Self-Discovery" by John Huie, director of the North Carolina Outward Bound School, in *OBA News*, Summer 1977.

A SCHOOL IN MINNESOTA

*My son attended Minnesota Outward Bound two years
ago. . . . He arrived in Duluth airport a little boy, frightened,
lacking self-confidence, angry with the world, and with no
ability to persevere. He bombed out of high school in his
junior year. His month with MOBS produced all the
miracles one might wish for, and on a lasting basis. He
knows he's someone special . . . even changed his posture
to be more erect. He has forgotten the words "I quit,"
persists in difficult tasks until he is on top of them. He
has staying power to reach for distant objectives. He has
tolerance for the flaws in others. He has accepted society
as necessary and stimulating. He has learned his real
limits are much greater than he ever thought possible. Ben
graduated in June from high school with honors. May you
continue to supply others those conditions that stimulate
people to reach their potential.*

— A Minnesota student's parent

I returned east to open up the new Outward Bound headquarters in New Haven, Connecticut. Bill Coffin, now an Atlantic Foundation trustee, had made office space available in Yale's Dwight Hall. Helen Rawalt came with me on a two-month loan from the Colorado School. My charge from the Atlantic Foundation trustees was to see that the Colorado School opened with a full enrollment the following June, to guide establishment of

Planning a route across the landscape beneath the high clouds of Southern California's desert country. (Photo © PCOBS, Kim Budd)

additional schools, conduct public relations, raise scholarships, and develop an alumni organization.

During the summer Johnny Kemper and Coffin had followed up my visit to the Pieh camp in Minnesota. They saw Shining Trails in operation, did a canoe reconnaissance and got a dunking, had a good look at the Quetico Wilderness from the air, and discussed an arrangement for leasing the facilities from the Pieh family. The aerial reconnaissance northward into Canada gave them an awareness of the utter wildness of the country, where an expedition could go days without encountering another human.

Coffin also had another matter on his mind. Before becoming headmaster of the Anniston School, Bob Pieh had taught at the Indian Springs School in Alabama, which was founded with money left by a Birmingham industrialist to create a model for secondary education in the state. Coffin was aware that the terms of the will originally restricted attendance to "white Caucasians." He had no sooner arrived at Shining Trails than he put the question to Pieh: What was a Yankee like him with his humanistic Antioch background doing in a school that placed such restrictions on its student body? Bob could satisfy him on that score because diligent efforts by trustees and faculty had succeeded in getting around the restrictive covenant, first for Jewish youngsters, and eventually for blacks.

Kemper and Coffin came away satisfied that the Pieh proposal was sound. Kemper made a second trip, to Minneapolis and St. Paul, where he undertook to interest a group of Andover alumni and others in helping to form a board of trustees for the proposed new school. Among them was Louis F. "Bo" Polk, one of the Twin Cities' brightest young businessmen. At thirty-two Polk was a vice president of General Mills.

On October 7, 1963, the Atlantic Foundation approved formation of the Minnesota Outward Bound School, to be opened the following summer. At a meeting two months later the Piehs made a progress report that included the names of the fifteen men comprising the school's board of trustees, with Polk as chairman. In addition to his own dynamic energies, Polk was able to involve other resources at General Mills. One of the people he brought on the board was John Burger, a member of the company's public relations department. Although Pieh was resigning his school post in order to be a full-time director of the Minnesota School, he had to finish out the school year in Alabama. Polk, Burger, and other members of Folk's staff became the ad hoc staff for the school in the months before it opened, responsible for publicity, promotion, scholarships, and recruitment. Burger, working at the task virtually full time, did a splendid job in getting out publicity and literature and building community support. I would go out to the Twin Cities, and John would have a staggering schedule of meetings set up for me, as many as four in a day. John would always be in the back of the room when I talked, giving me a three-minute sign, two, one, and then the cut gesture. He was a tiger on preventing overkill of an audience.

An Andover alumnus and former Andover teacher in Minneapolis whom Kemper had had no difficulty in proselytizing was A. Lachlan Reed. Because a relative had married a former Gordonstoun student who idolized Kurt

Hahn, Lach was already well aware of Hahn's work. He took on with Polk the task of raising funds to cover needed capital expenditures for construction and equipment. General Mills also helped by putting up $7,500 for scholarships for sons of their employees around the country. The Avalon Foundation and the Old Dominion Foundation each made a seeding grant of $25,000; $10,000 of the total was to help support Outward Bound Inc., which had just been established, the balance of $40,000 going to the school's scholarship fund.

During the spring school vacation the Piehs flew overseas for a round of visits to the British Outward Bound schools. They signed on Ralph Clough and Colin Bolton, an instructor at Ullswater, for the Minnesota staff. The Minnesotans too recognized the value of using British instructors to facilitate transplant of the Outward Bound philosophy and method to American soil. In June the Minnesota Outward Bound School opened the first of the summer's two courses with an enrollment of ninety-six students comprising eight twelve-man "brigades."

For Bob Pieh the Minnesota beginning was the "catching of a train for perhaps an infinite journey" that he very much wanted to be on. He had grown up in Madison, Wisconsin. A natural athlete, he played all sports avidly. Also, from when he was very young, he nurtured his growth on an affinity for the out-of-doors.

"I found a lot of religion in natural phenomena," he said. "This grounded my concepts of God and ethical development."

The Pieh family was hit hard by the Depression. After his father's death during his senior year of high school, Bob attended the University of Wisconsin part-time while working for the city of Madison. He was made assistant to the city's recreation director, became involved in adult education, and worked nights on a newspaper sports desk.

Browsing in the university library, Bob happened on something Kurt Hahn had written. Impressed, he continued to collect Hahn items. When he graduated from Wisconsin with a B.S. in biology, he had enough other credits to qualify him also to teach English, history, or physical education. A few years after joining the faculty of Antioch College in Ohio he was made chairman of its health, physical education, and recreation department, directing the academic program for students in the field and coordinating physical education for the student body. In the latter role, Bob extended the available electives far beyond conventional sports. He encouraged students to play the games of other nations as a way to gain insight into foreign cultures. He developed an "open country" program, a mix of trekking, campcraft, canoeing, and other outdoor activities that became more popular than any of the standard sports. There were also teams organized as clubs that represented the college, sometimes students and faculty together. Bob played on the soccer team. He sought ways to use physical education to help build a genuine college community.

"We encouraged the faculty to play too, and made sure they didn't feel inferior if they needed to learn skills or improve themselves physically. Our conditioning program included Swedish and Danish free exercises and some yoga. We were interested in why the Eastern yogi advocated physical purification before advancing toward the spiritual. At that time there wasn't much in print on yoga—I had to write the universities in Calcutta and Bombay. So we had a healthy mix, a crazy quilt of experience that I think Kurt Hahn would have approved."

In 1957 Pieh went to Alabama. Summers he ran wilderness outposts for private camps, leading their youngsters on canoe trips into the Quetico. He bought the Minnesota property, where the Pieh family developed a camp-and-canoe expedition base for families and student groups. Continuing to glean Kurt Hahn material, he became aware of the roots of Outward Bound in England and felt he was using a kindred approach in his own educational efforts. Then one day he read in *Time* magazine that a U.S. Outward Bound school had been started in Colorado. Suddenly events seemed to be passing him by. "I had this strong feeling that the train was starting to leave the station. I told myself, if this really represents what you most want to do, you'd better act." That was when he wrote to Kemper.

In that first summer of 1964 the Minnesota School operated under physical handicaps. New construction was incomplete. A generator provided limited electricity. The water system, while approved, was improvised. Meals had to be cooked in the old resort main building and carried up to the unfinished dining hall during the first course. Pieh gave the students a sense of belonging by making the unfinished tasks part of the curriculum.

None of these physical shortcomings at Homeplace—the name Piehs gave to the school base at Ely, Minnesota—diminished the positive aspects of the program. The students received ten days of basic training in canoe fundamentals, swimming, drownproofing, water rescue, camping and cooking skills, map and compass route-finding, fire fighting, and survival techniques, and took short training expeditions. A spectacular ropes course and a variety of initiative tests built positive attitudes and teamwork. An interbrigade competition was built into the activities. After the training period each brigade took off on a long canoeing expedition into the Canadian wilderness: two men to a canoe, six canoes per brigade, and a seventh for the instructor and his assistant. The routes threaded a maze formed by rivers and lakes, the portages often exceedingly difficult, the dense bush testing determination and endurance, the arduous day's run sometimes extending into the long northern twilight. A three-day solo, followed by a final expedition, the brigade making its way back to Homeplace on its own. The marathon, the students writing their course impressions, and home.

The shaping process I observed at Minnesota renewed my awareness, acquired in my British exposure, that each school, while adhering to the essential concept, develops its particular personality and ambiance. This is partly a matter of geography and environment, but mostly, I think, the product of the leadership. The Piehs put their own mark on Homeplace and the wilderness activities. In a later time Jerry Fieri was to think back, "U.S. Outward Bound was then heavily into the challenge issues. There was a heavy emphasis on that in the beginning, and I think rightfully so. We also had a hidden agenda. We wanted to emphasize as much the beauty of nature and the importance of human relationships and caring for other people as we did the physical side of the program. We consciously did things that were intended to help kids appreciate natural beauty, and to emphasize humanistic kinds of values."

Among the students in M-1 were Lach Reed's eldest son and a school friend. Lach remembered, "The friend was the son of a millionaire, handsome, bright, a good athlete, and obnoxiously conceited. A spoiled rich kid. I'll never forget picking up those two at the Greyhound station when they came back from their course. My son said, 'Gee, Dad, it was a great experience,' and he and this boy got in the back seat. I said to his friend, 'How was it for you, Mr. Reed?' He said, 'it's the greatest experience I ever had. For the first time I realize what a horse's ass I've been all my life.'"

Lach, who was with the Honeywell Corporation, got a second insight that first year into the salutary influence Outward Bound could have on a young-ster. James Binger, Honeywell president, gave money for two scholarships and told Lach to select the recipients, preferably from a Honeywell family.

"Just about then a toolmaker in my department came to me and said, 'I hear you're helping to start a survival camp or something up north. I have a son who's not worth the powder to blow him up. He's sixteen, he quit high school at fourteen, he lies in bed all day smoking cigarettes and is out all night. I've tried everything, and he's just a mess. Would you take him?' I called Bob Pieh and told him about this kid and the scholarship, and Bob said, 'Sure.' I saw the boy up there at the start of his course, and he did bear out his father's just-a-mess description. The boy completed that course, came home and got a job right away, and enrolled in high school at night. His father said to me, 'Lach, it's absolutely unbelievable how that kid has changed!' I kept track of him for several years. He finished high school and the last I knew he was still doing fine."

■ ■ ■

On January 9, 1964, incorporation papers were drawn up creating Outward Bound Inc. (OBI). They provided for OBI, as it would come to be known, to take over the Outward Bound responsibilities that the Atlantic Foundation had been discharging. The incorporators were the Rev. William S. Coffin Jr., John M. Kemper, Mrs. Ellen Z. McCloy, Joshua L. Miner, and John P. (Jack) Stevens Jr. These five were named trustees, along with General Bruce C. Clarke, H. Wentworth Eldredge, F. Charles Froelicher, Thomas B. Hartmann, and Fred I. Kent II. At the first trustee meeting, I was elected president of OBI. It was a full-time salaried position; I was now wholly committed to Outward Bound and its future growth and welfare.

In June we returned to Andover, where the Outward Bound headquarters would be located for the next six years.

A TRAGEDY

✳

For sorrow ends not when it seemeth done.

—Richard II

S eeing the Minnesota School in action, getting feedback from students and
parents, made clear that the Outward Bound dynamic worked as aptly in
lake as in mountain country. There was, however, a distinction. The high
mountain vistas proclaim their hazards. The dangers implicit in those soaring
peaks are all too apparent; one needs no special warning to know they are
there. The Quetico, on the other hand, its placid waters set like jewels in the
endless bush, has an illusory benign quality. One forgets that of all the earthly
substances, water is the most inimical to man. It was in that seemingly kind
northern country we suffered our first fatal accident and were taught our first
harsh safety lesson.

In August I was visiting the Colorado School when I received a telephone
message that hit like a blow to the head. A student in Minnesota's M-2 course
had drowned. When I reached Ely the next evening, I heard the story of what
will always remain an unexplained tragedy. After a day of paddling on the ninth
day of the course, two students, Dan Lucas and Larry Hanson, had been placed
by their instructors on the shore of a fairly small lake for an overnight "duo," as
a preparation for their forthcoming solo experience. While Larry made shelter
and other preparations, Dan went out in the canoe to try to catch fish for supper
(an action not in accord with the school's strict rules governing one-man
canoeing). When he was two hundred yards or more offshore, he either fell or

jumped from the canoe. The only witnesses were Hanson and another student on the opposite shore. They both agreed they saw Dan in the water but differed as to the circumstances. Hanson said that he heard a banging noise and saw Lucas kneeling in the canoe and clutching something "black and white and looked like a loon," and that Lucas then fell out of the craft. (On the way to the duo site, according to Hanson, Dan had suggested they might catch a loon.) The other student said that Lucas seemed to get in and out of the canoe several times, that he suddenly was in the water with the canoe drifting away. Both agreed there was a yell and a whistle but that they sounded more like cries of triumph than calls for help. They agreed, and this was confirmed by others, that later a loon was swimming in the water near the empty canoe.

When Hanson realized that Lucas was in trouble, he gave the distress call of three shouts. Three youths who heard the call paddled to where the canoe was drifting, but found no sign of Lucas other than his floating paddle. A search of the water directed by the instructors proved fruitless. Early the following morning Jerry Pieh arrived at the lake to organize an ongoing search. Scuba divers of the Silver Bay Rescue Squad were flown in and continued for days to look for the body without success. Other searches were conducted in the woods around the lake.

As the days dragged by with no positive result, I spent considerable time with Joseph Lucas, Dan's father. In the timeless setting of lake and forest we talked about life and its uncertainties, about parents and children, their hopes and aspirations, and the cruel forces that can suddenly, brutally take charge. A splendid man, he bore no ill will against the school for what had happened. Dan was a husky, athletic boy and had been a leader in looking out for other boys in his brigade less naturally able than himself. He had been ranked a competent swimmer of average ability and had successfully undergone the school's drownproofing and water safety training, including the test of remaining afloat for forty-five minutes. He had been taught what to do if a capsizing or loss of balance put him in the water—the first principle being to stay with the canoe, which is a natural life raft. There seemed to be no logical reason for his having drowned.

It is possible, we knew, for a person to inhale only a few drops of water into his windpipe and have his breathing automatically shut off. Virtually everyone has had the experience of a drink going down "the wrong way," precipitating a fit of gasping and coughing. The cough is the body's effort to expel any foreign body from the windpipe. Unless water that has entered the windpipe is dislodged, a person who has gone overboard can be asphyxiated in two to five minutes even while remaining at the surface. But the prevailing placid conditions and Dan's natural abilities seemed to cast doubt on that possibility. There was the strange suggestion that Dan had been grappling with a loon and that this somehow accounted for the accident, but the weight of the evidence was against that hypothesis as well. It was because the drowning was so hard to explain that we also combed the land areas.

Dan's body was finally discovered by state fish and game personnel twelve days after the mishap. The autopsy concluded that death was due to drowning, that there was no other finding to explain the death, no evidence of a major injury or trauma. I had concluded that it was OBI's responsibility to have the accident investigated by a committee of persons not associated with the school, and Bo Polk and Bob Pieh concurred. I named a three-man team— Philip Allen, an Andover neighbor who was a Hurricane Island trustee, William Dabney, a trustee of the Colorado School, and John McLane Jr., an attorney from Manchester, New Hampshire, whose son was enrolled at Colorado that summer. Assembling the evidence, the investigators rejected the possibility that young Lucas had caught a loon—on the grounds that loons are almost impossible to catch from any kind of a boat, that they are extremely dangerous birds to fool with, capable of inflicting serious injury with their powerful neck and sharp beak, and that there were no injury marks on Dan's body. They concluded that he accidentally fell out of the canoe for some unknown reason, was inhibited by the weight of his clothing, and inhaled water and became asphyxiated within a few minutes, thus preventing him from making any attempt to save himself.

Subsequently I had a letter from Fred Lanoue, in response to the copy of the investigating committee's report I sent him. I cannot know whether any of Fred's theorizing was correct with regard to the Lucas boy's death, but the points that he made are certainly cogent to water safety. He did not agree that the hampering clothes, including leather boots, were a major factor contributing to the drowning and suggested the possibility of three additional

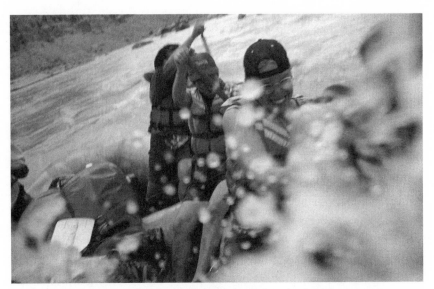

"All forward!" Getting wet on the Green River in Utah is the first step toward learning the lessons of whitewater. (Photo © Sanford Schulwolf)

factors. One, which would account for Dan's gyrations in the canoe, was cramps—quite common, Fred said, at the end of the first day of a canoe trip with relatively inexperienced paddlers. Another factor he thought could have played a part was an attempt by Dan to remove his shoes.

"When one feels the hampering effect of full clothes," he wrote, "the inadequacy of the kick contribution is immediately obvious, and so the first effort is always made to kick off the shoes. Using hands to remove shoes is lethal because one may be sinking all the time, whereas when attempting to remove clothes the legs are working all the time to remain at the surface. I have personally rescued a number of fair swimmers in pools and lakes from this specific situation."

A possible third factor, he suggested, was the complication of expelling water from the throat. "With no other complications present, a certain amount of success is probable by the usual orthodox uphill coughing with the head out of the water and face up. Downhill coughing with the head in the water is the only sure way to clear the throat."

U.S. Outward Bound's first fatal accident made us aware, in a way nothing else could, how simultaneously important and difficult the problems of safety in our program were going to be. The tragedy's many lessons included one of the most basic—when the hazard is not obvious, or does not appear to exist, it may most readily exact its toll. Unfortunately, this is not a lesson that any of us tends naturally to absorb from the experience of others; it is among the most difficult to teach and so save the learner the cost of having to learn it through personal experience.

One of the services performed by Ralph Clough and other instructors who came from England to help launch U.S. Outward Bound was to make the school staffs conscious of the fine safety tradition they were inheriting from the British movement. The schools gratefully accepted from the British Outward Bound Trust that body's safety policy, which provided a well-articulated set of guiding principles. The policy statement opens with the explanation that since Outward Bound students are encouraged to engage in activities where the risk of accident may be greater than in their normal way of life, those charged with their training have a special responsibility to take adequate, continuous care to protect them against accidents. The principle, it continues, is not to avoid activities involving danger but to prepare students, both by technical training and physical fitness, to deal competently with the risk. But hazards should not be sought for their own sake; they should be forestalled as far as possible, mastered through competence if they come. Safety, the policy states, is an integral part of Outward Bound's training and experiential process, exemplified by the words and action of each instructor. It involves not only overt precautions to prevent accidents but also a "what if?" attitude toward every experience. At its heart the policy states "The aim is to teach that the more adventurous an undertaking is, the more care and prudence it calls for if it is to succeed."

Each school implemented these principles by prescribing safe practices for its particular environment and courses, and by diligent instructor training and student instruction. Increasingly with the passing years, the directors coordinated their safety thinking and policies, and the schools exchanged information about their experiences of encountering hazard and the knowledge they gained in dealing with it. In time this led to the formulation and servicing of a national safety policy that has been much admired in the outdoor pursuit and education communities.

A SEA SCHOOL

*The sea, the granite quarries—nature herself—was
seen not as something to be feared as the enemy, but
to be respected and even loved. You were taught to be
in concert with nature. The sea, the rocks, the physical
elements of nature were the training tools. You were
not being trained to be an expert sailor or rock climber
but rather how to use your knowledge and respect for
them to make you a better person.*

**—The Rev. Thomas B. Kennedy, Trinity Church, Boston,
from a sermon based on his Hurricane Island experience**

It has been said of Peter Willauer that had he been born one hundred fifty
years sooner, he would have been a whaling captain. His mother was a
great-niece of Winslow Homer and had grown up in Fronts Neck on the
Maine coast. Like his architect father before him, Peter spent his boyhood
summers at Prouts Neck. He learned early to handle small boats, won three
national junior sailing championships, and competed on the U.S. Olympic
sailing team. At Princeton he enrolled in Navy ROTC, and for his required
two-year service duty following graduation he was appointed sailing
instructor at the Naval Academy in Annapolis. He lived aboard a barracks
ship where he supervised the African-American and Filipino sailors who, in
the Navy's way at that time, were mess stewards at the academy. Here, he
acquired some insights into race relationships.

His duty completed, Willauer went back to Princeton to work in the admissions office, decided to be a teacher, and won a teaching fellowship in mathematics at Phillips Academy—a good trick, since his college major had been international studies. At Andover he was much taken by the enthusiastic talk about Outward Bound from Reagh Wetmore and me. In particular, he was entranced by the fact that the original school at Aberdovey was sea-based. He spent the 1960–1961 school year at Harvard, earning his master's degree in education, and took a teaching and admissions job at the Groton School, where he also coached football, hockey, and crew. He had come out of Harvard not sure whether he wanted to teach in a public or private school. What decided him on Groton was the chance to work with John Crocker, one of the century's great headmasters.

"Jack was an inspirational character for Betty and me," Peter said. "He was a unique, special human being. His teaching and example as a terrific Christian and wonderful person were very much a part of why we were there."

During school vacations Willauer worked at Prouts Neck as manager of the yacht club's summer activities, coaching junior sailing and running the club's boatyard. He began to be uncomfortable about a sense of blandness in his life. "I was getting a little uptight with the summer bit of the social community, and finding that the year-round program had a sameness that made me conscious of how remote it all was from the rest of the world."

In the 1962–1963 school year he was director of admissions at Groton. I ran into him at a conference of admissions officers, and naturally I had to fill him in on the exciting developments on the Outward Bound front. When I told him that we were hoping to see a school get started in the East, he said, "Why don't you have a sea school?" We spent a good part of the conference kicking that idea around. In the spring he came over to Andover to tell Kemper and me that he was seriously interested in starting a school. We told him to get himself a board of trustees and a site and come back.

In Prouts Neck that summer, he read Kurt Hahn and did a lot of thinking about the kind of school he might create: "I knew I wanted a school based on a vessel that students could be independent in without having a captain aboard, so I discounted the large-vessel approach. That pointed to some kind of pulling boat that a dozen or so people could sail or, if there was no wind, could row. My thinking was influenced by a friend at Prouts Neck named Fritz Osther, a brilliant young scientist who had had a great career at Harvard and was working for Avco. He was a fine person to bounce ideas off, and he helped me research the pulling-boat idea. Another who guided me was Seymour Alden, a friend who had had my job at the yacht club before me, and who would be with us at Hurricane Island until he died. Seymour was a good listener and a steadying influence on a brash young man. Dan Bickford, whom I had known at Annapolis, and Rog Sherbrook, a Princeton sailing friend, helped to think through a program, and I had help from other Navy and sailing friends. Dick Homer, an architect friend of my father, got intrigued. Jack Crocker, who knew Kurt Hahn—Hahn had visited his school a couple of times—was giving me lots of encouragement. It was Crocker who gave us the key lead to a site."

Peter was envisioning an island as probably the best kind of location for his school. The coast was getting built up, and he liked the idea of the dramatic separation an island would give both mind and body. "The mystique you have in being isolated. Also, I realized we couldn't put a nonsailor in a boat all day, that you had to start out slowly and learn skills, leading up to expeditions at sea. So we would need a solid program on land as well as on water. I particularly liked the idea of drownproofing, which I had learned about from Reagh Wetmore. I thought it would tie into the curriculum nicely, and that it was a wonderful activity for the individual, as against the group stress experiences we were sure to get in a boat. I didn't know anything about rock climbing, but I recognized it was virtually a standard part of an Outward Bound program, so I felt we would want access to suitable rocks. I knew about the solo idea they had come up with in Colorado, and I bought that."

Jack Crocker summered at Vinalhaven, an island in Penobscot Bay off Rockland, on the central Maine coast. He suggested to Peter that Hurricane Island, a small island south of Vinalhaven, ought to meet his specifications. Hurricane had once been the location of an important granite-quarrying community; the Library of Congress building is one of the structures built in the late nineteenth century of Hurricane Island granite. The stone had run out, the stoneworkers had left, and the island had been uninhabited for decades. Because the excavated quarry was a natural catch basin for rainwater, it was well known to yachtsmen cruising Penobscot Bay, who often put ashore to do laundry and take fresh water aboard.

In September Peter and Betty Willauer sailed from Prouts Neck "down east" to Hurricane Island.

"It was blowing like hell from the northeast," Willauer recalled, "and we couldn't get ashore on what's now the main pier and Valley Cove side. We anchored over on the opposite, stone-beach side, off the quarry. We couldn't keep the anchor down, so Betty stayed with the boat while I rowed ashore and did a ninety-minute reconnaissance. I saw these granite cliffs and the fresh water, and the foundations of the old quarry village, and the mostly wooded island with the good harbor, and I thought, 'Gee, this is a natural!' and rowed back to the boat. I went down to Andover and told Josh I'd found the ideal site. We got a few trustees together, and they gave some encouragement. That fall with Dan Bickford I began negotiating with Jim Gaston, the owner, to lease Hurricane Island. The negotiations went on all winter before we finally worked out a deal."

All Peter needed now was money. At Andover's alumni weekend in the spring of 1964 I was in the rooms of Fred Peterson, a faculty colleague, when he introduced me to William Shallow, his visiting classmate. Bill Shallow was a New York advertising executive. Not surprisingly, with me in the room, the talk turned to Outward Bound. Shallow was for it immediately. I told him about the Hurricane Island possibility, and he asked, "What does it take to get it going?"

I said, "Cash."

He indicated he did not think cash was the world's biggest problem. I told Willauer about him, and he drove down to Connecticut to the Shallow home. It was his first fund-raising effort: "When I got there, I learned all the Shallow kids had some communicable disease like chicken pox, and I couldn't go in. Bill Shallow talked with me from a window. I told him about our plans and needs, and he said, 'It sounds good to me. I'll send you a check for five thousand dollars.' The next week the check came, and it was for ten thousand. That money enabled us to move ahead on our plans to build the school that summer. Also, the occasion gave us one of our very good early trustees. Shallow came on the board and was a real asset. Good judgment, tough-minded, willing to go out on a limb, and—obviously—generous."

Dick Homer drew up a plan for the school, and Peter, working through friends and friends of friends, lined up forty volunteer young people, most of them from secondary schools, to spend the summer of 1964 on Hurricane Island with him and some Princeton friends to build the base. The advance group went ashore on June 20, and the work moved forward from then until Peter had to return to Groton in mid-September. The work crews lived in platform tents. They built a pier, put up several buildings, including their own mess hall—now the laundry and generator building—and framed the big main structure that was to become the school mess hall and office. They cut roads to the quarry and hauled rocks. An electric generator was brought in on a barge; with special rigging and a lot of arm and leg power, they got it ashore and in place. Power was turned on August 20.

Tap Tapley, having completed the instructor training courses he gave in Colorado that summer, came on to consult and supervise the building of the ropes course. Another who showed up to help him was a twenty-three-year-old New Jerseyite named Phil Costello, fresh out of the Marines and preparing to start teachers college in the fall; for Phil this was the beginning of a long Outward Bound association. Tapley's coming added a new dimension to the island activities. It was interesting for a bunch of sailors to get together with a mountaineer for the first time and exchange knots, navigation, and orienteering techniques, and the like. For the youngsters, whose recreation up to then had been largely on the water side, Tap was the start of a new chapter. He got them up early each morning for a run and dip. He taught them how to build a fire, how to cook when it was wet in the woods, and how to hunt with a bowie knife. He introduced them to rock climbing, rappelling, and cliff evacuation in the quarry. With the kids, he took Wetmore's drownproofing course. When the ropes course was finished, he put them through it. He gave them fire-fighting drills, and did a ship-to-shore rescue drill with a kind of Tyrolean traverse arrangement. Each youngster also had a two-day solo on a Penobscot Bay island. Seymour Alden, a self-taught naturalist, briefed them on the edible foods they were likely to find.

During the summer, Willauer experimented with possible models for a pulling boat. When fall arrived, the design of the vessel that was to be the heart of the Hurricane Island program the following June was still an open question. Homer brought Willauer together with Cyril Hamblin, a Rockland yacht and commercial-fishing-boat designer and an expert in lightweight wood construction. The two decided that no boat then existed that could be sailed and rowed and had the sought-for simplicity and margin of safety.

The nearest thing to it they could find was the thirty-foot whaleboat that the U.S. Navy had used in the 1920s and 1930s off the old four-stacker destroyers. Part of midshipman training at that time was to be put overboard in the whaleboats and row around the mid-Atlantic for a day. Cy Hamblin took the Navy's old plans and reworked them against Willauer's demanding specifications. He added sheer for Penobscot Bay's steep seas. For sailing he designed a split rig (two masts) with a low center of effort, that is, short masts and a minimum heeling moment. The boat had to be able to carry fourteen—a full "watch," as the school's twelve-man cadre was to be called, plus an instructor and assistant—and gear for an expedition. Since it was expected there would be some sailing off beaches, it had to be light enough for a crew to launch. It had to have enough flotation so that even if it filled in the cold Maine waters, it would not sink, and even if it capsized, it could be righted. Willauer felt strongly about a boat for inexperienced sailors on the Maine coast having this built-in flotation. He had helped to design the Explorer class, which has a double bottom plus solid flotation in the wooden seat and bow, one of the early boats that could be capsized, righted, bailed, and sailed. The Hurricane Island pulling boats, in addition to their wood construction, have thirty-two cubic feet of Styrofoam built in the bow and stern and side thwarts. Every watch learns how to right a capsized boat.

For Willauer the collaboration with Hamblin was extremely happy. Years later he would say, "I was trying to get something that was sea kindly and also kindly to an inexperienced crew, with a gigantic margin of safety—even though the people in it would not be aware the margin was there. Cy came up with a design that gave us what we needed. When we had our second set of boats built in 1969, we made sixty small changes in design and construction detail, but it was still the same boat. All told, that boat has been sailed and rowed by close to eight thousand students the equivalent of four circumnavigations of the globe, with no mishaps more serious than one capsize, which proved routine, and two swampings when a boat broached on a jibe and filled in heavy seas."

A rappel is an exercise in trust of both self and belay partner. Students gain confidence through exercises in teamwork. (Photo © Ty Milford)

Opening page: A mountaineering student expresses the personal rewards of challenge, adventure, and character development on a summit in the High Sierra. (Photo © Ty Milford)

Backpacking in the vast expanse of the Beartooth Range, Montana, on a three-week course with Voyageur Outward Bound School. (Photo © Mark Zelinski, www.markzelinski.com)

"Gunnel up!" Kayaking on open waters allows students to feel at one with the elements on Puget Sound. (Photo © PCOBS, Jeremy Lucke)

Conquering your fears on the high ropes course is a challenging part of the Outward Bound experience. This one is at the Voyageur Outward Bound basecamp in Minnesota. (Photo © Mark Zelinski, www.markzelinski.com)

Opposite: Winter courses teach students how to adapt to the elements. Telemark skiing in Colorado's Rocky Mountains during a backcountry skiing course. (Photo © Brian Litz)

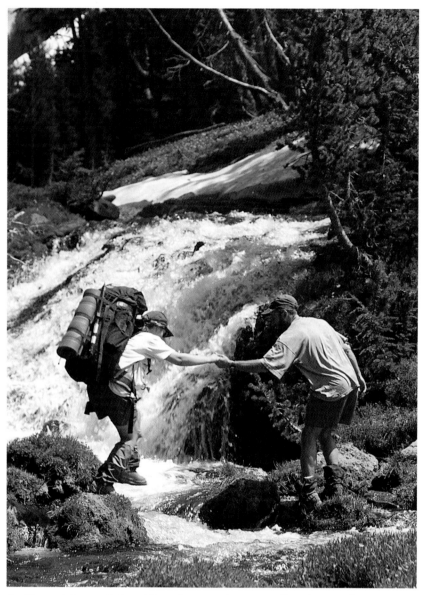

Problem solving on Outward Bound courses is a team effort that requires a significant amount of trust among the members to achieve the goals of the group. (Photo © Ty Milford)

Opposite: Crossing a meandering stream among the jagged peak and lush alpine meadow, students experience breathtaking natural wilderness on a mountain backpacking expedition. (Photo © Ty Milford)

A patrol of students crosses a mountain pass in the Minarets region of the High Sierra. Altitude, heavy packs, and long treks allow each team member to discover hidden inner strengths. (Photo © Ty Milford)

Opposite: Navigation exercises call upon observation, intelligence, and teamwork to succeed amid the vast landscapes of the High Sierra. (Photo © Ty Milford)

A moment of relaxation brings course members together in the natural wilderness of central California's High Sierra. (Photo © Ty Milford)

Opposite: Floating through Echo Park on the Green River with Colorado Outward Bound in the late 1980s. Reverence for the beauty of the environment is a large part of Outward Bound courses. (Photo © Mark Zelinski, www.markzelinski.com)

Social and environmental responsibility is important in any Outward Bound educational experience. Students learn and practice "Leave No Trace" skills at every camp area and on every trail. (Photo © Ty Milford)

Opposite: Rock climbers discover that hard work leads to success, as on this course in the granite crags of the Minarets. (Photo © Ty Milford)

Left: Joshua L. Miner III, founding father of the Outward Bound movement in the United States. (Photo courtesy Outward Bound USA)

Below: The Indian-style "war canoe" on a quiet lake in Minnesota's Boundary Waters region, during a Voyageur Outward Bound School course in the mid-1980s. (Photo © Mark Zelinski, www.markzelinski.com)

Opposite: A student develops strength and agility scaling Twin Peaks in the southern Sierra Nevada on a multi-element course in 1989. (Photo © Mark Zelinski, www.markzelinski.com)

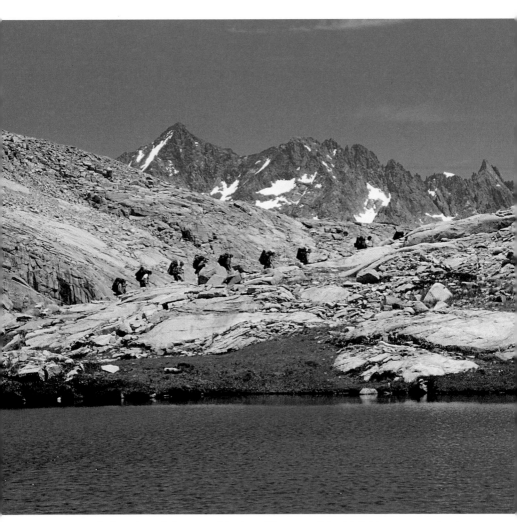

A patrol of students is immersed in the wilderness of the High Sierra, preparing to hike through the peaks ahead. (Photo courtesy Outward Bound Archives)

February came, and the opening of the Hurricane Island Outward Bound School was less than five months away. Willauer had his designs for the boats but no money to build them. Dick Preston, the trustees' president, was on a business trip. Peter caught him by phone in St. Louis. He said, "You know, we're not going to have a sea school if we don't have any boats." Preston told him to order one. He ordered five. They were delivered just before H-1 opened.

H-1 and H-2, in the summer of 1965, had 170 students, half on full scholarship. The planning in the building summer paid off; the curriculum worked smoothly, with few changes. The students were in twelve-man watches, instructed by a watch officer and an assistant. Hurricane's run and dip was an 05:45 call, a two-mile run up and down root-snagged paths through the woods and across great granite boulders along the water's edge, ending with a plunge into the icy ocean (48°F). For their first-day waterborne experience the students were towed in a pulling boat a mile out to sea and told when they were expected to be back for lunch—a fast lesson in the importance of self-discipline and teamwork that made for attentiveness during the subsequent instruction in seamanship and navigation. The students were on the water virtually every day. Practice in two-man peapods and seventeen-foot Marconi-rigged Explorers supplemented pulling boat instruction in rowing and sailing. A two-day cruise under instructor supervision—extended to three days in later courses—completed the training. For the final four-day expedition, the watch was on its own, usually sailing in convoy with two other watches. Instructors aboard a powerboat followed within emergency-aid range. Each expedition included a service phase.

A single season provided all the evidence needed to prove that in creating the Hurricane Island pulling boat, Hamblin and Willauer had devised a stress vehicle par excellence. A student on a mountain or desert expedition who wants to separate him- or herself from the interpersonal stresses of the cadre can drop back fifty yards on the trail for at least temporary isolation. But for twelve people in what is essentially a twelve-person boat (with two instructors also aboard, it's really tight) there is no escaping one another. Some may withdraw by occasional dozing, but enough must remain awake to man the helm, navigate, stand bow watch, assist at every change of tack, row when there is no wind, and prepare a meal for a hungry crew. Inseparable from the

Sailing an open boat on the waters of Puget Sound teaches skills of cooperation and confidence-building. (Photo © Andrew Dalrymple)

situation in the boat are the elements in which it is operated—the sea and the Maine weather. No two days are the same; conditions range from flat calm through fog, wind, and rain, to whole gales.

Among the watch officers were Adrian Middleton, an experienced Australian seaman and former instructor at the Fisherman's Point Australian Outward Bound School and Aberdovey; Barry Crook, a British instructor who had led thirty-five courses at the Ullswater, Aberdovey, and Devon Schools; and Jay Evans, who had taught at Colorado the previous two summers. Those without specific Outward Bound experience had equally fine credentials. The watch officers were assisted by specialists in seamanship and navigation, rock climbing, drownproofing, first aid, and fire fighting. Knut Smith, former Colorado as well as army and marine rock-climbing instructor, was in charge of the climbing in the old quarry. Euell Gibbons, famed writer-authority on edible wild foods, conducted a course in ecology and briefed the students on how they might eat well on solo.

Reagh Wetmore taught drownproofing—a ten-part course in the cold waters of the quarry pool, through to the final trials with hands and feet tied. The mile swim with clothes on tested mastery of the travel stroke. The fifty-yard underwater swim was an exercise in resistance to rising panic and fear of the unknown. Reagh's lifesaving instruction included a one-hundred-yard carry of a victim whose hands were tied behind his back—a surprisingly realistic experience for both rescued and rescuer.

"In an Outward Bound program," Willauer declared, "the place of honor must be held by the Rescue Services." He cited the heart of Kurt Hahn's programmatic thinking: "The experience of helping a fellow man in danger, or even of training in a realistic manner to be ready to give this help, tends to change the balance of power in a youth's inner life with the result that compassion can become the master motive." From Hurricane Island's beginning, each watch in a standard course has been required to do several twenty-four-hour tours of duty at the island's Rescue Station, which maintains a continuous radio watch for distress calls, fire alarms, and other emergency messages. Duty includes instruction in use of the school's fire-fighting equipment. The duty watch is charged with making the appropriate response to all emergency calls, under staff leadership.

For Willauer it was providential that on the final day of H-1, during the last tug-of-war in the interwatch competition, the general alarm sounded. Twenty acres of woodland were ablaze on Marshall Island, eighteen miles to the east. In a swift execution of emergency procedure, the duty watch, twelve students, and two watch officers led by fire-fighting specialist John Pingree were en route in the Rescue Unit *Penobscot* and in forty-eight minutes had water on the fire. The Coast Guard arrived soon after, and two other watches followed in smaller boats. Fifty men fought the fire until it was under control at 3 A.M. All hands returned exhausted to Hurricane Island, ate a late dinner during a predawn awards ceremony, packed, and at 0800 were aboard the ferry for Rockland, headed home.

THE DISADVANTAGED:
EXPERIMENT WITH DELINQUENTS

✵

I prefer the lawless to the listless.

—Kurt Hahn

Because so many of us involved in the start of U.S. Outward Bound were connected with independent schools, we were concerned lest the movement acquire a "preppie" stigma. We knew it would be fatal for Outward Bound's purposes if people came to think of it as available just to the affluent. We wanted a broad socioeconomic mix. Early on, therefore, it became Outward Bound policy that one-half a school's enrollment should be scholarship students. Some of these had partial scholarships, but many were economically and culturally deprived youngsters receiving full stipends. Most came from what a few years later would be called the "inner city."

At that time Andover enjoyed a close relationship with the Boys' Club of New York, a liaison that had come about through an alumnus named Peter Capra. Peter grew up as one of an immigrant family in New York's tough Little Italy. Before joining the Army in World War I, where he served as an orderly to a colonel, he had fought his share of fights on the streets, and he aspired to be a professional fighter. Just before Peter's discharge at war's end, his colonel discovered this ambition. He was wild. "You're going to make something of your life," he told Peter. "You're going back to school, to Phillips Academy and Yale, like I did." So Peter took the train to Andover and spent his last fifteen cents for a cigar that he smoked while parked on the front porch of the headmaster's

148

house. The maid tried to send him around to the back door, but Peter just did a sitdown until Al Stearns, who was headmaster then, found him there and took him into the school. The other students gave the New York kid a hard time. Finally Peter had to use his fists on a big jock who tried to bully him. After that his peer relationships were much improved. He went on to graduate from Yale, became head of the Boys' Club of New York, and chairman of Yale's Scholarship Committee. When we were getting ready for Colorado's first year, I went down to see Charlie Sikoryak, who headed up the club's educational program, and told him about Outward Bound. The club put up scholarships for ten kids a year. It was one of our early scholarship bonanzas.

Among the buses arriving at Marble for C-2 in 1962 was one carrying the first New York Boys' Club contingent. The students had to walk two miles from where the buses dropped them to the assembly area, where they lined up to get their gear and tent assignments. One of the New Yorkers was a sixteen-year-old black youth with an ebullient grin named Arthur Wellington Conquest III. As Arthur arrived at the assembly area, he took a wide-eyed look at the surrounding peaks, drew a knife from his belt, and with a whoop threw it high in the air. The assembled students scattered, leaving Arthur alone as the knife came down at his feet. Joe Nold, who had Arthur in his patrol, still relishes the incident: "It was Arthur's way of saying, 'Look, man, I'm here. I'm Arthur Wellington Conquest, I'm from New York and I'm black, and them mountains don't scare me!'" That was the beginning of a liaison between Arthur and Outward Bound that is still going strong.

The fact is that for all his clowning and bravado, Arthur was somewhat daunted by the mountains. Agile, he did well on the ropes course. The heights did not faze him. But he took less kindly to the grueling expeditions, the rock faces, and the strangeness of the high peaks. While he was able to absorb the culture shock that overwhelmed some of his peers in the abrupt transfer from city streets, his relationship with the mountains was an encounter rather than a love affair.

It was George, a patrol mate, who perceived that at times Arthur's clowning was a cover for his concerns. George, who was a good athlete and accustomed to the mountains, came from a well-to-do family. He tended to stay aloof from the group, and the others resented his indifference to the

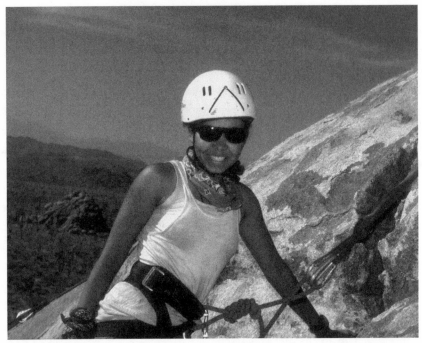

An Outward Bound student realizes her potential and that a sense of profound achievement is found not only in school or at home but also in the wilderness. (Photo © PCOBS, Kim Budd)

patrol's welfare. That changed as George and Arthur developed a warm friendship. On the expeditions George helped Arthur past the rough spots, and the day came when Arthur stood atop Snowmass Peak at 14,092 feet with the world spread about him. Back at Marble he recalled the moment: "It was then that I first woke up to life."

Later, on a visit to Bill Chapman, George reminisced, "It had never occurred to me that I would be needed to help somebody else. When I realized Arthur needed help, and saw what my help could do for him, something inside me changed. I found I was thinking about him and the patrol. That was a complete reverse for me. I'm a different guy now."

Today that sort of thing has happened often enough in Outward Bound that no one thinks twice about it, but to us in the early days it was an exciting social phenomenon. We used to say that if you had an Ivy Leaguer belaying an Urban Leaguer on a rock face in the morning, and in the afternoon the Urban Leaguer belayed the Ivy Leaguer in turn, and that night they shared a polyethylene tarp for a shelter, something happened! It was a dramatic discovery that you could take two youngsters with little or nothing in common beyond their youngsterhood and give them an experience that created a meaningful, perhaps even poignant, bond.

Something of the same sort happened to the instructors as well. Thinking back to that first summer of instructing at Marble, fresh from his teaching at suburban North Shore Country Day School, Joe Nold said, "I had never worked with Arthur before. That part of the experience was a great awakening of one's own awareness, and one's own self as a teacher. This is one of the things that is exciting about the Outward Bound involvement— that all of us in it have had to grow, and have grown."

Not that the socioeconomic mix always worked well. Not all those early New York Boys' Club kids and disadvantaged kids from Denver and elsewhere, some of whom were sent by the Juvenile Court, were having a gratifying experience. The difficulty was that if inner-city youngsters were recalcitrant or disruptive, we did not know how to work with them. When they created problems, there would be flack. Somebody would say, "Don't send us any more of those ghetto kids. They were troublemakers."

That attitude began to filter up to the school trustees and to the national trustees. Some of them began to say, "Why should we bother?" The man who took the decisive stand, who made Outward Bound history at that time, was Bill Coors, a leader among the Colorado School trustees. At a trustee meeting, the sentiment was voiced in a policy-making session: "If the kids of that type are going to respond negatively, why do we have them? Why let them spoil it for the others?" Coors stood up and socked it to that meeting. He said, in essence, "Listen, helping kids like this who have socially negative attitudes is part of what Outward Bound is all about." Nobody argued with him. It was a powerful piece of leadership at a time when resolute thinking was needed. Coors's stand influenced the entire movement. Awareness of it spread to the trustees of other schools, and in a remarkable way the precepts he stated became organizational policy.

In 1964 I read an article in the *Boston Globe* about the corrections institutions of the Massachusetts Division of Youth Services, which was part of the state Department of Education and carried out policy set by a Youth Service Board. The conditions the *Globe* reporter described were so bad I could not believe them. I called the director of the division and asked if I could come to see him. Dr. John Coughlan had taken this post years before, an able man who had established a reputation as a humane corrections specialist. Now he had white hair and a heart condition and lived with the fear that if he got too angry or too frustrated, he would have a relapse. Nevertheless, I would learn he was a brave man.

I said, "Dr. Coughlan, I can't believe that what you're running is as bad as this article said. I deal with young people, and I need to learn how to deal with the kind of young people you have to deal with. I'd like to look around."

He said, "I let this reporter look around on condition he show me what he wrote before it was published, which he didn't do. He's grossly distorted the facts and got me in serious trouble."

I said, "I'm not here to muckrake. I'm here to be educated. Maybe Outward Bound is something that can help. I'm not sure how, but I'd like to have a look at your institutions, and maybe we'll come up with some ideas." He gave his permission and turned me over to Herb Willman, one of his officers.

Willman first took me to the Roslindale Detention Center, where male offenders were taken when the court remanded them to the Division of Youth Services, usually referred to as DYS. A boy remained there while a sociopsychological diagnostic evaluation was made and his case was presented to the Youth Service Board for disposition. The building was intended to house about one hundred inmates for a few weeks, but the caseworkers and the system were so overloaded that as many as three hundred to four hundred boys were there, some for as long as six months.

It was a sight I shall never forget. Kids were scarcely treated as humans. Underfed, no furniture, bare floors, no recreation, no reading matter, no television. Defecating and urinating without toilets. The center was understaffed, the inmates frequently brutalized, the whole scene dehumanizing. It was unbelievable that this existed in the present day.

The Worcester Reception Center for girls was even worse. We visited the DYS training schools. In many dormitories bodies outnumbered beds—a violation of sanitary and safety laws. I found kids—recaptured runaways—in cages. Their heads had been shaved and they were kept on exhibition as object lessons.

I went back to Coughlan. "You know all about this," I said.

He said, "Yes, I do."

"What are you doing about it?"

"I'm doing the best I can. First, I'm trying to keep kids from coming in here. Then I'm trying to keep them from getting back in. There's very little I can do while they're here."

He had an educational counselors' program—specially trained and qualified counselors at good pay circulating through the schools, working with kids before they got into trouble and after they were released from incarceration.

I said, "Give us five of your youngsters. You pick them. I'll find the money, and we'll send them to the Colorado Outward Bound School. And we'll see what happens to them."

"Impossible," he said. "In the history of the Commonwealth of Massachusetts we have never sent an incarcerated person outside the borders of the state. Suppose they run away?" And he said, "My reappointment is coming up in January." And then he did it—he gave us five kids. It was a big gamble for him. It took courage.

As it happened, the Youth Service Board had its offices in the building of the United Community Fund, which was placing our Boston-area scholarships. Dr. Francis J. Kelly, a young psychologist who was on the board's staff, was in his office when the fund lady from upstairs looked in and said, "I have five scholarships for a summer camp called Outward Bound. Do you have five boys?" To Frank that was "like asking the Pope if he's a Catholic. I had two thousand boys under my care. Then she told me that this 'Outward Bound camp' was in Colorado, and I thought, oh-oh, that means sending Massachusetts-committed delinquents to another state."

On Kelly's advice, I went to see Lieutenant-Governor Elliot Richardson. He gave the needed authorization. Coughlan managed to get the support of his fellow board members, and Kelly steered us through the paperwork. The more Kelly and his people learned about Outward Bound, the more interested they became. They were professionally intrigued that it was not a camp, but a school with a curriculum based on wilderness challenges. They handpicked five boys they believed would respond positively to the experience.

Reports came back from Colorado that all five were doing fine. One was doing so well that Joe Nold asked to keep him on as a "sherpa" (a logistics helper) in the next course. The day the others were due back I went with Coughlan to the airport. The kids had flown out with escorts, and they returned with escorts. Watching as they came out of the aircraft, Coughlan blanched. "There are only four!" he said. I thought he was going to have that second heart attack. "Didn't you get my letter?" I asked. "What letter?" "I wrote you that they hired Robert Wilson[6] as a sherpa. He stayed on."

The next day Kelly called, excited. He had been talking with the four scholarship boys. "I'm impressed by their elation, their strong sense of well-being," he told me. "They're high as kites."

It was the same with young Wilson when he returned. He was a black youth who had run away from home in Ohio when he was just into his teens, had stolen money from a Massachusetts gasoline station and been caught. With no family to be sent back to, he had been kept in DYS institutions for four years, going to school. It was just a holding operation for him; he could not read or write. When he returned from Colorado, he got a dishwashing job in Boston and was living in a state police barracks. The next year the Colorado School wanted to rehire him. I went to see Robert where he was working. He was standing at a sink, his arms in suds up to the elbows, with his back to me. I told him about the job. He did not reply. I came around to where I could see his face. He was crying. "What's the matter?" I asked.

He said, "I can't take the job."

"Why not?"

"Because this is the first job I've had in my life and I don't want to quit."

I went to Willman and Coughlan, and we arranged for him to leave that job with honor and move to Colorado.

[6] This is not the boy's real name.

The next summer DYS sent forty boys to Colorado and Minnesota. Again they were handpicked. All but three completed the course, and nearly all of them had the same positive experience. Kelly followed these boys on parole, along with the original five, through the fall and winter and found they were compiling a remarkable record of keeping out of trouble. (Even several years later only five of the forty-two, 12 percent, had been returned to a correctional institution—a figure strikingly lower than DYS's expectancy rate of 45 percent for this age group.) By now Kelly was so high on Outward Bound that he was anxious to do some significant research. We helped him write a grant application for a demonstration study to the Office of Juvenile Delinquency in the Children's Bureau of the then U.S. Department of Health, Education, and Welfare. The proposal was that one DYS group—randomly selected this time—would take Outward Bound courses in the summer of 1966 while a matched group received routine treatment. Kelly and his associates would then make a study to compare recidivism—defined as return to a juvenile institution for violation of parole, or commitment to an adult institution for a new offense—of the two groups. Funding came through, and DYS contributed about $20,000 for tuition and other costs. We were excited. Here was to be a real test, the first anywhere, of whether Outward Bound had a substantively salutary influence on behavior.

One hundred twenty adolescent delinquent boys were selected for the study from the Roslindale Detention Center and two resident institutions. The criteria for selection were: (1) age fifteen and a half years and older; (2) good physical health; (3) absence of severe psychopathology; (4) minimum IQ score of seventy (to exclude severely retarded boys); (5) no history of violent assault or sexual acts; and (6) voluntary participation. Sixty of the selectees were randomly chosen for Outward Bound, to be paroled at the conclusion of the course. The other sixty went through the normal detention-center procedure or continued their institutional sentences.

The Outward Bound students were assigned to courses at Colorado, Minnesota, and Hurricane Island. Prior to the courses, the boys in both the Outward Bound and the control groups were tested to assess personality and measure their concept of self; the tests were repeated at the course's end. Relevant information such as background and school and court records were recorded from their social histories, and each subject completed a biographical data questionnaire. Scales were developed for use by the Outward Bound instructors to rate the delinquent youths in their patrols.

The project employed three Ph.D.-level social scientists as participant observers: Dr. Richard Katz of Harvard, Dr. David Kolb of the Massachusetts Institute of Technology, and Dr. Thomas D'Andrea, of Haverford College. Each observer attended at least one course; Dick Katz did one at each school. The participant observers completed the full course, recording their daily impressions of its impact on them and the boys, and of the interaction of the boys with staff. They interviewed each boy at the conclusion of his solo experience and trained the instructors to use the rating scales.

Every boy finished his course; that promise of immediate parole was a powerful carrot. Upon their return to Boston, the boys were retested, interviewed, and released on parole, to either their own homes or community placements, and the recidivism check was started. However, since the paroles of the control group members, who were still in institutions, would not start until their normal release time, all returns would not be in until 1968, two years hence.

THE MAINSTREAM POLICY

✳

I have multiplied visions.

—Hosea 12:10

The minutes of the May 1965 meeting of the OBI trustees read in part:

The remainder of the meeting was devoted to a discussion of the broad purposes of the Outward Bound idea. It was the spirit of the meeting that a new stage had been entered. The establishment of new schools is one aspect of this stage, but the broad application of Outward Bound techniques as well as its philosophy is being asked by a multitude of agencies, both public and private . . .

The board was taking cognizance of developments that were giving me growing concern. My mail and telephone were constant reminders that we had given substance to an idea whose time indeed had come—and that we were not up to reaping what we had sown. We were getting a steady flow of queries asking, "How can Outward Bound help us?" A lot of these came from more or less local programs—for instance, Montgomery County, Virginia—asking what we could do for their public-school system. But not a few of the letterheads or the signatures prompted a whistle of surprise.

■ From the Commandant, United States Naval Academy: How might the Academy work Outward Bound into its curriculum?

157

■ From the U.S. Army's STEP (Special Training Enlisted Personnel) program: About forty thousand potential draftees a year failed to qualify. All they needed was a little push—physically, attitudinally—to make them eligible. The Army had looked at all the youth movements in the country and decided that Outward Bound was their most likely source of help. Could we take on forty thousand kids a year if they paid for it?

■ From the Marine Corps' Mustang program, which selected outstanding noncommissioned officers who had been in the corps for ten to fifteen years and sent them to officer candidate school: The program was experiencing a heavy attrition. For some, the idea of making the leap to an officer's commission created a strong psychological barrier. Would Outward Bound care to look into the possibility of its playing a helpful role?

The Boy Scouts too were making interested inquiries. So were various YMCAs. Already one Job Corps Center had enlisted the Colorado School's advisory services. The Massachusetts Youth Service experience was producing a strong indication that the Outward Bound dynamic could be used, for positive influence on the self-esteem and values of adjudicated youth. An experiment with disadvantaged high-school youth in Trenton, New Jersey, financed in part by the Ford Foundation, was just beginning. Inquiries from schools and colleges were coming in every week. We were getting all kinds of calls for which we had neither a program nor resources with which to respond. With two or more additional Outward Bound schools in prospect, I felt I was carrying the organization about as far in expansion as was practicable. I was feeling half-submerged by the rising tide of demand for our services.

The upshot of the discussion at the May meeting was a special trustee meeting in September, called to discuss "The Future of Outward Bound in the United States." Jack Stevens was in the chair. He was carrying a bombshell and lost no time in tossing it on the table. Outward Bound, he said, had been extraordinarily successful to date. We had established three schools, had put two thousand youngsters through the program, and the schools were now enrolling a thousand students a year. The feedback—from the students, their families, their institutions—was highly gratifying. We had reason to be pleased with our results, but we should not fool ourselves. Our success to date was no more than a demonstration. A thousand youngsters a year against the several million who could be helped by an Outward Bound experience was a mere drop in the bucket. Even if we were to increase the number of schools tenfold, which was not possible, and put through ten thousand kids a year, that would still be but a small drop in a big bucket. For Jack, all this pointed to a clear conclusion: the future of Outward Bound lay in making its way into the mainstream of American thought and American education, and the central question facing us was how could we best do it? How best to shift from demonstration to full production?

The board was not, I think—any more than I—prepared for the force and sweep of Jack's remarks. His blunt how-do-we-get-into-production approach took the wind out of the sails of some of us. No one, however, quarreled with his logic or his mainstream thesis. The ensuing discussion produced a potpourri of ideas for implementing the mainstream idea that served to underscore how ill-prepared we were: Outward Bound must build an adequate headquarters staff. It should provide a pool of counselors and instructors. Facilities and programs had to be created for training instructors. Pilot courses should be made available to community leaders, government officials, school administrators, and welfare personnel, to give them an understanding of what Outward Bound was about. We should have our present program evaluated. We should bring experts together to plan a conference. We should establish a counseling section at headquarters, and a training center, with mobile training cadres working out of it.

Through all the brainstorming, Stevens stubbornly reiterated a single thought: we did not yet have a policy. We must come up with a well-defined policy, and the broadest feasible program based on it, before we let ourselves become involved in the specifics of any programmatic area. That program should have one overreaching objective: effective ways to project Outward Bound into the mainstream of American life. Nothing less would do. It was agreed that as a way of proceeding, I should prepare a preliminary planning paper and submit it to the trustees for reactions and suggestions.

Of the original Atlantic Foundation group who kept the U.S. liaison with Kurt Hahn alive by supporting his work abroad and ultimately attending U.S. Outward Bound's birth and growing pains, two in particular earned the everlasting gratitude of Outward Bounders everywhere. One was Johnny Kemper, the other was Jack Stevens. A successful businessman, Jack was equally successful in various endeavors for his fellow human beings. He was a born analyzer, a great person to take a problem to. He had a way of listening and then saying, "Now what is the problem?" You discovered you had not defined it, and that the defining pointed to the solution.

Jack was an enthusiast in the sense that he put his energies where his enthusiasms were. An inveterate birder, for a time he served as a trustee of the Audubon Society. He was a musician, an omnivorous reader, a great Civil War buff. He enjoyed giving; he considered himself a sophisticated donor and took pride in giving intelligently. When the Atlantic Foundation voted to support the proposed school in Colorado and he immediately contributed $10,000 to get the project rolling, it was not a spur-of-the-moment decision. He had been awaiting that moment for more than nine years.

Jack first met Kurt Hahn when he and my mother-in-law visited us at Gordonstoun. The two men, so widely different in background and experience, respected each other. When Jack asked him what he would think of a school that admitted youngsters primarily on the basis of their mental ability, Hahn said, "I would think that was as immoral as admitting them on the basis of how much money their fathers had." Jack understood and agreed. Another time Jack asked, "How important do you think brains are?"

Hahn replied, "I think they are as important as your arms and legs. They're useful to you." He meant, Jack explained, that brains don't make the man. One of Andover's mottos is *Non sibi*—not for oneself—and Jack had always said that Andover should teach more *non sibi*. It seemed to him that was what Hahn was doing. He was deeply sympathetic to Hahn's goals and saw them as too important to pursue in a limited way. Production!

Because I did not really understand the Stevens demonstration-production analogy, the next six months were as difficult as any half-year of my life. I had thought we were in production. No one was more aware than I of the evidence that Outward Bound had a greater potential than it was realizing, but I had assumed it was to be regarded as a potential, not a near-term objective. I had just succeeded in getting my first staff assistant, and our minuscule headquarters in Andover hardly seemed ready to attempt a massive infiltration of the

American mainstream. I went to see Jack a couple of times to get a better understanding of what he was after. I talked with Kemper at great length. What I eventually did was go back to the correspondence files, to all those requests for help that had come in and were still coming in, and make an analysis. I found they divided into three categories: one was education, the second was government agencies, the third was organizations such as the Boy Scouts, the YMCA, Boys' Clubs, and church groups. A fourth category was conspicuous by its absence: industry. In contrast to British Outward Bound, where industry was the primary source of enrollment, we had had no calls for help from American industry. Nevertheless, I included it with the other three as a mainstream component, a potential to be worked on. I drew up a paper that proposed a Mainstream (with a capital "m") policy of (1) endeavoring to persuade institutions and organizations in those four areas of the values inherent in the Outward Bound dynamic of utilizing challenge to develop self-growth, foster salutary interpersonal relationships, and nurture compassionate concern for one's fellow beings, and (2) seeking the means of helping them to weave Outward Bound methods into the fabric of their own programs.

Looking back from today's perspective, that special meeting of the trustees in September 1965 was a watershed occasion. It was the time when the organization first made the commitment to what, some years later, it came to call "Outreach," the policy of venturing beyond itself to proselytize institutions capable of multiplying its influence. It was a positive commitment that had positive results—even though no policy or program as cogently articulated and pursued as Jack Stevens asked for ever fully materialized.

All sorts of bedevilment of our effort to implement Mainstream lay ahead; all sorts of forces of circumstance would thwart an orderly growth of the implementation. We were not prepared, for example, for the mixed reception the Mainstream idea would, in the crunch, get from the individual schools—although we should have realized that the first concern of each school would have to be its own viability and the quality of its own program. We failed to face squarely the hard facts of how much in staff, resources, and money would be needed to implement a comprehensive Mainstream activity, or how difficult it would be for OBI and the schools to make the Mainstream effort pay for itself. We did not reckon with how precarious would be the status of adaptive programs born of Mainstream when they lost their original leadership and with it the enthusiasm, faith, and energy that launched them, or when their initial funding from a government or foundation grant ran out. We were comfortably unaware of the organic frustrations inherent in any undertaking to transplant new philosophy and method from a seminal to an established institution—and that those difficulties would exact a protracted amount of learning by doing, much of it harsh lessons in what not to do. Buoyed by our sense of mission, we did not stop to reflect that at a time when the new schools were still being formed and so much was needed in the way of strengthening the organizational mainframe, the attempt to pursue a vigorous Mainstream program might be premature.

Thinking negatively, one could say that even though the trustees supported my 1966 position paper, Outward Bound has never had a clearly defined, resolute Outreach policy. One would have to acknowledge that there continue to be those whose vision stops with asking why we should create competition for ourselves. Yet, again seen from today's vantage point, the remarkable fact is that the potential of Outward Bound for a positive influence on American life foreseen by Stevens and others has materialized in substantial measure. Mainstream did happen—successfully. Outreach is happening—successfully. It is a fact that Outward Bound has become a significant part of, and catalyst in, the educational mainstream across the gamut of elementary, secondary, college, and graduate-school levels. Virtually to its own amazement, it found itself spearheading a vigorous national experiential education movement, and has played a key role in formalizing that movement. It is being employed as a vehicle for helping a diversity of groups victimized by misfortune—the economically and socially deprived, the physically handicapped, the mentally retarded, the mentally ill—to deal positively with their disabilities. The successful employment of its methods as an alternative to conventional penal practice in dealing with delinquent youth, and to a lesser extent with adult offenders, has earned it a growing influence in the corrections community. Having removed all upper age limits in its own enrollments, and having outgrown its maleness, its influence now reaches into the worlds of educators, managers, career women, housewives, and the adult world generally.

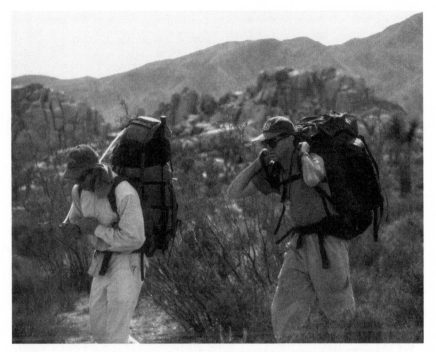

Challenge is mental, emotional, and physical in Outward Bound programs and requires personal commitment to complete the course. Adjusting a pack helps this student hit the mental "re-set button." (Photo © PCOBS, Kim Budd)

While the degree of success of a particular adaptive program may vary with a dozen factors, and the lessons of experience continue as a check on easy optimism, and while organizational policy may shift from one period to the next, within the Outward Bound experience is a dynamic that will out, even when no one proselytizes. The experience creates its own missionaries. When, to go all the way back to Dr. Zimmerman's happy phrase, "the bug has bit," there is no knowing how the "infection" may spread. Looking back to when Mainstream was given its initial amorphous shape, one is startled into an awareness of how extraordinarily far the movement came in a mere fifteen years. Jack Stevens's vision is still being realized—however impatient with the rate of realization he remained until the day he died in 1976.

YOUNG WOMEN

❊

These differences may be more of an
artifact of social or cultural restrictions
imposed on the female rather than a
result of true biological differences in
performance potential. . . .

—Dr. Jack W. Wilmore

S ince the student body at Kurt Hahn's school at Salem included both boys
and girls from the time of its founding in 1920, I once asked Hahn why
he had not made Gordonstoun coeducational. The blue eyes twinkling, he
replied, "You don't try to grow dates above the Arctic Circle." The British, he
had realized, were not ready for coeducation in 1934. His judgment, that it
was only a matter of time before they would be, was confirmed later when
Gordonstoun began to accept female students.

In this country things took a different tack. It was Bob Pieh who in 1965
broke the sex barrier in U.S. Outward Bound. On the heels of the Minnesota
School's first season, he announced that he planned to put a "pilot group" of
young women through the same course the following summer. Gene Caesar,
a writer who had observed and written about the Minnesota course, tried to
dissuade him.

"I did my best to reason with him," he wrote. "I reminded him that
everyone, from the President's Commission on Physical Fitness down
through the cartoonists who draw the junior-miss comic strips, has agreed

that the country's teenage girls are soft, pampered creatures. But Bob Pieh is an idealist, and idealists can be incredibly stubborn."

The first girls' course, designated MG-1, had two twelve-woman brigades. Most of the students were sixteen and seventeen, a few eighteen; there was one twenty- and one twenty-three-year-old. The young women in MG-1 had to meet essentially the same challenges the boys encountered that summer. They had the same training in canoeing, drownproofing, map and compass, rescue and first aid. They did the same run and dip, the same ropes course and initiative tests, ran the same obstacle course, climbed and rappelled the same rock faces, penetrated the same total wilderness on their expeditions, portaged the same sixty-five pound canoes and heavy packs, and dealt with the same deprivations on equally lonely solos. While the pace of the expeditions naturally accommodated to lesser female strengths in paddling and portaging, the Quetico wilderness did not mitigate the rigor of its challenges.

The first female course is well documented: it was covered by writers for two national magazines. Gene Caesar wrote for *Seventeen* an informative reflection of an adult male response to a young female phenomenon, which was enriched by his access to the journals of a number of the students. Barbara La Fontaine, one of *Sports Illustrated*'s top staff writers, did a two-part piece.

Caesar found his first sight of the student body, descending the bus from Duluth, a shock. "I had expected an assortment of muscle-molls, a native version of the Russian women's Olympic track team. Instead, I saw two dozen feminine young women, several of whom, as a north woods guide would say, wouldn't have weighed a hundred pounds wringing wet—which they were destined frequently to be." He had several occasions to note a kind of blitheness under stress recognizable by anyone who has known teenage girls in an Outward Bound environment. Going along on the "Quiet Walk" that was the Minnesota staff's welcome to the group—two hours of struggling through heavy bush and soft swampland in alternate spells of brisk striding and running, with crossings of the South Kawishiwi River in progressively swifter and deeper (but still safe) stretches of rapids—he was surprised by the contrast to the male behavior he had previously observed. While males had wallowed through waist-deep muck "like soldiers but griping and occasionally cursing like same," the young-women grinned, giggled, and made remarks about "lolling around in a lot of gook." Of another occasion, at the end of a day of rock climbing followed by a hike "with singing and laughing in a kind of triumphant exhaustion strongly suggestive of drunkenness," he wrote: "Long hours later, after taps had been sounded, high-spirited laughter was still ringing out in the tent village." Then he added, "There were almost certainly moments of despair as well in the privacy of that village. From the several diaries that were later shared with me in confidence, I'm certain that there was some sobbing too. But I wasn't permitted to hear it. The fellows had treated me like an unofficial chaplain with their complaints. The girls put on instant grins and brave smiles like magic make-up jobs."

Barbara La Fontaine participated in the entire course. Her *Sports Illustrated* report tells something about how it was for a thirty-four-year-old woman as well as for adolescent girls:

On the long final portage of the first day I think it was disbelief that sustained us. Betty started off with a canoe, missed her footing and subsided, with loud cries, into the mud. Carrying pack, paddles, and an armful of life preservers, I went in only up to my shins, but it seemed enough and my temper was very bad. My character, I felt, was not developing; it was shrinking to the size of a pea, a small dry pea. And it turned out to be a long portage, about a mile and a half of mud and treacherous footing. We didn't know how long it was—for all we knew it was endless—and at one point I felt almost panicky with weakness. As Polly was to say much later, "You just try to keep from screaming or crying or anything," and so you do—a matter of what the boys call "gutting it out." It turned out there was an end to the trail, and all the first girls who got to it turned back for extra packs...

The boys had commented on how the girls carried packs, going slowly, watching their footing; I think they didn't see that if we lost our footing, we were down and could not get up again. The mud, underbrush, hills, rocks, and fallen trees made it difficult to keep our balance and with The Monster [the biggest pack of all] I couldn't keep mine...I fell one day and had to crawl on my hands

The Outward Bound methodology, after decades of fine-tuning, creates instructors well-versed in technical and interpersonal skills. Here, a climber double-checks her harness prior to an ascent in Joshua Tree National Park. (Photo © PCOBS, Kim Budd)

and knees to a tree and pull myself up, gasping for breath. I had seen Polly leaning against a rock, almost in tears—"This isn't even Outward Bound, this is just torture," she had said. At this moment I could only agree . . .

It had been raining again and, besides, we had all got the idea by now that there was no keeping dry, and we slopped briskly into the water at all the portages. The flower of American girlhood, brought up on, "Get out of those wet clothes!" had learned a marvelous truth on this trip. When soaked to the skin, keep all that wet stuff on, and with body heat, a fire, and any luck

at all you may be dry by the time you have to try to sleep on the
ground.

From day to day each girl carried within herself the apprehension of
solo—three days and nights in that utterly wild country, alone except for
possible animal visitations, without tent, sleeping bag, food, and insect repel-
lent. For some—a matter of competence and temperament—the actuality
proved pleasurable. A few did well in the culinary department, preparing
varied menus of freshwater clams, crab, cattail roots, and leaf tea. For some
the actuality was as miserable as they had feared. Most were content and
miserable in turn.

All of the girls had stuck it out, most of them without eating,
though Joan had had two pairs of frogs' legs, some berries, and
"the inside of a tree," and Cathi had eaten 12 ants, in groups of
four. Genie had constructed an obstacle course and spent her days
running it and had memorized the label on her survival can and
the whole of her last letter from Bill (which, strictly speaking, I
don't think she was supposed to have with her at all). Max said
she had sat and sung to herself every song she knew. Sandy had
built what sounded like an exquisite ant trap, with a lid. She lured
ants into it and squirted them with antiseptic cream. We were all
of us somewhat enfeebled, and the girls looked more wan and
spiritual than they will probably look again for 30 years.

"Survival" over, the brigade settled into the expedition's final days. Fed
again, they were stronger "and rather competent."

Darcy took to carrying two packs, one back, one front, now that
the food packs were lighter. On long portages Sandy's interest was
in carrying the canoe the whole way without a rest, not just in
whether she was going to live or die. One day several of the girls
double-portaged a mile-and-a-half trail, thus making the trip with
packs three times, and then walked a fourth and fifth time, in the

rain, to help a vacationing couple they had met. I myself had
shaped up and could swim more than a mile and not feel winded.

Bob Pieh had told them that there was a rhythm to the wilderness that
would catch them, and now they found it to be true.

We had no watches, and we just went along, getting up after the
sun rose, going to sleep after it set. When we were thirsty we
dipped a cup over the side of the canoe and drank, or we drank
from our paddles. When we were hot we took off our clothes.
When we wanted to bathe we jumped into the lake. I brushed my
teeth in pools with minnows gathered to nibble at the cloud of
toothpaste, and I hung my clothes on a tree. Life was very simple.
We got tired, but that is a simple matter, too, and most of us
became very tranquil—even those of us who were most miserable
were tranquilly miserable.

Nearing the end, a student wrote in her journal: "We paddled all day and
made some hellish portages—over beaver dams, through swamps, etc. Early
in the afternoon, we reached the river that divides Canada and the United
States, so we went ashore and kissed the huge rock on our side. I have never
known such close friendship as with these girls." La Fontaine came out of the
wilderness a day ahead of the students. Up on Birch Lake the same evening a
student reflected: "Now we are sitting in our leaky tent as it rains buckets. A
fitting last night for this little expedition! But I have been thinking. A bar of
soap would be a luxury now. So would an orange. A little brown sugar to put
on the Bisquick we bake over the fire would be a real treat, if we had any left.
If only there was some way to go right on appreciating things! Wouldn't it be
cool if one could always get excited over something like brown sugar and
Bisquick?" The next day La Fontaine watched as the girls came out.

They were sick of the wilderness, and they wanted to go home. In
spite of this, their manners and their tempers had done nothing but
improve. If they looked a little gritty as they finally emerged, they

were more thoughtful, more gentle, and more ladylike by far than
they had been when they went in (something the so-called "best"
girls' schools in this country might ponder—that the Canadian
woods succeed where they too obviously fail). The girls had gone
into the wilderness teenagers and had come out human beings—no
small transformation. It had happened, and I had failed to see it
develop. Having made a point of going all the way to watch for it, I
had even missed the moment when it began. However, I am sure
the cause was partly pride. The girls had done a good job; they were
properly proud of themselves, and the dignity of their pride did for
them just what Kurt Hahn used to explain that it would do.

Months later, when queried, a number of the girls wrote of their feelings as they had crystallized with time. Some called the course a turning point in their lives, and at least two were ambitious to return as instructors. Several for whom much of the experience had been a hated ordeal were in retrospect among the most enthusiastic. One of these articulated the nub of the retrospect thousands of Outward Bounders have known: "Nothing seems as bad as it really was." (Twenty years before, a youngster had expressed the same idea to Hahn—"Magnificently, sir, except at the time!") One mother, however, took issue with La Fontaine's "ladylike" finding.

"I sent a graceful young lady with a beautiful skin and a lovely figure to Minnesota. I got her back with her feet and ankles swollen double, legs scabbed by mosquito bites, and talking like a lumberjack. There must be some easier way to find one's inner self!"

But her daughter saw it differently. "It's true that I was never so terrified and never pushed half so hard. But I never felt so *alive* before either."

Intriguingly, it was Barbara La Fontaine—then years ahead of her time as "a woman over thirty" taking part in an all-female course—who stated about as well as it can be stated the essence of what Outward Bound is all about: "None of us, I suspect, who was not an outdoorswoman before all this has become an outdoorswoman because of it, but that was never the point; in fact, whichever girl liked it the least has probably come off best, having learned more than any of us what she is capable of. And that is the point. We are better than we know. If we can be made to see it, perhaps for the rest of our lives we will be unwilling to settle for less."

■   ■   ■

The following summer Minnesota offered two female courses and enrolled close to one hundred. There remained the interesting question of how the other schools would respond to the precedent. One by one they came along: Colorado in 1967, Northwest in 1969, North Carolina and Hurricane in 1971. Due to the Dartmouth Center's early focus on college students and teachers, its public courses were coeducational from the start.

I happened to be at the Northwest School the first morning of NWG-1. Wanting to get his own sense of the group—and perhaps to deliver the message early that Outward Bound would be no brownie bake—Director Bill Byrd personally led the run and dip. The run ended at a stream whose source was in a melting Cascades snowfield. Bill plunged into the icy water and was out in a flash. "All right," he said to a group of girls, still breathing heavily from their run, "everybody in!" He waited, with a pleased this'll-give-'em-the-idea expression, for the first female scream. Seventeen-year-old Cinda Kittredge dove in and came up, shaking the water from her head. Instead of heading for shore, she slipped into a smooth backstroke, gave an exultant cry, and called to her companions, "Oh, it's great!" Bill's face was a study.

Experience has demolished early concerns about the wisdom of introducing the female element into Outward Bound. One apprehension was that women were not up to hard physical stress or to meeting traditionally male kinds of physical challenge. Another was the "Amazon syndrome"—a concern lest Outward Bound have a defeminizing influence on girl students, or attract "Amazon types" to staff jobs. Some of the schools responded to these concerns by making girls' courses easier, but this did not last long. Male instructors and students were treated, often to their bafflement, to demonstrations that, age bracket for age bracket, women are competent to meet the same physical challenges as men. It was highly disconcerting, for example, for an adolescent youth to be shown, as not uncommonly happened, that his female peers were better natural rock climbers. That sort of realization is less surprising today, in a time of superb female athletes, women's team sports, coed volley ball at the "Y," and the like. Already it is difficult to believe that the discovery females need not be Amazons to lead or come through an Outward Bound experience with flying colors was then cause for wonder.

There was another concern. Bob Pieh recalled some of the responses to his pioneer course. "Reactions in the Outward Bound community were mixed. There was strong feeling at that time among those valuing and cultivating Outward Bound's machismo image that the success of women in similar experiences would diminish that image. Regular Minnesota male staff felt the presence of mere women would cause 'changes.' That local resistance diminished rapidly when the willingness of women students and overall readiness and courage of both women staff and students became evident."

The fading of the machismo concern was a subtle matter. It is frequently described in terms of one of its aspects—that the Outward Bound influence transformed male attitude from one of regarding women as sex objects to one of relating to them as persons. The female incursion, Pieh said, "may have been a threat, until it was lived with." In the long run the entire Outward Bound community has shared the same lesson: Don't worry about the women; they can take the physical challenge, and will be no less women for the experience; and the men will be the better for it. In retrospect it is ironic that there was any hesitancy to offer distaff courses, for today the schools could not be viable without women students. More than 40 percent of the current U.S. Outward Bound enrollment is female.

NEW SCHOOL IN THE NORTHWEST

※

It's not that I'm not scared anymore; it's just
that I know I can function when I'm scared.

—A Northwest student's course impression

I n the early winter of 1965 I made a presentation in Portland, Oregon, at a meeting sponsored by St. Helen's Hall, an Episcopal private school. Samuel McKinney, the school's development officer, was much interested in the idea of an Outward Bound school in that area. Since we especially wanted to see a school founded in the Far West in order to achieve a continental span of activity, and since the Cascade Mountain range, running from British Columbia down into Washington and Oregon, offered dramatically beautiful and challenging terrain, this was a potential of strong appeal. Among the thirty or so persons present at the St. Helen's Hall gathering was Donald Vetterlein, a Portland businessman. In Maine the preceding summer Don had run into an old friend, Hugh Latham, who was an enthusiastic supporter of the new Outward Bound school being built on Hurricane Island. The two men sailed out to the island, where they had a look at the building activity and talked with Peter Willauer. Vetterlein came away impressed; months later, learning of the meeting at St. Helen's Hall, he got himself invited.

The occasion produced a core group of a dozen or more who were willing to pool their energies to investigate the idea of starting a school in Oregon. By spring the sentiment was strongly affirmative, mixed with uncertainties about costs, start-up problems, and the like. Vetterlein, who was going east again in the summer, volunteered to make inquiries en route. He revisited Hurricane, where Willauer gave him helpful advice and data. When he came to Andover, my most useful counsel was probably that the Portland group had only to journey one hundred miles south to the city of Eugene to find a ready-made school director—Bill Byrd.

After my meeting with Byrd in Colorado two summers before, at the time he was returning to Oregon from his Peace Corps duties in Puerto Rico, I had made a point of keeping track of him. In the spring of 1965, in the course of discussing some Colorado School matters, I suggested to Joe Nold that he get in touch with Byrd. Bill was living in Eugene, where, instead of going back to teaching school, he had set up a trial-preparation practice as a service to the city's plaintiff lawyers. Talking with him, Nold mentioned that one of the Colorado's School's problems was the physical limitations of the Marble base, which were limiting enrollment.

Byrd suggested that Nold experiment with a mobile course operating without a base. "Take advantage of the out-of-doors," he said. "It's there; you don't have to do anything to it. All you have to do is get out there, equipped. Run students out in buses, introduce them to the staff, provide them with their equipment, resupply them at designated points and times, and run your courses. Why fuss around with a big base facility?" Nold saw the merit in the suggestion, and the upshot was that Byrd agreed to come on that summer and direct an experimental mobile course in Colorado. While he ran it out of a tented training-and-supply base near the ghost mining town of Ruby, Colorado, it approximated the fully mobile model that later became his particular style.

When Vetterlein stopped at Marble to observe the Colorado program and get counsel from Nold, the latter likewise suggested that Byrd would make a good school director. Don drove over to Ruby to meet him. Byrd remembers, "Vetterlein said, 'Why don't you look me up in Portland when you get home?' But I just went back to Eugene and went to work. I was making money with this business I'd set up, and that was kind of fun for a schoolteacher. Then Vetterlein and a whole delegation came down to see me. By that time I was getting up to my eyebrows in the legal business. It was fun to make money, but I was getting completely out of touch with my family. I was thinking this is kind of silly—making money can't be all that important. So I said. 'You guys want to start an Outward Bound school, and you know damn well I do too. Working with kids is apparently my life, so how do we do it?' We had it going in six months."

Bill Byrd was a platoon sergeant in Charlie Company, 161st Regiment, in New Caledonia in 1944, taking part in General Douglas MacArthur's preparations to invade the Philippines. Finding he enjoyed instructing his men, he decided he wanted to be a teacher. "Even though it was the art of war, it was teaching. We'd lost so many guys we were full of new recruits, and for them there was an immediacy to the value of learning. You didn't have much trouble with attention span." The 161st Regiment still has the record for continuous front-line duty; in the Philippine campaign they were in contact with the Japanese for 178 consecutive days. Bill's platoon was turned over about four times.

But when he went back to college at the University of Oregon in Eugene, where he got his B.A. and went on to graduate work in education, Byrd found himself in a confrontation with the establishment. "It was disillusioning for me to see the price I had to pay to become a teacher, since I was already a proven teacher in the field under the most difficult of conditions. I got a sampling of some of the courses and thought, what a way to breed incompetence in the classroom." He switched to the law school. In his second year there he became involved with a group who felt the university was not meeting students' educational needs, especially those of returning veterans. The dissidents lost their fight—at least in the short run; eventually their chief faculty supporter became president of the university—and Bill dropped out. He went abroad, climbed in the Alps and Dolomites, and toured Europe on a bicycle until his money ran out. Back in Oregon, he worked in a logging camp, then got a job teaching at a small high school in the wheat country of central Oregon. Summers he was a mountain-climbing guide in the Petzoldt-Exum School of American Mountaineering in Wyoming. With some of his fellow guides he took two summers out to start a mountain-safety program and establish a rescue service in Teton National Park. Following his marriage in 1953, he returned to the university and "paid the price," getting his master's degree in education.

Byrd was appointed an English teacher in the McKenzie High School, a small regional school serving a group of unincorporated communities along the McKenzie River in Oregon. The district school superintendent was a remarkable educator named Ben Huntington, whom Bill admired greatly: "Ben encouraged innovation, however far out, so long as it was based on solid teaching, control of the classroom, and genuine communication with the students. The students were mostly the children of loggers and laborers and they got virtually no encouragement to higher education at home. Ben's idea was, 'How can we change this for the kids in school? How can we take advantage of what curiosity is there and sustain it and help it grow? How can we get a few of these youngsters into higher learning; if they have no aptitude, how can we get them the best skills training possible, so that they can function as resourceful, independent folk in society and have a little bargaining power with the system?'"

With encouragement from Huntington, Byrd and a fellow teacher named Bob Cooley came up with a radically new plan for adapting the school's resources to the individual abilities of the students. When the faculty voted it down, Huntington gave the pair one end of the school building and authorized them to use the plan with their junior and senior students. One of the first things they did was have the students make a community resource study. The youngsters discovered that along the McKenzie River was an assortment of retired people rich in experience—businessmen, professors, writers, artists, and so on. Byrd remembers, "We got these people down into the school. We had loggers teaching in the classroom because some were history buffs, or were great on local folklore. Some of them were artists, but didn't want anybody to know it. We had a great year. Kids who had just sat dumb for years were on their feet taking part. At first the parents were all over us, calling us left-wingers and Commies, but after a while they came around."

The second year the state people came in to evaluate what Cooley and Byrd were doing and decided to fund it as a "gifted child" program. Although the two teachers considered it an "all kids" program, they welcomed the endorsement. Byrd, however, found his concerns centering increasingly on the youngsters at the "non-gifted" end of the spectrum. He volunteered to take all the school's "rejects"—the students the teachers had fingered as troublemakers—into a single class. In the mornings he, or other teachers with whom he swapped classes, worked with the youngsters on the basics they had never mastered. He also spent time with them on a kind of "consumer education" that dealt with practical problems of living they would have when they left school. In the afternoons they were given a work release to part-time jobs, and in the evenings those who wished came back to the school for additional tutoring. This plan also won state approval and funding. It became known as the McKenzie Plan and was adopted as a model by the federal Job Corps.

When I was recruiting staff for the Peace Corps in the summer of 1961 and spoke with the Teton guides, Bill was more interested in getting back to teach his rejects. But he had a rendezvous with Outward Bound. The following November the school secretary took a call for Mr. William Byrd, "the White House calling." The caller was one of President Kennedy's assistants, who several summers earlier had been in a Teton climbing party with Byrd as guide. He told Bill he had just come from a top-level Peace Corps meeting concerned with staff needs in which Sargent Shriver had said, "What we need down there in Arecibo are people who know the Outward Bound–type things and also are educators."

The aide said, "I know a good one," and told what he knew about Bill. Shriver said, "Get him!" Would Bill please come to Washington for a meeting? In January, Byrd went to Arecibo to partner his old Teton buddy Al Read as a rock-climbing instructor. A few months later Grant Venn, director of the training center, became ill and resigned. Venn recommended Byrd to be his successor, and Shriver appointed him.

Byrd arrived at the training center just before Freddy Fuller returned to England. When he became director, he took over an evolving program that by then was staffed by people with no Outward Bound affiliation. Nevertheless, he recalled, the program continued to carry the Outward Bound stamp. "From talking with Fuller and with some Englishmen who stayed on, we still thought of ourselves as doing a heavy adaptation of Outward Bound. A lot of our off-hour discussions were about how nice it would be if we could do it pure some place—which we couldn't do there because of the special demands of the Peace Corps training. And wouldn't it be great, we said, to run it parallel to the American classroom type of education, to expose kids to this kind of challenge and self-discovery. Most of us, being educators anyway, couldn't help but explore the hypothetical limits of the particular philosophy we were trying to implement there."

The Oregon organizing group incorporated in the fall of 1965 and was chartered as the Northwest Outward Bound School, with Don Vetterlein as president. In January I went to Portland to help launch a fund-raising campaign, and by February the recruiting for courses NW-1 and NW-2 to be offered that summer was under way. The Forest Service granted the school a use permit in an area of mixed old-growth timber in the Willamette National Forest, at the base of the Cascade Range about seventy-five miles east of Eugene. Byrd set up a tented training base under a stand of magnificent Douglas firs—pyramidal, two-man miner's tents for the students, large tents for staff headquarters and cooking, no plumbing, and a ropes course. The site was on a small stream called Kink Creek, near the headwaters of the McKenzie River, five miles from the nearest settlement, a mile from Robinson Lake, a body of water fortuitously situated for the morning run and dip. A dozen or so hiking miles away were Mount Washington and the Three Sisters, the latter a group of three ten-thousand-foot peaks, the highest in the more southerly Cascades.

Forty-odd boys hailing from all parts of the country, half on full or partial scholarship, completed each of the two 1966 courses. After five days of training at the base, virtually all the rest of the course was carried out in a mobile mode. The students linked a basic expedition, an alpine phase of rock climbing and peak ascents, and a solo in a thirteen-day stretch. They returned to base for two days of interpatrol competition, including the marathon, then broke up into groups of four for a four-day final expedition on their own. Some of the final expedition feats in the second course, undertaken in response to challenges set in NW-1, were prodigious. Two of the groups covered routes just short of one hundred miles in the allotted four days.

In his final award-night talk to the students Byrd addressed the theme of "Know yourself, know where you're going, and be of service to mankind." From its beginning Northwest was among the staunchest of the schools in its

Mountaineering course members hit the trail on an early morning summit push up the South Ridge of Mount Adams, Washington. (Photo © Cobi Harris)

commitment to service. The senior staff that Byrd assembled were skilled in mountain rescue and stressed it in their training. The Oregon Mountain Rescue and Safety Council designated the Northwest School rescue team as the ready unit for the Three Sisters area. The Forest Service designated the school a fire-suppression team. In the second summer, which was exceedingly dry, the students contributed 1,800 man-hours to forest-fire fighting. The first-year students built a well-marked trail from the Kink Creek roadhead to Robinson Lake to keep fishermen and other recreation seekers from getting lost. In the two years, students removed some seven hundred seventy pounds of litter from public shelters, campsites, and picnic grounds. Other projects included rebuilding a footbridge and a miscellany of brush removal, grading, clearing, excavation, and barrier work. Altogether, service projects totaled 3,754 man-hours the first two summers.

In 1968, Northwest's third season, the school combined two weeks of staff training with a Wilderness Workshop open to teachers and others interested in gaining firsthand knowledge of Outward Bound educational principles and techniques. The workshop was led by Willi Unsoeld and Dick Emerson, Unsoeld's west ridge teammate in the successful 1963 American Mount Everest expedition. Another Northwest innovation took place in September, when the school offered a ten-day senior course, dubbed "Rebound," for men thirty and over. It was one of the first adult Outward Bound courses offered to the general public.

The Northwest School was the first to function without costly construction of a permanent base. In 1967, with doubled enrollment, the Forest Service had granted permits for two new training base locations, Foley Ridge and East Fork. With enrollment again doubling the third summer, the Foley Ridge site was retained, but two other central Oregon courses were conducted in the Mount Jefferson area on a fully mobile basis. Training was conducted on the trail, with emphasis on learning by doing. The course covered 150 miles but was shortened in subsequent seasons. Also in the 1968 summer, Unsoeld and Emerson led a mobile course in Washington's North Cascades.

The collective experience of that season confirmed Byrd's faith in the mobile-course concept, and in subsequent years the school's curriculum evolved into an all-mobile program. Eventually this enabled Northwest to operate in the three states of Oregon, Washington, and Idaho. The other schools were quick to note the positive values in Byrd's example. In particular, the schools operating from permanent bases sooner or later saw those bases subjected to the strains of overpopulation; when that happened, mobile courses provided a viable alternative. Today, all the schools run at least some mobile courses, and some operate entirely on the mobile principle.

■ ■ ■

The fourth school. We were growing. At Andover, OBI was beginning to look more like a national headquarters. In the early years fiscal constraints had limited me to a single staff assistant. My first good staff break came in 1966, when the Ford Foundation gave us money for salaries and I was able to persuade Bob Bates to take a leave of absence from teaching at Exeter. Bob is one of the country's top mountaineers, a former president of the American Alpine Club and co-leader of the 1953 American K-2 expedition. He had helped me with advice when Coffin and I were recruiting staff for the Peace Corps in Arecibo. Subsequently, he served as Peace Corps director in Nepal. Exeter gave him a year's leave to work with me. A fine person of high and versatile competence, he was an invaluable assistant.

At that time a trustee committee was searching fruitlessly for the right man to fill a new OBI post of "schools coordinator," who would work closely with the school directors. I tried to sell Bates on taking the job. He declined. "Willi Unsoeld is your man," he said. "He has the talents you want. He knows Outward Bound from his time in Colorado with his Peace Corps volunteers, he believes in it, his lifestyle and interests are in tune with it. And since he's about to complete an assignment for the Agency for International Development in Nepal, he's available." Bob called Unsoeld and offered the job on our behalf. Willi accepted. He came aboard in the fall of 1967 as my number two and chairman of the Outward Bound Coordinating Committee (OBCC),[7] the newly formed school directors group. A few months later he was named OBI's executive vice president.

■ ■ ■

Willi Unsoeld was a twelve-year-old Boy Scout when he looked up at the Three Sisters in Oregon's Cascade Range—his first sight of mountains—and experienced an instant desire to be a climber. Following army service in World War II and two years as an undergraduate at Oregon State, he spent another two years beating his way around the world, climbing mountains as he went. In India he lived for months in a cave with a Hindu holy man, and spent time with two American missionaries whose dedication to compassionate service "opened my eyes to Christianity." Back home, he got his B.A.

---

[7] OBCC replaced the Operating Committee (OBOC), the former school directors body.

in a year and took up graduate study in religion, first at Oberlin, and then at the Pacific School of Religion at Berkeley, California. He intended to return to India as a missionary, but by the time he finished seminary, India was surfeited with missionaries expelled from Communist China. Deciding to be a teacher, Willi earned his Ph.D. in philosophy at the University of Washington and joined the philosophy department at Oregon State University, where his field was ethics. Along the way he went on two Himalayan expeditions.

Although Unsoeld loved teaching, he was having doubts about being a philosophy professor when Bates asked him to be his Peace Corps deputy in Nepal in 1962. That was when Willi came to the Colorado School with his volunteers and took part in C-3. In Nepal he succeeded Bates as director after a year, but not before taking a leave of absence to join the 1963 American Mount Everest expedition. With Dr. Thomas Hornbein, he was the first to reach Everest's summit by its west ridge. The price was nine of his toes and the agony of recovering from frozen feet. One of the highlights of my life was the three years of hard work and close friendship with Willi Unsoeld at Andover. As Hahn would have said, he was the kind of fellow you like to steal horses with. He had intelligence, enthusiasm, a great sense of humor, supreme confidence, and a talent for partnership. Much in demand as a witty and inspiring speaker, he brought Outward Bound considerable limelight. He was a genius in human relations. One of his greatest gifts was getting to know people quickly; he never met a stranger. The ultimate instance of that was his meeting with John Laycock.

John was sort of the majordomo of the Andover skating rink. A Scotsman, he kept the skating club kids in line with an iron hand and much love. One day between halves of a hockey game I took Willi into the little room where John sharpened skates. I said, "John, I want you to meet a friend of mine. This is Willi Unsoeld—Willi, this is John Laycock."

John looked at Willi and said, "Who sent you, Willi?"

The two men stood gazing at each other. Willi said, "John, who's your guru?"

John replied, "Willi, you were sent. Who's your guru?" They exchanged guru names, and there ensued a dialogue quite outside my understanding. I had not known John could spell guru, let alone that he had one.

It was just a godsend to have Willi's collaboration on so many responsibilities that up to then I had carried alone. We were a good team. He had a faculty of listening carefully and understanding the essence of what you were saying, not letting the words get in the way of his comprehension. I always knew that when I went out on a mission with him, we would both get back intact, and that the mission would be accomplished. Hahn, on one of his periodic visits, observed us and approved. I remember Hahn once advising me about fund-raising. "Don't go alone. Alone, you are strident. Take Unsoeld with you. Remember, lions hunt in pairs."

Another staff member at that time was Dyke Williams, a young Bostonian who had joined us when Bob Bates left. Dyke had the indispensable zeal for Outward Bound, and talents to implement it. He spoke and wrote well and was a good fund-raiser. OBI was charged with raising the money for one-half the scholarships at all the schools, and Dyke had much to do with our achieving our annual quota. He was our proposal writer until he left to join the Minnesota School staff in 1970.

James "Gil" Leaf was a valuable staff addition in 1968. After graduating from Harvard in 1963, Gil had twice worked his way around the world, instructed at Hurricane Island and at Outward Bound schools in Australia and East Africa, taught at the Fessenden School in Massachusetts, been an assistant to Peter Willauer, a consultant to the state of New Jersey on an Outward Bound adaptive proposal, worked with Trenton Action Bound and with Massachusetts juvenile delinquents. We gave him the job of organizing Mainstream. Gil's enthusiasm, energy, and imagination together were a veritable idea factory. I had to put a sign on my door, "No one under 35 allowed after 11 A.M.," to keep Gil from overwhelming us with new ideas as we worked on those he had already given us. Outward Bound carries a debt of gratitude to both Dyke Williams and Gil Leaf.

TRENTON'S ACTION BOUND

�֎

*There are pitifully few channels in our society through
which young men can move with dignity, success, and a
sense of adventure from adolescence into manhood.
Opportunities for positive, character-forming experiences
are particularly limited for youngsters of low-income
families. . . . They are the ones who most often sink finally
into aimlessness and apathy, or who take out their frustrations on the institutions that have failed them in acts of
violence and hostility. . . . They need experiences that will
show them that they are not so limited as they think,
experiences that will give them confidence and enthusiasm
for the business of facing life, experiences that will assure
them that they can make it.*

—Gregory Farrell, in the application for funding of Action Bound

In 1963 Gregory Farrell, a Princeton alumnus who was working in the
university's admissions office, was driving to Boston with his friend Mike
Stewart when their car broke down at New Haven. Waiting on the repairs,
Stewart suggested they drop in on his friend Bob Kiphuth, Yale's great swim
coach. Stewart was a former Princeton end and Rhodes Scholar who had been
stricken by a wasting disease while serving as a naval officer in the Far East.
Kiphuth, whose competence as a physical educator and therapist approached
genius, had helped him rebuild his physique. While these two were chatting,

Farrell perused the bulletin board outside Kiphuth's office. His attention fastened on a quotation the Yale coach had posted:

In present day civilization five social diseases surround the young, even in childhood. There is the decline of fitness due to the modern methods of locomotion; the decline of initiative due to the widespread disease of spectatoritis; the decline in care and skill due to the weakened traditions of craftsmanship; the decline in self-discipline due to the ever-present availability of tranquilizers and stimulants; the decline of compassion, which is spiritual death.
—Kurt Hahn

Greg remembers, "I was struck both by what the man said and by the spiky, nineteenth-century language. I asked Kiphuth who Hahn was. He told me the little he knew and gave me some literature from the new Colorado Outward Bound School." Excited by what he read, Farrell wrote us a letter asking if there was a way he could become involved in the Colorado activity. Subsequently I met Greg and was instrumental in Joe Nold's offering him a place in the instructors' course Tapley would be giving in the summer of 1964. Farrell, who by then was a reporter for the *Trenton Times*, snapped up the offer.

He was twenty-eight. At Marble he found that most of his coursemates had two advantages over him. They were under twenty, and they had had the basic course. "The first five days," he said, "I thought I was going to die. I felt like a thirty-three and one-third record being played at seventy-eight." After the grueling first days, things went better. "I came to feel strong and good, very light-headed. I got to love Tap and his wife, and all the guys in the course. At the end of it I was really moved." He discussed the Outward Bound idea with Tapley, Nold, Petzoldt, and others. One of the thoughts he took back with him was that the Outward Bound method would be applicable to any educational environment.

Things happened fast to Farrell that year. A series of pieces he wrote about the Community Action project in New Haven, a pilot undertaking in the new federal antipoverty program, led to his being commissioned to write a book about it. Covering Trenton meetings where a project on the New Haven model was being planned, he was frequently able to contribute helpfully to the discussion. Before the year was out he was made director of United Progress Incorporated, the official agency spearheading action on Trenton's poverty problems.

At Colorado, Greg had seen ghetto youths responding positively to the Outward Bound experience. One of his first moves in his new post was to obtain funds to send youngsters from the Trenton ghettos to Outward Bound schools. He did the recruiting himself, making the rounds of neighborhood youth activities, telling the youngsters about his own experience, showing *Tall as the Mountains*, a new film about the Colorado School the Adolph Coors Company had made. Some thirty boys signed up, mostly African-Americans and Puerto Ricans, and in the summer of 1965 he packed them off to Colorado, Minnesota, and Hurricane Island.

One morning several weeks later he went to his office early. "I had hardly started working when 1 was surprised by a knock on the door. I opened it, and here were two kids, a Puerto Rican named Miguel Camacho and a black kid whose name I can't remember. They said, 'Hi, Mr. Farrell!' I said, 'Hey, what are you guys doing here?' and they said, 'We're back from Hurricane Island.' I said, 'But it's seven-thirty in the morning'—these guys never got up before eleven. They said, 'At Hurricane we get up every morning at five-thirty and we run around the island. So Miguel and I got up this morning and started running, and we thought we'd run down here and see how you're doing.' They were four feet off the ground. I was really thrilled, because it obviously had caught them so hard."

When the others got back, it was much the same story. Only three of the thirty had dropped out. Greg arranged for several of the youngsters to attend a meeting of the city's antipoverty committee, of which the mayor was a member. The youths told about their good experiences. The mayor asked them, "Now what are you fellows going to do?"

One black lad said, "We're going to set up a rescue service on the Delaware River, We're going to patrol the river and save people from drowning." The boy saw that the mayor and some of the others were skeptical. He said, "Mr. Mayor, do you know how many people drowned in the river in the city last year?"

The mayor did not know, so the boy told him. The mayor asked, "Why do you fellows want to set up a lifesaving service?"

The boy said, "Because then we can save Whitey instead of get Whitey."

Farrell and I talked a lot about the need for follow-up. He was responsive to my point that one person who goes to Outward Bound and comes back alone may be treated as an oddball, especially by ghetto peers; but several together have their own esprit with which to counter peer pressures to conform to the group. We discussed forms the follow-up might take, ways in which to facilitate transfer of an enhanced self-image and the new sense of what's possible that goes with it, as these youngsters returned to their street environment.

Farrell held a series of meetings with about twenty of the Outward Bound kids, looking to come up with an ongoing program with them as a core, along with a second group who would be receiving scholarships the following summer. They talked about how they might do Outward Bound in the city, discussed things like what kind of urban expeditions they could have, whether doing a solo in the city would encourage stealing, how they might set up a rescue program. Finally, this informal activity jelled into a plan, funded by the Ford Foundation and the U.S. Office of Education under Title III (innovative programs) of the new Elementary and Secondary Education Act (ESEA), for a special program called "Action Bound" for a volunteer group of students in the Trenton City High School.

The plan called for the Action Bound students to be together in their own homerooms and to participate in a combined school-time and weekend schedule of Outward Bound–oriented activities. The Trenton Board of Education gave somewhat uncertain support. Since nobody in the school system felt threatened, and the program proposed to deal positively with some of the more troublesome students, the school people went along.

Trenton was a new kind of challenge for us—the first time an urban community sought to use the Outward Bound experience of a few as a healing force that could be brought back into the community and somehow harnessed as a multiplier. At the same time it suggested one practical way to deal with the perennial question of Outward Bound follow-up. From the educators' viewpoint, it was a pretty radical undertaking. Alternative schooling was not then as respectable as it would become; what Farrell and others were to attempt in the next several years was a pioneer effort.

Farrell asked me to find someone to take charge of the outdoor-activity part of Action Bound. I nominated Barry Crook, an able young Britisher who had been an Outward Bound instructor in England and at Hurricane Island and was then helping to set up an adaptive program for New York's Horace Mann School at its nature tract in Connecticut. I had a helpful liaison at Trenton City High in Frank Nappi, the football coach, a charismatic individual whose experience accompanying some of the scholarship kids had made him an ardent Outward Bound supporter. Through Farrell I made another good Trenton contact in Warren Hill, president of Trenton State Teachers College. We helped Trenton State develop a three-part program by which students could get credit for the standard Outward Bound course. They started with a one-week precourse on campus, which I taught. Following a course at Colorado, Minnesota, or Hurricane Island, each student submitted a paper on how he intended to weave Outward Bound into his teaching practice. It was the first time a college gave academic credit for Outward Bound and, I think, the first time Outward Bound was explicitly related to experiential education theory.

A key purpose of the Trenton State scheme was to help provide Barry Crook with a staff. Half a dozen students signed on to work with him on Action Bound weekends, thereby earning additional college credits. Another Trenton State undergraduate whom Crook acquired was Phil Costello, the ex-Marine who had participated in the building summer at Hurricane Island and now was an instructor there. Also attending Hurricane that summer of 1966 was a forty-five-year-old former Flying Tiger pilot, ex-actor, and ex-nurseryman and landscape designer named Jose Gonzales, who was a special-education teacher in a Trenton junior high. The oldest individual to take the Hurricane Island course up to that time, he found it "the best challenge since my war days"—this from a pilot who had survived downed flights in three different World War II theaters. At Hurricane he met Phil Costello. Action Bound would intertwine and redirect the lives of those two.

That same summer Farrell visited a federal Job Corps Center at Camp Kilmer, New Jersey. This was one of a number of centers around the country where the Office of Economic Opportunity (OEO) was bringing together unemployed youngsters for academic and vocational training to qualify them for jobs with career potential. The youngsters lived in dormitories, each of which had a kind of resident "cottage father" responsible for their well-being. These leaders were taught a leadership process called guided group interaction (GGI), a group dynamics technique for bringing about peer influence on the side of positive behavior. Farrell sat in on a GGI session led by a young African-American named Joe Moore, who had graduated from Central State College in Wilberforce, Ohio, a year previously. Impressed by the effective way Moore related to his charges, Greg offered him the post of assistant director of Action Bound, and Joe accepted.

The director's post was still open. One day a young ex-theologian turned up in Farrell's office. Bob Hanson had recently left the Episcopalian priesthood in order to resolve problems in his personal life. In his new lay status he was director of a political action committee in Cambridge, Massachusetts, doing campaign organizing work for candidates who favored ending the war in Vietnam. In New Jersey as a consultant, he learned that the Trenton antipoverty program was seeking someone to head up an educational program. He went to see Farrell, who—with Moore and Crook's approval—hired him.

Some eighty-five students, sixteen to eighteen years old and primarily a mix of juniors and seniors, made up the three homerooms comprising the Action Bound enrollment. In addition to most of Farrell's Outward Bound bunch, there was a broad mix of others who were recruited—or "selected"—for the program. By and large they were youngsters who in the eyes of the school staff "didn't fit." Many were considered disruptive. Two-thirds were African-American or of Puerto Rican descent. Most were regarded as "problems"—discipline problems, learning problems, problems growing from family situations. They were problems in that the school did not know what to do with them.

In its first, tentative year, Action Bound had two primary components— one on weekends and the other at school. On alternating weekends, Barry Crook and his staff either trained the recruits in outdoor skills, first aid, and rescue, and led them in community-service projects or took them on expeditions. Winter and spring vacations were times for rigorous weeklong expeditions. During the week the students met with Joe Moore in an adaptation of his GGI process and for personal counseling. In evening meetings they explored leadership concepts and techniques with Barry and Joe.

Coming to Outward Bound out of the priesthood, Hanson had no difficulty with the concept. "I think I was convinced from the very beginning," he said. An incident that stuck in his memory occurred early, when the students were doing their first rappel, on the spillway of a frozen dam. "There was a great big kid who was something of a bully, overwhelming the others with his mouth, and particularly intimidating one small boy. On the rappel the big guy came first, scared to death. He couldn't bring himself to take that first step. For all their dislike, the others, including the intimidated one, were giving him moral support. 'Come on, take it one step at a time, you can do it.' But the bully never went down that day. The next in line was the intimidated lad. He rappelled down like a pro. From that time on the relation between the two changed markedly. The big guy no longer bullied. The little fellow, who had had no sense of being able to accomplish anything, suddenly in his own mind became a giant. And the two became friends. That kind of productive use of the environment helps to make a person whole."

Hanson's perception of the wilderness component came partly from his own experience. "I had been strictly putting on my suit and tie, getting in my car to go to work. All of a sudden one weekend I was running around the rocks of Stokes State Forest. The next I was in the Pine Barrens, which petrified me, because I knew there were rattlesnakes there. And the next I found myself paddling down a river in the freezing cold rain. My apprehension level remained high until we started to have problems, like an overturned canoe, or being stranded overnight in the Pine Barrens without food and freezing our butts. After I'd come through several of these, I really began to relax, and a lot of my whole sense of apprehension about what was happening in all of my life began to diminish."

Joe Moore took part in the weekend activities, then used them as "impetus" for his supportive services. He recalled, "During the week we would meet in the students' free time and discuss what the weekend experiences might mean to each individual. At the same time I was finding out what counseling needs they had, what their group needs were, and getting a line on their academic problems. Getting the kids to realize that we were really interested in what was happening to them, I was building a constituency."

At one point there were so many youngsters coming to Moore's sessions that the school library was the only room big enough for them. Hanson was impressed by how well Moore's work supplemented Crook's. "Outward Bound and guided group interaction were a beautiful marriage. It was not enough that a kid have a really good experience on a weekend. The experience had to be translated into feeling through articulation. Joe had those skills in spades."

By the end of the school year good reasons for confidence in the essential soundness of the program had been established. Particularly impressive was one research finding[8] that showed how teachers perceived change in the students. Rating "blind"—knowing neither the purpose of the inquiry nor to which group an individual belonged—they perceived a marked degree of positive change in the Action Bound students that they did not find in a control group. But it was also clear that Action Bound's success would be limited unless the school accepted it as an integral part of the institution. Ironically, despite the favorable blind findings, the institution did not respond favorably to the program. Hanson feels that much of the difficulty lay in a failure of understanding. "Here was a classical educational problem," he said, "that of kids coming into an institutionalized educational setting with a strong self-concept and being *penalized* for it. When you get a kid who says 'Hey, teacher' (and let's assume he's doing it politely), 'I've been through this unit in some other kind of experience, could I go on to the next chapter, or could I do an individual study project,' the teacher says 'No, we're all going to be on this page doing this thing at this time.' There are hundreds of gradations of that same problem. The kids would come back from the weekend feeling much better about themselves. They would go into class. They would see the old behaviors imposed on them, and bingo—right back to ground zero."

The rest of Action Bound's history was to be an effort to create a "school within a school." Sarah Christie, the assistant superintendent of schools, an old-timer not far from retirement, understood Action Bound and perceived its

---

[8] See *Final Report: Effect of Outward Bound Training on Urban Youth*, Harold M. Schroder and Robert E. Lee, Princeton University, Princeton, N.J., 1967. See also Arnold Shore's critique of this study in *Outward Bound: A Reference Volume*, (Greenwich, Conn.: Outward Bound Inc., 1977).

potential. It made sense to her to try to integrate the cognitive side of school with the weekend experiences. She assigned three teachers to serve half-time on the program staff. In its second year, 1967–1968, Action Bound had its own classes in social studies, earth sciences, and history, with experiments in using the Outward Bound component as a learning resource, in support of the classroom. Hanson was made acting assistant principal. There was now a small group of sympathetic teachers, but to the staff at large Action Bound remained "that project."

On my periodic visits I found the program functioning more and more on its own. The ties with those of us who had originally sparked it were increasingly tenuous. Farrell's promotion to head up the state antipoverty program took him out of touch. Barry Crook was drafted into the army. Another Britisher, Jeff Evans, took his place but stayed only a short time before moving on to be chief instructor of the Minnesota Outward Bound School. He was replaced by Herb Kincey, who came from Colorado Outward Bound and at the year's end would go to the new North Carolina School.

Joe Moore, whose growing administrative duties were leaving him little time for guidance and counseling, had come to be the one to whom the outdoor staff and the classroom teachers brought problems they were having with the youngsters. There were more problems than ever. Most of the gung-ho core kids who had helped Farrell dream up Action Bound were gone. While the recruiting effort continued to try for that kind of youngster, the "regular" school had found Action Bound a convenient repository for students it could not cope with. "One of the recruiting problems we always had," Hanson said, "was that the staff should not think of this as a program for dumb kids or troublemakers. But every time the counselors got a kid they couldn't handle, they would direct him to us. That would be the last the kid would ever be in trouble, the last time he'd ever be referred for discipline. His attendance would suddenly skyrocket. Nobody ever said this is terrific—we just kept getting all these referrals. Until finally Joe Moore had to say, Look, you guys are giving us kids nobody can handle, lay off."

Then the program lost Moore. Following a serious race riot at the school, the riot leaders were suspended. Sarah Christie turned them over to Joe, who started a school in a factory basement. Moore regarded that school as "probably the most powerful experience" of his life; students from the regular school were begging to get in. But this work took him from Action Bound for the rest of the year.

Remarkably, for all its vicissitudes that second year, the program actually grew stronger. The weekend expeditions continued to produce their catalysis. They became more educationally significant through being related to classroom activities. Hanson, growing skillful in the art of grantsmanship, was bringing in new federal funds to enlarge the academic staff and pay for staff training. Now too, in that time of racial tension, the program was beginning to be seen as a kind of safety valve. Action Bound never had serious racial problems.

In its third year, 1968–1969, the program was switched to a sophomore activity, formally sanctioned as a dropout-prevention undertaking. No longer could teachers and counselors be discouraged from steering the troublesome students into it. Many of the sixty or so youngsters had been put out of school at least once, and all of them were rated disruptive. That year the school-within-a-school was fully realized, embracing all required subjects and foreign languages except for the science labs. Before the year started there was an intensive week of staff training that included a wilderness expedition. Phil Costello, now a graduate student, was heading up the outdoor activity and also teaching. Moore was back, putting in a good deal of time training staff in the ways of working with ghetto youngsters. "We had a sensitive faculty, people who could understand some of the nuances where those kids were coming from. We concentrated on bringing out the kids' strengths rather than on their weaknesses."

The staff included several paraprofessionals—black women, some of them mothers of students, capable women who believed in the program and could relate well to the youngsters. They counseled, helped with personal problems, assisted the teachers. Some of them visited the students' homes to explain the program and its philosophy to their families. Action Bound began to build a parent constituency in the ghetto communities.

Costello got most of the staff to go out on many of the weekend expeditions. "That was important," Moore said. "If you had that teacher who taught you sharing the same pot of dehydrated food, things were on a different dynamic when you went back to class the following Monday. The response

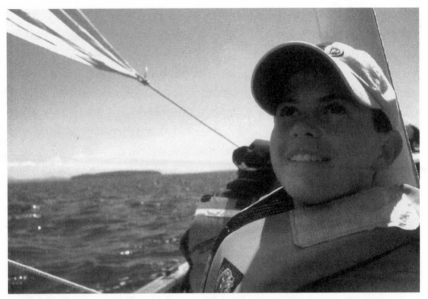

Outward Bound opens the eyes of a young life on the waters of the Pacific, with high winds in the sails and shipmates close by. (Photo © Andrew Dalrymple)

was different, the whole aura was different. It was extremely positive." In March Moore resigned to accept the offer of a deanship at Princeton. He could leave with a sense of accomplishment. "It wasn't the smoothest of operations, but it had good attitudes and feelings on the part of the kids. They enjoyed coming to school. They took to our nontraditional approach. It was very intensive. The twenty-four-hour, seven-day-a-week situation was a powerful experience for them."

Worried about the program's fourth-year funding, looking for other models with which to strengthen it, Hanson found the Philadelphia Advancement School, itself modeled on a successful experiment in North Carolina. He worked up an elaborate proposal to the federal Health, Education, and Welfare Department for a merging of the Action Bound and Advancement School concepts into an independent school within Trenton Central High. The Outward Bound elements were central to his proposal. "I felt then and I feel now that public education artificially separates the learning functions—

that we somehow pretend that the youngster is a disembodied mind—a blank slate we can simply write on without being aware of how he feels, or without being aware that he learns with his body as well. Outward Bound was the first serious attempt that I heard about to try to look at what happens to a youngster as he learns physical skills that he thought he was not capable of, as he changes his concept of himself, and with that changed concept of himself comes to a learning situation in the school that is integrated with the physical learning experience he had been having."

The proposal was an ambitious, daring venture, calling for a budget of a million dollars a year for five years. By then the Department of Health, Education, and Welfare had become highly sophisticated in what it required of grant proposals and in its evaluation of them. They rejected Hanson's first submission for technical deficiencies. He went to Washington for a week's briefing and started over. But in funding terms, a year was lost. In its fourth year Action Bound was scraping the bottom of the support barrel.

Yet the program had what in many respects was its best year. The teachers and paraprofessionals had acquired a surer sense of what they were about. While Moore was gone, Gonzales was back with Costello after a year of teaching in a storefront school. Felix Pace, a teacher fresh out of Yale, was a welcome recruit to the outdoor activity. Morale was good; the program matured. Part of the maturing process was a missionary effort to reach out to the rest of the school. Action Bound teachers offered to team up with "regular" faculty members to design and teach a course cooperatively. Costello offered the services of his outdoor activity to any team or individual teacher who wanted to use wilderness adventure in support of a classroom study. While the science and other departments did take considerable advantage of this offer, and a number of teaching teams were formed, the missionary effort met with considerable resistance. The communication lines were in too poor repair to deal with the frequently voiced suspicions that "that project" was trying to take over the school.

Still, the successes were impressive. Costello estimates that, in addition to working with sixty Action Bound students throughout the year, he and his staff took three hundred fifty others on one or more expeditions. By way of example he likes to tell the Freddy Burke story. Freddy was one of the least involved students in a largely uninvolved English class taught by Mary Ann Springle. In desperation Mary Ann asked Costello and Gonzales to take the class on a weekend expedition and try to motivate them. The youngsters were dropped off in groups of four in Stokes State Forest in northwest New Jersey. Each group received a bag containing a miscellany of items and a letter. On opening the letter the group learned they were the survivors of a plane crash on an island, cut off from the rest of the world, and they had to create their own society. The contents of the bag were all they had been able to salvage. The letter gave them a list of ways they could earn points—building things out of natural materials, inventing a new game, and so on, and a list of things they could make to trade for food. The youngsters had a fine time; an anthropologist passing through Stokes Forest would have been intrigued with the variety of cultures flourishing there. Two weeks later Mary Ann came into Costello's office holding a notebook. She said, "I've taught Freddy Burke for two years. He's never written a sentence for me. He went on that one weekend expedition with you and wrote a journal thirty pages long, and it is one of the most incredible stories I have ever read!"

Freddy, it seemed, had been the captain of the TWA charter flight that crashed, and his journal was being written twenty years later. He told every- thing that happened in the twenty years. He included a Christmas poem the foursome had written together on their fifth Christmas marooned on the island. Years later Costello still gets excited when he recalled it: "Talk about a creative mind, an imagination! This kid blew his teacher right off her chair! She said, 'I'm going to go out with you next weekend with ten other students and see what you do,' and she did. I started team-teaching with her, and we did a whole slew of things with that class. A lot of them came out of my happening on a paperback book called *Hooked on Books*[9] that gave about a hundred ways of getting kids into reading. Essentially they were techniques for finding out what a youngster was interested in and then giving him books about it. We took that idea and made it work. Kids Mary Ann had never been

[9] Daniel N. Fader and Elton B. McNeil. *Hooked on Books: Program and Proof* (New York: G. P. Putnam's Sons, 1968).

able to get to open a book, we would find out what interested them, what they cared about, we'd go find a paperback on it, and that kid would be reading. It was great for us because it tied Action Bound into the English Department. Mary Ann sold us to the others."

The staff persuaded people in the Trenton business and civic communities to sign up Action Bound students for various projects. Youngsters in the math classes had part-time jobs in a bank; others dug for Indian artifacts at an archaeological site on the Delaware River and helped set up exhibits in the state historical museum. One of the most successful projects was in a hospital across from the school, where a team of six students was given jobs in the emergency room. Action Bound taught them advanced first aid, and the hospital trained them in handling patients and emergency-room procedures. They worked in pairs after school, nights, and weekends. For the youngsters it was a dramatic way of being useful. A decade later, two of them were still on the hospital staff.

With the support of a $1,000 grant from the state, Action Bound did a series of joint expeditions with a racial mix—black and white—of police officers and youngsters. After six months a plan was afoot to set up an "advisory board" of inner-city youngsters who would work with the police on their youth problems. Unfortunately, by then the year was running out. And so was Action Bound.

The program had a dramatic high point when word came from Washington that the "advancement school" application, with its million-dollar-a-year budget for five years, had been approved. But the euphoria was short-lived. Soon after came the crushing news that Congress had failed to fund the supporting legislation; no money was available for the upcoming year. It was a death blow. Action Bound did not wither away; it was struck down in its prime. On the heels of the bad news, Hanson resigned. For Costello and Gonzales, it was a career crisis. Costello said, "We felt the things we were doing were the greatest things we had done in our lives in the way of making contributions to kids and education. We weren't about to give them up." He, Gonzales, and Pace resigned from the school system to start something they called Project USE—Urban Suburban Environments—a kind of Jersey-oriented Outward Bound. Project USE is still going strong.

There is an ironic postscript to the Action Bound story. The following year, in the winter of 1971, Washington informed Trenton that $800,000 was forthcoming to fund the proposal approved the year before. Project USE offered to help implement the program; the school said, Thanks, we're going to do it our way. Gonzales sat in on one of the "our way" meetings. "I couldn't believe my eyes or my ears," he said. "They were arguing about things we had worked out three years before. They dropped the Outward Bound adventure component, they dropped the paraprofessionals and the idea of liaison with the families, they dropped the part-time job experiences. They just about dropped Action Bound!"

The substitute program did wither away, with HEW dropping its support.

■ ■ ■

Historically the Trenton experience broke trail for Outward Bound's incursion into the educational mainstream. It remains a model both for what can be accomplished and the pitfalls that waylay efforts to effect institutional change. But when Trenton was happening, we did not know it was that significant. Nor had we yet discovered that introducing an Outward Bound adaptive program into an institution is analogous to an organ transplant in a human being. The reflexive action of the institution is to reject the foreign element. To counteract the reflex forces calls for a high degree of management skill, particularly in human relationships.

In the New York office where he was executive director of the Fund for the City of New York—and a much-involved national trustee of Outward Bound—Greg Farrell thought back across a decade to his launching of the Action Bound experiment. "Outward Bound does present and make real and quite palpable another possibility for behavior, a set of possibilities which it is quite energizing to discover. Out in the wilderness, under these changed circumstances, a youngster takes on a new role for which he may have had very little preparation or model, and all of a sudden he realizes, my God, I can be this, I don't have to be that. The possibility that emerges is often a shock and a delight. Those kids who were so high when they came to my office in Trenton that morning were experiencing just that. The thrill of this discovery and sense of capacity in themselves so excited them that they wanted to continue playing the parts in life that they learned they could play at Hurricane. It was quite thrilling to me, too. I should have remembered what Larry Paquin had told me. Larry was an ex-sea captain who became superintendent of schools in New Haven, and whom I met as a newspaper reporter. He had gone into the job with some ambitious ideas. One day I asked how his projects were going. 'Son,' he said, 'he who would change schools must learn to grow trees.' Action Bound was very imperfectly conceived. Still, for all our mistakes it worked well. I learned a major lesson about institutional change: the effort required for an Outward Bound adaptive program of Action Bound's scope is roughly equal to that involved in starting a new Outward Bound school. You need at least ten years to mature. You must learn to grow trees."

When Bob Hanson, a staff member of the New Jersey Department of Education wearing two hats—management consultant and program-design specialist—stopped by to say hello to his old friends at Project USE, inevitably the talk would run to the old Action Bound days. He said, "Had we not had such a radical turnover in the top staff of the school system, had we had some really supportive people over a long period of time, something much more substantial would have resulted. After all, we left them a fine legacy—a multi-million-dollar federal grant, a dedicated staff of twenty-one people, loads of equipment, a lot of achievement. We took youngsters nobody else wanted or could handle, potential dropouts, and helped them through school. We never had a staff member transfer out. And in four years of operating the wilderness program we never had a serious accident.

"I have lots of feelings of failure about my own involvement, that I was thrown into a management role without having been trained for it. But I know now that the experience we had was typical of all Title III programs, except those that happen to be a favorite of a superintendent or principal, and those cases are not the way change usually happens. Usually the innovation is asked for by a teacher or someone else who is not part of the power structure, and there is always that set of barriers to how you introduce change and how you incorporate the beneficial products of the change. In recent years a lot of thought has been given to the change process by the states and by the federal agencies. Today you can go to the shelves and pick off whole books directed solely to the change process in public schools, whereas at the time of Action Bound nobody was even talking about it."

Joe Moore, home from his daily commute, Princeton to Newark, where his work involves him in the long-term implications of the Supreme Court ruling that financing education through local property taxes is unconstitutional, recalled that first successful year of Action Bound when so many of the students went on to college, his evolving administrative role with its growing interpretive function between staff and students, and Action Bound's achievement in skirting racial dissidence. He also articulated, carefully, a dichotomy in his own thinking and feeling about "the transfer," about the difficult question of what the individual does with the self-discovery newly won in the wilderness when he returns to his own environment.

"I often think about the transference. I sometimes look back on that experience, 1966 to 1969, with some resentment because of the assumption Outward Bound made in terms of the urban environment and the urban youngster. We could take a kid away on a weekend, and he could have the thrill of his life, and normally did. We could normally provide a positive school experience for him. But often we did not appreciate all the kinds of problems the youngster had. It's naive to think that a kid who can scale one-hundred-eighty-foot cliffs can resolve all the problems that urban communities have. The basis of survival was not necessarily that of the wilderness, but of the day-to-day survival in the urban environment. That sometimes, I think, provided some of the misgivings that I personally had about the Outward Bound concept. Not that the experience was not good for the participant. It did stretch the kids, in terms of accomplishing things they thought they could not do. But you had a successful weekend experience and an unsuccessful environment. That was a negative factor—in that some of the youngsters had hoped that Outward Bound would not only change their lives but make a continued success possible, but the urban barriers were too great. I think most of the kids had very successful experiences on an individual level—kids that I still see today, who remember the program in a very, very positive light. There's no question about that. On the one hand we were providing very powerful experiences, but on the other hand we were augmenting frustration."

Farrell's learning to grow trees, Hanson's quest into change theory, Moore's caveat on augmenting frustration—all these and corollary lessons were gained through the Action Bound experience. Although we lacked the wisdom to derive these lessons early on—time, repetitive patterns, and a sharing of thinking about experience are probably imperative parts of this kind of learning process—we did come to recognize them. More and more, Outward Bound in its counseling role and the Outreach programs, with their accumulation of own and shared experience, are profiting from them.

Action Bound's failure to survive is less significant than the extraordinary degree to which it succeeded—and could have gone on succeeding. It continues to have a hold on many whose lives it touched. Often, when Joe Moore visited Trenton, he would run into some of the guys: "I can sit with those kids today and have a beer with them and talk about those experiences. 'Hey, Joe, do you remember Jose Gonzales helping us do this, showing us how to do that? Do you remember telling us that story around that campfire?' The level of relationship was probably as intense as you'll ever get in terms of closeness of adults to kids."

The Gonzaleses lived in the country by then, but when the doorbell rang, it was often a former Action Bounder stopping to say hi, or to discuss a problem. Phil Costello, walking along a Trenton street, bumped into Mrs. Meyers, Bobby Meyers's mother. Bobby was an Action Bound student, and his mother was one of the paraprofessionals who did liaison work for the program among her fellow parents in the African-American community. The two embraced and there on the sidewalk held a happy reunion, remembering the good days of the program. Or Costello was visiting in Alexandria, Virginia, and happened to see in the paper that the local high school principal's name was Susan Halbert. That had to be Sue Halbert, who taught social studies and English in Action Bound and did all the wilderness things. He called her up, and she said come on over to the school, and the two spent an excited couple of hours of reminiscing.

Freddy Burke? He graduated and was gone, and nothing was heard of him. Four or five years went by, and one day Costello's phone rang, and it was Freddy calling. He was in the Navy, home on leave. He was going to be married next week. Would Phil be his best man? Sure, Phil said, he'd be honored.

NORTH CAROLINA

✳

I didn't see why we had to do the things we did, like getting up at 5:30 a.m., and running and dipping. I didn't see any sense in going through the ropes course or standing out in the pouring rain all afternoon. I got sick of it all really fast, so I left. But, once I left, I just couldn't face myself. I guess I was just looking for an easy way out. I've always taken the easy way of things, and at first Outward Bound was not going to be an exception. After I left, I started thinking about my life and the way it's been, and I really got sick. I guess I felt like about the biggest cop-out alive. So, I came back and I've found that to be the best decision I've made in my life.

—A North Carolina student's course impression

I n April 1964 the *Princeton Alumni Weekly* carried an article about me and Outward Bound. One alumnus who read it with more than passing interest was Watts Hill Jr. of Durham, North Carolina, who had been at college a year ahead of me. Hill was president of the Home Security Life Insurance Company, had served in the state legislature, and was active in state civic and cultural affairs. He sent the article with a "this-may-interest-you" note to George Esser, president of the North Carolina Fund. The fund was a five-year project set up the previous year by Governor Terry Sanford to attack problems of poverty in the state through demonstration programs with monies provided by the Ford Foundation and two North Carolina foundations. Esser passed the article along to Jack Mansfield, his director of special projects. Mansfield, a Methodist minister who had left the pulpit for social activism, and his assistant, Marjorie Galloway, a recent honors graduate of the state university at Chapel Hill who had taught elementary school in England and Durham, were both greatly intrigued by Outward Bound and sought more information about it. One of their sources was Tom Hartmann, my old sidekick at the Hun School. This requires a digression.

In 1958 Hartmann became headmaster of St. Marks School in Dallas. In periodic trips east he visited us in Andover, always keen to know what was happening on the Kurt Hahn front. By the time the Colorado Outward Bound School was founded he had also come to know Chuck Froelicher as a fellow headmaster. He recruited students for Colorado and helped raise money for Outward Bound. When he returned to Princeton in 1963 to shepherd the merger of two Princeton day schools, the Atlantic Foundation elected him to its board. As noted, he was one of the original OBI trustees. Early on he was elected board secretary.

Through Tom I met Paul Ylvisaker, who was then director of the national affairs activities of the Ford Foundation. As the initiator of half a dozen pilot urban programs around the country, Ylvisaker was the conceptual father of the Johnson administration's antipoverty program. One evening in early 1965, Greg Farrell, Hartmann, Joel Sugarman, and I were dinner guests of Ylvisaker, who was interested in Outward Bound's potential as an antipoverty force. Subsequently he hired Hartmann as a consultant to survey innovative antipoverty programs and simultaneously to seek ways Outward Bound might be applied in the anti-poverty arena. Tom's survey brought him into contact with Mansfield.

When Mansfield and Galloway learned that the Minnesota School was starting the first course for girls in the United States, Marjorie went up to Ely for a firsthand look. At Homeplace she observed the female students undergo basic training, talked with the instructors and the Piehs, took note of the inner-city kids who were there on scholarship from the Massachusetts Youth Services and Trenton. One evening after supper Jerry Pieh suggested a walk. When they reached the ropes course, he persuaded Marjorie to climb up to the starting platform and then to do the initial traverse. Marjorie remembered, "I had watched the students do the ropes course and hadn't even conceived of attempting it myself. Once I'd started, I wanted to keep going. Down on the ground Jerry talked me through the whole thing. I finished on top of the world!"

As it happened, we were holding an OBI trustee meeting at the Minnesota School at the time. Mansfield came up for that. He talked with Tom and me about the North Carolina Fund's possible interest in starting a school. It was decided that Marjorie should go on to Colorado. There she went on a three-day safari with two instructors and the wife of one, checking students on solo. They carried live chickens, an experiment (not repeated) in solo cuisine that summer. It was hailing and snowing, and Marjorie shared a tent with the chickens.

"I found the reality of Outward Bound even more than I expected," she said. "The instructors were a terrific bunch of people. They really inspired me. I came back to Durham sold on Outward Bound as a proposition for the North Carolina Fund."

But when Mansfield drew up a proposal for the fund to found an Outward Bound school, the trustees decided they would be exceeding their charge in sponsoring an organization that would not be exclusively for the poor. At that juncture help came from another quarter. Hartmann, now deputy director of the North Carolina Fund, called me to come down. The occasion for the trip was a dinner at the home of Harold and Sibby Howe in Chapel Hill. Harold "Doc" Howe had taught at Phillips Academy; the year we arrived there he left to be principal of the Punchard High School in Andover, the first of a series of public-school posts he filled with distinction. In 1964 he became head of the Learning Institute of North Carolina (LINC), a private organization acting as a kind of holding company for a series of educational experiments going on in the state.

The Howes' dinner guests were George Esser, Hartmann, and I. We ran the *Tall as the Mountains* film, and I reviewed the organizational story. When I finished, Doc said, "All right, let's outline the steps to start a North Carolina Outward Bound School." Esser was sympathetic. He reiterated that the North Carolina Fund could not sponsor a school but offered to provide staff aid to do missionary work, seeking out citizens who would be willing to come together as a board of trustees. He gave that assignment to the Mansfield-Galloway team, who reported to Hartmann. I have always remembered Doc Howe's *amicus curiae* role that evening as a splendid demonstration of what an understanding, concerned liaison person can do in a situation where catalysis is needed. As events transpired, the timing was critical. Two months later Howe was gone from North Carolina, to be the U.S. Commissioner of Education.

In the fall of 1965 a piece of property in the Blue Ridge mountain region was offered to the North Carolina Fund. Mansfield and Galloway went to look at it as a possible school site, accompanied by Dave Mashburn and Herb Kincey, two Colorado instructors who were advising them. When the location was found not suitable for Outward Bound purposes, Mashburn and Kincey said, "Let's go to Table Rock. We'll show you some real pretty terrain, even though you can't have it, because it's U.S. Forestry Service country." Table Rock Mountain rises above the hamlet of Jonas Ridge, near the town of Morganton in the western part of the state; a great tablelike rock gives the mountain its dramatic apex and its name. While the site was well known at that time to a few rock climbers and the hunters and fishermen who frequented the adjoining spectacular Linville Gorge country, the general public did not impinge on it much, and it was remarkably wild considering its closeness to populated areas. Mansfield and Galloway resolved on the spot to investigate the chances of obtaining a special usage permit from the Forest Service. Their day peaked when Mashburn and Kincey put them through their first rappel.

The North Carolina board that Mansfield and Galloway recruited was incorporated, with Watts Hill as chairman, in January 1966. When Mansfield left the fund soon after, Galloway carried on as the board's agent. One of her first assignments was to pursue the Table Rock site. Richard Eriksson, the Forestry Service's deputy regional director, became an enthusiast for the Outward Bound idea and helped immeasurably in guiding her through the red tape. By spring the usage permit was assured, and the lawyers were working out a lease of eighty acres. The North Carolina Outward Bound School was chartered in April, with plans to open the following year and aspirations to become the first year-round school in the United States. Tony Mulvihill, a former marine officer and youth worker in New York's Harlem ghetto, who had worked for me in the Andover office, was hired as director of development. In June, he and Galloway, who was now an employee of the school, moved into an office in Durham provided by Watts Hill's insurance company.

In pursuit of their year-round objective, the board commissioned Vincent Lee, a Hurricane Island instructor who was a graduate student in architecture at Princeton, to design the school. His plans, which earned him his graduate degree, were an exciting concept for a mountain school organized on "dunk 'em and dry 'em" principles. The board's intent to offer courses ten months of the year, on the British year-round model, received an enthusiastic response from educators and youth workers around the state. Events, however, were to prove the idea overly ambitious.

The school site was a short distance below Table Rock itself and a mile off the gravel road that wound its way over the mountain. On a rainy night in October 1966, four young men, three of them under twenty, drove up the mountain and hiked into the site. Their leader was Lance Lee (no relation to Vincent), a New Englander who had had his first Outward Bound instructing experience at Aberdovey and then joined the Hurricane Island staff. On the two-hundred-mile trip from Durham they had picked up tools, lanterns, cooking equipment, and food. They pitched tents in the darkness and driving rain, bunked down, and at 6 A.M. began the first day's work of clearing the site for the new school. They were the first of many rosters of Lance's "woods crew," an ever-changing phenomenon of mostly willing, however unskilled, artisans who would build the school. "I recruited them from every place imaginable," Lance said. "We had dropouts from schools and colleges, from Cuba, from a reform school, and a mental institution. I would capture kids from the road, if they looked like they would work on the mountain. We got some of the dregs and fashioned them into quite a good woods crew." The initial group worked into December, closed down for the winter, and resumed in the early spring with the school's opening less than three months off.

The board appointed James "Pop" Hollandsworth as school director. He was dean of students and chairman of the science department at the Asheville School, with a thirty-year background of operating summer wilderness programs. They hired the usual new school complement of two experienced British instructors.

One of them was John Lawrence, an Oxford graduate who had been teaching at New Zealand Outward Bound; the other was Peter Sheehan, a British-born Eurasian from the Moray Sea School. Knut Smith, a Colorado instructor, was engaged to teach rock climbing. Dave Mashburn also transferred from Colorado; later Herb Kincey came.

When George Greene, a marine sergeant major just retired after twenty-six years in the corps, hired on as business manager in April, he found the one-mile access road cut in but not yet graveled. A crew was drilling for water, with no luck. The woods crew had completed the clearing work and were building platforms for six-man tents. They had acquired a boss carpenter in the person of Jesse Padrick, retired police chief of Wilmington, North Carolina. For Greene the woods crew's motley quality and long-haired kind of esprit were a sharp shift from the structured, crew-cut environment of the U.S. Marines, but he found the change not unrefreshing. "Lance had all these problem-type kids coming and going; most of them had hardly ever hammered a nail before, and they were building tent platforms under the leadership of an ex-police chief. Maybe working next to the chief would be a Puerto Rican kid on probation out of Spanish Harlem who didn't know anything about sawing a straight line, and didn't saw a straight line, but the old chief tolerated it, and the two would learn a lot from each other."

The only building put up the first year was a secondary structure in the Vince Lee plan; open on all sides, it included the kitchen and eating facilities, and would temporarily provide office and equipment storage space. Everybody pitched in—woods crew, instructors, volunteer alumni of other schools. The lumber was timbers from an old furniture factory recently torn down in Morganton. The great fifteen- by- twelve-inch beams were trucked up the mountain and put in place with block and tackle. Since there was no electric power, all sawing, drilling, and other work was by hand.

On July 2, 1967, the school was dedicated by Mrs. Emma Clark, U.S. postmistress at Jonas Ridge. Two days later it opened, with forty-seven students divided into four "crews." The summer courses went well, despite a plague of rain in July and a goodly assortment of other start-up difficulties.

The lack of electric power and a water system became part of the Outward Bound experience. The summer's students came from twenty-odd states. The desired socioeconomic mix, which was well met, included a number of North Carolina lads, white and black, from poverty environments, and a group of DYS youngsters from Massachusetts.

The North Carolina School did not include an age ceiling in its eligibility rules. An important reason for this was Lawrence Cohen and his Jewel Box Corporation, a chain of jewelry stores operating in the South and Southwest. Larry Cohen was one of the most enthusiastic and dedicated of the school's trustees. He believed in Outward Bound strongly enough to invest a considerable portion of the company's training budget in the program. For several years the Jewel Box organization enrolled some of its store-manager trainees in each course and contributed an equal number of scholarships.

In the fall, the plan to operate a year-round school ran into trouble. A September course did not fill, and after that the overall off-season schedule was not adequate to meet expenses. Since there were not enough courses to occupy the instructors, they were used for recruiting. Living conditions on the mountain were less than remarkable for comfort. Eight mobile homes were brought in to provide staff housing, but the task of putting down seven miles of underground electric power and telephone lines to the site was not finished until February.

The school was seriously strapped for funds, with little additional income anticipated before the new summer season. Greene remembers a gloomy rainy-night, lantern-lit meeting in one of the mobile homes, with Willi Unsoeld (who had recently joined us at Andover) and Peter Willauer sitting in, when a trustee group discussed closing down the school for several months. For George this raised the specter that it might not open again. "I think that night some people would have said, 'Let's give up.' Being an outspoken sergeant major, I let it be known that I thought that would be the worst thing we could do. I offered to work for nothing. Watts Hill said we should keep going, and he carried the day, but it was close. A few months later good things were happening, and we could see we were going to make it."

An aspect of the North Carolina story that gives it special interest is that it brought Murray Durst into U.S. Outward Bound. This was a happening that not only safeguarded the survival of the North Carolina school, but in the long run had considerable import for the national organization and ultimately for the national experiential education movement that Outward Bound was destined to generate.

■ ■ ■

Murray Durst lived his childhood in Brownsville, Texas, and his early adolescence in New Canaan, Connecticut, before the family moved to his father's native California. In 1950 he was a junior at San Jose State when the Korean War broke out. Rejecting the idea that the fortunate should be exempted from military service for having the advantage of being in higher education, he volunteered. His war experience affected him strongly in two ways. One was that in undergoing the army's training, of which he was critical, he became deeply interested in the processes of training and education. The other was the consequence of President Truman's executive order desegregating the army. "It exposed for us that two-world situation in which we had been living and probably were very comfortable. It really opened my mind to that whole issue and created the consciousness that led me later into concerns for dealing with the disadvantaged minority person. As a college kid who had grown up in the New Canaans of the world, the social interaction with the less-advantaged person that one gets through a citizen army was, I think, very key to the directions I took."

Having done his military service, including a year in the Korean front lines, Durst went back to college and got his degree. Knowing he wanted to be an educator but unwilling to continue in the classroom to gain teacher certification, he took a job with the state of California, working with private industry to encourage training and employee development activity. He steeped himself in the new literature dealing with management as a function. After three years he became director of training for Sacramento County, a densely populated governmental entity with a large, varied employee force. Five years later he was appointed a regional training director of the U.S. Bureau of Reclamation. From that post he was called to Washington to be director of training for the entire bureau.

It was the time when Lyndon Johnson was launching his "war on poverty," which included the Job Corps, a program for helping unemployables in an affluent society to become employable. One of the first proposed Job Corps Conservation Centers was to be at Collbran, Colorado, close to the home of Congressman Wayne Aspinall, whose chairmanship of the House Interior and Insular Affairs Committee gave him great political clout. The Department of the Interior, anxious to have a good operation in Aspinall's backyard, assigned Durst to direct it.

One of Murray's ideas was that the corpsmen should be encouraged to take a large part of the responsibility for operating their center. The implementing of this policy, however, was beset by a problem: "We were bringing kids into that center at the seven-thousand-foot level in the Rocky Mountains, forty miles from civilization up a canyon road, in what to my middle-class eyes was absolutely gorgeous country, but to those urban and southern rural eyes was a fearful place. We had not done the job of looking at the potential in the locations of Job Corps Conservation Centers. We had failed to see that we could use their very environments for learning purposes."

As it happened, Durst was seeking a way to deal with this problem at the same time Joe Nold was looking for ways in which Outward Bound might serve some of the issues involved in the war on poverty. As it also happened, Collbran was a mere forty miles as the crow flies on the other side of a mountain range from Marble. Still another happenstance was that the head of the Office of Economic Opportunity (OEO), of which the Job Corps was an agency, was Sargent Shriver. That simultaneity of interests led to a contract between the Collbran Center and the Colorado School to introduce Outward Bound concepts into the Job Corps training effort as a means of helping the center utilize its own environment for its educational goals.

The collaboration was successful. Nold assigned a staff to assist Durst in achieving his several purposes. The primary goal was to help the corpsmen transform their negative feelings about their environment to positive ones, giving them a confidence-building learning experience in the process. Another was to apply Outward Bound techniques to the training of those who showed promise of leadership capabilities for carrying out Durst's self-government policy. There was yet a third payoff, which Durst recalled gratefully. "We had a big public-relations problem because the general population viewed the centers as places where the U.S. government was bringing real risky people into these rural environments. So another important use of Outward Bound was directly to apply the service notion with which Kurt Hahn was so especially concerned—to train those corpsmen to serve as rescue teams in our mountain area. They made rescues in situations ranging from airplane crashes to floods. Their abilities, trained through the Outward Bound process, brought to that center a great deal of positive response."

Quite apparently the Durst method had merit, for in a time when the Job Corps generally was experiencing a dropout rate of 35 percent, the rate at Collbran was only 3 percent. Subsequently, after being called back to Washington to serve as deputy director of the Interior Department's Job Corps effort, Durst was twice returned to the field on rebuilding missions to troubled centers. In each instance he used the Outward Bound principles that had worked well at Collbran to contribute significantly to the turnarounds he was able to achieve. The second of these rescue tasks was at a large urban center in Grand Rapids, Michigan. Durst was still involved in his mission there when the center fell victim to President Johnson's new policy of cutting back on the war on poverty to help finance the growing American commitment in Vietnam. It was clear that the entire OEO program was beginning to run down.

"Knowing what was happening," Murray recalled, "I started wondering about where I might go. My first thought was Outward Bound—I had become so interested in that whole effort. So I called Joe Nold and asked, 'Que pasa?'"

Nold was aware that Hollandsworth was going back to his old school and that the North Carolina trustees were looking for a new director. He called us, and I arranged for Willi Unsoeld to meet with Durst in Chicago. Since I had come to admire the way Durst combined managerial competence with creative insight to Outward Bound as an educational process, I strongly supported Willi's endorsement of Durst's candidacy for the North Carolina post. As it was, Durst sold himself to the trustees, and they to him. His regard for the solid quality of the board's commitment was reenforced when it assumed an obligation that was imperative to the school's survival—a bank loan of $100,000 personally guaranteed by the board members.

Taking over in the spring, Durst made several basic decisions. He closed the Durham office and established an overall headquarters on the mountain, "where the investment was." Marjorie Galloway had left the Durham operation shortly before; she continued to serve on the board she helped to create and in 1980 became chairman. Tony Mulvihill also left at that time. As the official school history notes, "the long hours, personal dedication, and sacrifice on the part of Hill, Galloway, and Mulvihill provided the foundation on which the school was built." Durst also persuaded the board to abandon its ambitious building plans. Subsequently he concluded it did not at that time make sense to aspire to year-round operation.

Murray Durst was a new kind of school director, hired not because he was a highly competent outdoorsman-educator, but because of the managerial abilities that he combined with educational concerns. He had no difficulty in making the transition from the worlds of big government, management theory, and personnel development.

"In coming to grips with the whole translation of the Outward Bound learning process into the Job Corps setting," he said, "I had learned the process. I do have an affinity for the out-of-doors, and I understood the Outward Bound concepts—but more importantly, I think, I understood the processes of learning. I have been particularly intrigued with the process of learning out of consciously structured experience, and Outward Bound is nothing if it is not that."

And he did his Kurt Hahn homework. "I read all of Hahn's speeches and addresses I could get hold of. I went directly to the man, to avoid having to interpret interpreters of Kurt Hahn, and tried to interpret directly from him. I looked not for the forms that he espoused to fit initially his work in Germany and subsequently his work in Britain, forms reflecting those two societies, but rather the principles that he was articulating. There was then no difficulty in interpreting those principles into an appropriately comfortable form."

■ ■ ■

Five schools. As the organization continued to grow, and school enrollment with it, demands on the OBI staff and the scholarship needs of the

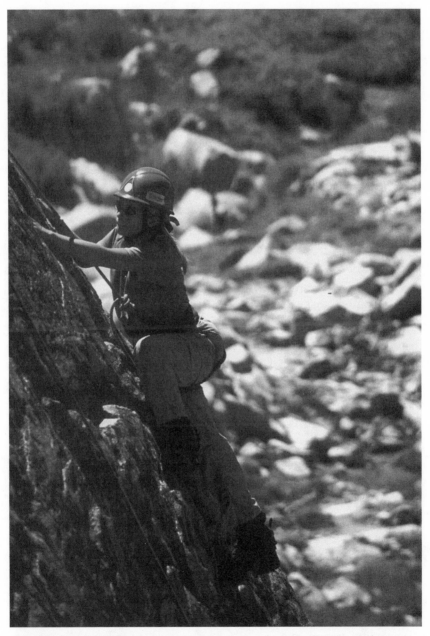

Climbing the granite crags of the High Sierra teaches coordination, balance, and teamwork on Outward Bound mountaineering courses. (Photo © Ty Milford)

schools kept increasing—and the perennial quest for funds became more pressing. In 1969 it was estimated that the total funding required to make full use of the school capacities was very close to $2.5 million. We were getting into the big time. Outward Bound never could have succeeded as it has without the generous contributions that individuals, corporations, foundations, and others have given to support its work. In 1969 we were treated to a vivid demonstration of how profoundly human generosity can advance the welfare of an institution.

When the Colorado School was inundated with applications after the appearance of Lydia Ratcliff's *Reader's Digest* article in 1963, I looked up the name of the magazine's publisher on its masthead and wrote Mr. DeWitt Wallace about the extraordinary response the article had generated. I was quite ignorant of the story of how DeWitt and Lila Wallace had conceived and created the world's most successful magazine. Nor was I aware of any of the lore that had grown up around their many benefactions. As the months went by, I wrote Mr. Wallace several times more, telling him of the impact the *Reader's Digest* was continuing to have on Outward Bound, and saying I hoped they were as pleased as we.

On a Monday in the fall of 1964 I answered my office telephone, and a man's voice asked for me. When I identified myself, he said, "Mr. Miner, my name is DeWitt Wallace, and I am associated with the *Reader's Digest.*" Lights went on and the adrenalin started pumping. I had visions of another article. He continued, "I've been watching the progress of your organization with much interest. Outward Bound's philosophy seems to jibe with my own. When you're in New York, I'd like you to come out to our offices in Pleasantville and talk with me about Outward Bound."

I said, "I'm going to be in New York on Thursday." He said, "Thursday seems a long way off." I said, "If that's the case, I could come tomorrow." He said, "You could? How would you get here from Andover?"

I told him I would fly to New York and rent a car. He said, "That seems to be putting you to too much of an inconvenience. I've checked into it, and find our plane could land at North Andover. Would it be an imposition if I sent the plane up for you to come down for lunch with me tomorrow?" The next morning I got on the *Reader's Digest's* twin-engine, twelve-passenger transport.

There were two pilots, a hostess, and me. In forty minutes we landed at the Westchester Airport, and in short order I was seated alone with DeWitt Wallace in the dining room of the *Digest* guest house. He was a tall, vigorous seventy-four-year-old, but appeared much younger. Mentally he was razor-sharp.

We talked about Outward Bound through lunch, and the conversation continued for most of the afternoon. Mr. Wallace kept asking me, "How much would it cost to put a school in every state?" My answer was, "It depends on how fast you want to do it. If you're willing to take twenty years, there's one price, if you want to do it next year, that's another." I knew we did not want a school in every state but I did not want to be anything but enthusiastically responsive to this lovely gentleman.

I left that meeting with a sense of having made a good friend. Not long after, out of the blue, the mail brought a check for $10,000 from DeWitt Wallace. Nothing like that had come out of the blue before. The next thing was that Mr. Wallace called to say he wanted to meet an Outward Bound trustee. He knew Jack Stevens's brother and was inviting Jack and me for lunch at the Pan American Club. The two older men hit it off beautifully. Mr. Wallace asked Mr. Stevens if he was supporting Outward Bound. Mr. Stevens said he was, that it was a worthwhile cause he enjoyed supporting.

Mr. Wallace said, "I have a proposition to make. Why don't we give it some more support, you and I together?"

"Wait a minute," Jack said, "I'm not in your league." Then he added, "But I'll be delighted to support Outward Bound with you." They came to an agreement whereby Mr. Wallace would give $50,000 and Mr. Stevens would give $10,000. I listened happily as another unanticipated $60,000 entered the till. As Jack and I left the club together, he said, "That was the most expensive lunch of my life!"

A year or so later the three of us met for another lunch. Mr. Wallace inquired if Mr. Stevens had kept his pledge. Mr. Stevens said he had, and made the same inquiry of Mr. Wallace. When Mr. Wallace said indeed he had, the two men made a second, similar agreement. There were other Wallace contributions as well.

All this happened at a time when we were struggling and trying hard to grow and very much aware of our potential. Mr. Wallace kept asking, "What is it you need most?" Stevens kept saying, "This guy needs money to get this thing rolling. He needs unrestricted funds to support an organization." But Mr. Wallace, it was clear, did not like to give that kind of money. He preferred to give for something tangible. In the spring of 1969 came one of his periodic calls: "I've never met any of the men who actually run the schools. Do you think you could get them all together? I'd like to have a lunch for them at the Pan American Club."

I said, "Wally, they'll be delighted!" and he named a date. It was May, and the directors were tooling up for their school openings; it was the worst possible time to take them away from their work. Only with the greatest dragging of feet did they agree to make the journey to New York.

I had butterflies about the meeting. On the night before, I met with the group and went over the ground rules. No laundry lists. We were not going to ask for anything. We were just going to do all we could to give a fine old gentleman a wonderful time at the luncheon he was giving us. Meanwhile, about a week before, Mr. Wallace had called me to say he was nervous about the luncheon; he would like to know more about these fellows so that he could ask intelligent questions. So I had made up a one-page information sheet on each director, with a picture and biographical information and the salient features of his school.

As the directors arrived at the Pan Am Club, Mr. Wallace went up to each new arrival and greeted him by name: "Alan Hale, you don't look as old as your picture!" After he had seated us, he turned to Joe Nold and queried him about his experiences as head of the oldest U.S. school. He went on to Bill Byrd and said, "Bill, you're the fellow who invented the mobile course, tell me about it. What are the good things about the mobile course, and what are its disadvantages?" And so on around the table to Peter Willauer, Murray Durst, and Alan Hale. By then he had the group in the palm of his hand. The entire luncheon became a happy affair. When the dessert and coffee came, Mr. Wallace turned to me and said, "Josh, these boys hardly ever get to New York. It's silly for them to travel all that distance and then go right home. I'd like them to stay in New York for the next two or three days and do anything they want, and I'd like to pay for it." And he slipped an envelope into my pocket.

The lunch over, we said our thanks and good-byes. Going down in the elevator from the top of the building, someone said, "What's in the envelope?" I opened it; inside was a letter and a check. I took a quick look at the check in the subdued light and said, "It's a check for ten thousand dollars!" Somebody said, "Holy smoke!" Bill Byrd, who was looking over my shoulder, said, "You can't read. It's for a hundred thousand!" Joe Nold said, "Let me see it." He took a look, then a closer look, and said, "My God, it's for a million dollars!"

We came out of the Pan Am Building six inches above the pavement. We just could not absorb the reality of it. The other five split to fan back across the country. I walked over to the Princeton Club and wrote Mr. Wallace a letter. I was deeply moved. It was not anything as simple as the money, although the levitating effect of a million dollars is extraordinary. It was the marvelous esprit of the man, the verve with which he continued to reach out to life in the eighth decade of a remarkably creative lifetime, and the generous spirit that shone through his acts of disbursing his wealth for socially creative purposes.

Mr. Wallace's letter specified that the money was for an endowment for scholarships, and there was a subsequent letter of instructions. Jim Wallis, one of our trustees, was a vice president of Guaranty Trust Company, where we had our account, and he would not let me loose until he had that check in his bank. Jack Stevens wrote a hard bargain with the bank. We wanted six percent return on the money and the principal was to be appreciated with the aim that it would always provide the same number of scholarships as $60,000 provided then. The bank moaned and groaned, but Jack had a way of getting what he wanted.

It was not the only million dollars that DeWitt Wallace gave us, nor was the second the last. For almost the entire span of U.S. Outward Bound's existence he has been its greatest benefactor. He has never asked anything in return—other than that we do our job well.

WINTER COURSES

�֍

*Winter is a resonant instrument that twangs
its own music.*

—Henry Thoreau

*Ambivalence is when nature is calling, and it's
ten below zero, and you know that you're
never going back to sleep unless you unzip
your bag and risk freezing your bleep.*

—Phil Plubell

*In the midst of winter I finally learned that
there is in me an invincible summer.*

—Albert Camus

I

A year after he graduated from Dartmouth, where he captained the 1961 swim team, Alan Hale and his wife, Anita, were looking to join the Peace Corps. Discovering that the Outward Bound camp at Arecibo had staff positions to fill, they decided instead to cast their lot with the Puerto Rican training mission. When Bill Byrd hired Alan, neither had an inkling that it was a case of one future Outward Bound school director bringing another into the fold. In Washington the Hales found Sargent Shriver and his people concerned about the prevailing six-month staff turnover in Puerto Rico. They made a commitment to stay two years. Their leave-taking in 1964, along with colleagues who had completed their tours, pretty much marked the passing of the Outward Bound era at Arecibo. It pretty much severed, too, the transcultural bonds with the local people that Bill Coffin encouraged initially and that Bill Byrd and others nurtured. When the Hales revisited the island, their old friends in the Arecibo countryside said, "After you people left, we never again saw any Peace Corps volunteers. They never came to our homes for coffee. They never bothered to talk with us." Alan said: "They were learning all their Spanish in a language laboratory when the roads, and the *tiendas* like the ones where we stopped for a beer after rock climbing, were full of people speaking it."[10]

In 1967 Alan was in business in the farming center of Jefferson, Ohio, when Bob Pieh offered him a place as assistant director of the Minnesota Outward Bound School. Subsequently he succeeded Pieh,[11] from whom he inherited a soundly grounded program and a first-rate staff. In time, as the Piehs had and as every director does, Hale put the mark of his own personality on the school. Looking ahead after the 1968 season he had two innovations in mind. One was coeducational courses, a development logically sequential to Minnesota's pioneering of courses for young women, the other was winter courses. Both were important developments within the U.S. Outward Bound family—winter courses in particular in that they were a key step toward year-round activity.

---

[10] This becomes the more significant on reading Kevin Lowther and C. Payne Lucas, *Keeping Kennedy's Promise—The Peace Corps: Unmet Hope of the New Frontier* (Boulder, Colo.: Westview Press, 1978). These two veteran corps administrators, strong adherents of the Peace Corps ideal, write a severe indictment of the corps' ultimate failure to get the volunteers to cope with their own ethnocentrism and to establish creative transcultural relationships in the countries where they served.

[11] Bob Pieh returned to college teaching, joining the Faculty of Education at Queens University, Ontario, where he built a distinctive academic record in the areas of experiential education, adult basic education and retraining, and community service. In 1973 he returned to Minnesota Outward Bound as acting director for that summer. Subsequently he was appointed director of the new Canadian Outward Bound Wilderness School in Ontario, combining that post with his university duties for several years.

It would be hard to find a more testing environment for confronting winter's challenges on starkly implacable terms than the Superior-Quetico country. In winter it is a land of fiercely unyielding cold. Temperatures that seldom get as high as zero Fahrenheit plunge to sixty below in the long nights. Winds tunnel their deadly chill factors across the open lakes, driving the snow into drifts that make the going even more difficult. The rule of thirties is commonplace: thirty below zero, thirty knots of wind, thirty seconds to freeze bare flesh. The vast white blanket builds, storm after storm without retreat, burying trees and obliterating the lacework of lakes and streams. It is a brooding environment, innately hostile to the human body. The cold that crackles spit in midair threatens to drive the blood inward to the visceral core, exposing the bodily surfaces and extremities to frostbite and the body itself to the insidious toll of hypothermia. Ten seconds with a glove off and the hand goes numb, in instant prelude to frostbite. One must keep testing the body for signs that some part may have lost sensation. In the first stages of hypothermia, the brain falters, prey to hallucination.

Because there was no U.S. precedent for a course conducted in so severe a winter environment, Hale sought help from the one source of expertise on cold-weather operations in worldwide Outward Bound. A letter to the Outward Bound Trust wangled him an invitation to take part in the British Army Outward Bound's winter course in Norway. The reply from London was cordial: even though the manuals made no provision for an American civilian's participation in a training exercise of Her Majesty's soldiers, the military liaison people were disposed to accommodate the American warden.

With Alan scheduled to leave for Norway in January, Jeff Evans, his chief instructor, conceived of a bon voyage present from the staff. Jeff was a highly capable British instructor who a few years hence would become director of the new Canadian Outward Bound Mountain School at Keremeos, British Columbia. He told Hale that at Christmas vacation he would assemble a group of instructors at Ely and lead them on a reconnaissance course to check out the winter terrain and a cold-weather mode of operation. Deeming the proposed expedition overoptimistic, Alan doubtfully gave it his blessing. Christmas came, and Evans and twelve staff members headed north, filled with pioneer zeal. They drove to Lake 1, an end-of-the-road spot in the wilderness east of Ely, about thirty miles short of the Canadian border. Getting there was an initiative test in itself. The original plan had been to head north into the Quetico on a beeline expedition across the frozen lakes, but a warning that the lake ice was thin under several feet of insulating snow had induced cautionary second thoughts. Now the plan was to start from Lake 1 at the west end of the Kekekabic Trail and follow it east for about forty miles of rugged, hilly country to where it intersected Gunflint Trail, which runs north into Canada, then double back.

At the trailhead the participants must have seemed a motley bunch. Nobody quite knew what the best equipment would be or what methods would work. Most were on snowshoes, with limited experience in their use. Although none had been on cross-country skis, three were using them. Individuals were carrying gear in everything from pack frames to rucksacks. Evans had got hold of two Norwegian heavy-duty-aluminum rescue toboggans for carrying supplies, and these had to be towed.

In 1968 the Kekekabic Trail was hardly broken out, difficult enough to follow in summer. In winter, with the snow level above the tree blazes, it was virtually nonexistent. Two hours after the start the expedition was lost. Doug Page, one of the expeditionaries, remembered: "We were off the trail, bushwhacking through this horrible morass of hills, deep snow, and trees— six-, seven-, eight-foot trees with only the tops sticking out. Breaking trail in the deep snow in that up-and-down country was exhausting. The toboggans were a major problem—they just weren't designed for that kind of overland travel. The skiers had no waxes, so they couldn't help pull them. At times they had to take off their skis to get uphill. Once one of them hit a hole and sank up to his chest with his skis on. Some of the guys on snowshoes were falling. We were all done in in the slow going."

According to the best estimates offered in the many debriefings that have been given on the "Great Minnesota Winter Recon," the expedition covered between one and one-half and two miles in nine hours. As darkness closed down the short winter day, bivouac was a fresh challenge. The toboggans held an assortment of two-man and four-man tents. "Ensolite pads for insulation were new then," Page recalled. "We'd heard about them but we didn't have any. Some of us had cut up old pieces of wool. Guys scrounged around, some used pillows, one took a pad from a toboggan. In the night the temper-ature got down to thirty-five below. In the morning, when someone hit against your tent, hoarfrost that had built up from frozen breath and body moisture cascaded down on you."

After breakfast a retreat was agreed on. The second day was a repeat of the first in the reverse direction, except that everyone was less strong and less gung-ho. One man became ill and had to be carried on a toboggan. It was dark again when the expedition staggered back to its starting point at Lake 1. In two days they had covered between three and four miles. They took another eight hours getting the cars started, using everything from ether to open flame to warm up the motors. In the morning the caravan limped into Homeplace. That was where Hale, who had driven up from Minneapolis to await their return, found them. When he took off for Norway, he carried their bon voyage present with him, in the form of a brief informal report: "You can never have a winter course."

It is a striking coincidence that in the same Christmas week, half a conti-nent to the west, a Northwest School group of three instructors—Steve Wennstrom (later Northwest's program director), Vernon Bush, and Adrian Todd—and six Northwest alumni attempting an experimental six-day "winter trek" on skis were forced to abandon the expedition on the third day. A combination of deep, drifting snows, rising winds, low visibility that necessitated skiing by compass bearing, cold, and heavy packs finally proved too much for the expeditionaries, who well after midnight put in to the hospital at Bend, Oregon, for emergency treatment of frostbitten fingers and toes. It was, Wennstrom reported, the end of "the most exhausting ordeal most of them had ever endured." Then, less than two weeks later and three thousand miles to the east, as part of the new Dartmouth Outward Bound Center's course for undergraduates bucking to be instruc-tors, a cadre of students and leaders had a comparable experience in a whiteout atop Mount Moosilauke.

Learning through failure is one effective mode of the experiential method. It was a healthy thing for the movement that widely separated, virtually simultaneous early essays into three quite different kinds of winter wilderness taught the same memorable lesson. There is a connection

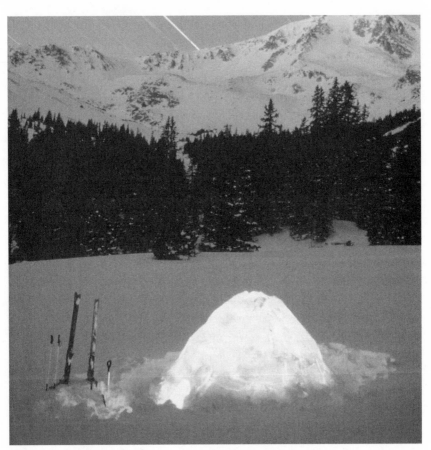

Winter Outward Bound courses present a different set of challenges for students, including developing skills for traveling across snow and ice, and creating shelter from the elements. (Photo © Brian Litz)

between those lessons and the fact that in the ensuing dozen or so years the Outward Bound schools put thousands of students through cold-weather courses without serious mishap.

■   ■   ■

Learning through failure is motivational. The motivation made Alan Hale all the more appreciative of the expert tutelage in winter expedition leadership he got at the Outward Bound School in Norway. This was an auxiliary unit run by the British First Army Corps, with key instructors from the Norwegian military, to give young officers wilderness training. Hale's presence was strictly "non-reg." On the roster he was Lance Corporal Hale, First Tank Battalion, Hertford. As the course expedition was ending, he was cautioned to lie low because an inspection party was at the base to which he was returning. Skiing along a mountain trail on the expedition's final day, he was last in line. Suddenly a group of officers in smart uniforms were skiing past him. The colonel in charge of the inspection group ranged up alongside. "Pretty cold last night, son!" the colonel said. Because it was still cold, Hale had his balaclava, a stocking-like knitted headgear, pulled down to cover most of his face. He gave the colonel the briefest possible glance befitting military courtesy, uttered an overclipped "Yessir!" in his best Hertfordshire accent, and resumed his head-down poling. Back at the base he was the butt of much kidding. The colonel had come in and spoken directly to the commandant: "There's an American on this course!" The commandant did not bat an eye: "No, sir. You must have met Lance Corporal Hale. Born of British parents and brought up in Brooklyn, New York. Terrible accent, sir!"

The Hales ran Minnesota's first winter course out of their lodge at Homeplace in January 1970, with twelve students, Alan and an assistant instructing. The next winter the school scheduled a full offering, January through March, of twenty-three-day "standard" and shorter skills courses. Budgeted for ninety-six students, it drew one hundred twenty-seven. Hale's original course closely followed the Norwegian model. The brigade was issued U.S. Army surplus skis, which were solid and sturdy. Each student carried a Bergen pack—a rucksack on a small metal frame—and the brigade pulled a "pulk." This was a homemade version of a Scandinavian-type snow vehicle—half-sled, half-toboggan, with canvas sides that could be tied to form a cover over the load-designed to function as a supply carrier. While the pulk was a burden—its superiority to the rescue toboggans used on the ill-fated recon-naissance expedition was mainly a matter of degree—its greater attribute was that it freed the students from having to carry everything on their backs and made skiing much easier.

Not all the staff, Hale recalled, was happy with the original scheme. "After Jeff Evans left, my new chief instructor and some of the other instructors, most of whose orientation was to the mountains, wanted to shift to a faster way of going. They used aluminum pack-frames, and they thought it would be better not to take the pulk, which literally was a drag, and carry everything on the back. I said, 'Well, try an experiment for a course or two, and then we'll make a decision.' While the experiment didn't go very well, it was defended because people didn't like the pulk. But many of the students skiing with very heavy packs were falling down so much that they were not learning to ski, and they certainly were not enjoying themselves. What worried me most was the risk. If someone sprains an ankle, what do you do with his pack? So they started taking a very small pulk-like vehicle to carry a few extras. That didn't work well either. They tried homemade sledges on ski runners, and those fell apart. Things were getting ridiculous. I said, 'Let's settle on one method so we can concentrate on process.' So the next winter we went back to pulks—this time we imported the genuine article from Norway—and Norwegian ski stretchers. We used medium-weight touring skis, and packs. Having proper equipment, designed for the purpose, made a world of difference. I felt we finally had something we could take pride in calling an Outward Bound course."

II

The Colorado weather in May 1969 was something to remember. Five feet of snow fell on the mountains and foothills, and the thaw flooded the roads on the Denver plateau. The plan to stage a Manpower Challenge[12] course in the foothills proved impractical, forcing instructor Rick Medrick to improvise in various parts of the mountains. He and his patrol ended up in the San Juans, a range in the southern Rockies, slogging through the deep, soft snow of Uncompahgre Basin. Until each midmorning the going was good. The crust that had refrozen in the night was strong enough to bear the patrol, climbing

---

[12] Manpower Challenge was a course for chronic unemployed persons that was developed by the Colorado School in collaboration with the Adolph Coors Company, the Gates Rubber Company, and the Mountain States Telephone Company, as part of the National Council of Businessmen's program to provide jobs for socially disadvantaged people. Company supervisors took the course along with trainees. For the trainees the objective was to break the syndrome of failure; for the supervisors an opportunity to gain new insights into working with the disadvantaged.

on foot, but by 10 A.M. the crust softened, and the climbers were in snow up to their thighs. Struggling, the Manpower Challenge students, some of them newly out of the penitentiary, gave full range to street vocabularies.

Struggling with them, admiring the more creative maledictions his charges were pronouncing on their objective, Medrick gazed at the upward sweep of virgin snow and wished for skis. High above, the summit of 14,309-foot Uncompahgre Peak offered a worthy expedition objective. A year hence, he promised himself, he would return to lead a ski-mountaineering course in this terrain. The Colorado School, mindful of the avalanche dangers, sub-zero temperatures, high winds, and other hazards, did not yet have a winter course in the mountains. The May environment, with its ameliorated above-snowline temperatures, would provide a useful laboratory.

■ ■ ■

How Rick Medrick came to be at the Colorado School is representative of a good many instructor histories that tell as much about Outward Bound as about the instructor. At Dartmouth, where he followed Alan Hale by one year, Rick was successively president of the Mountaineering and Outing clubs. Winters he spent as much time as he could—even dropping out for a semester—as a ski patrolman at Suicide Six at Woodstock, Vermont, summers as much time as he could climbing in Wyoming's Teton Mountains. Eventually the mountains won; he still lacked graduating credits when at the end of his senior year he left for Jackson Hole to serve as an apprentice Teton guide in Glen Exum's mountaineering school. Subsequently he picked up the credits in the process of moving into a Ph.D. program in philosophy at the University of Colorado in Boulder. He combined his graduate studies with ski instruction and each summer went "home" to the Tetons, moving up in the Exum staff hierarchy.

Somewhere in that time Medrick had his first awareness of Outward Bound, when a fellow guide left to join the staff of the Colorado School. "My impression then," he recalled, "was that this was a militaristic boot-camp type of outfit. In any event, as a professional mountain climber who conceived of the mountains as a sanctuary from society, I couldn't see myself associating with an organization that was using the wilderness for a social process."

Three years into his Ph.D. regimen, he found himself more and more out of tune with a philosophy faculty that had a traditional orientation from which his own intellectual interests increasingly diverged. In that same time he was no longer finding the mountains the haven they had been.

"I guess I had grown as disillusioned with the life of a professional mountain guide and professional ski instructor as I had with a future life as a philosophy professor," he said. "My wife, who was a schoolteacher in Boulder, had been making me conscious of political and social issues that I had lost concern for after my undergraduate days. Looking for a way to give my life new direction, we decided to join the Peace Corps."

The Medricks were the first Americans at a remote secondary school in Kenya that had formerly been run by the British. Making themselves active members of the African community, they had a happy experience there. While Rick had some doubts about the value of the American presence in Africa, he had none at all about the value to himself of his volunteer service. Halfway through his two-year commitment, a Peace Corps green-sheet listing of potential jobs for returning volunteers brought the tidings that his old Teton sidekick, Willi Unsoeld, was now an executive of Outward Bound.

Medrick remembered, "My orientation had shifted enough that I liked Willi's description of what Outward Bound was involved in. Still, I wasn't going to let him off easy. I wrote him, in effect asking what he was doing in this militaristic summer-boot-camp-for-rich-kids type of organization. Willi wrote me back a letter in which he said he had gone through three stages as a climber. First, as a young buck where you had to climb the hardest thing you could find, make your reputation, and develop your craft. There were the 'second-year winners' who flame out the third year and climb no more; you had to get past that and undergo the process of becoming a mature climber. The second stage was where the climber had to look to making a living through his craft, where the process was simply one of exposing people to a mountain experience, and sending them away better off for what you'd done, with you better off for being able to stay in the mountains on the money you had earned. I understood that; that was the way I had felt. Then, Willi said, there came a further stage when you began to look at the mountain as a means of serving social ends. The way he portrayed that to me was that Outward Bound was an opportunity to use the mountains to share the opportunity they had provided us in developing our philosophies. This was so congruent with my own thinking at the time that it was all I needed. I wrote Joe Nold and applied for a job at Colorado a year before I came back."

Medrick reported for duty at Colorado in March 1969. His first course was a contract course, leading a group of students from Mitchell High School in Colorado Springs, where there had been a student riot. His patrol—three African-Americans, two Hispanics, and five whites—included the opposing riot leaders as well as one of the school's most popular athletes and a student council leader. It took place in the Baja, the peninsula on Mexico's Pacific Coast formed by the Gulf of California and the Pacific Ocean. Medrick learned what the Outward Bound process was by letting it happen.

"I had read the literature and been well briefed at Denver, and with my guiding and Peace Corps experience I was at ease leading the group. But since I had no experience with the dynamics of the Outward Bound process, I decided I would not try to structure any of it, as I would have later, but would just let things happen. Those students were at each other's throats a lot of the time. Two of the rival riot leaders had a fistfight over who had taken more peanuts. One day I introduced the trust-fall exercise.[13] It broke the ice in enabling us to explore the feelings in the group. A real neat rapport began to develop, with a grudging appreciation of one another. We had a lot of discussions about problems at the school, why the riot had evolved, students' attitudes toward each other. We developed a very close relationship where I could share the benefit of my experience and they theirs. I remember one of the black students saying, 'Man, I just like to sit and listen to you talk.' It all seemed to fit naturally into the experience, and I came out of the course with some real insights as to what Outward Bound was about."

In May came the Manpower Challenge experience and the resolve to do something about a winter mountain program. The following winter Medrick

[13] In this exercise, often used in Outward Bound to promote a better group feeling, each member successively stands on the edge of a platform several feet off the ground and lets himself fall backward, holding himself rigid and trusting the group to catch him.

planned and promoted a twenty-day ski mountaineering course for the coming May. Eighteen signed up, mostly a mix of high-school and college students and others who had dropped out of college to "ski bum." Two female students made it one of the first coed courses. Two patrols were organized under instructors Harry Friscman and Mike and Carol Lowe, with Medrick as course director.

As the basis for a winter course, Medrick decided to experiment with skiing into high mountain terrain that otherwise would be unapproachable. The students brought their own equipment—downhill skis with bindings that could be adjusted for touring, laced boots, and climbing skins. For most of them it was a first experience with ski touring, climbing skins, climbing ropes, ice axes, and snow camping. Their initial expedition was a strenuous three-day climb from snowline to a plateau at twelve thousand feet. En route they got their first indoctrination in such skills as map reading, knot-tying, avalanche safety, and search and rescue. They slept in tents and cooked on gasoline stoves. On the plateau they dug and lived in snow caves.

The first expedition climaxed with a climb to the summit of Uncompahgre Peak, the students going as high as they could on skis, then roping up to complete the ascent. There was a long downhill run from the plateau back to snowline, on trickily variable snow that sent the skiers pack-over-head-over-skis. Rock climbing and rappelling, another peak excursion, a three-day solo, and a final expedition that included a full-moonlight ascent of 14,048-foot Handies Peak and a bivouac above thirteen thousand feet. Lessons were learned in such forms as sleeping bags soaked by dripping snow caves, a tent burned in consequence of careless stove use, loosely packed bags that rolled away and had to be retrieved from far below in an exhausting descent and climb. In a key respect the experience echoed that of so many courses before; one student put it, "I didn't expect the total involvement with the people I was with. You had to get tight with them to make it."

Medrick reconnoitered in advance throughout the course, creating it as he went, simultaneously thinking ahead to the deep-winter adjustments that would have to be made the following January. At intervals he rejoined one or the other patrol for a safety check; each fresh snowfall was adding to the avalanche danger. Trekking out to make a resupply rendezvous, he brought back fateful tidings. The course coincided with the American invasion of Cambodia and the shootings of students during an antiwar protest at Kent State University in Ohio. In contrast to the normal course, which shuts students off from the "real world," this one was deeply affected by events outside it. "A dialogue had been evolving throughout the course," Medrick remembers. "Everything seemed to come together the day before it ended, when we all sat down for an afternoon and tried to get a grasp of what had happened 'outside' and what our own experience had been worth. There was a strong feeling of its being a unique, special time, and of having been 'out of time' for a short period and having felt the idea that if people can get together like this in this environment, why isn't it possible to carry it back in some way into other communities? For me, anyway, the course became in microcosm the whole concept of using an Outward Bound experience as a means for people to explore values and their commitment to involvement with the processes of society. And on the program side it opened up a new horizon of possibilities for the school."

Colorado offered its first true winter ski-mountaineering course in January 1971. While incorporating the lessons of the previous May, its design had to accommodate the much more severe seasonal elements of a Rocky Mountain midwinter—notably, temperatures of as much as forty to fifty degrees below zero and the corresponding wind-chill factors. It was necessary to set up emergency-stocked cabins that could be heated and serve as refuge during the high mountain storms. The cabins also came to provide occasional overnight stopping places where a patrol could come together for an evening's conversation, furthering the group dynamics that function more slowly in the winter courses. The course was repeated in April. The next year it was offered each month from January through April.

The Northwest School likewise started winter-mountaineering courses in the Cascade Range in 1971; it now also offers a ski-touring program in the lovely Wallowa Mountain country of northeast Oregon that was once the habitat of Chief Joseph and his Nez Perce Indians. As noted, the Dartmouth Outward Bound Center started cold-weather courses as early as 1969. North Carolina, which actually had pioneered winter operation with a special course for Jewel Box managers in 1968, initiated regular winter courses in

1972. In that winter the Hurricane Island School conducted a special course in north-central Maine for students from Lincoln-Sudbury High School (Massachusetts). A year later Hurricane opened a winter mountaineering program to the public, confirming its new amphibious status. Presently all the schools run courses of varying lengths.

The advent of winter courses was a significant advance in U.S. Outward Bound's growth. On one score it was the beginning of year-round operation. On another, it introduced to the curriculum one of the most formidable of nature's challenges—deep cold. Will Lange spoke to this in his director's report on the Dartmouth Center's first courses. "In conclusion I would say that the cold was essential to the program. It required everyone to think constantly about his physical welfare; it kept everyone under a constant stress and brought human qualities out into sharp focus; and merely surviving, let alone being creative, under these conditions gave all the students a real sense of accomplishment."

But this gets ahead of the Dartmouth story, which is coming up.

THE DARTMOUTH CENTER

�֍

*Be not content with the commonplace in character any
more than with the commonplace in ambition or intellectual attainment. Do not expect that you will make any
lasting or very strong impression on the world through
intellectual power without the use of an equal amount of
conscience and heart.*

—William Jewett Tucker, ninth president of Dartmouth College

A faculty colleague at Phillips Academy who became deeply interested in
U.S. Outward Bound during the movement's early years was Charles
"Doc" Dey, a Dartmouth alumnus, class of '52. Charley was among the first to
conceive that important learning potential lay in finding ways to integrate the
Outward Bound philosophy and method into academic environments. When
he left Andover to join the Dartmouth administrative staff, he had in mind
the idea of establishing a liaison between Dartmouth and Outward Bound.

In 1966 Dey was appointed dean of the William Jewett Tucker
Foundation, an independent endowment within the college charged by the
trustees with furthering the moral and spiritual work of the Dartmouth
community.[14] Among its activities were a number of program vehicles, such as
off-campus internships, enabling undergraduates to translate their social
concerns into constructive action while also learning. Reflecting on new paths

---

[14] Dey was appointed president of the Choate School and Rosemary Hall in 1973.

the Tucker Foundation might take under his leadership, Charley perceived Outward Bound as one appropriate vehicle. He came to Andover for a meeting with Bob Bates and me. At that time Secretary of Defense Robert McNamara's proposal to broaden, so as to include nonmilitary activity, the kinds of service that would qualify for national selective service was getting serious consideration from a presidential advisory committee. Charley's initial idea was for an Outward Bound school under the wing of the Tucker Foundation that would train instructors for service programs.

Dey remembered: "There were a variety of ways in which we were working with Dartmouth students to help them confront some of the tougher issues of life, thereby to reach beyond themselves in service to others. I believe that's an important experience as part of a liberal education. The purpose of a higher education is not simply to take courses and amass information and worry about yourself. Outward Bound seemed to be one vehicle through which a college student, at a highly egocentric point in his career, could be put in a situation where he had to give himself to others."

In this aspiration Dey had the support of Dartmouth's then president, John Sloan Dickey, a strong believer in the educational potential of the out-of-doors. For our part at OBI, we saw a means of strengthening our ties to the educational community and implementing both our own internal training needs and our commitment to the service ethic.

As it happened, the nation's deepening involvement in the war in Vietnam precluded any liberalization of the selective service law. It took another two years for Dartmouth, working with the New Hampshire Department of Education, to arrive at a plan giving the college a satisfactory service rationale for a campus-associated Outward Bound activity, and OBI a sound basis for issuing a charter. Under the plan, undergraduates would be offered Outward Bound instructor training with related academic study, followed by an opportunity to conduct a course for New Hampshire secondary-school students. In developing the plan Dey had a staunch faculty ally in a sociology professor, Wentworth Eldredge, a longtime adherent of Hahn's ideas who was one of OBI's original trustees.

The Dartmouth Outward Bound Center was formally chartered as a component of the Tucker Foundation early in 1969. The idea of a chartered "center" as differentiated from a "school" was a concept that evolved in response to a need we saw in the Dartmouth situation and that might well arise again. There was a logical possibility that an educational or other nonprofit institution operating under a trustee governance for its own purposes could simultaneously advance those purposes and the Outward Bound cause by offering sanctioned courses and consulting services. For such a special kind of school within an independent institution or agency, we hit on the center designation.

Thanks to Peter Willauer's interest, the Dartmouth Center was activated *de facto* under the cooperative umbrella of the Hurricane Outward Bound School ahead of the formal chartering, when Will Lange, a Hurricane staff member, came on campus as director in the fall of 1968. A graduate of Wooster College in Ohio, Lange had been a high-school teacher in the Adirondack region of upstate New York. One day in 1964 he happened on a feature article on the Colorado School in a back issue of *Life* magazine.[15] It was the first he had heard of Outward Bound. He promptly wrote to ask how he could get an instructor's job. I referred him to the school directors, and Willauer hired him. At Hurricane he developed into one of the school's top instructors.

D-1-I (Dartmouth instructors' course number one) began in January 1969 with an enrollment of six Dartmouth undergraduates and one graduate. The students were required to carry two regular academic courses, making special relevance arrangements with their professors. The Outward Bound activities, along with lectures, seminars, and required papers, earned the students credits as a third course, designated Education 41.[16] The first week, based at the college-owned lodge on Mount Moosilauke, was given to basic skills training and indoctrination in Outward Bound philosophy and method.

On the third day the group set out on a winter training expedition that proved a remarkable echo of the Minnesota group's debacle on the Kekekabic Trail just a fortnight before. The plan was to climb Moosilauke's eastern slope, spend the night in the summit cabin, descend the western side of the mountain to a Dartmouth Outing Club cabin on the second day, and circle

[15] "Marshmallow Becomes a Man," *Life*, August 7, 1964.
[16] Dartmouth's academic year then consisted of three three-course terms twelve weeks in length. The college now operates year-round, offering four terms ten weeks in length.

back to the lodge on the third. Nature had other plans, Lange remembered. "We had not anticipated that breaking trail would be such tough going. The new snow was so deep and light that our snowshoes sank more than a foot with each step. Several times somebody disappeared completely when he stepped on a buried treetop arching over an air pocket. Our climbing rate was half a mile an hour, and we did not reach the summit until four o'clock. Above the tree line, fog was creating a virtual whiteout. If you let the nearest person get twenty feet away from you, you could no longer see him. In that white soup we could not find the summit cabin. We were losing our bearings, and it began to get dark and colder. The footing was extremely icy, and we were having the utmost difficulty in keeping the group together.

"We headed back down the summit cone. By the time we reached the tree line it was dark, and we called a bivouac. Using snowshoes for shovels, we dug a two-level shelf about seven by twenty feet, laid our ponchos out over the dug area, and climbed into our sleeping bags. Since the trees and under-brush were coated with ice, there was no fuel for a fire. We started the Svea stove and cooked up a concoction of cocoa, coffee, sugar, dried soup, Coffee-mate, and sour balls. Tinctured as it was with burnt sugar, the mixture was extremely tasty. At least, it took the edge off the chill. We slept well, except for calls of nature. For breakfast we had another portion of the previous evening's menu. We packed and retreated down the mountain by a route made very difficult by the deep snow. Back at the lodge a day ahead of schedule, we licked our wounds and held a highly educational debriefing."

Lange found the experience fortuitous. "In a few hours, early in the course, all the instructors were indelibly impressed with the lesson that somehow and sooner or later they had to learn—of how subtly deadly the winter wilderness environment can be for the unwary or the unprepared. Even Paul Ross, our British-trained rock-climbing specialist and a fine mountaineer with alpine experience, gained new respect for the New Hampshire mountains."

After ten days in Hanover to get a good leg up on their academic work, the students traveled north to the Dartmouth College Grant, a forest area close to the Canadian border classified by the U.S. Air Force as subarctic, for their second period of wilderness training. Back on campus for another academic period, the students also kept up the morning run, did drownproofing in the college pool each day, compiled an instructors' manual, and prepared for the advent of the high-school students enrolled in D-1, the course they would now instruct under the supervision of the center staff.

The D-1 students, thirty-one youngsters from high schools throughout the state, were put through a twenty-two-day winter course. They seemed a good deal more content after they moved from the Moosilauke lodge training base, with its compromising comforts, to living outdoors at the College Grant in two-man tents or snow caves. They were miserable, they said, but were they not there to discover themselves through hardship? The cold ranged from twenty degrees below zero to thirty-five above, with three to ten feet of snow. Despite the cold, or perhaps because of it, the solo proved a surprisingly positive experience, as it had for the undergraduates who were now their instructors. Any staff concern that the high-school youngsters might not have had an authentic Outward Bound experience was dispelled by a reading of their course impressions. They felt they had been tested as never before, physically, emotionally, and morally. Their enthusiastic endorsement of their experience on returning to their schools helped to recruit students for future courses.

The wilderness phases of D-2-I, the second instructors' course, took place entirely in the still snow-mantled College Grant. In the concluding phase the undergraduates sailed and rowed two pulling boats from Boston to Hurricane Island, where they became assistant instructors in Hurricane's May course.

Starting that summer the Dartmouth Center offered thirty-day courses for teachers that helped to pioneer a three-pronged development in the national movement: teachers' practica, adult courses, and coeducational courses. "In terms of affecting the human condition we were highly successful with the teachers in our summer courses," Lange reflected. "Whether or not they went back to start their own outdoor projects, as some did, almost all reported themselves to be different *people* as teachers—not hiding behind the book or the assignment, relating to their students much more as human beings, having a much greater sense of caring and feeling about their work."

Lange's second-year staff consisted of Perry Gates, another fine instructor who had come with him from Hurricane Island; Mike Stratton, a D-2-I student who had graduated in June; and, unofficially, Will's wife Ida. The center had a strong "pop and mom" aspect in the early days. While primarily

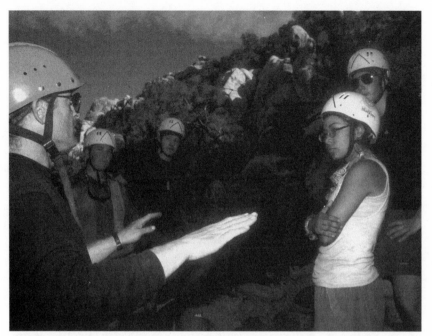

Easing the concerns of his Outward Bound students, a rock climbing instructor outlines the day's lessons as first light touches the surrounding peaks. (Photo © PCOBS, Kim Budd)

a response to low-budget imperatives, this was also thanks to the fact that from the time the Langes first went to Hurricane Island, Ida had responded affirmatively to the Outward Bound environment. That is not always easy for an instructor's wife. Ida's recollection of the family's summers at Hurricane Island points up the problems of women married to Outward Bound instructors. "It's a difficult existence, especially for a young woman with two or three children. She does not feel her husband is her husband—he's there but he's not. When he's not off on an expedition, she may see him across the island, but he may run right by her with a bunch of students and not even say, 'Hi!' She may see him in the mess hall with his Outward Bound kids, but she's the one who has to make their three kids behave. And he comes home to their tent and says, 'Hello,' and collapses; when he is there, there's nothing left of him. You both have to face the fact that his first priority is his students. If he comes back at night, and the two of you are having an important talk, and a student comes knocking on the door and says, 'I'm going home,' your husband forsakes you and goes off with the youngster for a heart-to-heart talk. The best way to lick it is somehow to join it, to take on some volunteer helping task that makes you part of the school. If you as a wife lose your identity, it's bad. If you look on it as finding another corner of your identity, and become involved in it, you're okay."

In its second year the center's undergraduate program was getting marks as a successful experiment. An imprimatur was placed on it when the Dartmouth faculty of arts and sciences accepted a refinement and elaboration called the Outward Bound Term, which became part of the college curriculum in the 1970–1971 year. The term had six segments: a preliminary reading period; a standard three-week Outward Bound course (also open to students from other colleges) with added seminar components; an intensive three-week academic period; the Outward Bound course for secondary-school students under undergraduate leadership; a critique and evaluation period; and the writing of a major paper. Partly because of the highly interdisciplinary character of the academic components, but presumably also due to gingerly handling of the question of credits for the experiential innovations that were a central feature of the term, students successfully completing the requirements received the equivalent of full credit in the form of a three-course reduction in the degree requirement, from thirty-six to thirty-three, in Dartmouth's twelve-term, three-course system.

The term earned the center a significant feedback in the form of recognition by faculty members of the educational value of an Outward Bound experience. For some this was the result of participation, for others of perception of effect on students. English Professor Robert Siegel became aware of Outward Bound when a student turned in a short novel after completing a Dartmouth Center course.

"It was a fictional analysis of the self along the lines of Dostoyevsky's *Notes from the Underground,*" Professor Siegel reported. "It vividly evoked the intensity of an individual's feeling on facing the cold and the group and then finding himself in relation to the group. The pressure of the experience gave the piece an arresting authenticity. It was clear to me that this man's Outward Bound experience had driven him to a brilliant depth of introspection that I feel sure will have carryover impact on his life and what he does with it."

Professor George Theriault, Lincoln Filene Professor of Human Relations in the sociology department, was among the first to perceive the center's value as an academic resource and to employ it for exposing students in his courses to appropriate experiences. In retirement he remained an enthusiast, saying, "I believe strongly that the most effective way to teach is to combine a student's experience, either through natural or contrived situations, with what he's trying to learn."

■ ■ ■

In 1970 Lange asked Robert MacArthur, a former curate of his church, to join his staff. A member of Dartmouth's class of '64, Bob had pitched varsity baseball on a championship team, sung in the glee club, been active in the Episcopal student association, belonged to a prestigious fraternity, and been one of a handful in his class elected to Casque and Gauntlet, a senior society. Three years later he graduated cum laude from Berkeley Divinity School (now part of Yale Divinity). Having enjoyed a success-oriented youth, he reacted all the more keenly to the career and personal difficulties he encountered after leaving divinity school. He accepted a job offer from the rector of St. Thomas's Church in Hanover, New Hampshire, involving work in the hospital, the college, and the parish. The two years he spent there, a time of rising tension in the college community over the war in Vietnam, proved a hard period for him—"although very rich in retrospect"—as Bob recalled: "I became aware of how difficult it can be to reconcile a prophetic ministry—in the sense of the role of the prophets in both Testaments calling people back to the right path—and a pastoral ministry, in which the clergyman stands with people throughout the personal crises of life. In order to stand with people, you can't stand over or against them. It's very difficult to balance those two callings, particularly when you're young and just out of the seminary.

"I believed we were wrong to be in Vietnam, conducting the war the way we were, and I felt strongly that part of the Christian witness was to proclaim this. My conflict was symbolized by the commandant of the Navy ROTC unit at the college, who was a parishioner. His daughter was a pillar of the youth group, and his father had recently died, a sadness which brought me quite close to the family. He invited my wife, Peggy, and me to sit in the reviewing stand at the ROTC commencement. It was a painful dilemma, since I was active with both the student and faculty groups who were trying to protest the war, and they were planning anti-ROTC demonstrations at the exercises. Peg sat with the family to acknowledge our relationship with them while I ended up going to a corner of the field by myself, unable to associate totally with either viewpoint and feeling very frustrated. The incident focused my feeling that at that point in my life I was not prepared to deal with the conflicts and ambiguities of the parochial ministry in relation to the war."

Because he was interested in community life, Bob took a job at a folk school in the mountain country of southwest North Carolina. The school was a three-hundred-sixty-acre farm community based on the model of the nineteenth-century Danish folk-school movement, with the purpose of revitalizing the Southern mountain population. Bob remembers it as a time of ironic crosscurrents: "You had college people from the East coming back to the land, while the indigenous people were reaching out to the more urbanized life that the college people were rejecting. Unfortunately, from my point of view, the folk-school people were not serving the indigenous population. I became rather critical of the leadership and was fired after eight months."

Aware of Bob's skills with people and learning of his availability, Lange offered to make him his assistant at the center. Bob took the post with little more knowledge of Outward Bound than what he knew from his wife, who as secretary for the Tucker Foundation had been a part-time secretary to the Outward Bound Center. "Peggy used to come home from her work with much amusement and strange tales of this crazy bunch of people who were pursuing the grail in their own way. Outward Bound seemed to bring together my athletic interests and my enjoyment of the outdoors in a new way, and I was intrigued by that. As for its place in the Tucker Foundation, I saw it as another arena for encouraging the capacity of individuals to examine their resources and improve their ability to relate to other people within a compassionate framework."

Realizing that the first thing he had to do was take an Outward Bound course himself, MacArthur signed up for a teachers' practicum at Colorado in the summer of 1970. The experience had a bad start. "I was in a low state of self-esteem, having just been fired, which was my first failure experience of any magnitude. The course director happened to be the skipper on my raft on our trip down the Green River. While we were preparing the rafts, I got into conversation with him. When he found out I was a minister, he told me bluntly that in his mind a minister was the lowest form of male human being. He was chagrined that I would be working with Outward Bound. I'm sure that my performance reenforced his stereotype of me. I'd never been on a river before, and he put a lot of pressure on me when it was my turn to captain the raft. We locked horns repeatedly throughout the course. On one occasion he told me he got bad vibrations from me, which was a big putdown in front of the group. I was then very susceptible to the mystique of the elite Outward Bound instructor—the image he portrayed of the fit, strong, keen, resourceful individual. Because I had no credentials of merit to offer, I had little skill with which to counter his judgmental criticism. I have since learned that he was not a representative course director in the eyes of his peers at Colorado, and I realize now that he had his own insecurities. I can look back on what happened with more humor, but at the time it was a shattering experience. Yet on the whole the course was a positive experience for me. Which says something for Outward Bound. I think there's something organic in those basic activities and in the structure of the course that enables the individual to grow in ways he needs to."

Two years later MacArthur came off a course he had led at North Carolina to learn he had been selected as the new director of the Dartmouth Outward Bound Center. The appointment came at a time of major change for the college, which in turn called for transition within the center. That year Dartmouth went coeducational; simultaneously it initiated the "Dartmouth Plan," a scheme for operating the college year-round. MacArthur's first response to a coeducational student body was to bring Sharon Goodyear, a highly regarded instructor at the North Carolina School, to Hanover as Outward Bound's first female program director.

The Dartmouth Plan presented a major problem, in that it rendered the Outward Bound Term academically unviable. Since the plan reduced the degree requirements for all students from thirty-six to thirty-three credits, it was no longer feasible to employ the negative credit device. A year's modus operandi was afforded by the Education Department's offering of three course credits for a term that linked the Outward Bound phase of the old plan to a high-school teaching-counseling internship. Meanwhile MacArthur, charged by his Tucker Foundation superiors to build more bridges between the center and the academic community, developed two programs that have proved the strong core of his directorship, the Outward Bound Laboratories and the Living-Learning Term.

■ ■ ■

The laboratory idea was based on the Outward Bound method of involving people in initiative-demanding situations that generate strong learning experiences. MacArthur invited the faculty to use this competence as an experiential resource to assist their teaching. As a consequence of that invitation, groups of Dartmouth students found themselves in an extraordinary assortment of environments not normally thought of as ancillary to classroom endeavor. The environment may be a strange woods a hundred miles from Hanover. ("You have been dropped behind the enemy lines without food. Do not engage strangers in conversation, use roads, or trespass on private property.") It may be rowing all night in a pulling boat, or bunking down in the cell of a maximum security prison, or using a subway train as a traveling base from which to carry out a scavenger hunt. Individuals who until now have only known each other as fellow students across a classroom aisle may be called on to take up communal residence in a tree for two days and nights. Or a group may be led blindfolded into the pitch blackness of an elaborate World War II bomb shelter and left to organize themselves into a resourceful and cooperative community for the next forty-four hours.

Professor G. Christian Jernstedt of the psychology department was among the faculty members who used the center extensively. He incorporated an optional series of three Outward Bound weekend laboratories in his highly popular Psychology 22 course on Learning. "Outward Bound and Psychology 22 have a number of critical similarities," Chris Jernstedt told his students. "Both are concerned with one's understanding of the behavior-change process in oneself, both provide one with experiences that will carry one beyond the limits of the course, both encourage one's personal freedom and responsibility in a directed educational venture, and both involve a period of intensive individual learning."

The Psych 22 laboratories provided a slice-of-life resource that otherwise had to be obtained by secondary means. Since the course required some kind of real-life situation to which the students could apply the learning principles it elucidated, the normal method was to use a novel, such as John Steinbeck's *The Grapes of Wrath* or Joseph Wambaugh's *The New Centurions*. Those who signed up for the laboratories could use their Outward Bound experiences instead. "It makes the course more work— they have to give those weekends, as well as lose several days of other classes," Jernstedt pointed out. "But it's such a rich experience that there is always a considerable number who want to do it. Their papers are better than those that deal with the novel because they're writing of something they feel strongly about."

The scheme was symbiotic. The students examined the philosophy and techniques of learning presented in the course in the light of their laboratory experiences, and examined the individual and group learning that occurred in these experiences in light of what they learned from their reading assignments and in the classroom. The first two laboratories of the course were typically an overnight ropes course and rock-climbing experience and a three-and-a-half-day pulling-boat expedition out of Hurricane Island. The third varied from year to year, the objective being to place the group in a context different from any they had known up to then and to break up the group patterns formed in the first two experiences. One of the most successful was a weekend so structured that the group was chronically stressed by change. The participants were divided into two crews who made separate planning decisions based on different information; then half of each crew was switched. Reunited in the bomb shelter and having organized themselves on the assumption they were in for a long stay, they were blindfolded and whisked away. Two hours later, in their windowless vans, given fifteen seconds' notice to select whatever they wished to take with them, they were deposited in Harvard Square in Cambridge with a new set of instructions. Each time they became set to cope with a new environment and new rules, the environment and rules were shifted.

After learning teamwork, leadership, compassion, and social and environmental responsibility, students head home traversing California's Joshua Tree National Park. (Photo © PCOBS, Kim Budd)

"They really enjoyed the experience," Jernstedt said. "It opened up a lot of questions for them about what kinds of skills you bring to new situations, and how you can prepare yourself; about leadership, and how to make decisions. They voted on a lot of things, and they didn't like that; it was inefficient. And they were stressed, which was part of the purpose. When they came to write, they had a lot to write about. All sorts of good issues had been created that they could discuss in their papers."

The center has serviced courses in sociology, psychology, geography, government, education, environmental studies, economics, and a graduate-level course at Dartmouth's Tuck School of Business Administration. When Tuck School Professor Roy Lewicki incorporated a long weekend's pulling-boat experience into his sensitivity training "Seminar in Interpersonal Behavior," he found it an effective way to enable the class to "dominantly focus on individual and group *behavior*, rather than the *discussion* of *behavior*." The center also devised and serviced therapy elements for treating patients at the Dartmouth-Hitchcock Mental Health Center and provided team-building exercises for the Mental Health Center's staff.

■ ■ ■

A Hurricane Island conversation between Professor Lewicki and MacArthur produced the skeletal idea for the center's Living-Learning Term, an experience in community life that integrated wilderness activities, academic endeavor, cooperative living, and community service. Launched in the spring of 1974, then offered year-round, the Living-Learning Term was conceived in part as a vehicle for bringing to on-campus life some of the values that students derived from Tucker Foundation off-campus internships. In the Tucker model, MacArthur explained, off-campus situations gave rise to an intensity of experience through people working together as a team, with valuable by-products gained from the cooperative activity. In the Living-Learning Term the center developed an intense on-campus program combining the unity-of-participants, common task, and group living features of an off-campus program with elements of an Outward Bound course, while integrating academic life more fully with residential life.

Each term, ten to twelve students—preferably an equal number of men and women—shared a residence that they operated cooperatively, including food budgeting and purchase, cooking, and household chores. In addition to the two academic courses they selected individually, the students took one course together, as a common intellectual task and to make for interaction with faculty outside the classroom. An Outward Bound instructor lived in the residence as counselor and energizer. The residents held periodic group sessions for purposes of communication and planning, interpersonal feedback, and self-examination of the ways a group develops and functions. This residential and academic regimen was intertwined with wilderness and service activity.

The Living-Learning Term began with an Outward Bound wilderness experience in the ten days preceding the opening of the college term. This usually turned out to be a good way for a dozen strangers who would be living together for a fairly stressful ten weeks to initiate their family arrangement.

"From the start there was a nice attitude of helping those who weren't as strong," instructor Knox Johnstone said about the expedition, which had kicked off the winter term for which he was then counselor-in-residence. It had been a ski-and-snowshoe trek that peaked in a final night sleeping in the fire tower atop Mount Cardigan. "With a little bit of luck, when you take people on a nice adventure like that, you give them a real common denominator to build their living experience on." During the term there were two additional wilderness elements, a three-day-and-night solo, and a four-day final expedition that the students planned and carried out on their own. Thus the term was in part an extended Outward Bound course, but in a context much different from the standard experience.

The Term House was one of several campus-living experiments that the Dartmouth administration observed with interest in its ongoing quest for advantageous alternatives to traditional dormitory living. Peter Bryant, the center's program director and one who has had the residence "duty" a number of times, considered the return on the term's communal living to be a major value. "I am sure that along with the Outward Bound challenges, virtually all of our Living-Learning alumni would award top marks to the term for having given them a sense of place, of living in a family kind of atmosphere that allowed them to express needs they somehow put away when they go into a dormitory. Those who go back to a dormitory talk especially about this."

The service project—normally some form of assistance to children, or elderly or handicapped persons, or adolescents who had been in trouble with the law—was another important element. The students were usually involved in a commitment—building a children's playground, for example—that was part of a community project administered by the Dartmouth-Hitchcock Mental Health Center.[17] In Bryant's view, a significant aspect of the service project was that it gave participants an opportunity, rare for college students, to test their values. "It's easy in a college setting for students to be theoretical about the values they feel they have. When the Living-Learning students go into communities in the Mascoma Valley, which is a federally designated poverty area, and are called on to relate to economically deprived families in an open, under-

---

[17] The Dartmouth-Hitchcock Mental Health Center is a joint operation of the Dartmouth Medical School and the Mary Hitchcock Memorial Hospital.

standing way, they have a chance to find out if they are up to doing what until now they've just idealized themselves as doing."

The Outward Bound Center's association with the Dartmouth-Hitchcock Mental Health Center grew in a progression of successively more ambitious undertakings. Expansion of their joint activities began in 1975 when Bryant and Robert "Sparky" Millikin of Outward Bound, Kristi Kistler, director of activities therapy at the mental health center, and Dr. Gary Tucker, director of psychiatric residents at the medical school, undertook a five-week experimental therapeutic project with seven disturbed adolescents and young adults. Not least of the reasons the mental health staff were pleased with the results was that the patients themselves—who had been given to feel the activity was a chance to do something "normal" rather than a form of treatment—felt they had had a successful experience.

Following this encouraging start, a regular weekly schedule of activity with inpatients at the mental health center was established. In 1977 the Van Amerigen Foundation made a grant to underwrite a substantial enlarging of the program, support evaluation and research, and provide a coordinator and research assistant. For the coordinator post the college tapped Tom Stich, director of the Wilderness Program of the Forensic Treatment System in the New Mexico Department of Hospitals and Institutions. Stich had originally gone to that post in a consultant capacity when Colorado Outward Bound was engaged to help the New Mexico agency set up a wilderness program for prisoners, including the emotionally disturbed. In his first year at Hanover, in addition to expanding the inpatient activity, Stich initiated a comparable program at the Veterans Administration Hospital in White River Junction, Vermont, where the psychiatric unit was affiliated with the Dartmouth Medical School's Department of Psychiatry and some of the staff were members of its faculty.

The Dartmouth Center expanded its public course offerings to virtually a year-round operation. These included two courses in the development of which the center played a pioneering role. One is a cycling version of the standard course. The other is the Adult Leadership Program (ALP), a course the center first conducted in 1975 for adults who were primarily interested in adapting Outward Bound to their schools or agencies. In 1981 Dartmouth initiated two three-month semester programs, one of them jointly with the Minnesota and the North Carolina Schools.

HAZARD AND ADVENTURE

�֍

*Out of this nettle, danger, we pluck this
flower, safety.*

—Henry IV, Part II

A powerful Outward Bound tradition of intelligent respect for hazard and the responsibilities it places derives directly from the founder. In his book *Impelled into Experiences*, Jim Hogan, first warden of Aberdovey, the first Outward Bound school, related how Kurt Hahn constantly insisted it was Hogan's duty to understand all the factors affecting safety. "Certainly," he wrote, "the early operations at Aberdovey gave ample material for concern, and there were periods when Hahn telephoned hourly for news of our adventures," and then:

> *There is no doubt that the Outward Bound schools could not conceivably have established themselves with their remarkable record of freedom from accidents had it not been for Hahn's almost obsessive concern that there should be no trace of carelessness or recklessness in our affairs.*

At the time of our first fatality in U.S. Outward Bound, I wrote Hahn the sad tidings. In reply he urged us to spare no effort in seeking the accident's cause, making good use of impartial experts. He suggested that we share our findings with all kindred institutions in order to pool knowledge and prevent similar tragedies. And he bade us to carry on, keeping in mind that two enemies of Outward Bound are "the safety-firsters and the toughness worshipers."

■ ■ ■

The morning of July 23, 1978, was clear and warm in the northwest North Carolina mountain country. The twelve members of Number Two crew of NC-118, with instructor Aram Attarian and assistant Virginia "Ginny" Davis, were on the final day of their main expedition, day eleven of the standard twenty-three-day course. They spent the morning bushwhacking up the north side of Bandy Cove Mountain to a roadway, where they stopped for lunch. The weather was changing. Sensing that a storm was brewing, the instructors took the occasion to brief the crew on the lightning hazard.

There are several things that everybody ought to know about lightning. Two of them are cardinal rules—one for avoiding injury, the other for treating injury if it happens. The first is to get away from mountain summits and peaks, as well as from open rock faces and high rock outcroppings wherever they may be. Seek protection on low, flat ground or in shallow declivities. In the woods, don't stand under tall, isolated trees; take shelter instead under thickets of shorter trees. A deep cave or overhang gives excellent protection, but a shallow cave does not, nor do narrow ledges or stream gullies, because of the danger from ground currents generated by nearby lightning strikes. When someone is hit by lightning, the cardinal rule for treatment is not to assume that the victim is dead because no breathing or heartbeat can be detected. Quite commonly the victim suffers from arrest of breathing, and often from heart arrest, as well as burns and involuntary muscle contractions. Breathing can be revived by the swift application of mouth-to-mouth resuscitation. If the heart has stopped CPR should be employed.

All this was part of the briefing to Number Two crew. Twenty minutes after they resumed their trek a hard rain began, and crew and instructors stopped to put on rain gear. Having donned theirs, Aram and Ginny waited, seated on their packs about thirty feet from the students. By now there were lightning flashes—coming closer, Aram noted. The students too were checking the time between strikes and how long it was taking for the sound of thunder to reach them. They had just counted a strike two seconds (about two-fifths of a mile) away when a ground current[18] from yet another strike hit the group. Afterward, crew members reported a blue flash, a bright flash, smoke, a booming sound, and seeing Aram and Ginny thrown to the ground. Four students likewise were knocked down, but not hurt. Another was "jerked and jolted" and a sixth felt a "tingling sensation." The others experienced no sensation from the lightning.

When the students reached Aram and Ginny, neither was breathing, and Ginny was unconscious; both had heartbeats. Crew members, who had been well coached in first aid by their instructors at the start of the course, immediately started mouth-to-mouth resuscitation. After twenty to thirty ventilations, both instructors began to breathe. The students treated Aram for shock and second-degree burns on the lower right leg and foot. Treating Ginny for shock, they monitored her closely.

Help was summoned from the North Carolina School's base camp and the Burke County Rescue Squad, and the injured pair were transported to the hospital at Morganton, where they were treated and admitted. Ginny, still only semiconscious, complained of severe pain in her lower back. Aram was discharged three days later and returned to his crew on July 29, day sixteen of the course. Ginny was discharged three days after Aram and returned to the crew on August 1.

As is the practice in Outward Bound, the accident was written up by program director Mike Fischesser, and the report was circulated to the other schools for their information and guidance. It was noted that a supplement to the instructor field manual dealing more thoroughly with lightning was being distributed to the staff, and that future staff training would amplify coverage of the lightning hazard. Also, because the school and rescue squad had lost

---

[18] As the North Carolina *Instructor's Field Manual* notes, "The current which flows in a lightning bolt does not dissipate itself at the point of direct hit; it tends to flow along the easiest paths of electric conduction on the surface of the earth. These may include wet, lichen-covered rock, cracks and crevices filled with water, natural fissures and chimneys, wet ropes, cables and the like along the ground, and 'spark gap' areas [when the ground current takes a short straight path through the air, rather than a longer path around through the ground]." Investigators from the North Carolina School found no physical evidence of a direct lightning hit in the accident area. The type of discharge that struck Aram and Ginny remains a mystery.

time in locating the victims due to incorrect information, a telephone report form had been designed to minimize similar confusions in the future. Among Fischesser's comments on the accident and its outcome was this: "It shows that in-depth first aid instruction reduces the odds for serious injury or fatality when taught at the earliest time during a program." To which Director John Huie appended: "Training works; preparation matters. People acting wisely can make a difference."

This was an accident with a happy ending. Accidents frequently do not have happy endings, and Outward Bound has had its share with truly tragic consequences. We related this particular incident because it dramatically points up the primary concern for the safety of students and instructors in the conduct of an Outward Bound course. A great deal of instructor training relates to accident prevention and to rescue technique. Instructors are taught that an integral factor in their relationship to the cadre is the setting and maintaining of a tone of concern for safe performance. In the first week, students receive a basic grounding in first aid, and throughout the course they are briefed on how to protect themselves and their fellows.

In U.S. Outward Bound's first nine years of operation the mysterious drowning of Dan Lucas in 1964 was the single student fatality. Even though marred by that still unexplained tragedy, and by two equally tragic instructor deaths,[19] this record reflected the diligent efforts of the schools to conduct their courses as safely as possible. Then in the summer of 1971, with calamity's brutal suddenness, fatal accidents occurred at two schools. First a male student, Walter Kennedy, drowned at Minnesota, in circumstances as strange in their way as those surrounding Dan Lucas's death. (Starting on his one-mile swimming test, young Kennedy dove into the lake water and raced away from shore while the accompanying canoe was being launched. Within a short distance he was in serious trouble and disappeared suddenly, just as the canoe caught up with him. If the students in the canoe had not been wearing life preservers, they might have been able to dive for Kennedy in a second or two while he was sinking.)

[19] In 1965 Lew Covert, a Colorado instructor, was killed on a peak ascent when struck by a falling rock. In 1969 Colin Henderson, a British instructor on the staff of the Colorado School, drowned in the Green River while on instructor training.

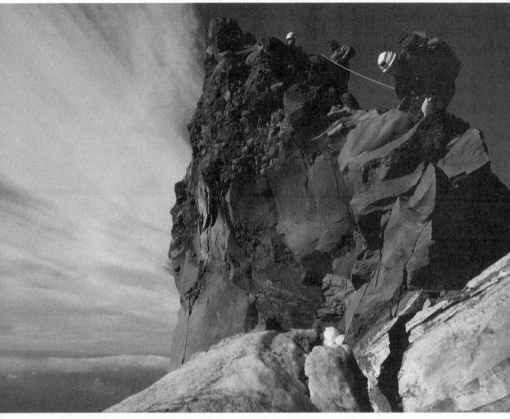

An ascending student reaches the top of Mount Adams via the White Salmon route during an Outward Bound mountaineering course. (Photo © Cobi Harris)

A short time later three young women on their final expedition at the Northwest School were caught in severe, prolonged storm and low-tempera-ture conditions. When the group failed to seek adequate protection away from an exposed slope above timberline, two of them, Joyce Howden and Lorene LaRhette, died of hypothermia (exposure).

Altogether, in the nineteen years through 1980, thirteen students lost their lives in eight fatal occurrences in U.S. Outward Bound schools. It would be a mistake, however, to conclude from the chronology of these occurrences that Outward Bound courses grew more hazardous with time; if anything, the opposite was true. The fact that most of them occurred in the 1971–1978 period reflects the great increase in the exposure factor as the number of students grew from a 1962 enrollment of 100 to nearly 3,800 in 1970 and around 8,000 in 1979. The exposure figures indicated a student was safer, statistically, on an Outward Bound Course in the wilderness than in a motor vehicle on a public highway. No comfort, however, is to be drawn there. No statistics can minister to the heartsickness of all those touched by the tragedy of a life lost.

The irony of virtually all adventure-oriented accidents is that they could have been prevented without diminishing the adventure. Safety, in fact, is essential to the adventurous experience; this is apparent enough when a disabling accident puts an end to participation. Reviewing the record of all Outward Bound deaths—ten drownings, three falling-rock mishaps, two cases of hypothermia—what strikes one most forcibly is that most of them either occurred in seemingly low-risk situations, such as an apparently competent swimmer in still water or a group bivouac in the desert on a starlit night, or where people had been lulled into relaxing their guard against such hazards as swift water, loose rocks, or the possibility of a cloudburst. They reteach the most retaught of safety lessons—that the first rule of safe passage is constant vigilance.[20]

Earlier we related that, from the beginning, each school implemented the guiding principles the British Outward Bound Trust provided us by prescribing safe practices designed for its particular environment and courses and supporting these through instructor training and student instruction. In choosing staff, program directors placed increasingly heavy emphasis on maturity, sense of responsibility, experience, and technical competence. It was felt that these attributes, in conjunction with the accident prevention and first-aid and rescue doctrine, staff training, and supervision at the course-

---

[20] However many times it may be retaught by bitter experience, this rule cannot be repeated too often. It is universally true for all hazards. In his penetrating analysis of nuclear-energy risks, nuclear physicist Dr. George L. Weil quotes Dr. Edward Teller: "The real danger occurs when a false sense of security causes a letdown of caution."Dr. Weil also cites the instance of the prelaunch exercise in the Apollo spacecraft in 1967 when three of the original astronauts lost their lives in an oxygen-fueled flash fire. A National Aeronautics and Space Administration official suggested that "alertness . . . had become dulled" by previous successes in the Mercury and Gemini programs. The New York Times editorialized: "It is true that astronauts and others have worked in pure oxygen atmospheres hundreds of thousands of times without incident. But that only means that the probability of accident was small, not—as the designers seem to have assumed—that an accident was virtually impossible." (George L. Weil, Nuclear Energy: Promises, Promises. Washington, D.C., 1973, privately printed.)

director level, would come together in the leadership skills and attitudes that made for a safe program.

There has never been a reason to discard this approach. In time, however, the school directors came to feel that there ought to be a more formal structuring and coordinating of the schools' safety standards and practices than was afforded by the informal coordinating activity that had come about spontaneously during the organization's formative years. In 1971 the OBI safety committee and directors jointly agreed on the need for the national office to develop a national safety policy to which each school would be committed and for which each school would be subject to a periodic evaluative check.

The main burden of formulating a national safety program and implementing the structure for carrying it out fell on Ralph Puckett, who held the post of national program coordinator in OBI. Ralph consulted with national leaders in the accident-prevention movement, top industrial safety engineers, and experts in various phases of outdoor safety. At the same time, the supervisory staff and instructors of each school contributed to the thinking and the eventual consensus that made an all-school safety policy possible.

As finally adopted, the National Safety Policy was prefaced by the British Trust's policy declaration summarized in an earlier chapter. Bound loose-leaf in anticipation of periodic revision, it defined the national safety organization and its responsibilities, set administrative procedure standards, and detailed safe operating and expedition practices. Achievement of the policy was an organizational milestone. Its success is due in great measure to the fact that the school directors gave it their strong backing and made certain that its intent of dedicated self-discipline by the schools toward safe conduct of their courses was realized. Their implementing of the policy integrated a continuing concern for the well-being of students and instructors into the day-to-day activity at all administrative and operating levels, to a degree of success not otherwise possible.

Inevitably, the National Safety Policy evolved. A primary difficulty arose because often there is more than one right way to do things—for example, to tie in for a rock climb. The impracticality of making a central document satisfy all conditions at the local level eventually led to a "local operating procedures" policy permitting greater initiative at the school level. The National Safety Policy defines the safety objectives of Outward Bound in the United States, establishes the roles and responsibilites of key board and staff individuals and groups in regard to safety management, and stipulates the nature and frequency of incident reporting and accident investigations. The policy also specifies the requirements for conducting regular safety reviews of operating programs, and the selection and training of both staff and students. Each school then determined its own local operating procedures within the parameters of the national standards.

Each school has its own safety committee, whose responsibilities include approval of local operating procedures, ensuring that they do in fact conform to the National Safety Policy, and an annual on-site safety review of the school's programs. The national safety committee consists of the school committee chairmen, the president of OBI, an OBI staff assistant who is responsible for coordinating the committee's activities with the schools, and an OBI trustee who chairs it.

The duties of the OBI staff member assigned to the national safety committee are so considerable as to make him virtually a full-time safety officer. He is expected to keep familiar with safety practices at all schools, to ensure that the useful experiences of one are communicated to all, and to investigate and respond to safety questions referred to him. He recommends changes in the National Safety Policy in light of new developments, provides an annual summary of accident reports submitted by the schools to OBI, and monitors and reports to the national safety committee concerning the activities and effectiveness of the school committees. One of his most important duties is to lead a team in a periodic on-site safety review of each school.

When Hank Taft appointed John Rhoades program coordinator at OBI in 1973, John inherited the safety job, including the inspection responsibility. Studying the accident report files, John was struck by the fact that historically there had been no serious accident or near miss attributable to defective equipment. He concluded that the big problem was in the area of human judgment and that inspections should center there. "The problem I set myself," he recalled, "was how to evaluate that human element, recognizing that there were built-in resistances to my coming in to do the evaluation. One of the first things I did was change the name of what we were doing from inspection to safety review. My goal was a consultative model, not one that was pointing fingers, taking names, and kicking fannies, but one that used a team of people to come in and ask the school administration—the director, program director, and course directors—what their safety concerns were, what they particularly wanted us to look for. We would do our job with a view to giving them the most helpful feedback possible as to whether what they wanted to be happening was in fact happening."

Rhoades and his review team associates put in as much time as possible in the field. They asked the students questions—"What's in that first-aid kit? What would you do if you got lost right now?"—as one way to obtain feedback for the administration. They worked hard for a rapport with the instructors. "To get that rapport," Rhoades said, "it was absolutely essential to get into a consultative mode, where any one of us could ask, 'You've been instructing here for three years; what do you worry about most? Where do you think the system is soft?' In the normal inspection system that kind of data doesn't appear, because it's to your best interest to cover up, or to answer only those questions that are put to you directly."

The safety review that Rhoades, building on the foundation of Puckett's work, developed and defined over four years, was the model Bob Box inherited when he held the post of program coordinator at OBI from 1978 to 1980. Box came to OBI after five seasons as chief climbing instructor at the North Carolina School. In his instructor training there, he had done an exemplary job of making safety a central concern of the climbing program without diminishing its challenge and had created one of the most competent mountain rescue teams in the East. He took up his new post with an experience-based conviction that, in Outward Bound, adventure and safety belong hand in hand.

"The review as I see it," Box said, "has two functions—control and staff training. On the control side, the school administration gets an outside perspective on how well the school is living up to its safety responsibilities as defined by the National Safety Policy. On the training side, the school is getting feedback on how it might improve its program in any number of areas. Also, the flow goes both ways. The review-team members from other schools take home a tremendous amount of spinoff, knowledge that they put to work in their school. They may see a problem, and a team member may think, I'd better check that out in my own school. Or they may see a creative answer to a problem. For example, at Hurricane Island we discovered that their admission procedure included an outstanding system for screening applicants' medical reports. We said, 'You guys are doing this better than anyone else—let's share it!' With Peter Willauer's permission I sent it around to all the schools. That kind of thing happens a lot; people doing the reviews told me it was a staff-training function for them as well."

The review team normally consists of three to five persons, led by an OBUSA safety staff specialist. Other reviewers may include school or program directors, other senior staff members and experts from outside Outward Bound with special competence in the activity, environment or participant population being reviewed. Reviews normally take five to seven days to complete.

Box pointed out that since it is not possible to draw a line defining where safety concerns stop, the review has a broad reference base. In essence, it is a chance for the program director to be evaluated by his peers, not only on safety but in any aspect where the review team has expertise. It starts with the how-can-we-help approach. "The very first question in a safety review is, 'What do you especially want us to look at?' and as often as not the program director says, 'I'd like you to see how well I'm communicating with my staff. Tell me if my expectations are being met in reality.' This won't be in the review report, but the team will give the feedback verbally, and they can do that on any number of requests."

In Box's view, the valuable function of the review team was looking at systems. The team does not often find that the students have their carabiners turned the wrong way or that techniques, equipment, and procedures are incorrect or deficient. They focus on the supervision, the staff training, the follow-up procedures needed to assure the safety program's smooth running. The review customarily starts with a once-over session with the school and program directors, to become familiar with the safety scheme of operation, check on the previous review's recommendations, and learn where the school feels its problems lie. The team examines the files with special attention to what feedback the top echelons are getting from course directors and instructors in the field, and to see how effectively headquarters is responding.

In the field the team splits, each member going with a different cadre, observing and talking with instructors and students, then reunites to compare notes. Box explained, "They probably have gone out there with questions that grew out of their interviews, their run-through of the files, and so on. They're making a reality check. Say an instructor has reported the students are not eating properly on winter courses, where calorie intake is important. If the team then goes out in the field and sees students are not eating properly, that's two important observations. One, the procedural one of the need to tighten up, make sure of calorie intake. Second, the school is not listening to its own staff. That could be the larger of the two problems."

Box affirmed the importance of time for talking with staff. "Probably the best feedback we'd get in the whole time was the informal conversations with instructors and their course directors. They'd clue us into things we ought to look into. For the most part they are professionals first. They're concerned about safety: they've got those ten to twelve kids out there. They have the ability to ask the hard questions rather than just cover their own rear ends to avoid any problems."

A safety review is hard work. "The high energy level is sustained throughout the review," Box said. "You're running in planes and cars and on the trail, in constant contact with your teammates and school personnel. For me the most debilitating part was the nervous and emotional energy I expended. You deal with real sensitivities. Regardless of how openly the team comes in, and how receptive the school may be, there's always that element of these guys are here to tell us what's wrong, and that makes them nervous. As a team we spent a lot of energy being sensitive to that and counteracting it, to break down those barriers of communication. Sometimes they don't break down, and that's even worse."[21]

After the field review the team huddles to develop the framework of its report, agreeing on the key issues and other observations and suggestions they want to make. They share these orally with the school administration

---

[21] Bob Box left OBI in 1980 to accept the post of program director at the Southwest Outward Bound School. He was replaced by Ted Moores, a former program director of the Minnesota School.

and safety trustee. Much of the report ends there; the observations and less significant suggestions are noted by the school, to be acted on as it may determine. The key issues are set forth in the written report that the OBI representative writes upon return to his or her office. When the full team is in agreement on the report content, including all recommendations, the report is formally sent through the president of OBI to the school director and safety trustee. The school is required to reply to the recommendations within thirty days. If the school does not wish to comply with a recommendation, it states its reasons. The review team may accept the school's response as valid; if it does not, it restates its case, perhaps revising the recommendation. If an agreement cannot be reached, the issue is referred to OBCC, which arbitrates it and makes the final decision.

Over the years, the annual school safety reports became increasingly sophisticated; they inform in greater detail and employ a uniform system of statistical analysis. These reports become a part of the National Safety Committee's annual report, so that each school benefits from the others' experience as well as its own. A good instance of this is the fortuitous consequence of an incident at North Carolina, when a student's severe allergic reaction to a bee sting caused him to stop breathing and necessitated his hurried evacuation to a hospital. Two years later students suffering similar allergic reactions on North Carolina and Dartmouth courses received an emergency injection of epinephrine from staff in the field, a treatment that prevented severe trauma. The change of procedure over the two years was directly attributable to the shared recommendations in the report on the first incident.

An essential part of the accident reporting system is that covering "near misses." The difference between little or even no injury and serious or even fatal injury may be more "accidental" than the accident itself. It is just as important to have information about serious accidents that almost or might have happened as about those that did. In either case a hazard existed, and the incident has shed light on how to deal with such dangers or on the need for a preventive strategy. The schools follow a policy of circulating full reports on all "safety-related incidents that had the potential for critical injury or fatal results, but resulted in no injury or minor consequence."

In 1978 Outward Bound requested the National Executive Service Corps, a volunteer citizen organization, to conduct an outside, independent review of Outward Bound's safety systems. Following an in-depth review at each school and of the national system, the team of three reviewers[22] submitted its report in December 1979. The report said in part:

Taken as a whole we felt that the Outward Bound people are extraordinarily talented and dedicated and are committed to giving the students a challenging, adventurous and educational experience but with continuous and unremitting attention to safety. In a few instances, we concluded that improvements were very much needed and that they could and should be made. . . .

Following receipt of the report by OBI, the national office and the schools made positive responses to all the team's recommendations.

■ ■ ■

The self-education of the schools to better deal with hazards in order to have finer adventure is a continuing response to that discipline placed on Jim Hogan some four decades ago: "Hahn had constantly insisted it was my duty to understand all the factors affecting safety." The founder's iron rule still prevails. In the final passage of *Impelled into Experiences* Hogan reflected on an effect of the growth in popularity of adventurous outdoor pursuits, for which the success of Outward Bound is in considerable measure responsible: "Many of the well-meaning adults who lead young people in such pursuits are insufficiently aware of the dangers involved and the technical training that is essential to safety." The reflection caused him to recall that most memorable of Hahn aphorisms, which had given him the title for his book, that it is culpable neglect not to impel young people into experience. He concluded:

[22] The team was Howard W. Blauvelt, retired president and chairman of Conoco Inc.; Marian S. Heiskell, then president of the Community Service Society of New York; and Charles A. Anderson, retired president of Stanford Research Institute.

To those who seek to adopt Hahn's precept one would like to stress that behind all his practices there was a passionate concern that youngsters should not merely survive the experiences in which he plunged them but that they should emerge strengthened. If Outward Bound has demonstrated anything, it must surely be that adventure should be used as an ingredient in education only by those who have accepted the restraints and disciplines which are essential to successful practice.

Hogan's commentary on the heart of the founder's philosophy itself became a precept for those entrusted with carrying on his work. To it let us add the observation of another British Outward Bound philosopher, who likewise acknowledged a grateful allegiance to the founder's wisdom. In 1966 Tom Price, warden of the Eskdale Outward Bound School, addressing the Royal Society of Arts on the meaning of Outward Bound, spoke directly to this point: "If one disregards safety, one in effect holds life cheap, and that is contrary to the whole spirit of a training which devotes so much time to first aid, mountain rescue, lifeboat work, and other forms of service."

THE ADJUDICATED

🏵

A great part of [the frightening rate of increase in crimes of violence] is not individual violence; it is fed by the gang spirit, which is a degraded form of the comradeship, the platoon-spirit in an army. The gang, the cell, is an immensely strong unit. It may be easier to convert it into a shock-troop for some good purpose than to break it up into individuals. It must be admitted, though, that such "gangs for the good" would lose their strongest cohesive force: the disapproval of society.

—Dennis Gabor

I had been to some of the state and county [training schools] and God, I was repulsed—to think that we were paying something like $10,000 a year just to keep a kid in a cage without any type of rehabilitation. It was just really horrible. And I figured that if I didn't do any other damn thing while I was governor, I was going to [change] that system.

—Francis Sargent, former governor of Massachusetts

In February 1967, Frank Kelly, who by then had left the Massachusetts Division of Youth Services to teach psychology at Boston College, called me. He had a bulletin on his research project tracking the sixty delinquent youths who had attended Outward Bound schools the preceding summer. After seven months only eight had recidivated—been committed to an institution for a new offense. Since the normal expectation was twenty—one in three—this report was encouraging. But we still had to wait a year for processing of comparative data for both the Outward Bound group and the control group who had been treated in the normal institutional routine.

The project report by Kelly and his Boston College colleague, Professor Daniel Baer, was published in June 1968.[23] Containing much comparative data for the two groups, the report centered on a recidivism comparison, initially for nine months, subsequently updated for a year. In the first twelve months of parole, thirteen of the Outward Bound group (20 percent) recidivated, as against twenty-five (42 percent) of the control group. The Outward Bound group's rate was half that expected for boys of their age committed to DYS, while the control group's was about as expected. The superior record of the Outward Bound group was rated statistically significant.[24]

In analyzing their data Kelly and Baer noted that in addition to the Outward Bound experience, several "background variables" appeared also to relate to the recidivism. One of their surmises was that Outward Bound might have a greater influence on those whose offenses were against persons or property than on those who were committed as "stubborn or runaway children" ("status offenses" that have no adult counterpart and usually reflect familial conflicts expressed in disobedience, incorrigibility, and running away from home). Even so, although the recidivism rate for the stubborn/runaway category in both groups was high, it was twice as high in the control (83 percent) as in the Outward Bound group (40 percent).

[23] Francis J. Kelly and Daniel J. Baer, *Outward Bound Schools as an Alternative to Institutionalization for Adolescent Delinquent Boys* (Boston, Mass.: Fandel Press, Inc., 1968). Includes a Participant Observers' Report by Richard Katz and David Kolb.

[24] Kelly and Baer have since made a five-year follow-up. While the difference in recidivism rates continued to favor the Outward Bound group (38 percent versus 53 percent), the difference was no longer considered statistically significant. Noting that the increase in recidivism among the Outward Bound group occurred in the second half of the second year, Kelly commented, "This suggests that Outward Bound had an effect on some delinquents sufficient to sustain them in the community for a longer period than traditional treatment, but that the effect eroded before the onslaught of negative environmental pressures." The offenses of the control group tended to be much more serious than those of the Outward Bound group.

The Kelly-Baer report, along with other papers the two subsequently published, had a considerable impact on the corrections community at large, on DYS, and on Outward Bound. In my first call on John Coughlan, in 1964, I told him I thought Outward Bound might be something that could help. Now we had solid empirical support for what had been little more than a gut feeling. Others—people who could put this knowledge to work—were made aware of it. In particular, young social and behavioral scientists who had entered corrections work aspiring to find more productive ways of dealing with young criminals and potential criminals were receptive to the implications of the DYS experiment. Since then we have had amply more indication that Outward Bound has something valuable to offer the juvenile corrections community. In recent years, in fact, corrections professionals have increasingly sought out Outward Bound and Outward Bound–derived agencies for aid in developing programs alternative to incarceration for young offenders.

DYS was sufficiently impressed with the Kelly-Baer findings to continue the Outward Bound liaison, again sending sixty boys in 1967 and 1968. This was expensive—$600 per individual on average to cover tuition, transportation, and miscellaneous. But since it would cost between $3,000 and $4,000 to maintain each boy in an institution for a year, the alternative was rated a good investment. At the same time the Outward Bound success inevitably raised a question. If the method worked so well with youngsters sent from the institution, why not introduce it directly into the institution? The query was not an easy one. To superimpose the Outward Bound process on a homogeneous delinquent group on what was essentially their own turf would be quite different from integrating several delinquent youths into a standard course in a totally strange environment. Still, it was a challenging idea. In 1968 the Hurricane Island School contracted with DYS to provide a staff and program for one living unit at the Lyman School for Boys. Lyman was the state's largest institution for youthful offenders, with a regimen of remedial education in classrooms and rehabilitative treatment under counselors.

The conventional wisdom is that the story of the Lyman School experiment is one of honorable failure. It deserves a better testimony. Moreover, it supplies a linkage in the evolution of the thorniest of Outreach undertakings—bringing the Outward Bound dynamic to bear in society's attempts to deal with adjudicated youth and their antisocial behavior.

The program ran ten weeks, from the end of January 1968 to early April. Peter Willauer assigned three of his staff—Adrian Middleton, Hurricane's chief instructor, Baha Uddin Abdul-Malik, and Gil Leaf—to staff the Lyman project. Middleton, an Australian who had come to Hurricane Island via Australia Outward Bound and the British school at Aberdovey, was project director. Abdul-Malik, a music major graduate of the University of West Virginia, had been one of Malcolm X's chief lieutenants before that Black Muslim leader's assassination. He was from New York and had worked at the Urban League's Harlem Prep, a street academy. Leaf, a Harvard graduate, teacher, and staff assistant to Willauer, had helped to set up the Hurricane Island School and had instructed there and at the Outward Bound schools in Australia and Kenya. Author of Hurricane's report on the first phase of the Lyman experiment and still its oral historian, he reminisced:

We were the first Outward Bound program to be residentially located in a reform school, and we went in ill-prepared. None of us had training for dealing with a homogeneous delinquent group, although Baha's skills in working with kids from the inner city, both black and white, were fantastic. Nor had we done any kind of pedagogical homework before leaping into this situation. They gave us Oak Cottage, a funny little three-story building almost as old as the school, which was founded in 1846. The school was full of euphemisms like cottages and cottage masters. We had twenty-four kids, mostly sixteen and seventeen years old, about sixty-forty percent white and black. They were a mix ranging from 'stubborn children' in mild trouble to real psychopaths or to kids who would tell you, 'I got a bum rap,' and then you'd learn this was their umpteenth conviction. The mix was disruptive and diminished a good deal of what might have been accomplished. The first day there were a lot of fights as the pecking order got sorted out. We named the project the Overlanders and divided the group Outward Bound–style into two patrols. We had four cottage masters and a counselor assigned to help us. Three of the cottage masters did make a real effort. They didn't know what we were about, but they tried to be open-minded. They were dubious because we started breaking all the classic rules of the institution, and they were just waiting for us to fall on our faces, which we did a number of times.

In the standard cottage plan at Lyman the boys kept their personal gear in lockers in the basement and slept in rows of beds on the third floor, surveyed by a watchman. The Overlander staff put the beds in three rooms on the second floor, had each student place his locker by his bed, and gave him some personal wall space to use or decorate. They took the boys out of the uniform-like nightshirts that were obligatory for others at Lyman. Because they wanted mealtime to be an important part of the group experience, they maintained dining quarters at Oak Cottage, two boys fetching each meal from the school cafeteria. Fairly rigid rules for sharing and organization and cleanup were enforced. Many of the boys took kindly to this as a sort of surrogate home atmosphere. Some of them—presumably those who had worked with their mothers—were extraordinarily house proud, zealous in cleaning up. Part of that, Leaf thought, was a way of escaping from threatening interactions with other inmates.

The curriculum consisted of classroom work at eighth- to tenth-grade levels, outdoor pursuits and gymnasium, a ropes course, initiative tests, drown-proofing, weekend wilderness expeditions, trips to museums and the like, maintaining and drilling with the school fire engine, operating the big bulldozer that the Reverend Bob Brown, the school chaplain, had got hold of, and service projects, with letter and journal writing and recreation in the evening. The basic plan for the daytime schedule was to alternate ninety-minute academic and action-oriented periods. The staff learned early that while the general intelligence level of the boys was higher than expected, their attention span was quite limited. Midway in the course the period lengths were halved, and efforts were made to increase variety and action in the curriculum.

The staff gave the students considerable rein from the outset and soon regretted it. They realized they had made a serious mistake not structuring a transition from the completely regulated Lyman regimen to the responsibility

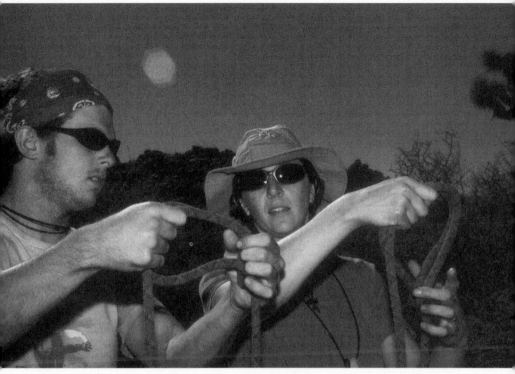

Instructor and student compare knotting techniques on a desert trekking course in the late afternoon sun. (Photo © PCOBS, Kim Budd)

and initiative inherent in their open-cottage pattern. The boys were quick to seize advantage of what they took to be supervisory weakness, and the result was a kind of seesaw balance of power. "These kids had us in their element most of the time," Leaf said. "They could have destroyed the program at will. In many ways our ineptitude and naiveté were our strength. When the boys found we were such pigeons, they sort of carried us out of curiosity. We also had the outdoors and the wilderness as our allies; there we had them more in our territory, which made a huge difference."

The counselor assigned to the project gave the staff no help. At the same time the staff found their own efforts at counseling going for naught. "It's a real myth," Leaf said, "that you can work with these kids effectively one on one. You would have a fine talk and think you were really communicating with that boy. You were absolutely kidding yourself because five minutes after you put him back with his peers, his behavior pattern was entirely different. Most of the psychiatric social workers we saw could not work with kids in a group because they were scared of them. Yet the core of what we were trying to do was to get at these kids' problems—deficient sense of delayed gratification, lack of some kind of internal discipline system, need for some kind of values training—within the context of the group of peers."

The staff became aware of a three-way contrast: the standard Lyman disciplinary scheme, the approach that worked effectively with delinquents at Outward Bound schools, and the peculiar conditions creating difficulty for the Outward Bound method in the Lyman environment. The traditional Lyman structuring, as the Overlander staff saw it, was designed to detain in a highly regulated atmosphere, cut off from decision making and responsibility, well suited to creating a docile and passive attitude. The archaic cottage system was built on the concept of a ratio of thirty, forty, even fifty boys to one cottage master. To make the machinery of the daily schedule work, the cottage master ruled by the clenched fist. "It became quite evident to us," Leaf said, "that most of the cottage masters had a good sense of humor and a general affection for the boys. But the system denied them the opportunity to be much other than guards. As a result the boys, who frequently came from violent backgrounds, had their previous experiences reenforced by an institutional system dependent on physical force."

By contrast, Leaf pointed out, Outward Bound operates on a different disciplinary basis that in residential courses is effective with delinquents. Since all students are on strange ground and placed in situations of interdependence, group pressure is highly effective. "The predominantly middle-class ethics system is very powerful and supportive to the delinquent kid. In that setting he has to conform to the majority's will. Invariably the positive elements in a twelve-man group outnumber the negative forces. Boys are given great responsibility and respond remarkably to the challenge. There is little or no incidence of bullying, as situations demand total group cooperation. But at Lyman we had a homogeneous delinquent group, albeit of all different gradations. In the all-delinquent community you don't have the kinds of mechanisms you have at an Outward Bound school. The pecking order becomes a far more powerful force."

The most striking fact about the Lyman experiment was that the Overlander staff was able to carry the course to completion. Seriously under-staffed to begin with, an expedition injury to Leaf and much less help from the cottage masters than anticipated aggravated the situation close to the breaking point. In the latter part of the course Miles Becker, a Northwest School instructor, was a welcome addition. But the staff had to keep running just to maintain the daily routine, with no break in the stress. In light of this unrelenting pressure, Middleton's fortitude as leader was the more remarkable.

"Adrian was the real heart of the program," Leaf said. "His sense of personal morality, his incredible Christian behavior, was the primary force working for us. Adrian fostered the idea that the Overlanders would be something special within the school. He was just a tower of strength, and delinquent kids reacted to him in a fascinating way. He was the squarest, most out-of-it character you ever want to meet, and the kids loved him for it. So many of the adults they had dealt with seemed to be devious, or exerted their power. Adrian never played the power business with them. It was quite extraordinary."

While the course was a mix of plus and minus values throughout, as it progressed the plus side gained. Performance levels improved, generally as much among the smaller or less aggressive youngsters as among the "tough guys." The boys found rock climbing, which started late due to the weather, scary and thrilling; many exuded a new confidence as a result of their climbing achievements. While most were initially terrified of operating the big bulldozer, they all came to handle it competently. Never before, the Reverend Bob Brown remarked, had he seen a group of Lyman boys combine confidence, attention, and skill in such an activity. This and other performances encour-aged the staff to believe they had made real progress in building self-esteem. Many of the boys enjoyed keeping a journal, as long as the writing period was established for them, and letter writing was a favorite activity. Surprisingly, some of those who had tested poorly in verbal aptitude seemed to write the best prose—a finding that reenforced the staff's suspicions that motivation, or lack of it, played a large part in the group's test performances.

The Overlanders responded especially well to community service. Trained to use the school fire truck and equipment, they handled emergency calls when the nearby town of Westboro was hit by a flood, pumping out a factory and the basement of a private home. They were extremely proud when an open letter thanking them was published in the Worcester newspaper. With the cottage masters, they put in a three-day service effort for the Massachusetts Fish and Game Commission, wielding bushhooks, axes, and saws to clear a large picnic area in a state forest. Cottage masters and boys alike returned to Lyman with high morale and new pride. The pleased commission marked the area with a sign that read, "Cleared by Overlanders I, 1968—Rogers and Henson Patrols."

Throughout the ten weeks the wilderness expeditions, growing increasingly difficult, were the program elements where the students experienced the greatest sense of personal achievement. There too, the cottage masters were forced to regard the youngsters in a new light. Taken out of their cottage where they had reigned supreme, the masters were now thrown into situations where the boys could hike longer and had learned better how to orienteer, so that the men had to follow them. "For the first time," Leaf said, "the masters saw their charges as kids rather than young bums." The youngsters' behavior on the expeditions and in the periods directly after their return was at its best. On one such morning, a Sunday late in the course, Middleton's log read:

> Boys up at 0630, had all beds made etc. 0700 breakfast brought up to staff! All ready for church. Cottage v. clean.

Although youngsters ran away from Lyman all the time, often despite locked doors, no Overlander ever ran, even though they had keys to the cottage and could come and go virtually at will. By the course's end most boys cared about staff opinion and tended to be upset with themselves when they did not perform up to standard. In the third week from the end there was an incident that had a telling effect on the entire experience. Some member or members of the Overlanders stole a ring and money from a visitor in the gymnasium. It was 9:30 P.M. when Middleton got everybody together and delivered an emotion-charged ultimatum: They would sit there until the stolen items were returned, or the project would be terminated.

The boys were shocked. "They were truly conscious of the personal dedication and affection for them that Adrian had shown throughout," Leaf said, "and his intention to fold the project if compelled to shook them profoundly. He appealed to their sense of honor and their treatment of visitors. He restated the meaning of the unofficial Overlanders motto: 'Liberty is the right to discipline oneself so as not to be disciplined by others.' For the first time its meaning hit home."

The culprit's identity was not known among the boys. As the night dragged on, they negotiated among themselves and between the two patrols. Emotions ran high as suspicions were voiced and indignantly denied. One boy made a false confession, but this was seen through. Finally, at 4 A.M., the boy who had stolen the ring turned himself in to Baha, and in the follow-up inquiry another who was involved gave himself away. The entire group was sent to bed but roused at the usual 6:30 hour. On rising they were called together for a secret ballot on whether to expel or keep the thieves. By large majorities they voted to dismiss both from the program. "The whole issue of returning the ring, the rightness and wrongness of it, was very effective," Leaf said. "It was not lost on them at all. From that night on they seemed to take a greater pride in their group. They amazed us by self-administered discipline with their swearing."

The final expedition, an eleven-day journey to the Pemigewasset Wilderness in New Hampshire's White Mountain National Forest and on Vermont's Long Trail in the Green Mountains, was a capping success. On their three-day solos without food, only three boys broke. Near the end youngsters who had thought covering five miles a day in deep snow was almost impossible managed to do thirty-four miles in two and one-half days. When they returned "home," as they had come to call Oak Cottage, self-regard was obviously strong, and the euphoria was sustained through the final three days. The boys took pains to wear their Overlander shoulder patches everywhere. A peak final occasion was a dance, with guests from a nearby girls' school. The boys conducted themselves as gentlemen, without incident during the pleasant evening.

Thinking back on the experience a decade later, Leaf essayed an evaluation: "I think it was a reasonably successful experiment. It was clumsy, but I think was the best that could be expected in terms of our lack of training and our lack of logistical support. We were run down because of the emotional climate. Some of the kids were very unstable personalities so that you became very uptight yourself. You had to keep the kids busy all the time, or you were in trouble.

"At the end we didn't know what the impact would be on the kids. That would have had to be measured over a long period of time, and still would have been fuzzy. I think whatever impact we had was second to the impact on the institution—forcing the state to reexamine its process. We certainly messed with the minds of the cottage masters, at whole different levels of trusting kids. A series of things of that nature were, I think, more significant than our rather amateurish performance with the kids. I think we provided a nudge to Jerome Miller toward what he eventually did, closing down the institutions."

■ ■ ■

Dr. Jerome Miller was the innovative—some would say maverick—individual brought in as commissioner of a new state Department of Youth Services in 1969. In the course of the next several years he closed down all but one of the state institutions for youthful offenders. The fact that the exception was Homeward Bound, an Outward Bound spinoff, indicates that Leaf's surmise was sound. There was in fact a connection between the Outward Bound influence in DYS and Miller's ultimate dramatic actions.

By the time Miller came into office, Hurricane Island had run a second Overlander activity in the winter of 1968–1969. Learning about the Kelly-Baer study, the Overlander history, and the department's continuing success with scholarship students, Miller found Outward Bound's accessory participation in the department's work to be one of the few aspects of what the department was doing that he approved of. In addition, he discovered that Alan Colette, superintendent of the DYS forestry camp at Brewster, Massachusetts, had already started an activity with a potential for becoming the department's own Outward Bound–type treatment.

The Stephen L. French Youth Forestry Camp in the state forest on Cape Cod had been activated in 1960 as a facility to which youngsters committed as first offenders were sent for six to nine months. The rationale was that in the course of working in the woods they would learn silviculture and other forestry skills. But when Colette transferred from the Lyman School staff to become the camp's assistant superintendent in 1965, he found no silviculture or related instruction. The inmates were functioning primarily as maintenance crews in the state park, picking up litter, cleaning the latrines, and the like. While at Lyman, Colette had accompanied DYS scholarship youngsters to Minnesota Outward Bound, where the school's method had impressed him. In 1967 he obtained a scholarship to a teachers' course at Hurricane Island. Considerably overweight, and in less than the best of physical shape, he suffered greatly throughout the course. "Nevertheless," he said, "I learned an awful lot." Returning to Brewster, he persuaded the then superintendent that Outward Bound offered a fresh new approach to rehabilitative work with delinquents. His superior agreed to let him set up an adaptive program for the final month of the inmates' stay. The kids dubbed it Homeward Bound.

Miller, enthusiastic about what he found at the camp, encouraged Colette in his ideas for building up the adventure-experience element and cutting back sharply on the overall length of stay. A series of Hurricane Island instructors—Arthur Conquest, Bill Hughes, John Conant, and others—were brought in to help structure the program. By 1971 only the Outward Bound element remained—eventually its time span was whittled down to one month—and the entire Brewster operation was being called Homeward Bound. Having made up his mind to phase out the other institutions, Miller used Homeward Bound to divert youths who would otherwise have been assigned to the training schools and transferred others there for a final Homeward Bound experience prior to parole.

The shutting of the Massachusetts institutions for young offenders, with the exception of Homeward Bound, was virtually completed in January 1972 when, on Miller's authorization, a caravan of cars manned by University of Massachusetts students carried off the remaining thirty-nine inmates of the Lyman School. Two years later Herb Willman, by then an executive assistant in the department, would say in retrospect, "If you want to close down the institutions, start a Homeward Bound." Nearly a decade later the complex of alternative treatments that Miller initiated to replace the training schools was still operative, and Massachusetts remained unique in its radical dealing with the delinquency problem. A matured Homeward Bound, with the beginnings of a plan for maintaining a follow-up relationship with its students, was going strong.

SCHOOL IN THE SOUTHWEST

✳

I have learned the depths of strength and trust that are present in me and my fellow man. I shall try to remember that any of my neighbors or fellow workers could have belayed the climbing rope for me or given me his hand when I was slipping off a steep slope. I may forget, but I will try to remember.

—Reporter Allen Hall, writing in the *Dallas Morning News* about his course in the Texas Big Bend

The year 1970 saw important developments within the organization. Late in 1969 we named Murray Durst national executive director of OBI. In two years as director of the North Carolina School Murray had convincingly demonstrated his managerial competence. We now sought that competence to implement the OBEX (Outward Bound Executive Committee) policy that "the paid president is not responsible for the operation or administration of Outward Bound Inc." Willi Unsoeld had been largely relieving me of those responsibilities, but now the Unsoelds planned to return to their beloved Northwest. At midyear they departed for Olympia, Washington, where Willi had accepted a place on the founding faculty of new, innovative Evergreen State College. Much as I regretted Willi's going, I would have been even more desolate had I realized how few times our paths would cross thereafter. I was among the thousands whom tragedy deprived when he and one of his students were killed by a snow avalanche on Mount Rainier in 1979.

In the fall of 1970 Durst and his staff moved to offices in Reston, Virginia. Going with him as director of operations was Lee Maynard, whom I had hired as OBI business manager shortly before Murray joined us. My president's office remained in Andover. Durst's move was dictated by the trustees' sense that with the increasing recognition being accorded Outward Bound as an important educational movement, it was time to relocate the national headquarters closer to "the action." The choice of Reston was based in part on the increasing difficulty of obtaining federal funds for educational purposes in the Nixon administration and the feeling that it would be advantageous for the national office to be in the Washington area.

The increasing scope of Durst's task in response to the growing needs of the schools was one reflection of Outward Bound's growing significance on the national scene. In 1971 the student total leaped from 3,800 to 5,300. For ten years the annual enrollment increase had been averaging twenty percent, a record few other educational programs of the period could match. OBI was responsible for helping sustain that growth, meeting the scholarship funding quota that grew with it, and satisfying other expanding service requirements of the schools. By 1971 every school was conducting women's courses, coeducational courses, contract courses, and offering a host of educational experiences ranging in duration from five to eighteen days that were broadening the Outward Bound appeal—to teachers, businessmen, adults generally, juniors, and special groups. Each school now had some form of winter program and with each passing year was approaching closer to the goal of year-round operation. The calls from schools and colleges for help in establishing adaptive programs were mounting. Outward Bound was winning academic acceptance; a growing number of colleges were recognizing Outward Bound as a valid educational experience for credit, all the way up to doctoral programs. In another area of social concern, Outward Bound's usefulness as an alternative to incarceration for juvenile delinquents was receiving respectful attention from youth service agencies.

At the same time developments in the management area were building our institutional vigor. OBEX membership was revised to provide for representation of the schools, assuring them a role in the decision-making process on national policy and operation. Procedures for regular evaluation of school operations were emerging. One of these was a peer review plan initiated by the directors through OBCC, whereby each was periodically evaluated by a group of leaders—usually directors and program directors—from other schools. Cooperative activity between the national trustees' safety committee and OBCC was leading to the school safety review plan.

The organization was also being offered the opportunity for another growth leap. We had a charter application for a new school.

■ ■ ■

In our earlier years the school directors met regularly in their identity as the Outward Bound Operating Committee (OBOC). There was a period when these meetings were held in cities unconnected to the schools, chosen as likely places for recruiting students and spreading the Outward Bound word. In the winter of 1967 the Colorado School, whose sponsoring turn it was, chose Dallas. The meeting generated considerable interest among a group of Dallas citizens, not just to send young people to Outward Bound but also to initiate some form of permanent activity in the Dallas area. For a time the Colorado School considered setting up a subsidiary operation as a means of seeding a new school in Texas. Subsequently Dick Galland, a Texan who was on the promotional and instructional staffs at Colorado, persuaded the Dallas group to seek a school charter. His father, Richard I. Galland, took the lead in the organizing work. A committed group of prospective trustees incorporated in mid-1970. The board of twenty included twelve from Dallas, two from Fort Worth, and six from Houston. On an evaluating visit Durst was impressed by the quality of the support for the proposed new school. With the senior Galland he worked up a gradualist modus operandi for bringing it "on line" and reported an affirmative recommendation to OBEX. In November 1970, OBI's trustees voted a charter for the Texas Outward Bound School.

The Texas development strategy was to proceed slowly, centering first on organization and conduct of Outreach programs on a contract basis. In February 1971 the trustees appointed Dick Galland Jr. executive secretary and set up an operating committee to work closely with him. They provided $10,000 for scholarships, mostly for teachers' practica, at other schools in the 1971 summer. Dick's main tasks, in addition to publicity and fund-raising, were to reconnoiter potential areas for conducting courses and promote Texas Outward Bound's availability for contract services among schools and colleges in the state. The course site search revealed the merits of the Big Bend National Park area. Named after the "big bend" of the Rio Grande that forms the dip and rise of the border line between southwest Texas and Mexico, the area is a spectacular combination of desert, mountain, and canyon country. Galland made two reconnaissances there and won permission of the National Park Service and neighboring ranchers to use the area.

Texas Outward Bound's first program was a ten-day orientation course for the freshman class of St. Marks School in Dallas in August 1971, with eighty students and faculty sharing a mountain-river experience. Among nine 1972 contract courses for schools and colleges was a mini-semester for a large coeducational freshman group from Tarrant County Junior College in Fort Worth—the first junior college adaptive program of such scope in the country. The school conducted its first standard courses for the general public in the summer of 1972, with the younger Galland as director. A year later Texas Outward Bound was in full operation.

By then it had become apparent that the entire Southwest was rich in environments ideally suited to Outward Bound programs, and that a school more centrally located could better serve an area with the potential of reaching from Texas to California. In 1974 the name of the Texas School was changed to Southwest Outward Bound. The following year the school moved its headquarters to Santa Fe and enhanced its trustee membership to reflect the new regional realities. Lee Maynard, who after leaving OBI had served as vice chancellor of Prescott College and president of Prescott Institute, was the new director. The school expanded its operating terrain—to the Grand Canyon, the Gila and Pecos Wilderness areas of New Mexico, the Gulf of California, the Sierra Nevada in California, and even overseas to Nepal. Maynard stepped down in 1978, and although the school's program offerings had broadened considerably in geography as well as enrollment, it stopped functioning as a chartered school sometime in the early 1980s.

Maynard's successor was Rafe Parker, who came from his post as associate director of the Hurricane Island School. For Parker, the sharp shift from the ocean environment of the Maine coast to the desert and mountain ambiance of the Southwest was another stage in a multistage life journey that gives insight

Outward Bound students have fun in the canyons of Utah during a multi-element course. (Photo © Sanford Schulwolf)

to international Outward Bound. Born in Sussex, England, Rafe lived most of his youth in Cyprus. On that island in the eastern Mediterranean that once harbored Phoenician ships, he became an ardent sailor, and he won his mountain-climbing spurs in the ranges that form its double spine. He was sixteen when terrorism bred by ethnic tensions among the Cypriots caused his family to return to England. A student at Sandhurst, the royal military academy, he ocean-raced on its sailing team, captained his college rugby team and competed on the college shooting team, taught judo, climbed in the Alps, and won the Queen's Medal in Military History for his thesis on the French-Algerian conflict. Commissioned in the Royal Corps of Signals, he qualified for duty in the Special Air Services, an elite corps comparable to the U.S. Army's Special Services. Along the way he picked up skills in gliding, underwater demolition, and winter warfare and won a bronze medal in the royal military fencing tournament. As he was taking part in a simulated air invasion in the NATO exercises of 1962, his parachute malfunctioned. Severely injured, he was invalided out of the army and hospitalized for three months. Of the parachute mishap he said, "I packed it myself so I'm entirely to blame."

At twenty-two Rafe had a go at the business world. His enjoyment of the work was diminished by a sense of having little in common with his colleagues. He was in much more congenial company when Freddy Fuller hired him to instruct at the Aberdovey Outward Bound Sea School. After ten courses at Aberdovey he went to East Africa as chief instructor, and subsequently deputy warden, of the Outward Bound school just then opening up in the new Republic of Zambia, formerly Northern Rhodesia. Rafe remembered the Zambian experience as an exciting time: "The first couple of years we had a substantial percentage of white students, but that changed rapidly with the changeover from the colonial pattern to the new black-governed status. The main rationale for the school was to give black Africans from tribes all over the country an experience together. Zambia is a large country with a tremendous diversity of tribes. It is very important for those tribes to nurture a national identity and work out a common understanding toward developing their country. We were putting through seven hundred students a year. We started the first girls' course in African Outward Bound and adult courses for executives. We pushed hard at turning out people qualified to teach rescue and first aid. We organized an alumni association and developed to a high degree the sponsorship needed to make the school fiscally viable. I felt it was on sound footing when, after three years, I left."

Now married, Parker had decided he wanted to make a career with Outward Bound, but in a new theater. "It was important for me to go to America rather than back to England. From my African perspective I could see American Outward Bound as a much more dynamic, fluid program that allowed a great deal of creativity and imagination to be used by the instructor. I was disappointed by the way the British-oriented schools in Africa had tended to implant the British concept rather than try to mold the process to the African needs of the African students. It was the good old colonial attitude; I had contributed my share in Zambia. Also, Outward Bound was a great deal more accepted by the mainstream of education in the United States than in England. That was important to me because I felt strongly, as I still feel, that the Outward Bound process has a place in education."

Parker came to Hurricane Island, where Adrian Middleton, his old sidekick at Aberdovey, was chief instructor, as a watch officer in 1968. Four years later, when Middleton returned to his native country to become warden of the Australian Outward Bound School, Parker succeeded to the chief instructor post. He was successively promoted to be program director and associate director.

■ ■ ■

After the Reston move, my office in Andover was primarily a development office. My chief responsibilities were general promotion of Outward Bound, fund-raising, building a broader national trustee base and close liaison with school trustees, and liaison with Outward Bound in other countries. "General promotion of Outward Bound" was a broad mission. An evidence of the recognition being accorded the movement was that I found myself on frequent call for TV and radio talk shows. On the television game show *What's My Line?* I just about blew it when one of the "imposters," in answering a question, said Outward Bound had no courses for women, and I indignantly cried out, "Oh, yes we do!"

When appearing on NBC's *Today* show, one has to rise at 5:30 A.M. and get over to the studio early to be made up. On arriving, I was ushered into a room with three barber chairs. Barbara Walters was in one, Hugh Downs in another, with an empty one between. As I entered, Walters looked around and said, "Here comes muscle boy!" I was very nervous and I did not need that at that moment. While I was being made up, a producer came in and said to Downs, "Hugh, here are the Outward Bound film clips. You'd better have a look at them." When the clips were run, my heart sank. They had clipped our new film, which had sequences from each of the schools, taken only the dramatic and sensational scenes, and spliced them together. Downs said, "What do you think?" I did not know what to say; I decided, What the hell, I'll tell him exactly what I think. I said, "I think it's awful. It's like 90 percent of the publicity we get, which just plays up the sensational, makes us look like a toughness program, and misses the whole point."

Downs said, "Well, do you have one word to summarize Outward Bound?" I said, "Yes, I do. It's 'compassion,'" and I quickly told him about Kurt Hahn and his concept of serving those in danger and in need. Downs said, "There's certainly nothing compassionate in those clips, or in the questions I've been given to ask you." Then he said, "Look, we have just seven minutes. Let's sit down and see if we can't figure out the questions you'd like me to ask you."

In seven minutes, plus time during the commercials, we wrote our own script. Downs did such a beautiful job of it, and he showed such compassion himself, that soon afterward we made him a trustee.

INTO THE EDUCATIONAL MAINSTREAM

✳

*I realize that the treatment of me, both at the rock
climbing and the rappelling, has several implications for
my teaching. First of all, set the goal high enough, so that
the person will have to extend himself to reach it.
Second, let the person know you consider it to be well
within his capabilities. Third, where possible stay with
them until they accomplish it. All the while being calm,
patient, and giving emotional support. Outward Bound
seems to be an attitude, a way of doing things.*

—Student in an early teachers' practicum

Early in 1967 Arthur Bragg, coordinator of student activities at East
Denver High School, attended a dinner at which Joe Nold was the
speaker. Bragg's excited reaction was that Nold talked the same educational
language as Robert Colwell, his principal at East High. When he brought the
two together, they struck sparks. Nold told Colwell about Outward Bound.
Colwell told him about East High, Denver's oldest high school. Its 2,500
students in a forty-year-old building comprised a cross section of the city's
economic and social strata. Its enrollment was about 50 percent white, 40
percent African-American, and 10 percent Hispanic. While the racial situation
within the school was better than on the outside, the inherent tensions were
there, and Colwell was looking for ways to counter them by breaking down
social and communication barriers in the student body. Wanting also to make
academics more effective, he liked what he heard about the Outward Bound

emphasis on experience as a learning tool. The upshot of the Nold-Colwell dialogue was a grant from the Phipps Foundation of $25,000 a year for three years to the two institutions for an undertaking to try to find, as they expressed it, "the moral equivalent of the mountain in the city."

As a seeding device, a number of East High students and seven teachers were given scholarships to Outward Bound courses that summer. Significantly, two of the initial effects were on Outward Bound rather than on the high school. The first resulted from Colwell's proviso that no East High youngster would be denied a chance to take an Outward Bound course because of race, creed, or sex. Sex was the problem; the courses were for boys only. It was to accommodate East High female students that Colorado offered its first girls' course in 1967. A further difficulty arose from Colwell's persuading seven teachers, men and women, to take part. But there were no courses for adults. Nold dealt with that by giving assistant instructorships in the girls' course to some women and placing the other teachers as "partici-pant-observers" in male or female patrols.

The response of the teachers to this experience led to the high school's second impact on the mountain school. "That following fall," Nold recalled, "I couldn't get Bob Colwell to talk about kids, because he wanted to talk about what had happened to his teachers."

Colwell admitted that the exaggeration, if any, was mild. "The results I could measure most readily were those with the teachers. One of them was a very sarcastic beginning instructor in science. A few years later he became head of the department, but at that time, because he was so abrasive, I had seriously considered not keeping him. The Outward Bound experience smoothed him out a lot; he came back much more sensitive to the needs of other people. On the opposite end was a Hispanic girl, one of our Spanish teachers. She knew her Spanish beautifully, but she was so shy in the class-room that the kids could hardly hear her. When she came back, she was still quiet, but in the classroom she was forceful and driving and became one of our best Spanish teachers. Those were the two extremes, and there were others in between."

To Nold this was a revelation. "We thought, if this is what a participant-observer role can do for teachers, how much more we should be able to achieve with a course designed expressly for them!" The following summer (1968) the Colorado School, jointly with Colorado State College at Greeley (now the University of Northern Colorado) offered the first Outward Bound practicum for teachers. This was a month-long course starting with an urban experience of several days in a Denver slum and followed by Colorado's standard course. It concluded with a several-day seminar wherein the students considered together how the experience had affected them as individuals and teachers and what, as a result, they might take back in the way of new insights to classroom method and special programs. Thirty-six men (Colorado did not essay a coed course until a year later), virtually all classroom teachers, took part. Student and staff evaluation concurred that the practicum filled a valuable educational need.

This success had a considerable impact on U.S. Outward Bound. In 1969 Hurricane Island and the Dartmouth Center joined Colorado in offering teachers' courses; the other schools soon followed suit. Almost as soon as the practica were initiated, they were made coeducational. At the same time, as a departure from the sixteen-and-a-half-to-twenty-three age rule that had largely been observed up to then, they exposed the age ceiling as arbitrary and artificial. The schools began to offer coeducational courses for adults at large and had little or no trouble filling them. The opening of Outward Bound to adults was a natural evolutionary step, but a decade would pass before we fully realized its import.

In 1969 the Carnegie Corporation accorded solid legitimacy to what was happening in the educational sector with a three-year grant of $110,000 to OBI. The grant provided for our hiring someone to coordinate and service the teachers' course activity and in particular to be a follow-up resource for the teacher-students when they went back to their schools and undertook to introduce adaptive programs. A key stipulation was that the teachers' courses should carry graduate credit from an accredited college or university.

Some Carnegie funds were used to obtain an independent evaluation of the 1969 practica by a group of educators at the University of Massachusetts School of Education headed by Professor Glen Hawkes. Using a subjective method of inquiry, the evaluation committee found the practica "a valuable and innovative strategy for teacher education." Teacher comments are interesting for the diverse course values they reflect: gain in understanding and appreciation of other people, boost in self-confidence, discovery of the joy of helping less able course-mates, greater courage to confront others, more willingness to risk failure as against "going the easy and nonparticipatory way." Many went back more empathetic with their students, better able to understand their feelings and see the educative process through their eyes. Others felt much less threatened, if at all, by students, were much more at ease with them, more willing to communicate on a personal level and to reveal weaknesses as well as strengths. There was a new willingness to give students more independence and to encourage student participation and decision making, and much less concern about dress codes, haircuts, and the like. ("More lenient due to more self-confidence," one wrote.) But while many were less concerned about the lesser behavioral matters, they remained strict—or grew stricter—about student achievement. Said one, "Since I faced up to many challenges that I thought I could never accomplish, I have now given my students much more to do. They are much more capable than I ever thought they were."

In the spring of 1969 we were looking for the right individual to carry out the Carnegie Corporation's charge. As luck had it, the person we were seeking was simultaneously looking for us. He was Robert Lentz, a young schoolmaster who had graduated from Brown in 1961, earned a master of arts in teaching degree at the Harvard School of Education, was head of the upper school of a private day school in Ohio, and led canoe trips in the northern Ontario wilderness in the summers.

In Ohio Bob Lentz had become increasingly concerned about what he saw as a dichotomy between the classroom and the world outside. "As a teacher and administrator it troubled me that too often in school we just deal with experience vicariously, through books, that we deny many kids experience outside that classroom, and if they do get it, we can't relate anything within the classroom to what's going on out there. My personal frustrations from that were compounded by the fact that there were several boys whom I saw during the year at school and then saw in the summer canoe tripping. I would be with them on long, eight-week expeditions. I could see that they were growing in a variety of ways up there, and somehow that didn't keep happening when they got back within the conventional school environment."

Bob started a program at the school in which tenth- and eleventh-graders were required to put in two weeks on an outside project, working with an institution. While the program went well, it did not end his frustration. "We got back report after report on these kids about what a lively, alert, intelligent, responsible student this is. And you would visit this student on his project and, my God, he was alive and alert and responsible. You'd look through his records and ask teachers about him and the answer you'd get was, wasn't alive, was lethargic, wasn't alert, wasn't responsible. A kid would come back in off his project, for a few days he'd be alive and alert, then his old behavior would come back. That simply said to me, We're missing some vital things here. I decided to make a move. One of the people I wrote to was Outward Bound."

We hired him for the post of director of education programs. This was a milestone in implementing Mainstream. For the first time we had a staffed multiplier program on a comprehensive scale, well thought out and adequately financed, tying directly into the educational mainstream, and serviced by a follow-up resource. One hundred six teachers were enrolled in the practica in 1969, nearly double that the next year, a still larger number in 1971. Many returned to their schools to start an adaptive program. Others were content to bring Outward Bound into the classroom through new ways of teaching, or simply by virtue of being changed persons. Sometimes, Lentz recalled, it meant that a teacher moved from one school environment to another that would be more supportive.

Lentz left us in 1972 to become director of Project Adventure at Hamilton-Wenham High School in Hamilton, Massachusetts. At that time he had a unique perspective on our teacher education program. "I see it as perhaps the most important thing that Outward Bound ever got involved with. When you get involved with teacher training, you're relating to the country's ongoing educational system, where 98 percent of kids spend a good bit of their time. You have the opportunity to evaluate what the Outward Bound process means beyond just the context of a twenty-six-day course involving four thousand kids a year, which is about the size of one good-sized urban high

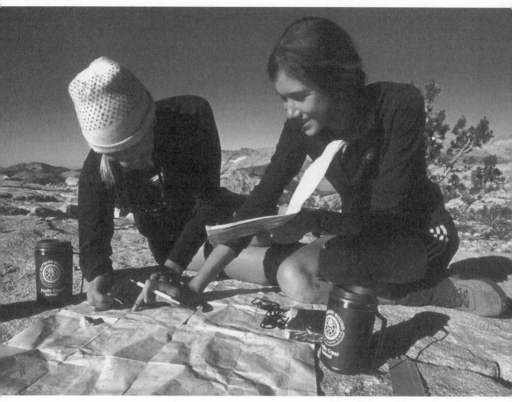

Armed with the basics—a map, a compass, water, and friendship—two Outward Bound students plan their route in the High Sierra on a mountaineering course. (Photo © Ty Milford)

school. It's good to have that impact on those four thousand kids, but if the process speaks in important ways in the development of young people and of teachers as well, then teacher learning may be the most important thrust." It was an echo of the old Jack Stevens thesis, seven years along in the Mainstream activity launched by his stubbornly held position.

Lentz saw the consequences of the teachers' courses as important in several ways. They had brought us to the realization of an adult constituency, whom we had to address somewhat differently from the youthful one. They had caught up a growing number of educators in the stream of Outward Bound enthusiasm and had begun to open up university affiliations, with a powerful potential for influencing teacher education. They had generated all kinds of growth in the way of adventure programs in high schools and colleges. The development was still fragile, but the involvement with schools that had been so tenuous was now much less so.

Lentz also put his finger on some key Mainstream problems. "School superintendents, state departments of education, federal funding sources, teacher educators, school committees, that whole world that feeds, sustains, and grows upon itself, is hard to crack. Outward Bound is a strange institution in relation to that establishment, as you discover when you try to fill out any form that asks who you are. In a sense that lack of fit gives you freedom. But it also means you have to deal with frustrations other institutions don't have. It also creates a danger within Outward Bound that you become very insular. You just talk among those people who don't ask you, 'What's Outward Bound?' and you become almost intellectually incestuous. The need is to bridge the two worlds. The teacher program is a crucial first step."

◼ ◼ ◼

From courses for mixed cadres of men and women teachers, it was an easy and inevitable step to coed courses for adults at large, a major new source of students. It also completed the departure that began with Minnesota's first girls' course in 1966. With both young and grown women comprising a substantial part of the student body, Outward Bound became a fully coeducational institution.

A profound effect of women students was their corollary: the growing presence of female staff. The entry of females into a very male world was bound to create problems—the more so in that at times the males would be slow to perceive that the problems were there. Joe Nold, for one, candidly recalled "the days when Outward Bound was very much a male chauvinist organization." The situation was compounded by the coincident tensions generated by the feminist movement as it surfaced in the late sixties.

While this story has a happy ending, the resolution of those problems and tensions did not come easily or in the course of a season or two. There was a period of considerable female grievance—that the early girls' courses were made too easy, that the men did not trust the women instructors and treated them as "borderline incompetents," that the women were paid less than the men, were denied promotion to girls' course supervisory positions, and so on. Susan Rogers, who notes that she was "the first female instructor not married to a male instructor," became Colorado's first woman senior instructor in her third season and then was told, "You did a good job, but we are not yet ready for a woman course director." Sue Kinne, who three years later did become Colorado's first woman course director, recalled a preceding period of distaff unhappiness at two schools. "It's difficult now to separate out how much was paranoia, which we intensified by talking and thinking about it a lot, and how much was a function of the male administration not feeling comfortable having us out there. I think both played a part."

Today women course directors and women in upper echelon administrative posts are common throughout the U.S. Outward Bound community. When Bob MacArthur selected Sharon Goodyear to be program director of the Dartmouth Center in 1972, it was both a pioneering move and a special case, as Dartmouth was just then starting to admit women. But five years later it caused no great stir when Minnesota School Director Derek Pritchard appointed Andree Stetson to the school's number-two spot, or when Director Gary Templin promoted Leslie Emerson to be the Colorado School's program director, giving her top-echelon responsibilities in the country's biggest school. The gratifying fact is that in the outcome Outward Bound successfully met this family "initiative test"—a kind of psychosocio bushwhack through thickets of stubborn mind-sets and strong emotions while holding to the correct compass bearing. The analogy is not as farfetched as it may sound, for the Outward Bound spirit undoubtedly played a built-in role in working through to the happy ending.

One school curriculum development was a particular testimony to the influence of women staff. At the 1974 Conference on Experiential Education jointly sponsored by the Colorado Outward Bound School and the University of Colorado School of Education, one of the workshops was "Experiential Education Planning for Women." The presenter was Dr. Jean Kugler, a clinical psychologist working with college students at the Counseling Center of the Claremont Colleges in California. Jean had already organized an informal outing club at Claremont when she took a teachers' course at the Colorado

School. She was thirty-nine—ten years older than the next most senior member of her patrol. Her professional reflexes stimulated, she began to analyze the Outward Bound process: "I see Outward Bound as a process that takes people out of their situations and gives them a meaningful experience around which insights are articulated in such a way that they understand, or feel, or find out what it is to learn and solve their own problems, independent of the process or the group. It puts people into a context of other people where they have to learn things they need to know about their own learning processes. A person learns his or her own learning style, own way to make decisions, and he or she can go back then and do that in the real world." She came out of the course with the bright light of an idea burning in her head. If this coeducational course had been so helpful to her, a woman approaching forty with grown children and pursuing a professional career, would not Outward Bound courses designed specifically for adult women fill an important need? This was the central idea she broached in her conference workshop.

Among Jean's listeners was Ann Ketchin, a veteran Colorado School instructor—one of those who had started as "a female instructor who was married to a male instructor." Ann was just turning thirty. She remembers: "It was a happy circumstance where Jean Kugler's workshop happened to find a number of us from different parts of the Outward Bound community around the country thinking along the same lines. It seemed that a lot of women like me had suddenly realized that not only had Outward Bound been relevant to them in personal growth, but that there was reason to pool our sense of this and create a course that would be relevant to older women generally."

Jean's proposal and the discussion that followed ignited a group conviction that this was the moment of truth for the idea they had been sharing without realizing it. The workshop produced a task force of Outward Bound women who, with some male support, designed and sold to the organization a plan for courses for "women over thirty." OBI appointed Clare Rhoades and Ann Ketchin to be a two-woman promotion and coordinating team to advance the project. The pioneer courses, with their appeal and challenge to women in "midlife transition," were successful, in some instances dramatically so. The schools now offer a variety of courses in all seasons, seven to fourteen days in length, for adult women.

THE ALTERNATE SEMESTER

�֍

*I got so I hated riding on that damn yellow bus and listening to
the bullshitting that went around like a disease. A lot of times
I felt very lonely because I didn't trust a lot of people and
because they didn't seem committed to anyone or anything. I
was sort of trying to protect myself from having all that rub off
on me. It's only now that the realization of leaving Seminar is
hitting me. And it's only now that I'm finding out how much it
is a part of me and how much I really dug it. I've gotten closer
than ever before to people in a learning situation. And I've
learned from them even more than I've learned from the
sources we sought for information and example. I've learned
new depths in feeling people and understanding them since
Mexico. I've learned a lot about life and myself. I've found out
that it's going to be that way—learning and growing—for the
rest of my life.*

—Student in the first Senior Seminar, Denver East High

I

When Denver's East High opened in the fall of 1967, after the first
groups of students and teachers had been to Marble, the school
looked for ways to work Outward Bound into its own scheme of operation. A
first step was to start up a mountaineering club, the Aufsteigers, with instruc-

tors from the Colorado School. Bob Colwell later thought this was a mistake. The club attracted mostly upper- and middle-class youths who became a kind of elite, feeling superior to their nonmountaineering peers. A more productive train of events followed a Joe Nold talk to the faculty. One of his listeners was Craig Spillman, a young history teacher. "Joe showed us his movie," Spillman remembered, "and asked us, how do we find an educational interpretation of the Outward Bound concept in the school context? I was teaching in the very traditional, necktie, lectern-style approach. I'd never heard of Outward Bound and I'd never been an outdoorsman. But Nold's questions intrigued the hell out of me, and soon I was in a dialogue with him."

Nold asked Spillman to help Arthur Bragg and John Timmons, another teacher, organize a service expedition during Christmas vacation to San Felipe, a Mexican village in Baja California that had suffered a tidal wave. Four faculty members and about forty youngsters wound up painting the village school. "Overall, the expedition was a success," Spillman said. "We learned lots from our mistakes. One was going as a single large group. I was to learn that the most interpersonal growth occurs in a primary group—a dozen kids and one teacher."

Other teachers led other service expeditions and weekend mountaineering trips. English teacher Ellene Franzen Austin took the lead in developing a white-water rafting program. (This was how Colorado Outward Bound's rafting program got its start.) Spillman and another history teacher teamed up to teach a class in which students did volunteer work in the city, and resource people from the city—everybody from the mayor to the head of the Black Panthers—came to the classroom. They organized an expedition to the Navajo reservation in northern Arizona that revealed useful cross-cultural possibilities. During the next Christmas vacation Spillman took a vanload of students to Greenwood, Mississippi, where they did a service project in a black community center. The East High–Outward Bound collaboration was feeling its way in bits and pieces.

It was on a second trip to Mississippi that Spillman's youngsters planted the seed that would bring it all together. "We had just camped overnight on a Civil War battleground. As we drove down the Natchez Trail Parkway every kid in the van crowded into the front seats to talk about how could we create a full-time school environment where students could learn in the field. That started me thinking. I went to Bob Colwell and proposed a full semester where we would do, on an academic basis, the kinds of things we were then doing extracurricularly on weekends and vacations." With Colwell and Nold's encouragement, Spillman, Austin, and several other teachers developed the idea over the summer of 1969. In the fall the school decided, with the support of Assistant School Superintendent Richard Koeppe, to conduct an experimental "Senior Seminar" in the second semester. The seminar would be organized into a series of off-campus educational modules, kicked off by an Outward Bound kind of experience. The seminar was open to about one hundred student applicants, chosen by lot from ethnic categories in ratios matching those in the school population at large. An exception to the lottery procedure was the recruiting of twenty-five dropout and near-dropout students who, while unmotivated, were thought to have a potential for post-high-school academic work.

"An important thing about the way we organized the seminar," Colwell said, "was that there were no criteria for entry in terms of good behavior, or academics, or anything else. In fact, we deliberately tried to make it representative of a cross section of the senior class—racially, sexually, academically. Some of the kids were in advanced placement courses; some we dragged in off the streets. The cadres also represented this cross section. One of the things the kids accepted was that they were not going to choose whom they were going to camp with."

The two-and-a-half-week Outward Bound adventure module that launched the seminar took place, following a marathon bus trip, in western Mexico. Four teachers accompanied the ninety-odd students; adding four graduate-student practice teachers from the University of Colorado provided eight leaders for as many primary-group cadres. Returning to Denver, the students opted alternatively for a module in "Politics and Power" or "Urban Arts"—one a firsthand study of government processes centering at the state capital, the other an exposure to individuals and groups involved in creative arts. All took part in a module on the Navajo reservation, studying the Navajo pastoral, non-community society. Each student lived with an Indian family, many in isolated hogans, helping to herd sheep and goats, shear wool, cook, and share in other chores. Back again at the Denver base, the students chose between "Space Technology" and "Man and Hispanic Culture."

All participated in the "Urban Design" module, in which they collected trash with city sanitation crews, visited urban-renewal construction sites, talked with city planners, and through other leads explored the challenges confronting a city at once aging and growing. The seminar ended with a twelve-day white-water rafting expedition, with the original Outward Bound module cadres reunited on the Green and Yampa Rivers in northwestern Colorado. Seminar staff and park rangers exposed the students to geological, ecological, paleontological, anthropological, and historical aspects of the Dinosaur National Monument region through which the rivers flow.

Joining the students for two days and nights, Colwell found the tumbled barriers and communication among the students that he had set as a prime objective in the early talks with Nold. "First of all, I saw competence. Here were kids who two months before had never slept under the stars who were so comfortable living outdoors that you wouldn't believe it. They were clean. Girls were washing their hair in the river. A white girl was teasing a black girl's Afro, and a black girl was braiding a white girl's hair. The second thing I noticed was that the preoccupation with sex that you see at the school had disappeared."

On the second night he circulated among the campfires, from one group of cadres to another. "I asked them, 'What is the primary group like?' and a girl over in the shadows said, 'It's like a family,' and I heard general assent. They had adopted family as the only word that would adequately describe the relationship among those kids and their teachers. Another girl said, 'Yes, we love each other.' The kids picked that up and explained, 'We know who's going to be late getting up in the morning. We know who's going to be short-tempered at night, and who's going to be short-tempered in the morning. We know who the best cook is, who the one is that doesn't care about cooking but doesn't mind cleaning up.' And so on—this whole gamut of things that people who live in a family and understand each other will accept because they love each other. They got into a discussion as to whether they were as adequate without their teachers as with, and they agreed they weren't. I came away from the experience with a great soaring confidence in what kids can do."

A striking consequence of the Senior Seminar's first year was that thirteen black youngsters, most of whom had been in the dropout or near-dropout group, took a special qualifying program at Colorado University that summer and entered the university as freshmen in the fall. In 1973 seven of them were still in college as juniors, some of them making B averages. The seminar won strong support from parents of the participants; one stated to the Board of Education that he could not find words strong enough to urge that it be put into effect in all the city's schools. A story in *Life* magazine won it widespread recognition. It became a model for alternate semesters from Massachusetts to California and was an inspiration for others choosing different formats.

Despite the fame and praise, with the Phipps funding running out there was doubt the program could continue. The 1971 seminar was made possible by supplementary contributions from parents, money earned by students, and a $10,000 gift from Charles F. Kettering Jr. to buy buses. In the third year when Spillman joined the Prescott College staff, fellow teacher Emil Ziegler became seminar director. The Outward Bound module was strengthened by increased emphasis on on-site study of marine biology and desert ecology. A live-in with a Mexican family was added, along with a visit to a remote Seri Indian village. The official evaluation of the 1973 seminar reported: "The Mexico Outward Bound module, because of its strong impact on students and staff, has proven to be a most effective way of starting the Seminar. The experience forces students and teachers to confront and solve personal conflicts, to discover personal strengths and weaknesses, and, probably most important, it provides success for those accustomed to failure."

By then the seminar had achieved a solid status in the East High community, although it had yet to win its battle for permanent status. A strong majority of respondents in all categories—seniors, staff, parents, seminar alumni—believed that it should be "continued, as is" or "expanded."[25] The alumni, looking back with the perspective of time, reported that it had helped them to understand themselves better (96 percent), to "understand our society" better (92 percent), to value education (92 percent), to continue their education (83 percent), to develop useful skills (89 percent), to make friends (93 percent).

---

[25] In 1977, still under Ziegler, who had continued to build up its academic content and rigor, the seminar was made a permanent course in the East High syllabus. In 1978 it was declared open to students at all Denver high schools, and a year later it was made operative in both semesters.

Colwell, who would be promoted to executive director of the Denver schools' new Department of Alternative Education in 1974, could point to several significant offshoots of the seminar: "For one thing, the desire for field experience has become important to East High teachers. For another, I am convinced that doing things with the curriculum that more nearly met the needs of the students is one of the things that kept the school on an even keel in turbulent times.

"What we did not even contemplate when we started the seminar was the affectionate cross-cultural association we developed with the Mexicans, the Chicanos, and the Navajos. The Mexican and Chicano families now send their youngsters to us in an intercultural exchange, and there are many instances of East High youngsters taking their parents to visit their Navajo parents on the reservation. When our kids go to a live-in with a Navajo family, they are not observing a culture, they're living in it, and many healthy things have come out of this. The kids come back from the Navajos with manual skills they never would have got in any other way—many of our girls now can weave a Navajo rug. But more than that, a lot of our kids come back with the realization that money isn't what makes a family. One of the things we've lost in our country is the idea of the proud poor. The Navajos have it. Here is a hogan with dirt floor where the love a kid receives from his Indian family is as great as—in many cases greater than—the love he gets from his own family at home.

"Another offshoot that's very interesting is that about 25 percent of the parents report that the seminar experiences have noticeably narrowed the generation gap in their homes. When you stop to think about it, this would naturally be the result of the Outward Bound experience—self-realization, understanding yourself. Kids have written about it in their journals: 'I suddenly realized my parents have problems too.'"

II

The most valuable role of the East High–Outward Bound alliance was that for which, in fact, it was chiefly created—to help the school weather the racial crisis of the late 1960s and early 1970s and achieve a relatively happy resolution. Because the school was apparently doing a number of things right, the crisis was slow to develop there. Principal Bob Colwell remembered: "The black revolution hit us with the murder of Martin Luther King Jr. in April 1968. Until the shooting of King, this school, we felt, was well on its way to becoming a truly integrated institution. The idealism of the kids for integration, and their drive to achieve it, were very high. The shot that killed Martin Luther King, I think, will go down in history as being just as important as the shot that killed Lincoln. The day after King's murder was hell around here. Nobody was seriously hurt, although there were several beatings. Some heroic things also happened. About noon two black boys were beating up a white kid in front of my office. A black girl of pretty fair proportions grabbed both the black boys and said, 'Lay off him; he didn't do it!' Black boys took white girls home in their cars to protect them. A mob of black students gathered in the street, and our black teachers went out there and worked to control them—those kids wouldn't look at a white teacher that day. But the main thing was the feeling on the part of both black and white kids that the world was falling in pieces."

Regis Groff was a black teacher at East High who Craig Spillman recruited for the first Senior Seminar. He was not however, keen on participating in the Outward Bound module. He agreed to drive one of the buses to Mexico with the proviso that he could then fly back home. But at the airport the authorities insisted that since he had entered the country driving a bus, he must leave with it. Regis had no choice but to take part in the Outward Bound experience. "I had absolutely no intention of enjoying any of it," he said. "I had it figured out why I wasn't going to like it, why my background would not let me get excited by that kind of experience. And shoot, I still got shot down. One of those first nights I was lying in my sleeping bag, watching all those stars over my head, and my pillow started getting wet—it wasn't raining either. Something happened, working with the kids and running into some brand-spanking-new challenges.

"It was the same at the end of the semester when we went on the river. I had no intention of going through the Warm Springs Rapids. Then someone said, 'Okay, Regis, you're next,' and I took a paddle and jumped into the boat because I was expected to. We went through those rapids, and it was the kind of experience a person almost has to have. I felt some kind of exhilaration I never felt before, and I've never felt since. I had to splash water on my face so the kids couldn't see all that stuff slipping out of my eyes wasn't river water."

Most meaningful to Groff was the effect of the Outward Bound experience on the students of his own race. "It takes a lot of hate out of you. I think that's what happened to the black kids. I don't know one who went to Mexico and went down the river and came back and said he didn't like it. I don't think they lost their anger, but they lost their hate. They still get uptight, they still have some rage, but the hate is gone. You just can't hate some guys you spend all that time with in the desert or on the mountain or on the river, cooking and drinking out of the same thing and struggling up the same hill; you can't hate him. I came back fifty feet off the ground. Really, not only did my armor get destroyed, but I got pushed way over on the other side, which doesn't happen that much when you've got your mind made up on it."

One of those in the "near-dropout" group who went on to college from the first Senior Seminar was Marshall Chambers. Colwell had a vivid memory of his first meeting with Marshall. Several teachers had stopped the principal in the hallway to alert him that a boy named Chambers had been sent to his office. They added such remarks as "You'd better get him out of here," and "I don't ever want to see him again." When Bob reached the office, a seventeen-year-old black youth who was sitting on the counter outside greeted him: "I thought they'd get you in here!" Then, poking the principal in the chest, he said, "You and I will get along if we understand one thing. You're a white racist son of a bitch and I'm a black racist son of a bitch. If we understand that, we'll be lucky."

Marshall Chambers transferred to East High from Cheyenne, Wyoming, when, at the age of sixteen, he moved to Denver with his mother and two brothers. East's bigness daunted him. On his first day he stood outside his homeroom, afraid to go in. In junior high in Cheyenne he had been a leading athlete, city wrestling champion in his age group, and a member of a prize-winning drum and bugle corps. Now, in the strange new big-city environment, he eschewed extracurricular activity, did well in his studies. Then came the murder of Martin Luther King. In the months that followed Marshall became, as he puts it, "a very political person." He grew to feel that the black students were being discriminated against in the quality of their academics and that the school community made its judgment on the black students either ignoring or in ignorance of conditions in the black community. His texts became contemporary works like Robert Conot's *Rivers of Blood, Years of Darkness,* and Eldridge Cleaver's *Soul on Ice,* and he became the leader of the dissident black activists in the school. During Christmas vacation he went to Los Angeles for a conference where he listened to H. Rap Brown and other radical leaders. Back at East the confrontations between him and the school and police grew more intense. "One day in front of the school," he remembered, "a policeman told me I was bound for jail because smart-ass niggers like me just didn't make the scene. He said, 'We're going to get you,' and I said, 'How can you get me? I'm not a thief, and I don't believe in ripping people off. I do believe in speaking out and being strong and believing in what I say.'" Soon after that Marshall was arrested for loitering. The loitering charge didn't stick, but he was fined $32 for having called a policeman a pig.

About that time something happened in his thinking. "I thought everything was going all wrong, and I had to get away from all the hassle and all the people. In February, when my eighteenth birthday was coming up, I went to Wyoming and stayed at a place my mother had that was vacant. I didn't communicate with people for quite a while. I was mentally drained. I couldn't even read a book. I pretty much came to the conclusion that it wasn't worth my effort anymore to fight the system, that the system was a massive powerful social force that the social laws had set apart, and they weren't going to change or be flexible to the needs of the people. They were simply going to say, we're going to put you in jail, or we're going to eliminate you altogether. This is the way I felt the system works—you're going to work with it, because you simply cannot work against it."

In the fall of 1969 Marshall persuaded East High to let him back in. He needed ninety hours of credits to graduate; the normal load was sixty. He was taking six courses, missing only one day of school in the entire term, when Craig Spillman prevailed on him to sign up for the Senior Seminar the following semester. The seminar was an educational eye-opener. "We were doing 'Politics and Power,'" he said, "and I thought, I've spent all this time studying history, and now they've taken me out of school for one semester, and I've learned more by going down to the capitol than I did the entire time

I was in school. I thought, How can it be? I really became involved in the seminar. It was taking me away from all the things I had been involved in. I felt a change in myself. I was still very radical, but I related to people better; I didn't try to maintain that facade that made people reluctant to speak to me because I might tell them to go to hell or drop dead. I enjoyed the river trip. On the last day of the river trip we were sitting around, and I was thinking, Well, what are you going to do now, Marshall?"

He was a while finding out. That summer he took two summer-school courses and a third via television to earn enough credits for his high school diploma. In the fall, junior college was a disappointment. So was the world of employment and a second try at college. In the winter of 1971, through the intercession of Howard Hoffman, an East High teacher and Outward Bound instructor, the Colorado School signed him on as an assistant instructor and recruiter of minority students. The Outward Bound association completed the process of turning Marshall's life around. He helped Hoffman develop a spring-vacation orientation course for inner-city youngsters who were slated to take an Outward Bound course in the summer. Two years later, in charge of the program and with a successful third orientation course completed, he had a clear view ahead. His job arrangement enabled him to attend college part-time, and he was looking past his education to ideas he had for becoming a resource person for young adults in the ghetto. His philosophy for beating the system had crystallized: "I think all people should decide what they want to do; once they've done that, they can pretty much achieve the goals they want. Once you have that commitment, there's nothing that can stop you, no barriers that will hold you back. That's one thing that Outward Bound has made me realize, the fact that I can achieve any goals I want."

III

As word of East Denver High's Senior Seminar spread across the country at the end of the 1960s, it coincided with a rising tide of student dissatisfaction with conventional schooling. School people were ready to try alternatives that promised to help repair a widespread failure to motivate many youngsters, both well and ill prepared. East High's example led a number of schools—a cluster in Colorado and others as far away as California and Massachusetts—to try a similar alternative term. The Massachusetts alternative is perhaps of special interest, in part for the teacher evaluation of the Outward Bound element and more particularly for the well-defined ambivalence it created among some fine teachers.

In the spring of 1971 a group of students at Lincoln-Sudbury Regional High, a school for some two thousand students living in two Boston suburbs, approached one of their teachers and voiced their discontent with the character of the schooling they were getting. At that time, Lincoln-Sudbury had a first-rate adaptive program, Nimbus, that had been created by the Hurricane Island School and placed under Joseph Kleiser, head of the physical education department. Instead of seeing the new outdoor program as a threat—a not-uncommon athletic department reaction—Joe embraced it, simultaneously articulating Nimbus into his department's program and making it available to the academic side of the school for assisting classroom projects. Nimbus received strong support from Superintendent Willard Ruliffson, a staunch convert to the Outward Bound idea from the time he observed the effects of Hurricane's pilot course on both his students and teachers. So it was not surprising that the teacher who was approached by the unhappy student group turned to Kleiser for counsel.

A consequence was that two classroom teachers and Kleiser journeyed to Denver to observe and be briefed on the Senior Seminar at East High. When they reported back, the excited reaction of the students was that this was what they were seeking. Ruliffson gave the go-ahead for an alternate semester, provided the students did the organizing and fund-raising. He made English teacher Dixie Pierson the faculty member in charge.

The student body for Lincoln-Sudbury's Alternate Semester was quite different from the carefully devised cross section of the student body that comprised East's seminar enrollment. Pierson describes the original seminar group as academically oriented, very bright, with initiative and confidence—and disaffected. While their intent was to have all kinds of students in the seminar, that did not happen the first year. Most of the thirty-five juniors and seniors who signed up were the intellectual elite. What these kids wanted was an experience-oriented alternative to classroom learning. They wanted a decision-making role in their own education; the planning phase of the semester was very important to them. They wanted a sense of community. Many felt lonely, alienated. They were looking to explore new roles with each other and with teachers—they no longer wanted to see teachers as teachers. They also wanted to relate to the larger community through experience.

While Lincoln-Sudbury employed the East module structure, the nature of the modules was different in that the main emphasis was on internship projects. One module, however, was decisively retained; the students strongly supported the precedent of starting with an Outward Bound experience. The module was contracted to Hurricane Island. Land-based in north-central Maine, it was Hurricane's first winter course; once again it was a case of an adaptive program stretching the capability of an Outward Bound school.

"Outward Bound was perhaps the most overwhelmingly successful unit," the faculty evaluating group reported. "It appears in retrospect to be the one which came closest to meeting its goals of establishing group unity, building individual self-confidence, expanding self-awareness, and encouraging appreciation of the wilderness." They reported that after four months of other experiences the students still stressed the impetus the intense opening experience had given the entire semester; many cited ways in which it had influenced them throughout the program and perhaps changed them personally. The staff concurred, noting that it had taught the students to work together and helped break down barriers between staff and students. They were impressed by the way it had affected individuals:

All seemed touched by it in some way. There were no dramatic changes in character, no instant solutions to deeply rooted personal problems—it would be naive to expect either—but there were significant changes in attitude. . . . Many left feeling better about themselves in some way—and their behavior bore witness to these things throughout the semester. Outward Bound held out certain values which were a continual source of personal and group strength.

While both student and staff evaluations of the overall Alternate Semester were positive, they differed significantly. The students stressed its experiential character, that they were able to do "real work," shape their own education, and explore and nurture relationships in which they came to trust and care for others. The teachers, however, while rating the experiment a success and favoring its being offered again the following year,[26] had reservations in the form of deep personal concerns. The dilemma of the teacher dedicated to scholarship as the sinew of our culture, who at the same time acknowledges the educational values obtainable outside the classroom, may never have been more poignantly stated than in the staff report signed by teachers Dixie Pierson, Barry Copp, and Karen Sargent:

Our most profound reservations about the program are philosophical. We watch all the praise pour in. Most employers were enthusiastic; many students claim it was the most important thing that has ever happened to them. But we remain skeptical and cautious. We speculate about what all this adds up to and question by what criteria an experience like this can be understood. As a staff who, although still young, are really the product of another system, we cannot avoid feeling threatened on some level by a program which so basically calls the academic approach into question. We see that this program released incredible amounts of productive energy, that the students exercised more self-discipline, wrote more articulately, and showed greater curiosity than they do in most of our classes. And there is no doubt that for some students this provided a very valid learning experience. But, at the same time, we question very seriously an approach which seems so oriented to the concerns of the present, so hostile to academic pursuit and so disinterested in intellectual and cultural heritage.

It may be, as Arnold Shore has tentatively suggested in his commentary on the research literature on Outward Bound, that the anti-intellectual bias is

[26] The Alternate Semester was still in the Lincoln-Sudbury curriculum in 1980–1981. However, both Nimbus and the semester's Outward Bound component were casualties of time and other factors.

overstated and itself indicative of a narrow sense of what constitutes learning. These teachers, however, did perform their responsibilities to the Alternate Semester on a dedicated level, did testify to its impressive results, did support its continuation. They were, as we interpret them, articulating a question more than affirming an answer. It is a valid question, and the answer is not as simple as some on either side would have it. However, much in this book makes clear that there is no inherent contradiction between conventional classroom and experiential approaches to learning, and that in fact the happiest results are obtained where a symbiotic relationship exists. In any event, the final thoughts in the staff's evaluation appear to resolve whatever doubts they shared about the Alternate Semester's value. In part they were influenced by their students' evaluation.

> *We also hear the students saying how profoundly Alternate Semester affected them. If in fact this is true, if they do feel significantly better about themselves, if they do feel they have exercised control over their education and assumed responsibility for the direction of their own lives, then we most definitely believe it is worthwhile.*

In part, they were persuaded by the experience's influence on their own feelings:

> *We also look at ourselves and find that, despite all the difficulties, we have come to understand and care for these young people in a way that never would have been possible in a classroom. We think we have a better comprehension of their needs, a clearer idea of what is important to them, and thus a far sounder justification for our involvement in education.*

COLLEGE ORIENTATION:
THE MOBILE TERM

❈

*It is our belief at Prescott College that through
the medium of the mountains, the sea, canyons
and rivers, the qualities of style, compassion,
integrity, responsibility, and leadership can be
fostered and encouraged.*

—Ronald Nairn

I

Prescott College opened its doors in Arizona in 1966 as a new kind of private, four-year, liberal-arts college "unfettered by any tradition that could limit its opportunity to relate itself dynamically to the emerging 21st century." In light of its ill fate eight years later, the declaration became ironic. Prescott made its mark on higher education, and its influence continued even before its remarkable revivification. In the generating and shaping of that influence, Outward Bound played a prominent part.

Prescott's first students made do with an informal physical-education program based on the availability of a new combined field house and gym and an athletic field. As Dr. Ronald Nairn, Prescott's founder-president, wrestled with the decisions of shaping a long-term physical education and athletic policy, his thinking was governed by three primary considerations: The college was poor; it lacked funds for a formal athletic program.

Geographically it was isolated; competitive athletics with other institutions would require much travel. It was situated in glorious country, close to some of the greatest natural challenges in the continental United States.

Raised on a ranch in wild, back-country New Zealand, Nairn had enjoyed an adventurous youth. A World War II fighter pilot in Britain's Royal Air Force at seventeen, he had returned to find the rugged countryside of his boyhood considerably tamed. By then Outward Bound had come to New Zealand. Nairn identified with its purpose to expose young people to the kind of wilderness challenges that had been his natural lot. Later, as an educator in the United States—he obtained his doctorate and taught at Yale—he kept tabs on the spreading U.S. Outward Bound movement. Now he conceived of a physical-education program grounded in Outward Bound kinds of activity. He put the proposal to Charles F. Kettering Jr., a Prescott trustee and a principal benefactor. Kettering, who lived in Denver and had already become interested in what the Colorado School was doing, endorsed the idea. The college engaged Joe Nold as a consultant and on his recommendation hired Roy Smith, a British instructor then working for Colorado, to organize a physical-education program along Outward Bound lines.

Roy met heavy student apathy to Outdoor Action, as he called his program. "I talked to the whole school and said I wanted to get them out into the Southwest, to get them excited about things like backpacking, mountaineering, and rock climbing. It was pretty strange talk to them. These were fairly spoiled middle-class kids. Only a few were academically inclined and even fewer were inclined to my area. I used to walk around the commons at mealtime, and knock on dormitory doors to line up students. My battle cry was, 'Get involved!'"

Gradually Smith's involvement process took hold. "Out of the climbing came mountain rescue. I explained the service idea, had the sheriff come up and tell how mountain rescue would help the community. Now the students were excited. We formed a mountain-rescue team that was deputized for Yavapai County and later in Grand Canyon National Park." He trained ten student assistant instructors for a more ambitious program the next year. The program broadened to include white-water kayaking, sailing, scuba diving,

A class "gunnels up" for lessons in sea kayaking in the clear waters of the Sea of Cortez, Baja, California. (Photo © COBS, Chris Brown)

rafting, horsemanship, and, for a time, gliding. The water-activity people formed a water-rescue team.

The increasingly ambitious expeditions included winter mountaineering, Grand Canyon river trips, the first sea-kayak exploration of the Golfo de California between Baja (Lower California) and the Mexican mainland.

In the midst of this expanding activity the program that made Prescott famous, its freshman orientation, was conceived. Smith remembered the idea getting its start in a conversation with Nold. "He asked me how things were going, which prompted me to say what these kids needed before starting college—not for my purposes but for their own benefit—was an experience to shake them up. I told Joe they had no idea of their potential as people—not as backpackers but as people. They needed to discover what they could do. They needed an Outward Bound experience before they came here."

Starting with the fall of 1968, Prescott began the freshman year with a three-week wilderness-based orientation. It was essentially a standard Outward Bound course designed to help prepare students for life at the college—the first time an institution of higher learning tied the Outward

Bound experience directly into its curricular scheme. Together with the offbeat physical-education plan, it won Prescott national publicity that brought a flood of applications. In effect, Outward Bound solved the college's recruiting problems. The character of the student body changed remarkably. Smith no longer had to proselyte. Now the students arrived with their rucksacks and climbing boots, gung-ho for what he had to offer.

In his president's office, Ronald Nairn reflected on Outward Bound's impact on the Prescott campus. The time, and the student climate, was 1973: "I think Outward Bound is one of the country's more important movements. In this particular climactic time, young people have virtually no roots—hence they cannot heed the old Chinese aphorism, 'Have roots, yet soar like an eagle.' If one has roots, one can afford, especially in adolescence, to experiment, explore. If one has a perch to come back to, one can soar—but otherwise one is lost out there in space. Outward Bound has a particular quality in that when you deal with a mountain, a river, with cold or heat—these natural issues—you are dealing with total honesty. It's there. It is, if you like, a root. While I don't think that Outward Bound is going to provide a substitute for those intrinsic roots in our society—family, church, school, justice, and so forth—that all seem to leave so much to be desired, it is very important in default of these things. In our freshman orientation those students come back here totally different from any freshmen that I've ever seen in my life, as cohesive, ready-to-get-at-it young adults. The transformation in three weeks is just extraordinary."

Twenty months later, in December 1974, Prescott College closed its doors, a bankrupt victim of a presumed helping agency's fraudulent manipulation of funds. The closing was an educational tragedy. But although the institution's plant and campus were lost, its esprit did not capitulate. Following on the closedown, two-fifths of the students and all but one of the faculty returned for the final semester of the 1974–1975 year. They borrowed classrooms where and when they could, made generous use of the out-of-doors, made do with the faculty's personal libraries. Many of them graduated. The following year, with accreditation lost but a stubborn faculty nucleus holding on, student enrollment was down to fifty in the Prescott Center for Alternative Education, a phoenix seeking to rise from the Prescott ashes. The struggle for survival was led by Jim Stuckey, another who came to the Prescott staff from the Outward Bound community. By 1980, now Prescott Center College, the institution was carrying on under Stuckey's presidency with growing strength. The final step in accreditation appeared to be close at hand. A documentary film about the college was being made for showing on public television. Its title: *The College that Wouldn't Die.*

Even apart from Prescott's survival, education in the United States continued changed from what it would have been had the college never existed. Outdoor Action and the Prescott freshman orientation proved to be important models for other colleges and secondary schools. Challenge/Discovery, the extension of Outdoor Action that Roy Smith started at Prescott as a summer program for youth from the general public, carried on under Smith's direction at Crested Butte in the Colorado Rockies. A number of Outward Bound adaptive programs that Prescott alumni founded or helped to initiate—among them the Boojum Institute in San Diego and Arizona's Adobe Mountain School for incarcerated youth—were also manifestations of a once-presumed-dead institution's living spirit.

II

Our classroom covered 6,000 miles of road, 150 miles of trail, and 20 miles of river. In contrast to campus life, academics were not separated from our every day living. There was no distinction between days of the week to give us a routine to follow. Our whole selves were involved, not always by choice—spiritual, emotional, intellectual growth merging together. Intensity and integration were two words of which we gained a fuller understanding.

—Student report on Southwest Field Studies, Earlham College, 1976

Earlham College is a coeducational, Quaker-affiliated college founded at Richmond, Indiana, in 1847, with a student body of about one thousand in 1981. In the late 1960s, four members of the faculty—geology professor

Charles Martin, biology professor Cameron Gifford, mathematics professor Richard Rodgers, and history professor Douglas Steeples—began to talk seriously of ways they could share educationally with students their interest in the outdoors and so give them kinds of experiences they would not gain otherwise. During that time several Earlham students who had received Outward Bound scholarships brought back enthusiastic reports to the campus. The press and the intercollegiate grapevine were spreading word of Prescott's Outward Bound–based freshman orientation. Doug Steeples recalled students periodically prodding the faculty group for activity involving real physical and psychological challenges "to make a little more true the college's rhetoric about educating the whole man." Steeples finally set about providing Earlham's president, Landrum Bolling, with information for a grant proposal.

In April 1970 the Reader's Digest Foundation made a grant of $100,000 to Earlham to fund an "adventure program" in a wilderness environment. That summer a faculty member and a student were sent to Minnesota Outward Bound, another student to the Colorado School, and three of the faculty core group took wilderness skills courses at the National Outdoor Leadership School (NOLS) in Lander, Wyoming. In addition to his NOLS course, Steeples twice visited Prescott for briefings on its orientation program. We sent Bob Lentz twice from OBI, the second time with Dyke Williams, to offer counsel and encouragement. After considering several alternatives, a faculty-student planning group concurred on the idea of a month-long wilderness expedition as an orientation to the college, with coeducational cadres, to take place prior to the college's formal opening and earning one academic credit. Dick Rodgers was released from his teaching duties to serve as director.

Earlham's first Pre-term, as it was called, took place in August–September 1971 in the High Uinta Primitive Area of northeast Utah. The course design combined the Outward Bound and NOLS models, including Outward Bound's solo, with academic elements and other specifically Earlham content. The patrols were led by student instructors. A faculty member functioning partly as counselor, partly as learning resource, accompanied a pair of patrols, and largely succeeded in cloaking the collegial status that gave him ultimate veto authority.

The program was endorsed by the faculty, who were generally agreed that classroom and other contacts with students bore out the report of professors

Rodgers and Steeples. In their summary of "what worked," these two observed that the Pre-term had expanded the participants' moral sensitivity, nourished their self-confidence and eagerness to meet challenges, and enhanced their awareness of the relationship between mind and body in a balanced life. It had effectively oriented participants to the college. Another important plus, Steeples noted, was that the Pre-term's coeducational policy had done much to break down stereotyped attitudes about the sexes. "In our student debriefing one of the more prominent themes was that for a number of the fellows it was now possible to view girls as something other than sex objects. They had become human beings in their own right."

Earlham was fortunate to have in Landrum Bolling a president who was quick to perceive the value of a wilderness program to the institution. During the planning year, Alan Hale came down from Minnesota to North Carolina Outward Bound to conduct a three-day minicourse for a group of Earlham faculty members and spouses, which included Dr. and Mrs. Bolling.

"Here we were," Dr. Bolling said, "two middle-aged past-fifty types, climbing up a cliff and hanging by ropes and this sort of thing.

"It was an exciting new experience and great fun. It gave me a kind of inner gut feeling that the students must get from learning these skills, and you could see what it would do to help a person. I've had many talks with students who have been through the Pre-term. There are two themes they stress over and over. One is, 'I found myself doing things I never thought I would or could do, and this helped me to have a more confident feeling about myself.' The other is, 'I learned that in a close, tight, stressful situation I could trust and cooperate with other people in ways I had never experienced before."

"Self-confidence and trustfulness toward others are two things I think our society very much needs. As I see young people today, and the kinds of problems they wrestle with, it does seem that one of the most persistent points of tension and difficulty is low self-esteem. This seems strange, with all the advantages they have, but the fact is, I think, in our modern, industrialized, gadget-ridden society in urban settings, most young people in one sense really grow up to maturity as parasites. They've never had to do anything particularly useful. They're always in a sense parasites on their parents, on the community, on the school, and so on. They're not really contributors, as people who grew up in a farm community would be.

"I think there's a kind of psychological scar that even the most well-adjusted kids carry from growing up in a setting where they don't really count for very much. There's a deep inner hunger in a lot of young people to feel a sense of personal worth and confidence, and I think the Outward Bound experience gives them that sense to a remarkable degree—belief in themselves, a fundamental inside feeling that they can meet a challenge. And I think there is a kind of transfer of this kind of experience in the wilderness to other stressful situations. I think the experience has demonstrated its value and can be fitted into a college curriculum."[27]

In their memorandum following the first Pre-term, Rodgers and Steeples took particular note of the value of reliance on student instructors, with faculty members filling less obtrusive roles as experts in some fields and model learners in others—which, they maintained, is the actual teacher status, however less apparent it may be in a conventional academic setting. "The result," they said, "could be a sense of a genuine community of learners, largely free of the common expert-novice polarity and threat." This prophecy was to prove more apt than its authors realized.

Margaret Lechner, Earlham '72, was one of the two students initially tapped to take an Outward Bound course and join with the faculty group in developing a wilderness program, and one of the original Pre-term instructors. Following graduation as a biology major, she instructed at Minnesota Outward Bound, then in the second Pre-term, after which she returned to the college for a visit. A classmate, Ben Foster, was also back. A geology major, he too had been a Pre-term instructor and now was fresh from a summer's instructing at North Carolina Outward Bound. One evening in a conversation with friends, the two advanced the idea that some kind of a term-length academic program, designed on the mobile field learning pattern of the Pre-term, could provide an educational experience in which the values of that program would be multiplied. "Write it up!" their listeners urged.

---

[27] Dr. Bolling subsequently was made president of the Lilly Endowment in Indianapolis, and later became president of the Council on Foundations, the representative organization of private foundations in the United States.

During and subsequent to a backpack trip in the Sierra Nevada, they put their concept on paper.

"Our basic point," Margaret recalled, "was that Pre-term was fine for its purposes, but we wanted to go beyond people getting acclimatized to the wilderness, being exposed to personal challenge and the interpersonal process, being introduced to a wide variety of subject matter, getting adjusted to college, and that sort of thing. We knew how wilderness experience had helped us academically, and we wanted to extend that kind of opportunity to other students. For example, I was a plant buff who was completely turned off geology until I traveled in the wilderness with Ben. We began to build a plan of what we could do if we had a full academic term to work in."

In December they submitted to the college a proposal for a mobile term in the Southwest embracing three courses—"Regional Natural History," "Land and Resource Uses," and "Outdoor Education." Revised and refined with faculty assistance, the plan was accepted on a trial basis. The program was made available to students at member colleges of the Great Lakes College Association (GLCA) and funded through a joint grant from the Lilly Endowment and the Reader's Digest Foundation. The first "Winter Wilderness" term, as it was initially called, took place in Earlham's 1974 winter term, with an enrollment of seventeen students. Lechner and Foster were the instructors; Professor Orland Blanchard, a plant botanist, and geologist Charles Martin joined the group part-time in the field.

By the fourth year (1977), now titled "Southwest Field Studies," the term had evolved to a two-course curriculum, "Regional Natural History" and "Experiential Outdoor Education," earning three credits. The content was interdisciplinary, embracing biology, geology, and education as the primary areas of study and including aspects of geography, land use, meteorology/climatology, and history. Three major natural areas—the Grand Canyon, the Lower Sonoran Desert on the Arizona-Mexico border, and Big Bend National Park on the Texas-Mexico border—were used as outdoor classrooms. In addition to the two faculty leaders, Lechner and biology professor William Buskirk, the students had access to local resource persons. A number of these were embarked on research, education, and land-management projects, in careers of possible interest to the students.

Other useful resources were such people as park rangers, ranch managers, a town mayor, and a Mexican goatherd.

Still another resource was the students themselves—primarily but not exclusively upperclassmen who had acquired a degree of expertise in their fields of study. While peer teaching and learning had been contemplated from the outset, it got an assist from dynamics that proved to be built into the experiment. "The one big lesson we learned the first year," Lechner recalled, "was that we were putting people into a unique educational situation, a twenty-four-hour, peer-group learning situation, and this produced significant course content. There was a tremendous amount of useful course material generated around questions like 'How come this feels so different from school, even though we're dealing with the same subject content?' We hadn't planned that. We said, 'Hey, let's put in educational philosophy as part of the outdoor education course, because it's happening anyway.' We consciously made the decision to use what was happening to us within the group as a sociological and psychological resource."

Biology professor Bill Buskirk's involvement was instructive. His appointment as one of the two 1977 staff leaders was a response to the Curriculum Policy Committee's recommendation, in postponing final action on the experiential term's permanent status, that the natural science component be upgraded so as to "combine the special advantages of field study with a level of academic expectation equal to that typical of classroom instruction." The previous year he had been a part-time faculty participant, leading the group through a two-week comparative vegetation study of the Sonoran and Chihuahuan deserts. (A Buskirk dictum: "When we learn to respect the desert for what it is rather than what it is not, we learn to respect and like it.") Prior to that, his only exposure to the program had been in attending a slide-show report by the students who had taken part in the 1975 term. Thinking back to that occasion a year later, he recalled, "I felt a very high level of group coherence and togetherness in the program. It came off as strongly experiential. As a teacher on campus I felt that maybe I'd never be able to produce a learning experience that had excited people so much and sharpened their thinking so about the educational process. I thought it was commendable that the program had done that. But I also sensed that these people coming back might be very challenging in their attitudes toward education once they were here."

But then he had done his two weeks with the 1976 term and had come to have a quite special feeling about students in his classes who had taken part in "Southwest Field Studies." "I'm always glad if any of these people are involved in a group exercise in my course because I feel there's a certain amount of leadership there. The group interaction capabilities are much higher, as is motivation to learn for themselves. On the average I feel much more comfortable with these people than with other students. I feel open to them, and that they're open to both criticism and criticizing. They are more ready to tell me what they like or don't like. But I have never felt it in a way that was threatening to me. I've always recognized that they were genuinely interested in what I was doing and how I was doing it, and how it reflected on them—as opposed to other feedback you sometimes get that's, say, more divisive."

As he spoke in the spring of 1976, he was anticipating with concern his leadership role the following winter. "I'm amazed at what can be done at the level of personal growth and in peer learning in this program. Margaret, this last winter, seemed to be able to generate an atmosphere in which everybody pulls together for their own learning and shares a lot. In thinking about teaching with it next year, I think there may be a tendency, if a full professor with whom they've had some prior experience in courses shows up, that it's going to become more directional as far as information flow is concerned, and not this more synergistic sort of relationship. I'm very concerned that it not become a strongly academic program alone. Its uniqueness in the past has come from a blend of the two."

The empirical evidence—an enthusiastic student report on the 1977 term—indicated that the experience served to remove the concern. In the spring, the faculty accepted "Southwest Field Studies" with permanent status in the curriculum.

In pursuing the story of "Southwest Field Studies," it may seem that we became a phase separated from Outward Bound. In a strict sense, it was not an adaptive program. It derived from Outward Bound, contained Outward Bound elements, and employed Outward Bound learning principles. Growth and interpersonal phenomena comparable to those common to Outward Bound experiences occurred in it. It was not, however, a stress program, and it is not characterized by severe physical demand. In the beginning Lechner and Foster thought that it would be. But early on, they came to realize that the time and energy required for full personal and interpersonal challenging had to be conserved for academic endeavor. Nevertheless, Earlham's "Southwest Field Studies," along with the rest of its Wilderness Program, was a significant chapter in the story of Outward Bound, for it shed considerable light on a question that, while not quite a mystery, is nevertheless difficult to explain: How did Outward Bound become a spearhead of the experiential movement in U.S. education? The phenomenon is best elucidated by the case method, and the Earlham story is among the most cogent of the case histories.

■ ■ ■

There are natural laws, not always understood, governing the development of human organizations. In 1972, U.S. Outward Bound was eleven years old, relative to the date of the Colorado School's incorporation. I had served nine years as president or chairman of Outward Bound Incorporated. It was apparent that the organization was now in a period of dynamic growth, with the kind of problems such growth produces, where it would be well served by a president who was somewhat less an educational administrator and more a practitioner of those managerial skills that are usually gained through experience in the business world. Also, Theodore R. Sizer, dean of the Harvard School of Education, was appointed headmaster of Phillips Academy following John Kemper's untimely death.[28] Ted offered me a new challenge as director of admissions. Less interested in the selection process, he wanted to expand the applicant pool from 1,100 to "over 3,000." Plans were being made for the academy's bicentennial; coeducation was on the horizon. So was the largest fund drive in the history of secondary education—fifty million dollars. Ted was determined to refine the emerging "house" or "cluster" structure, and he was dedicated to an increased foreign student constituency. Most important, he offered a recommitment to the founder's constitutional mandate that the academy be "ever open to requisite youth from every quarter." He had

---

[28] John Kemper died of cancer in December 1971. He was one of Andover's greats, and no less so in the annals of Outward Bound.

dreams of realizing this last objective to an even greater extent than had been the case at any time in the last century.

The challenge was exciting. I returned to Andover in the fall of 1972, where I continued with my Outward Bound responsibilities until the OBI search committee found the man with the elusive combination of attributes they had set for the new president.

The committee's man proved to be Henry W. "Hank" Taft, whom they finally located in the top echelon of the Bristol-Myers Company. Hank had attended the Taft School, which his great-grandfather Horace had founded, Yale, and Harvard Business School. Interlaced with his formal education were two hitches in the U.S. Navy, in World War II and the Korean War. Coming out of the Harvard Business School, he got in and out of the plastics industry fairly rapidly and joined the publishing house of Doubleday and Company, later becoming its treasurer. In 1959, at a time when he was considering a career change, a friend with whom he had just played a game of squash stuck his head out of the shower and said, "Hank, would you like to go to the South Seas?" Hank said, "Yes." His friend's lead was to three California men who were planning a flight from the "rat race" by sailing to Tahiti in a forty-six-foot ketch. Hank joined them.

The adventure took a year—three months living aboard the ketch in Sausalito, California, while outfitting it; a voyage of a month and a half, with island stops, to Tahiti; three months living on the Tahiti waterfront; a seventy-two-day eastward voyage with only one anchoring before making a landfall in Peru; and the final northward voyage, through the Panama Canal to New York. It was a self-made, super–Outward Bound experience. Hank felt it changed his life for the better in many ways.

He went to work for Bristol-Myers, was made the company treasurer, and later became vice president for acquisitions. He was executive vice president of the Products Division when the search committee found him. He was also a trustee of the Taft School and chairman of the board of trustees of the Rye Country Day School, and had been thinking he would like to become directly involved with education. The committee felt it had done well to ferret out a highly able businessman who had a yen for adventure and a deep interest in education. They would be proved right.

UPWARD BOUND AND
OUTWARD BOUND

❄

Higher education has usually limited enrollment to those who were already known to be bright and had the background needed to get in. Few higher education institutions have had experience in educating the type of youngster who does not have the conventional talents, conventionally measured. How can we educate some of these young people? I am sure that there are scores of ways of educating people that none of us has ever used. Whatever Upward Bound does, I would hope that it identifies and systematizes many of these ways.

—Dr. Richard T. Frost, National Director, Upward Bound, 1971

The sixty-eight passengers in the bus that took off from Middletown, Connecticut, for Morganton, North Carolina, at the end of May 1969 were an odd mix. Predominantly ninth-grade boys and girls, they also included teachers, staff members of Wesleyan University's Master of Arts in Teaching program, and members of the Harvard Motivation Achievement Development Project. About half the youngsters were black, a number of others Hispanic; the adults too were a racial mix. This was the entire student body of NC-12, a course contracted by the North Carolina Outward Bound School to Wesleyan Upward Bound. As a contract course primarily for disadvantaged youngsters with a coeducational and student-teacher peer-level mix,

NC-12 achieved a new level of uniqueness among Outward Bound courses. At its conclusion the experiment was adjudged seriously flawed. Time, however, has proved it the successful start of a significant strand in the Outreach story.

People who do not know what Outward Bound is sometimes confuse it with Upward Bound, and vice versa. Upward Bound, a federal War on Poverty project initiated by the U.S. Office of Education in the 1960s, is a precollege program for high-school students from low-income families, sponsored by colleges and universities as a service to their area. Its task is to identify economically and culturally deprived youngsters about to enter the ninth grade who have college potential but whose attitudes are apathetic or negative, perhaps even hostile, and to motivate them, follow up with development of academic skills, and eventually assist in college placement. It is not surprising that sooner or later Upward Bound and Outward Bound should have found each other.

An Upward Bound program was established at Wesleyan University in 1966. Richard Brown, a recent Dartmouth graduate who had worked under Charley Dey with the A Better Chance program in Hanover, New Hampshire, was director. In 1968 Peter Budryk became his assistant. Budryk, who would succeed to Brown's position two years later, had graduated from Boston College, taught high-school English for seven years, then earned a master's degree in school administration at the Harvard School of Education. He is a self-described poverty-hater: "I grew up in urban poverty amidst all of its concomitant pathologies, which touched me, my family, my friends. My reaction to poverty was, and still is, hatred bordering on revulsion."

Following the 1968 summer of the Wesleyan project, Brown and Budryk were dissatisfied with what had become more or less a standard pattern for most Upward Bound summer phases—a seven-week campus residence with primarily remedial study and recreation. The theory was that living in a campus ambiance would itself prove a motivational experience, turning on underprivileged youngsters to the idea of going to college. Budryk said, "It created a kind of plastic bubble world for kids that was totally unrelated to their home experience. And it created a huge baby-sitting job for the staff. We felt it wasn't working. We wanted something that was really going to hit at the kid's sense of failure, his sense that he couldn't control his own life, and at his failure to read the signals about negative behavior he was picking up from his environment. What would give the kids an opportunity to look at themselves in a different light? We wanted something organic we might do—like a model farm. We researched the possibilities and discovered Outward Bound."

They came to us at Andover seeking ideas. Out of a series of meetings with Bob Lentz and Dyke Williams from OBI and Murray Durst, then director at North Carolina, came a plan for the North Carolina School to conduct a contract course with the primary goal of building self-esteem and self-confidence in the Upward Bound students. The teachers who would have the students in the subsequent academic part of the summer session and in the school year to follow were to participate on a peer level with the students. This would, it was felt, give the teachers a more palpable sense of their Upward Bound mission and increased confidence for their task, and make for a more productive student-teacher rapport. The Harvard representation was a group of black psychologists who had organized to apply motivational methods developed at Harvard by Professor David McClelland in their work with minority children; they were to help develop student and teacher strategies for applying the gains of the outdoor program to the classroom.

"Pretty far out when it's stacked up against other Upward Bound programs," was the comment coming back from Washington. But the timing was fortunate. Both the educational community and Congress were then giving respectful attention to the Coleman Report on equal opportunity in education that the Congress had mandated. Among the Coleman group's key findings was the tenet that a youngster's sense of controlling his own destiny is by far the best predictor of academic excellence. Washington gave its approval for a summer's experiment.

NC-12 got off to a bad start, triggered by the severe culture shock of the overnight shift from Connecticut urban streets to the North Carolina wilderness. The initial unhappiness was aggravated when the articulate youngster who emerged as the leader of the dissidents created a racial issue. "It's not that we want to go home because we're finding it hard. We want to go home because this is a whitey outfit; it doesn't really fit us kids." The Upward Bound staff had no crisis management plan; in particular they had not built a strong parental support that could have stemmed the dropout tide. Twenty-two of the sixty-eight students, mostly black, opted to return home after the first week, and two went later.

Most of the Outward Bound staff were ill-prepared to work with hostile inner-city youngsters, the more so since these were younger than the students they were accustomed to. "Our kids were spewing epithets at the instructors that had the hair on their chests curling," Budryk said. "The response of some, speaking metaphorically, was to stick fingers in their ears and walk around in circles. When the kids saw this kind of ambivalence, they just drove the wedge in deeper. Then some of the instructors started to lower the course standards, which was the last thing we wanted. Our kids are very perceptive at picking up this kind of thing. There was an implicit but very clear message to a lot of them that you're poor, you're black, you're dumb, we can't expect you to do what the upper-middle-class bright kids can do, so we're going to water down the course. There was a little friction between our staff and theirs about that. On the other hand, there were also a number of instructors like Karl Rohnke, Jed Williamson, and others who were very good at handling the situation."

Williamson was one of the Colorado School instructors who had worked with Durst in the Job Corps project at Collbran three years before. Anticipating the need for perceptive staff work with the NC-12 students, Durst had summoned Jed and his wife, Perry, from New Hampshire. Jed remembered, "There were very few instructors who were in tune with where those kids were at. The kids were thirteen, fourteen, fifteen, and you just had to change gears completely. Perry and I enjoyed it. It drove Perry a little bit up the wall because she was so oriented to doing what you're supposed to do, and these kids weren't. But one day she was teaching some of them how to string up a shelter out of plastic when suddenly it hit her that these kids didn't have enough self-confidence to believe they could tie a half-hitch. And of course, the urban kid's response, when he doesn't feel he's going to have a success, is to say, 'That's chicken-shit. I ain't going to do that shit.' They're not like nice middle-class kids who say, 'I don't understand how to do that.' Rather than look bad, they come up with all kinds of bravado."

Jed recalled walking into a tent where a dozen or so black youngsters "on strike" were lying around. "I said, 'Any of you here can read maps yet?' 'Yeah, I can read those mother maps.' So I put a map on the side of the tent and I said, 'Okay, there are two or three here from my crew, and I want to give you a piece of information. This shows you where we'll be at noon today. Not only will we be there, but your lunch will be there.' One kid said, 'We're going to eat in the cafeteria,' which was what they called the mess hall. 'They're not serving lunch in the cafeteria,' I said. 'You see, everybody's leaving the base today. If you want to eat your lunch it will be out here at X.' That's how I got mine back."

Progressively, Outward Bound fashion, the situation righted itself. "The kids who stuck it out were glad they stayed," Williamson said. "They were glad it was over, and so were we, but they felt good about themselves." The Upward Bound staff gained perspective on what had initially seemed a disaster. "Part of the reason we had wanted to change the summer format," Budryk said, "was that we had been having a lot of dropouts. So when we lost all those kids in North Carolina we were traumatized. But then things improved. For those who stayed, and for the staff, the course was a success. Even the boy who led the go-home agitation, but then didn't go, had a good experience and afterward worked with us until he went to college. The Office of Education evaluator gave the course a glowing report despite the negative factors. And even in the matter of the dropouts we were in for pleasant surprises later."

The students who were still in the program continued with four weeks of academic work. "It is no surprise," reported the evaluator, "that the Wesleyan Upward Bound students who ran the whole distance were able to articulate the relationship between scaling a rock face and climbing the walls of ivy." At the same time there were indicators that the dropout episode was not a closed book. A factor that seems to have been an influence was that in the black communities of Middletown and Meriden parents of the youngsters who had stuck it out in North Carolina took a superior attitude toward parents of the dropouts. Whatever the psychology or sociological chemistry at work during that summer, a payoff came when school reopened. One by one the dropouts, seventeen out of twenty-four in all, showed up at the Upward Bound office and asked to be taken back.

To Budryk and his staff, those individuals were a phenomenon. In the past, dropouts had simply dropped out of sight. "We didn't make it easy for them to come back in," Budryk said. "We sat down with them, stretching it out over the winter, getting them to think about why they wanted to be in the program and what they wanted to achieve in their futures." He thought it likely that some of the effects of Outward Bound on the others had rubbed off on them. "In any event, the process of reenrolling that they initiated and we sustained with them seemed to be a very valuable maturing force. They did generally well."

Becoming director at the start of the new college year and convinced that the Outward Bound dynamic offered the motivating energy he and Brown had sought, Budryk researched the university's land holdings. He found they included a fifteen-hundred-acre wilderness preserve called Great Hollow in southwest Connecticut. Work was rushed to make the Great Hollow Wilderness School ready for the summer of 1970. Durst, now at OBI, gave counsel and moral encouragement. Jed Williamson, who had grown up in nearby Quaker Hill, New York, was on-site consultant. Jim Merritt, a Trenton State College and Northwest School alumnus who had instructed in Trenton Action Bound and at North Carolina as well as Outward Bound schools abroad, helped to set up a ropes course and was made chief instructor.

Budryk, not wanting to risk a recurrence of the previous year's dropout debacle, set about enlisting parental backing. Staff members met privately with each set of parents, describing the difficulties, fatigue, loneliness, and pain the students would encounter.

"We put it right on the line," Budryk said. "What would you do if your youngster called you from a pay phone at eleven o'clock at night and he was crying and telling you he was miserable, was being starved and overworked, and he wanted to come home? In most cases we were able to convince the parents to trust us, that this was going to be a good experience for their child, and if they gave in to him or her, the child's chance to grow through it would be lost."

A second tactic that guarded against dropping out was scheduling the crews so that from day two to day seventeen they were separated from each other, one at the base camp, the others on expedition. They had no opportunity, as had occurred in North Carolina, to get together and reenforce their misgivings. The two tactics, together with a staff prepared for difficult behavior, worked. No students left the Great Hollow course that summer. For Budryk the lesson "confirmed our belief that young boys and girls labeled 'undermotivated' and 'underachieving' can succeed where expectations are clear and consistent."

The 1970 experience established the summer-program pattern of a twenty-one-day "motivational ignition" course at Great Hollow, followed by four weeks of academic skills development plus enrichment workshops and athletics. Upperclassmen frequently continued their wilderness learning experiences in subsequent years, assisting adult leaders or as assistant counselors in a community camping program.

One of the black staff members in Great Hollow's second summer was Arthur Conquest, a former Hurricane Island instructor. This was the same Arthur Wellington Conquest III who nine years before, freshly separated from high school for truancy, took the C-2 course at Colorado on a New York Boys' Club scholarship. Arthur's self-styled "stern but loving parent" instructing style worked well with the Upward Bound youngsters. At one point on the trail, stricken with food poisoning and vomiting yellow bile, he came close to stopping and sending for a doctor; instead, conscious of his role-model responsibility, he pushed on with his crew. He thinks the kids got the message; none made a move to drop out. The only would-be defector was a teacher. Conquest told him, "Just like the kids, you start this thing, you finish." The teacher stayed. The following year, in 1972, Conquest was made chief instructor.

■ ■ ■

At sixteen, living with his mother and brothers in New York's East Harlem ghetto, Arthur Conquest was a zealous participant in all activities at the Jefferson Park Boys' Club. He was on the club swimming team and a good all-around athlete for the Monitors in the intraclub competitions. Since the club was located in the Italian section of East Harlem, most of the Monitors were youths of Italian descent. If you were black or Puerto Rican and lived in East Harlem at that time, you were very careful where you walked; east of Second Avenue, where the Italian neighborhood started, was pretty much off limits. Arthur was one of only a handful of blacks who prized membership in the club enough to venture there. "Looking back," he said, "I can see that I was chosen to go to Colorado because I could get along with whites." Only one other of the nine-member Boys' Club contingent was black; the rest were white youngsters of academic promise who were attending prep schools on club scholarships.

Arthur remembered, "I had some problems going through the course, partly because of my inability to understand the long-range goals. But also it was a matter of other people not understanding me and where I was coming from." The utterly strange mountain environment tested him severely. He vividly recalled his patrol's first practice climb and his inept effort to build a fire for cooking his lunch. "I ate almost raw chicken and raw potatoes. Joe Nold took us up to twelve thousand feet and he said, 'It's five o'clock, we've got an hour and a half to get off this mountain before dark,' and he begins to run off the mountain. Here I am a city kid and never been off a piece of concrete, and Joe Nold's running down the mountain. It was unreal. I was sick from eating the raw food and I was running down this mountain, bumping into trees, stumbling over rocks, and falling into dirt, getting to base camp in the dark and going to the nurse, telling her that I'm half dead, and she said, 'Take two aspirins.' I could have killed her."

He did not find it easy as the only black in his patrol, one of two in the entire course. Defensive, he was not letting anyone forget he was from East Harlem. There was a series of confrontations and other incidents. Once, at thirteen thousand feet, he had a fight with an older boy after which, he believes, the school considered asking him to leave. "I kept telling myself, I can't wait to get out of this place. But the most important thing, I never said I was going to quit."

Gradually things got better. A strong friendship grew between Arthur and his tentmate George, a student at the Thacher School in California. George became Arthur's sturdy advocate when tensions developed in the patrol. On final expedition, Arthur acquitted himself well in his group of four. In the marathon he finished tenth. He remembered Helen Rawalt saying, "I didn't expect you to do so well."

Toting his gear down to the bus on the final day, tears welled in his eyes and spilled over. "I kept thinking, I'm going to miss this place."

Young Conquest had no sense then of having forged a lifelong association with Outward Bound. Back home from Colorado he worked at various jobs and went to night school. When he was eighteen, he joined VISTA. Placed in one of Mayor John Lindsay's mini city halls on New York's Lower East Side to deal with slum tenant complaints, he discharged his responsibilities with more diligence than his VISTA superiors appreciated. Once he brought a band of tenants whose building the landlord had abandoned to stage a sitdown in the city building commissioner's office. Another time he punched an inspector who refused to order a new window installed and insisted instead that the tenants move to a hotel for welfare families. Eventually Arthur and VISTA agreed to part company. "I was a free spirit," he said.

Not long before, he had attended an Outward Bound alumni reunion at the downtown New York Boys' Club. He went because he was broke and knew there would be food. The club director asked him to show Peter Willauer around the building. As they made the tour, Conquest told Willauer his story. Peter offered him a chance to compete for a staff job at Hurricane Island. Conquest was one of six who won assistant watch-officer jobs for that summer. In his third summer at Hurricane, when he was twenty-one, he was promoted to watch officer. He worked at Hurricane for five years. Following the third summer he was one of the Hurricane group who comprised the second Overlander staff at the Lyman School. A year later he went back to Lyman for a time as a cottage master. In 1970 he was doing work for Jerome Miller at one of the state detention centers when a job offer came from Wesleyan Upward Bound.

Taking over the chief-instructor post at Great Hollow, Conquest made the course more difficult, despite the misgivings of Budryk and Ronald McMullen, Budryk's assistant and himself a member of the Middletown black community. Arthur's confidence when working with disadvantaged youngsters is an act of faith, both in himself and the youngsters. "If I don't know anything else," he said, "I know poor kids and delinquent kids. I believe in them. Because that's where I come from—and if I could do it, they can do it. Believing in the kids is all it boils down to. These kids will take you to great lengths to test if you really believe in them. They make you give second, third, fourth, and fifth effort. I made the course a little tougher, and people didn't think the kids would do it. But they did. Sure, they were leaner, and they had been through a hard experience. But I think in the end—and I don't just mean the end of the course, but when the kids have to deal with life—

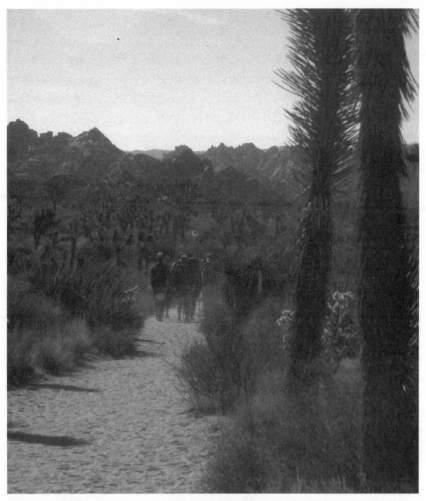

Desert environments allow Outward Bound student groups to learn self-reliance and teamwork skills necessary to survive in difficult climates. (Photo © Kim Budd)

they'll have whatever it takes to go to the well. That's what an Outward Bound course for these kids is for—when things get tough, you've got to really believe in yourself, persevere, go to that well, and do all the things you're capable of doing. My four years at Great Hollow were good ones. I'm always fascinated by things growing, and Great Hollow was growing."

By its second decade, Wesleyan's was one of the longest running and most successful Upward Bound programs in the country. All new staff members at

Great Hollow, however well qualified in outdoor skills or experienced as Outward Bound instructors, were required to take a university-accredited course in the group skills of working with disadvantaged youngsters.

The special training is necessary, Budryk maintained: "Our kids need a hell of a lot more support and encouragement and warmth, at the same time that they need high standards and firmness and direction. Due to both their age and cultural condition, they don't have the kind of aggressiveness and social responsibility that middle-class kids bring to the Outward Bound experience. For example, with middle-class kids there's a great deal more sharing of responsibilities. Our kids have what we call a vulture syndrome. While one gathers wood and another cooks dinner, the rest sit around the edges, letting the same kids handle the responsibility each day. When the food's on, they swoop down, get theirs, and swoop back to the edges. If they were in a preponderantly middle-class group, they might get the lesson themselves. But with our kids, that kind of negative group behavior is dominant, and there have to be ways of processing it.

"Or the ten-bananas syndrome. If in a typical Outward Bound patrol one of the kids wiped out the banana supply, the other kids might deal with that in a group way. The way it would register with our kids is, he was back to camp first and got the ten bananas. Next time I have to be back to get the ten bananas. It's these kinds of behavior we have to sensitize our staff to handle.

"Also, we have to prepare them for a constant daily high frustration threshold. An easy solution would be to remove the source of the frustration. But the whole charge of our program is not to do that, is to come up with some means of living with it. We have to help give our instructors the ability to reach down into their bag of expertise, training, humanity, and come up with something that's going to make for a positive relation with the kids. We constantly have staff who, even though they are conditioned not to ask outright to get rid of a kid, come to us making noises that clearly say please get rid of this kid. But it's unlikely that we will."

After a dozen years of working with it, Budryk had lost none of his conviction about the value of the Great Hollow adaptation of the Outward Bound dynamic. Each year the objectives manual that he prepares for his academic staff carries his statement of that conviction:

The completion of our Outdoor Program delivers an almost inestimable boost to our youngsters' sense of achievement and self-esteem. There is nothing "phony" about the challenges they have met, and this discovery hits strong and runs deep. Their confrontations with nature have shown them a new layer of self—a self with more mental, emotional, and physical endurance than they have ever had the opportunity to discover before.

There is no "conning" these youngsters into believing they've had an expanding experience—they feel it in their guts and muscle fiber—their very beings vibrate with this new sense of awareness. We are convinced there is no greater programmatic tool for igniting motivation.

Project Adventure headquarters, Hamilton, Massachusetts, spring of 1977. Karl Rohnke, thinking back eight years to the North Carolina contract course for Wesleyan Upward Bound when he was the school's chief instructor, recalled: "That was NC-12. I don't think you could go through that course and not say it was pivotal in the growth of the North Carolina School. It was the first time we did a course for all disadvantaged kids. It was our first coed course. It was the first time we had teachers in peer relationships to their students. And it was the time we began to make concessions to students. Up to then, everything had been pretty hard-ass—push, macho stuff. Then we got a bunch of kids who weren't going to go along with that type of thing. I remember a black girl, she said, 'There's no way I'm staying here. I'm going home.' Just as a lark—I knew she was a big smoker—I said, 'Will you finish the course if I give you a cigarette?' That was blasphemy. She said yes. I gave her the cigarette, and she finished the course. Some of the instructors thought that was a terrible thing to do—going against the smoking code—but she finished the course and she got the experience. So it started my thinking in a little different vein.

"The course shook up a lot of instructors, particularly dealing with black kids in that number. It was kind of easy on our part, the upper echelon, to sit back and say do this and do that, but the guys who were really in there putting up with it didn't want to put up with it. It wasn't their background, it wasn't their previous Outward Bound experience. They were into having kids do what they wanted them to do. After the course was over, and we looked back on it, there were big discussions about whether we should have that type of student come to Outward Bound. Some said, 'If they don't want the experience, we don't want them here; if we don't have motivated kids, we're spoiling it for everyone else'—that kind of thing. When it became clear that we would continue to have kids like that, I think it made a change in the program from that point on. It wasn't all macho, bust-your-ass type of experience. It was more sensitive to the type of student you had."

■ ■ ■

Nottingham, New Hampshire, summer of 1979, in Jed and Perry Williamson's house. It was after midnight, and Arthur Conquest was winding up an evening's reminiscence that reached from his course at Colorado in 1962 to his graduate studies at the University of New Hampshire. The previous spring he had been awarded a master's degree by the university's School of Education. Now, holding to a bizarre high-energy schedule of work-study, family concerns, and physical fitness, he was pushing toward his doctorate. The way from the days of skipping school in the inner city to his status of graduate student and family man was a long poke, and Arthur reflected.

"I wish that more inner-city kids, more black kids, more delinquent kids could have an Outward Bound experience and come away like I did with something positive. The kind of experience where you just feel so powerful about yourself, you feel so strong, and it's way down in the gut, just inside your belly button. An Outward Bound experience along with a few other things would be one of the answers I can think of that might be able to change the way inner-city or delinquent kids think about themselves. I've certainly taken what I got from Outward Bound and transferred it to other kids who've been through courses with me—the enthusiasm and the joy and the good feelings. I know what it feels like. I also know what it feels like to be on the street. And I've been close enough to failure to know how it feels, and I see it all the time among my boyhood friends when I go home to East Harlem."

PROJECT ADVENTURE

�֎

*. . . our culture is so urbanized and soft and our
school systems foster so much competition and
isolation—we need healthy counterbalances and
alternatives. Project Adventure proved to be an
invaluable beginning.*

—Hamilton-Wenham High School parent evaluation

Jerry Pieh left Andover to be assistant to the dean of the School of
Education at Harvard in 1966 and two years later entered the school as a
doctoral candidate. Studying educational theory at the graduate level, he
found his own philosophy being shaped as much by what he had learned
about teaching and learning when helping his father run the Minnesota
Outward Bound School as by what he was getting from his books.

"It didn't seem to me," he said, "that the critical things in the Outward
Bound approaches to learning were twenty-six days or the age of the students
or expeditions or anything like that. There were more fundamental issues
involved that were applicable in almost any educational setting: The use of
challenges with kids. The notion that people learn best in situations where
they're stretched, where they have to do more than they think they can.
Where they learn quickly whether or not they've been successful, and where
a failure is a learning experience, not a negative thing. The openness. The
stress on caring, on human values and the importance of people. The idea that
it's healthy to know your limits, and that it's healthy to expand them. Those

kinds of things were going through my mind as I thought about the process that took place in what happened to be a twenty-six-day wilderness format.

"It seemed to me that the important teaching principles were to establish a high level of expectation with students, to place them in unfamiliar situations that would confront them with their own limits, and to give them opportunities for experiences that would take them beyond those limits. There is an incredible amount of energy that comes when you break through what you have felt were barriers to your ability and discover a new kind of strength. If that energy could be harnessed into schools and into traditional learning situations, I felt we could accomplish much more than we were. That became the focus I took, the bent I went."

That was Pieh's focus and bent when he was appointed principal of Hamilton-Wenham Regional High School, serving some eight hundred fifty suburban Boston students, in 1970. He went to his new post with a keen aversion to the concept he had encountered in some of his reading—that of the school as a production system wherein the product is considered to be output in terms of number of students graduating, number of Merit Scholars, number going on to post-secondary education, and the like. He had equally strong convictions about the model he believed in. Here again, he drew on his Minnesota experiences:

"In an Outward Bound school everybody is conscious that the changes occurring within students is what the school is there for. The instructors organize the experiences that make for the changes in the students, and it's a very important role, but what the students do with the experiences is the actual learning that the school is meant to produce. The instructors place things before kids, but they don't lead them carefully through a problem step by step. They give them a problem to solve and get out of their way. Sometimes they let them fail, if the cost isn't too high, so they can learn from it.

"That relationship of the instructors to the students is very clear. It is not like that of a teacher who dominates a class and conveys information and then asks students to give back that information. There isn't the confusion between learning and teaching that sometimes happens in schools where the most important person is thought to be the teacher."

Thus in the Pieh model, the student—since he is the only one who can apply himself to the learning and changing—is the "first-line worker." The teacher, rather than being the first-line worker as commonly thought, is a first-line supervisor providing a series of resources of vital importance to the change process. The product of the schooling process is *change in students*— in values, knowledge, physical strength, skills, behavior, and so on.[29]

In his first year at Hamilton-Wenham, Pieh created a vehicle for carrying out his educational ideas that long produced reverberations in the nation's schools. The vehicle, made possible by a $94,000 Elementary and Secondary Education (ESEA) Title III grant, was a curriculum innovation called Project Adventure. The project had two main phases. First, a personal-growth course fashioned on Outward Bound principles was to be developed as the physical-education requirement for all sophomores. Second, the Project Adventure staff was to serve as a resource, providing students with off-campus experiences to enhance classroom learning and facilitate service to the community. The plan called for subsequently extending the staff's services to other area schools and creating a regional teacher-training and curriculum-development center.

Pieh hired Bob Lentz to direct the project. Much as we regretted losing Bob, we were pleased that his competence was being enlisted by what we saw to be a Mainstream development of major import. His associate director was Mary Smith, a teacher who had been in Laos under the aegis of the International Voluntary Service. Completing the staff were Karl Rohnke, who left his post as program coordinator at North Carolina Outward Bound, and Jim Schoel, a Hurricane Island instructor who had been teaching in a Harlem street academy. In addition, four of the school's physical-education teachers and a biology teacher took Outward Bound teachers' courses in the summer of 1971.

Under Rohnke's direction a ropes course—a decade later it remained one of the finest in the country—was built on the school grounds. The major part of the new sophomore physical-education course, taught in the fall and spring, consisted of progressively challenging ropes-course tests, focusing primarily on each student's sense of personal competence. A second part,

[29] Pieh's model was developed more fully in his doctoral dissertation, which dealt with the origins and implementation of Project Adventure and evaluated its first two years.

taking place mostly outdoors in January and February, included initiative tests and discussion problems, fire building, map and compass instruction, first-aid training for cold-weather hazards, and special snowy-day activities. Its primary concerns were with small-group dynamics.

In carrying out the other phases of their mission—to give students opportunities for experiential learning to reinforce their classroom endeavor—the project staff's method was first to induce a teacher to articulate a need.

"We made a couple of decisions early on," Lentz said. "One was that whatever we did with academic subjects should be something that over time those teachers could pick up and do on their own. So the kinds of things we helped initiate had to be things the teachers were interested in doing. Another decision was not to create separate structures—the school-within-a-school kind of thing. We said, 'Let's see what can be done within the assumption that the school doesn't have to adjust to us in any fundamental way.'

"So we began a series of conversations, saying here are some things we can do, some resources we have in terms of time and dollars, and here are some things we're concerned about, like how do kids learn, how to connect up things that are talked about in class with things outside of class, how to make better use of the community. In almost every case there was at least one teacher in a department who said something like 'Gee, I'm having a problem with colonial history and there's a lot of it around here; there ought to be a way to put these together'; or 'I'm very concerned with ecological concepts, and with all the living illustrations in the area we ought to be able to make a connection'; or 'I have a group of kids who don't like to write and think they have nothing to write about; maybe you could help us there. That would be a start.' We wanted at least the germ of the idea to come from the teacher, so it could be teacher and project staff working together."

Projects coming out of these collaborations were as diverse as, on the one hand, a biology class's slog through a swamp in a body-and-hands-on study of everything from wetlands plant and animal life to town history and, on the other, a social studies class's investigative trek to Boston's ethnically mixed and black ghetto neighborhoods in pursuit of concern with urban and minority problems. Students in the colonial-life module of an American history course divided into small groups to make a series of cemetery researches. An art class

A twin-masted longboat slices through Puget Sound during a two-week compre-hensive sailing course, the ideal team-building exercise. (Photo © PCOBS, Jeremy Lucke)

in advanced design took a "texture walk" from the school, finding textures in great variety and doing creative things with them. A social-problems class and a media-studies class joined forces to set up and operate a community paper, can, and bottle recycling project. Sixty high-school students signed up to tutor elementary-school and junior-high youngsters. Supporting Pieh's belief that the experiential projects should have a strong service element, the tutoring scheme was to prove among the most durable.

Project Adventure conceived the "action seminar"—a semester-long course scheduled in half-day sessions, with its subject content bridging several disciplines and offering options. In "The Sea as Teacher," for example, study of navigation, weather, salt-marsh ecology, and the design and use of oceanographic equipment provided credits in science; local history, town profiling, interviewing techniques, journal writing, a survey of the crab industry, and a history of the dory tied into social studies and English; boat design and dory building into industrial arts; and rowing, rock climbing, hiking, and jogging earned physical-education credits. Students used what they learned—for example, the boat they built. Life skills were learned with academics; carpentry, *Moby Dick*, and oceanography went hand in hand.

No other innovative educational proposal spun off from Outward Bound enjoyed greater success with the educational establishment than Project Adventure. When the state evaluating team made its first on-site evaluation in March, it reported "The team obtained an extremely favorable impression of the Project, confirming the Title III Supervisor's opinion that this is one of the very best Title III projects that we have." The second year, the school's physical-education staff took over the sophomore course, enabling the project staff to start working with other school systems in the region, thus broadening its base of financial support. In its third year the project was "validated" by the U.S. Office of Education (USOE) as a program "innovative, effective, transferable, and reasonable in cost," and designated a National Demonstration Site. The National Advisory Council of Title III bestowed its Educational Pacesetter Award. The state provided funding for diffusion to schools in the state, and a second office was opened in western Massachusetts.[30] Simultaneously, USOE made the project nationally available through its National Diffusion Network.

By 1980, Lentz and his associates had conducted workshops for administrators and teachers countrywide, keeping up student ties in their Massachusetts school programs. Lentz noted an ongoing happenstance tying the project to Outward Bound: "One of the things we seem to do that others don't do as precisely is say, for example, you're an English teacher, we'll help you develop something you can do with your English students. So we can help folks who have picked up the Outward Bound idea and like what they hear, but who are still left with that hanging question of what does it mean for me as a teacher in my school. Some of our strong states have been New Mexico, Colorado, Wyoming, Minnesota, South Dakota, Missouri, North Carolina, Maine, and you can recognize there states that either have Outward Bound schools or are regions that have been influenced by the Outward Bound movement."

Visiting Lentz and Co., we drove the few miles from national Project Adventure headquarters to Hamilton-Wenham High, where, we discovered, the fount model was alive and well. The tenth-grade physical-education

---

[30] The project also moved its headquarters from Hamilton-Wenham High to Wenham.

program, still known as "Project Adventure," was solidly entrenched. Biology's mud-walk and urbanology's city expedition had become curricular norms. "Every year we just run the urbanology field trip like clockwork," social studies chairman Richard Aieta told us. The science department's adventure-learning expedition to Acadia National Park or Cape Cod was an annual highlight. The tutoring program, in Principal Isa Zimmerman's view, was getting better every year. Project Adventure people were helping with an annual orientation session for the ninth-graders.

Dick Aieta, who had become chairman of the social studies department the year Jerry Pieh arrived at Hamilton-Wenham, harked back to the project's advent on campus. "They came to us with this idea of 'adventuring' the curriculum—this idea that learning had a more forceful impact and staying power if the students were somehow exposed to a challenge, somehow put to a personal internal test that wasn't necessarily cognitive. The first thing they did was adventurize our staff. They took them to Boston and had them do the things we would be asking the kids to do. There was a spirit at that time of a renaissance, a new feeling, and it was a nice, positive, alternative way of looking at things. The ideology wasn't new—it was with us when we went to school in the 1960s. The problem was, How do you institutionalize it? In my opinion, the success of Project Adventure is that they do their homework. It's not a 'let's go and swing from the trees and have a good time on a field trip' approach. It's very purposeful, deliberate, systematic, carefully thought out and planned."

Aieta was enthusiastic about the new Project Adventure–inspired activity to which his department was keying the economics elements of the Social Studies I course taken by all ninth-graders. Three times each year, one-third of the class travels to the nearby city of Gloucester. Working in teams of four, they visit and conduct interviews at some forty-five locations that together reveal a cross section of the economic life of the city, which is largely based on the fishing industry.

Although Aieta's primary concern was for the cognitive uses of the experience, he also valued its affective impact. "The adventure of that curriculum is that fourteen-year-olds have great trepidation about approaching an adult and asking him or her anything—particularly something the adult knows more about than they. They learn on their own what to do when they don't know what to do. And don't overlook the environment these kids are coming from. They live in comfortable suburban bedroom towns. They've had virtually no ethnic exposure. The original response of many kids in our community is, 'If it's different, it must be bad.' It's healthy for those kids to meet up with men who are wresting a livelihood from the sea and talk in heavy Italian and Portuguese accents, and with the members of the fishermen's wives organization, who made the government go back to calling their husbands 'fishermen' instead of 'fishers.' Also, this is valuable for me as a teacher. I had a real adventure going into that strange city and setting up those forty-five contacts. I've grown and I've learned a lot."

Sally Woodsom, chairman of the physical-education department, took us to see the ropes course. It lived up to its billing. Even the visitor who had seen a number of impressive courses looked up in awe at some of the tests. "Can fifteen-year-olds do that?" Each youngster, however, decided for himself what challenges he or she would try. "It's not how much you do or how high you go," Sally told us. "It's the attempt that's made, and how sincere that attempt is, that counts most."

A member of the Hamilton-Wenham staff since Pieh's day, she had firm convictions about the value of the tenth-grade phys-ed course. "I think we would be losing a lot if we ever eliminated it. I wouldn't want to be at a school that didn't have a program like this. The kids would suffer. It enhances their growth so greatly, makes them more understanding of each other and of themselves. They get a dramatic sense of accomplishment from doing something they're afraid to do and being successful. The response of some when that happens is phenomenal. It's a superthrill for both me and the students to live through from day to day."

Sally, who was one of the four physical-education teachers given Outward Bound scholarships at the project's start, reminisced about her course at Colorado. "I went out there thinking Outward Bound was almost entirely a physical experience. Even though I was in good physical shape, I was afraid because I thought I wouldn't be up to it. Then I found that, even more than the physical aspect, it was dealing with other people and with oneself that was what it was all about. The solo was a highlight, with all those things I'd never experienced before coming together for me. I had taught here for six years.

When I came back, the students talked about how I had changed. I really feel that at that time I became a person rather than a teacher. I was afraid of changing back; I didn't want to go back and be what I was. I know that some of it has gone, but I think most of it hasn't, because I still feel I'm a successful teacher. It was one of the great experiences of my life, and I don't expect to find its equal. That's why I think this is so important for these kids now. It's something that most of them are not going to experience anyplace else. It's something we can give them that's going to make them better people."

Back at Project Adventure headquarters we talked a bit more with Bob Lentz.[31] The conversation got onto the shifting fashions in funding. Lentz reflected on the policy line to which the project had adhered, to stay in the area of its particular competence and not be tempted to change focus by the changing purposes for which public and other monies became available. "We have tried very hard to have some sense of what we were about," he said. "You can really prostitute yourself." But he noted that it was important for the project to find new things to keep a sense of being challenged. "Right now one is 'special needs.' In our definition, special needs are pretty much kids who are in school but have learning disabilities or are behaviorally disordered. We're always looking for that new thing that can be begun here to be put through the network. Because it regenerates us."

Still, he had concerns. "With kids who have special needs getting so much funding and attention, one of our fears has been that if we began to work significantly in those areas, it would breed the idea that adventure, or experiential, or outdoor stuff is just for kids with problems, and all the others would be denied it. It's very easy today to get money for labeled kids, and it's damned hard to get money for kids." He told of a recent case in a nearby city where it had been necessary to cut back on a Project Adventure program. "They said to some of the students, 'We're sorry, you don't have any special needs, so we can't work with you.' Every youngster going through adolescence has a whole series of needs that he or she knows are very special. There was that look of pain and misunderstanding on the kids' faces as they were told, 'We're sorry, we know it's been good, but you don't qualify anymore, you don't have any needs.'"

[31] After nine years with Project Adventure, Lentz resigned in the summer of 1980 to accept appointment as a high-school principal in Birmingham, Michigan.

INSTITUTION FOR TOMORROW

❄

A race preserves its vigour so long as it harbours
a real contrast between what has been and what
may be; and so long as it is nerved by the vigour
to adventure beyond the safeties of the past.
Without adventure civilization is in full decay.

—Alfred North Whitehead

But a certain Samaritan, as he journeyed, came
where he was: and when he saw him, he had
compassion on him.

—Luke 10:33

In 1991, U.S. Outward Bound's thirtieth year, the total enrollment of the schools reached its high point of over 9,700 students. Throughout the nineties, enrollment hovered between eight and nine thousand. A breakdown of the comparative figures of enrollment is informative, for the years from 1999–2001:

BY AGE

18 and under	58 percent
19–22	12 percent
23–plus	21 percent
Not specified	9 percent

BY SEX

Male	55 percent
Female	45 percent

BY GEOGRAPHIC DISTRIBUTION

East	24 percent
South	22 percent
Central	12 percent
Southwest	6 percent
Mountain	6 percent
Pacific	17 percent
Foreign	13 percent

The raw figures sum up a remarkable growth and evolution in an institution that began in 1962 with one hundred male students, most of them youths in their late adolescence, half of them from the state of Colorado. By the late 1970s, two-fifths of the students were adults over twenty-one—or, if we define adult as the Constitution defines voting age (eighteen and over), the adult total was more than two-thirds. Two-fifths of the students were women; each year the percentage inched higher. The student body was drawn from every part of the country and abroad.

The evolution in the course offerings was fully as striking. Whereas the sole 1962 offering was a "standard" twenty-six-day course, based largely on the British model, today's prospective student has an extraordinary range of choices. The current standard course[32] varies in duration from twenty-one to twenty-six days, depending on the school and the season. A sampling of standard course titles attests to the variety of activity and emphases offered:

[32] The national standard course curriculum provides that the course would be formed and trained as a search-and-rescue unit available for public service. It provides for the first-week fitness training and instruction in safety; field-food planning and preparation; use of equipment; search, rescue, and emergency evacuation and first-aid procedures; map and compass, and route finding; traveling skills appropriate to the environment; knots, rope handling, and belaying; expedition planning and control; and use, care, and protection of the environment. For the curriculum subsequent to the initial training phase, the standard course specified experiences in training expeditions, rock climbing and rappelling, solo, final expedition, a marathon event, a service project, and periodic readings and discussions to help participants interpret the values underlying the course. Participants were encouraged to keep a journal.

"Mountaineering," "Mountaineering/River Running," "Canyonlands," "Canoe Wilderness," "Sailing," "Cycling," "Desert/Canyon/River Exploration," "Forest/ Mountains/Canyons," "Ski Mountaineering," "Winter Camping/Skiing/ Snowshoeing," "Winter Mountain Wilderness," "Winter Tropical Expedition," "Practica for Educators and Helping Professionals," "Cross-Cultural (with Foxfire)," "Leadership Development," "Junior," "Himalayan Trek." One key development dating from the 1970s is full-semester (three-month) courses, some offered jointly by two or more schools.

Short courses ranging in duration from sixteen days down to five days include virtually all the standard course activities and others as well (e.g., Sailing/Natural History, Grand Canyon/Cross Country). These are adapted to an open-ended list of special populations, e.g., Alumni, Troubled Teen, Physically Disabled, Women Only, Life Career Renewal, and others.

If the adult-at-eighteen standard can be applied to institutions, Outward Bound was about to enter a new life phase of youthful maturity in 1979. Some such thought was running through President Hank Taft's mind as he considered the variegated nature of the organization's growth. The time had come, he concluded, for Outward Bound to do some serious stocktaking of its institutional posture, of where it wanted to go, and how it intended to get there. When he proposed that the organization initiate a formal period of long-term planning in 1979–1980, it responded with a strong assent. Some activity was already in place. OBI had an active futures committee, and each school had a comparable trustee group. The consensus was that it made good sense to integrate the futures thinking of the individual schools and the national body.

As I became one of those involved in the futures process, I could not help thinking back to whence, and how far, we had come. A considerable part of that progress, I reflected, had been a response to the energies generated by the very act of our coming into being and finding that we filled a significant need. I could understand Hank's sense of the organization's having attained a watershed time, wherein simply growing on the strength of its successes was no longer adequate. In the more mature phase on which Outward Bound was embarking, the institution needed to exercise a greater degree of control over the directions in which its energies could carry it. Too many critical alternatives were at hand; it was imperative to think through the questions governing which of those alternatives would prevail.

My reflecting on the past was more than just the natural reflex of the "early settler" or charter member. It was inevitable also, in seeking to nourish my own thinking about the future of Outward Bound, that my mind should reach back to some of the teachings of the founder. I was, however, recalling him less as founder than as the most talented future watcher I had ever known. Kurt Hahn.

■ ■ ■

In the 1960s Kurt Hahn made periodic trips to this country. His visits to Andover were great occasions—for renewing our friendship, hearing his views about the state of the world, telling him about developments in U.S. Outward Bound, getting his counsel. He took a keen interest in my Outward Bound briefings. In the beginning it pleased him greatly that we had been drafted to set up the final training for the Peace Corps. He was enthusiastic about the American innovation of the solo; in his philosophy, periods of solitude were an essential human need.

"You cannot harvest the lessons of your life except in aloneness," he said, "and I go to the length of saying that neither the love of man nor the love of God can take deep root except in aloneness."

Sometimes he had concerns. Were the schools giving first aid its place of honor in the timetable? Did this or that school operate so far into the wilderness as to get away from other people and hence from opportunities to give aid or effect rescues? Only once, however, in my time as Outward Bound's president, did he give me a directive: "You will not let the word Christianity creep into Outward Bound. You will simply practice it."[33] He was captivated by the adaptive program phenomenon, so different from what had happened in Britain.

Invariably his counsel enriched us. Usually the advice I sought was on some question of strategy or tactic, and he had a way of elevating the discus-

---

[33] Hahn joined the Anglican Church in 1945. He remained deeply attached to his Jewish heritage. Speaking at Hahn's funeral service in 1974, the Right Reverend Lancelot Fleming, Dean of Windsor, said, "Kurt made it very plain that he was proud to be of 100 percent Jewish origin."

sion to one of principle. I remember once asking him who at Phillips Academy he thought I should go to for help in weaving Outward Bound philosophy into the fabric of the school. He said, "There are two people—your doctor and your leading historian. If the doctor is worth his salt, he is concerned about the physical well-being of young people and their future well-being as adults. If the historian is worth his salt, he will have detected the symptoms of a decaying culture and will be sympathetic to what you're trying to do."

He spoke often in aphorisms. On teaching: "Teach as little as possible. When you teach someone, you deprive him of the opportunity to learn." Of a non-admirer: "I don't think he includes me in his prayers." An all-purpose commentary: "Human nature is very prevalent." He contributed his share of merriment, although his jokes did tend to be distinctively Hahnian. One visit came just after we had moved into our new home. The previous owner, who had been a big-game hunter, had mounted his prize specimens in one of the rooms, which now required some remodeling for our less esoteric purposes. I explained this to Hahn as we looked in at the workmen. Smiling, he said, "And here you will mount the heads of the academicians you have shot down!"

He and John Kemper grew to be fast friends. Kemper came to enjoy the lessons in headmastering he received from the older man. One time when some of us on the school staff were trying to decide if a boy should be expelled, Hahn told Kemper, "Never let a committee expel a boy. A committee has no conscience. Use it to investigate and advise, but you must make the decision. That boy will carry his expulsion through life. There must likewise be someone who will always carry the decision on his conscience—someone who can think back and ask himself if the right thing was done." That way, he believed, came wisdom. He told me, "I have expelled boys I was right to expel, and others I should not have. And I have kept boys I should not have, and others I was right to keep, but I feel best about the ones I kept."

For all of Hahn's intense interest in what we were doing in Outward Bound, I was aware that his main concerns were elsewhere. It is a remarkable fact that in his long, intimate association with the Outward Bound movement, he never held an official position. He was an inventor of institutions, and it was a part of his genius that he was content to leave their administering to others. On most of those visits his primary interest was in advancing the

Atlantic College (later United World College) movement that he and Sir Lawrence Darvall had generated. For that institution it was seven years from dream to reality. Atlantic College—now United World College of the Atlantic—opened in Llantwit Major, Wales, in 1962. Now there is also a United World College of the Pacific in British Columbia and a United World College of South East Asia in Singapore, with others to come. Recognizing that international understanding cannot be treated in the classroom alone, the program of every United World College has a distinctively Hahnian component, referred to as its "humanitarian curriculum"—rescue and community services to those "in danger and in need." The late Earl Mountbatten of Burma, long the movement's international leader,[34] confirmed a heartfelt Hahn thesis: "It's hard to hate someone when you're both helping to save a life."

That is a variation of Hahn's, "Whoever saves a life will never take a life." No other human being, perhaps, responded as avidly as Hahn to William James's call to seek "the moral equivalent of war." He recognized that Tennyson's "peace of the broken wing"—peace that softens rather than tests moral fiber—was itself a menace to peace. The answer, Hahn was convinced, lay in "the passion of rescue." His moral equivalent of war was "to enthrall and hold the young through active and willing Samaritan service, demanding care and skill, courage and endurance, discipline and initiative." With each new visit I observed the conviction grow more resolute.

■ ■ ■

Some three dozen members of the Outward Bound community gathered at Lake Geneva, Wisconsin, in the fall of 1979 for a "Mission Conference" that had been organized by Greg Farrell, chairman of OBI's futures committee. The gathering included school directors, school trustee representatives, members of Greg's committee and other OBI trustees, of whom I was privileged to be one, and a scattering of outside resource people. For four days consultant-leader Warren Ziegler took us through a fascinating, intensive process that he called "Futures Invention."

[34] Prior to his assassination in 1979, Lord Mountbatten had relinquished his post as president of the International Council of the United World Colleges to Prince Charles of England.

At the outset Ziegler asked the question "What would you like to see Outward Bound achieving in the year 2005?" Each of us listed what we thought were the critical items that ought to be part of the organization's successful mission twenty-five years hence. Our leader then bade us group ourselves according to like interests. He did not care, he said, whether it turned out to be two or ten groups: It turned out to be seven. Each group was instructed to draw up a joint statement. That negotiation of a statement that everyone in a group could agree on was really hard work. At the end of a day and a half, the seven statements were in hand. Ziegler then said to each group in substance, "Here are the long-term objectives you have established for Outward Bound. Now go back, refine them, and ask yourselves, how will you know you are there? For each objective, prescribe several test measurements that together will show you have indeed arrived where you wanted to be. Also, set down what assumptions you have made about the state of the world—economic, social, political, whatever—in 2005."

When we all returned with this assignment accomplished, the conference was halfway into its third day. Then our leader said, "Now we're going to invent the future." He told us that we were not going to say, "This is 1979, the trends are such and such, how do we get from here to there?" Instead we would say, "We are now in the year 2005, and Outward Bound is just where we wanted it to be—how did we get there? What were the factors that made for success, what key events occurred along the way, what important trends were operative? Who were the people who played an important role?" That way, instead of being stuck with all the dross of today, all the pause that the state of the economy and the political state of the world would have burdened us with, our minds were much more open to the possibilities. It was inventing the future as history.

What our seven groups finally produced was written up and circulated to the schools. The school trustees were encouraged to put themselves, with their staffs if feasible, through a telescoped version of the process. The OBI board did likewise. Farrell then collected all the material that had been generated. From it he winnowed the principal "themes" under which important policy questions that had asserted themselves tended to group. There were seven themes: growth, performance audit/quality control, special target groups, reenforcement and follow-up, leadership, educational and other [e.g., corrections] models, and service and community responsibility. Farrell wrote and circulated a document summarizing the issues that had been raised in the seven theme areas and that needed to be resolved in order to permit planning and implementation to proceed.

The OBI Futures Committee then initiated an iterative process between itself and the schools to arrive at a new updated mission statement for Outward Bound. After back-and-forth revision and refinement, an official mission statement was adopted in October 1980. It read:

Outward Bound's purpose is to develop respect for self, care for others, responsibility to the community, and sensitivity to the environment. The Outward Bound process assumes that learning and understanding take place when people engage in and reflect upon experiences in challenging environments in which they must make choices, take responsible action, acquire new skills, and work with others. Outward Bound implements its educational and social purposes by providing leadership in experience-based programs, offering courses in its schools, conducting demonstration projects, and helping others to apply Outward Bound principles.

Outward Bound seeks to: strengthen its organizational effectiveness; improve the quality of its program; and expand the influence and application of its principles.

The mission statement was a solid achievement. The first part clearly defines, for insider and outsider alike, the endeavor we are in. The second part establishes the three paths for determining priorities and implementing that endeavor. This is the phase on which the organization embarked.

■ ■ ■

In 1968 Hahn made what proved to be his final journey to the United States. Deeply concerned about the worldwide violence generated by youthful rebellion and racial conflict, he was looking for guidance from the American experience. Long before, he had given to Sir Robert Birley, headmaster of Eton, counsel that Birley never forgot: "Whenever you have to deal with a boy who is a rebel, remember that you must get him to face the question: Are you going to be a fighter or a quarreler?" Now he was looking for ways to harness productively the fighting spirit of young people in revolt.

For two months he crossed the continent and back, from Harvard to West Coast campuses, from Harlem to Watts, seeking new knowledge about student and racial tensions, new leads to healing forces. Fred Glimp, who was dean of Harvard during the student riots there that year, still marvels at Hahn's keen comprehension of the issues and events on the Cambridge campus. Five years after his 1968 visit to the headquarters of the National Urban League's street workers in Harlem, they had vivid recall of the eighty-two-year-old gentleman from England who came up the stairs two at a time. On Hahn's visit there, a boy who had recently returned from a course at Hurricane Island told him, "It gives you a feeling of great power if you breathe life into a dead person." This was one more affirmation of the message he was carrying on his cross-country safari: "The passion of rescue releases the highest dynamic of the human soul." As he made that safari, his sun-induced affliction was heavy upon him. At such places as New York's Horace Mann School, Wayzata, Minnesota, and the Athenian School in Danville, California, people still remember the dim, imposing figure at the front of a darkened, crowded room, tirelessly answering—and asking—questions, offering his ideas ("I am anxious to carry conviction on this") in response to theirs.

He was intent on inventing a new institution. His dauntless mind worked toward a grand plan under which a "Service by Youth Commission" would coordinate forces enabling young people to contribute productive energies that otherwise would be spilled in confrontation or drained by frustration. Central to the plan was the removal by aid-and-rescue agencies of age restrictions preventing service by adolescent volunteers, and an international call to young men and women to help in the fight against unnecessary death and suffering. "Lifesaving," Hahn kept telling his American audiences, "is the job of the layman. The less serious things we can leave to the doctors."

In the Watts section of Los Angeles he listened eagerly for two and a half hours as Ted Watkins, chairman of the Watts Labor Community Action Committee, talked about his work with ghetto youth. Ted told him about the Watts young people painting telephone poles to spruce up the streets, starting a chicken and pet farm, converting derelict lots to "vest-pocket parks." Ted said, "Every youngster should be called on to make a sweat investment. He needs something he can protect." Hahn liked that. He made it a theme of his Service by Youth plan.

As his grueling safari ended, his affliction worsened. I drove him to the Boston airport with blankets blacking out the car windows. He wore the homburg hat with the broad, turned-down brim, an arrangement of green felt lined with lead foil shielding the back of his neck, and two pairs of dark glasses. At the plane's door his hand came up in the familiar farewell gesture. I was wrenchingly aware of that aircraft carrying off one whose comprehending concern for our sick world was irreplaceable.

Back in London and Scotland he worked on the Service by Youth plan. For all the grandiose scale of his thinking, the ideas he set down were cogent, down-to-earth, feasible. In a very real sense, I believe, he foresaw the coming tragedies of student shootings at Kent State and Jackson State and was working to prevent them. But he was not able, as he always before had been, to exert the force of his personal drive in support of that project. Struck by a car on a country road near Gordonstoun, he never fully recovered from the accident. Yet he turned even that misfortune to opportunity. The mishap gave him a new idea. He wrote Prince Philip, urging his support for a plan to reduce road deaths by including first aid in the driving test. The prince did take up that cause, giving it his earnest backing.

In retirement at last in Hermannsburg, Germany, living in an apartment at one of Salem's satellite schools, Kurt Hahn died on December 15, 1974. He was eighty-eight.

■ ■ ■

The new Outward Bound mission statement adopted in the fall of 1980 was circulated to the schools with three sets of policy questions relating to the three areas of activity indicated in the statement's second part: strengthening organization, improving program quality, and increasing influence in the mainstream of American life. In the winter of 1981 the organization was engaged in a procedure to determine which of those questions it wanted to focus on initially.

For Hank Taft the purposeful advance of the long-term planning process he had sparked was a double satisfaction, in that he had announced his intention to resign the presidency in June 1981. After eight and a half years in office he had, he believed, brought the organization to an "exciting node," poised for a new surge forward; he saw the time as right for the institution's bringing in a new leader. He had done a splendid job of shepherding the organization through a period when the total enrollment, and the total budget for operating Outward Bound in the United States, had nearly doubled. He had earned the sense of a task well carried out and an organization well launched on a new stage of maturity.

Participating in the conference at Lake Geneva, I was inspired by the creative spirit prevailing among that group so representative of Outward Bound leadership, as they solidified their ideas for the institution's future. The spirit was creative in the sense of being nonprovincial, broad of vision where it might well have been narrow, far-looking where it could have been nearsighted, questing for optimum institutional usefulness to society, concerned more for the people the institution can serve than for self-serving by the institution. This spirit is reflected in many of the policy questions that were circulated with the mission statement. For this Outward Bounder—and, I would assume from the discussions, for many others as well—among the most intriguing of those queries were two that relate to a principle I have always considered central to the Outward Bound mission.

The first is "*Should we seek greater emphasis on and sharper understanding of the role of service?*" I agree with Joe Nold and others who have expressed the opinion that the service commitment of Outward Bound has not yet been carried out as fully and fruitfully as it should be. While some of what is being done is excellent, the service elements of the Outward Bound curriculum still have an untapped potential. In the matter of "sharper understanding," one suggestion is that we can yet inquire more productively into the potential values that Kurt Hahn foresaw when he spoke of according first aid "the place of honor in the timetable" or employed such seemingly old-fashioned phrases as "passion of rescue" and "aristocracy of service." Hahn, of course, would have fiercely insisted that his ideas be evaluated not on the basis of their having come from the founder but simply on their merits.

The second, related query is "*Should we seek the development of community service and other programs for alumni?*" In the colloquies at Lake Geneva and later, I could not help being delighted to hear support voiced for this proposal, for it tended to confirm an old hypothesis: that there are self-asserting forces in the Outward Bound dynamic that influence its programs toward increasingly Hahnian kinds of practice. I can best explain this by trying to repair what I believe to be a serious misunderstanding in the areas of "follow-up."

U.S. Outward Bounders frequently do an unconscious disservice by quoting out of context the closing line of Hahn's address at the 1965 Outward Bound Conference at Harrogate, England, where follow-up had been one of the important debated subjects. His concluding words were "Outward Bound can ignite—that is all. It is for others to keep the flame alive." The line is usually quoted under the impression that Hahn in a sense was negating the follow-up question by relegating the responsibility to a vague, undefined "others." The error in the impression lies, I think, in failure to appreciate (perhaps not even to have seen) what the context was. For in his preceding paragraph Hahn had quite clearly defined whom he meant by "others," and quite clearly stated the form he believed follow-up should take:

> *I believe that the challenge of Samaritan Service, if properly presented, rarely fails to capture young people, body and soul, not only in the Western World. I hear encouraging news about the young behind the Iron Curtain—many of them look westward, with distrust but also with hope. They ask a question which makes us blush: "Are you in earnest about the ideals you profess?" Who shall give an answer? Young men and women who render hard and willing service to their fellow men in danger and in need.*

A few months later, visiting in Andover, Hahn gave me a photograph of himself. Part of the inscription, in the form of a charge, was an even more explicit restatement of the thought he had left with the conferees at Harrogate:

To Josh Miner . . . May he remember that the best service he can render to Outward Bound is to recognize its limits: Outward Bound can kindle the flame but it will be extinguished in many cases unless the Outward Bounders, returning to their schools and workshops, are confronted by the challenge and the opportunities to go on active service to help their fellow men in danger and in need. Their resolution to do so will be strengthened if we can build up an aristocracy of service throughout the free world, whose example will create a fashion of conduct.

That "aristocracy of service" was the new institution the eighty-two-year-old Hahn was seeking to invent in the aftermath of his 1968 U.S. safari. The lengthy memorandum he wrote upon his return home and sent to his Outward Bound and other American friends is a kind of testament to all of us who care about the well-being of his institutions. In the memorandum's final paragraph, using the designation "helper" for those performing Samaritan service, he stated the salient, consuming idea one more time:

One would hope that one day the status of helper would be recognized throughout the Western world—thereby a new and challenging avenue of distinction might be opened. Such development would go far to solve the baffling problem of the "follow-up" for Outward Bound and kindred enterprises.

Hahn expressed it as a hope. Can we now hope it will prove to be prophecy?

THE URBAN SCENE

❖

I was always a Bronx girl. My mother forbade me go outside my block. That's all you know when you grow up in areas like I grew up in. You do not move farther; you have to stay there. So I didn't know Manhattan, and when I did my Urban Exploration, I couldn't believe it. I was a New York City kid, and I'm going to Manhattan for the first time at 15! It was a whole new world. And as soon as I tasted that whole new world, I wanted more.

—Carmen Martinez, New York City Outward Bound
alumnus and staff member

By the end of the 1970s, Outward Bound had established itself in this country as an expert and trusted source in the field of education in the outdoors. Attendance jumped from seventy-seven students learning at one wilderness school the first year (1962 in Colorado) to more than 8,500 at five schools by 1979. We saw countless others adapt Outward Bound techniques across the country, but we wanted to do more. Teaching through the mountains and the sea was just one way to impart the Outward Bound philosophy, but we felt, for a variety of reasons, that we could be just as effective in the city as we had learned to be in the wilderness.

We began to consider our next major step: developing courses specifically geared toward urban youth and running them where those students live. Over the years, we had engaged in a recruiting and scholarship effort in cities—Hurricane Island, for instance, had a storefront office in Harlem—and we brought individuals and school groups from cities across the country to our courses. But we found that, as rewarding as it was for these boys and girls to attend our wilderness schools, they returned home to find no support system in place to make the lessons last. As Greg Farrell, who had seen the phenomenon up close in Trenton, put it, "We take kids from tough circumstances, give them a great experience, and then drop them back where they came from. Surely that can't be enough to make a difference in a high percentage of cases." We wanted Outward Bound to be more than a once-in-a-lifetime experience.

We also felt that the idea of service so central to our philosophy might be especially meaningful in the cities. Service begins in Outward Bound with the care of the other members of the small, interdependent community in which the course is experienced. On wilderness courses, it may end there, for want of apparent opportunities to come to the aid of others outside the group. But it's a different story in the cities, where service to those in need can be the central and most compelling lesson, and where there are plenty of opportunities to help others. So we decided to "bring the mountain to Muhammad," creating sustained relationships with the students, their schools, and their communities.

The reaction of some people to this idea—both then and now, inside and outside the organization—has been that we don't belong in the cities, that we are a wilderness operation, pure and simple. That feeling has decreased over the years, but it hasn't vanished entirely. What the critics may be forgetting is that Outward Bound is not inherently a wilderness program. When we brought Kurt Hahn's philosophy to the United States, wilderness courses were just one option for reaching people. As it turned out, they were not only the easiest to fund and the quickest to get off the ground, but extremely popular, due in part to their novelty.

In truth, though, working in cities and with schools brings us closer to Outward Bound's roots. Hahn started Outward Bound as a school outreach effort; an Englishman named Freddy Fuller later created the first urban program, called "City Challenge," in the 1960s. Much of Outward Bound's work in both The Netherlands and Belgium is urban-based as well. Hahn's focus was on service and self-discovery—lessons that can be learned in any environment. As long as we keep our eye on what he was interested in—the things that make us different from other kinds of youth programs—it doesn't make much difference where we do it.

Our board members began to feel this way as well. With the impetus of the 1980 mission statement, that Outward Bound should "expand the influence and application of its principles," we immediately began looking into ways to establish ourselves in urban areas, while continuing our outreach work. As longtime board member Lee Klingenstein recalled, "It dawned on people that, with a little attention to detail, a lot of what we were doing was applicable to urban environments. That if you wanted the experience that comes from climbing, you could do it up the side of a building." By 1985, this notion would take a step toward reality at a systemwide planning conference in Keystone, Colorado, when president John Raynolds and others raised the idea of creating a new Outward Bound school or other entity in New York City. Brooks Thomas, who was board chair at that time, recalled the ensuing discussion: "A lot of people said, 'Of course not.' But there were others who said, 'Why not?'"

While we were considering starting an operation in New York, a citizen-led effort was gearing up in Baltimore that would soon bring us into that city; and during the next few years we would develop a dedicated presence in several other urban areas, including Boston, Atlanta, and Philadelphia. (The programs and centers that developed in these cities came about in different ways—through decisions by our national board, efforts by our wilderness schools, and local citizen action—and didn't necessarily take the same shape. Organizers in New York, for instance, initially focused on bringing Outward Bound experiences to the city and to its young people; Baltimore's founders wanted to make use of their local natural resources and avoid traveling to our nearest schools, in Maine or North Carolina; and Boston's Thompson Island sought to serve that city's youth by bringing students to a patch of wilderness in their own backyard. While subsequent developments have brought their goals closer together, the identities of these separate urban centers remain distinct.)

During these formative years, we were also continuing other ventures that became valuable models for our later work. In addition to providing scholarships for disadvantaged youth, our wilderness schools reached out to students and teachers in places like Denver, Minneapolis, Los Angeles, and New York. As a result of these and other efforts, we had several especially successful programs to look toward when we began planning our "new" work in cities.

In Florida, the Short Term Elective Program (STEP) had been working with the state's juvenile offenders since 1975, taking them out of the city for month-long canoeing expeditions and "reality therapy," a form of counseling popularized by Dr. William Glasser and intended to help its beneficiaries "reconnect with people they need." STEP was a cheaper and more effective alternative to building prisons and keeping young people in them—a new way to send them "down the river." A judge from Jacksonville praised STEP for taking these young people "out of the concrete jungle and [making] them work their butts off and depend on others." The program, run by Hurricane Island Outward Bound, has seen thousands of offenders come through its doors; one study showed that a year after completion, 73 percent of participants have no repeat violations.

Lewis Glenn, now our national vice president of safety and programs, served as the director of STEP in the 1980s and as an instructor from its inception. He recalled his first experience leading a group of troubled youth, paddling with the tenets of reality therapy scrawled on his hand. "On a STEP course," Glenn pointed out, "everyone paddles the same miles, swats the same mosquitoes, cooks and eats the same food. If someone burns the rice, you all eat burned rice." He said that a level playing field introduces adjudicated youth, who are used to a certain hierarchy, to new possibilities.

STEP has continued working with young offenders and today runs three residential programs with their own public schools. It has also moved on to create Families In Need of Support (FINS), which invites parents to bring in boys and girls on the edge of trouble, that together they might "head them off at the pass." For the last two decades, the voluntary program has provided a chance for discussion, adventure, and counseling—and changed lives. In 2002, STEP was set to expand into South Carolina and had been invited to start operations in Georgia.

In a sense, STEP paved the way for sustained work with city youth. Based on the experiences of instructors in Florida, we created the *Outward Bound*

Instructor's Guide to Managing Adolescents in the Field, which is used by schools throughout our system. Though students in urban areas are not "troubled" by definition, Glenn pointed out that the lines between adjudicated young people and typical students are increasingly blurred. As a result, he noted, "staff once looked at askance are sought after for their ability to work with youth." STEP, which taught the rest of Outward Bound invaluable lessons about working with youth, has in turn has begun incorporating academics into its traditional adventure offerings.

Another endeavor blending adventure and academics was created in the early 1980s at the urging of the city of New York. Mayor Ed Koch wanted to send local students to prep schools in the summer to raise their reading levels. His youth coordinator, Marian Schwarz, asked Greg Farrell—who was then on our national board and running the Fund for the City of New York (a Ford Foundation offshoot created to engender change in city government)—to help her put it together. Farrell remembered, "I suggested that Outward Bound schools could probably do as good a job of intensive literacy development as Taft or Andover." So Summer Scholars was born, with the Hurricane Island and North Carolina Outward Bound schools hosting students from South Bronx High School and Brooklyn's Boys and Girls High School for the first time in 1984, and Thompson Island hosting it in later years. Though Hurricane Island and Thompson Island eventually found they couldn't continue, North Carolina runs the six-week literacy program to this day. "They developed a kind of spiritual attachment to it," explained Farrell.

Today, our New York City center runs a version of the program as well, in the Adirondacks. Combining canoeing and climbing with writing and reading, Summer Scholars was one of the first compelling examples of a formula that would prove to work well for Outward Bound: a combination of adventure and academic learning, producing results that schools could measure. Anecdotal as well as documented evidence suggests that students who attend gain an average of two to three grade levels in reading, writing, and listening, and their dropout rate is fifty percent of the norm in their schools. Most rewarding of all is the eye-opening experience that urban youth receive from Outward Bound. Carmen Martinez, a student from New York City, described reaching the top of a peak in North Carolina and realizing "Life is worth living.

Every time I feel like I'm going to have a hard time in my life, I have to remember moments like that."

Then there was Urban Adventures, started in 1979 by Maryann Hedaa, an Outward Bound alumnus and former nun who adapted our methods to serve inner-city youth. Starting with a staff of three, she developed lasting relationships at several schools, including South Bronx High School and Eastern District High School in Brooklyn. When we started our center in New York, there was an overlap between our board of trustees and goals and those of Urban Adventures; eventually, Hedaa's group, which we had in some sense inspired, merged with us, providing contacts and even equipment to help us meet our shared goals.

■ ■ ■

With experience with urban populations under our belt and the conviction that Hahn's ideas could be relevant in the city, we began looking in earnest at the idea of locating a center in New York. It was a likely place for us to establish a freestanding center for two very practical reasons: Outward Bound was well recognized there, thanks to the recruiting work of both Hurricane Island and North Carolina; and the board had what Tom James—a vice dean of education at New York University who helped us research and plan the new urban center—called "deep access" in the city at that time: ties to corporate, government, and nonprofit arenas that facilitated research and fund-raising. In 1986, at the annual national trustees' meeting in New York, our board participated in an "urban experience." After exploring a "course" with activities like rappelling out of Fire Department Academy windows and sleeping on the deck of a ship at the South Street Seaport, they were sold. As Brooks Thomas said, "We realized that wilderness was not the only metaphor for Outward Bound. You can have an Outward Bound experience riding around in a police car or on the subway."

Greg Farrell and fellow board member Bill Abelow took on the task of developing plans for an independent urban center. Abelow was a lawyer in the city who, after reading about our adult courses in a magazine in 1974, took them at North Carolina, Hurricane, and Voyageur and started a New York metro area alumni association. With the help of such New Yorkers as *New York Times* publisher Arthur Sulzberger Jr., head of the city council Andrew Stein, and Rick Guttenberg, who was then heading up research and evaluation for the city's Board of Education but would later come to work for us in Boston, they began to envision what this new entity might look like. Tom James and two research assistants from the Board of Education spent months contacting and visiting schools, nonprofits, community-service organizations, and other groups that were doing things similar to what we imagined. In the vision paper that resulted, James wrote that Outward Bound's "finest instructors should be exactly where the problems and the human prospect exist in their most concentrated form. The city confronts existing models; breaks them apart; demands new responses; asks harshly whether we mean what we say; opens the door to challenging opportunities for service; and thus gives life to the social vision that drives Outward Bound as a form of education." He concluded, "Outward Bound should be right in there, deeply embedded in the urban scene, with the most powerful programs it can muster."

And so our plans went forward. James remembered that "there was a fear that the wilderness schools would have the danger of being somewhat marginalized economically, because they're tuition-dependent." So the New York organizers agreed that the center would not offer courses to the public, but would work directly with schools or run courses by invitation or contract only. In 1987, with funds from the city and other sources, the New York City Outward Bound Center began its first projects: working with classes at South Shore High School in Brooklyn and hosting invitational youth-adult courses, pairing teens who were wilderness school alums with civic leaders to explore the local landscape.

Richard Stopol, a lawyer who worked in youth programs for the Fund for the City of New York, had become involved in the planning process and later went on to head up the center. Though Stopol had no prior experience with Outward Bound, he has devoted the last fifteen years to this "experiment," recently shepherding the center into a brand-new facility—complete with climbing wall—at the foot of the Fifty-Ninth Street Bridge in Queens. The center has developed close relationships with other schools, including South Bronx, Eastern District, and Brooklyn's Erasmus high schools. Its instructors

have a regular, year-round presence in about a dozen schools and work periodically with nearly fifty others, training teachers, working in classrooms, and
taking kids on explorations of the streets. Among other endeavors, the center
also sponsors a teen mentoring group, Rebels with a Cause; offers private
wilderness expeditions for universities and other organizations; promotes
corporate team-building with the Outward Bound Professional (OBP) course;
and runs an outdoor leadership and community service program for its alumni.

"We found that New York, as a course area, has limitless possibilities,"
Stopol said. "There are special opportunities to take advantage of things
Outward Bound has always had as part of its value system, but that are harder
to do in a wilderness context, like service—there are opportunities for service
on every corner in New York—and the opportunity to bring people together
who have different backgrounds. Every neighborhood is different in New
York, so there's the opportunity to interact with people who are different
racially or ethnically or socioeconomically—all that was here waiting for us to
take advantage of it."

These urban groundbreakers also found that there were some issues that
would take on new dimensions for Outward Bound. "I'll never forget going to
a [systemwide] safety meeting where everybody presented significant
incidents over the last year," Stopol said. "My Colorado colleague was running
courses in Alaska and told about a grizzly bear invading camp and how to
address that. Then I got up and talked about what we call 'hostile bystander,'
when kids are exploring a neighborhood in the city and run into people who
give them a hard time. That's just not something you encounter in Alaska." It
was obvious from the start that our formal safety requirements, which had
been designed with the wilderness in mind, would need amendments: things
like how to keep from blocking a narrow sidewalk when wearing a large
backpack, remembering to wait for a walk sign, knowing what to do if you get
separated from your group on the subway.

Lewis Glenn, who oversaw those changes, said, "We grappled with how to
apply what we had done in the wilderness environments to urban environments. The urban environment is replete with hazards that exceed anything
in the wilderness. Human beings are less predictable than avalanche hazard,
white-water rivers, or other factors you can control or predict." Just like the

wilderness schools, the urban programs would undergo safety reviews and prepare incident debriefings. "The challenges were new and different," Glenn said, "but the procedures were the same."

Those challenges might lie around any corner. The students canoe in Jamaica Bay or the East River; they climb in Fort Tryon Park or the Cloisters; they cook meals for homeless men and play a little basketball with them while they're visiting. After the tragic events of September 11, 2001, the center put together a "unity course," a series of weekends for student leaders focused on adventure, culture, and service. The result of all of these activities is that the students learn about their city and themselves. In a 1987 piece in the *New York Times* on the then-nascent center, a young woman named Ary talked about her view from the bay. "I looked at the stars and listened to the water. I looked at the city and started seeing it in a different way."

Though Stopol and Abelow, who became the center's deputy director, are quick to point out the difficulty of reaching every child, due to the vastness of the city school system—it serves more than a million pupils—the center has made an impact. "There are so many stories and examples of young people and groups of young people whose lives we have affected," Abelow said. "I am hopeful and excited, and continue to be turned on by what we are doing." He added that he is "firmly convinced Outward Bound works in the city. The students are from the city, we're in the city, and it's an opportunity for us to have a continued presence in their lives."

A group in Baltimore, Maryland, sought that continued presence at the same time we were planning the New York center. In 1983, Mayor Donald Schaefer (who would be elected Maryland governor just a few years later) created the Parks and People Foundation, asking campaign volunteer and influential Baltimorean Sally Michel to chair it. Through a local connection, the group became aware of Hurricane Island's continuing efforts to reach urban youth, and began raising money to send its young citizens north. With the help of the school system, which loaned its buses for the nearly twenty-hour drive, Parks and People sent a hundred boys and girls from Baltimore to Hurricane Island the next two summers—black and white, rich and poor, from public, private, and parochial schools. (They also found help in the form of matching funds from the Robert and Katharine Garrett Foundation,

Hurricane Island's oldest endowment and, coincidentally, a fund with local ties. Robert Garrett was an Olympic medalist and Baltimore resident who had set up sports-related opportunities for local kids decades earlier. Grandson Jim Garrett—who helped build the facilities at Hurricane—grew up in Baltimore, serves on the boards of Hurricane Island and the Baltimore program, and works with Lewis Glenn delivering staff trainings across the country.)

On that first bus trip in 1984, the children discovered that the only thing they had in common with one another was knowing the location of a single street in Baltimore, York Road. But on their return it was a different story. "They came in [to a board meeting] in shorts, with their scratched-up legs," Michel recalled. "'We're a family now,' they told us. 'What do you want us to do?'"

As in other cities, the lack of productive follow-up was a problem. After sending a second group north in 1985, Parks and People floated the idea of hosting an Outward Bound school right there in the city. It would cost less, allow them to use local resources like the Potomac River and the mountains of western Maryland, and make follow-up a reality.

George Armstrong, who was then vice president of Hurricane Island, remembers going down to meet with the department of recreation and Parks and People representatives. The Baltimore program came together "in a matter of months," Armstrong remembered, "almost instantly." With the help of a grant from Baltimore Orioles first baseman Eddie Murray, the school started up in 1,300-acre Leakin Park—an ideal location, as it's near public transportation and is a place where "you can get lost in the woods—in a good way," noted program founder Dick Frisch. Organizers hired two graduates of a wooden boat school in Maine to build four pulling boats for explorations in Chesapeake Bay. Hurricane Island stepped up to own and operate Baltimore/Chesapeake Bay Outward Bound, with Parks and People continuing as a major sponsor and fund-raiser. The first two directors, Phil Costello and Arthur Pierson, were both former Hurricane instructors. In 1988, David Starnes, who had worked at STEP and interned at Voyageur, took over the reins.

Today, Starnes oversees the school at its home in the park's Crimea Estate, running a combination of wilderness and urban programs from that historical base. The 1990s saw a new emphasis on urban and school-based work for Baltimore/Chesapeake Bay, with the goal of becoming a primary partner with

Outward Bound rock climbing courses reveal personal strength, agility, and finesse. (Photo © PCOBS, Kim Budd)

local schools. "When we started the Baltimore program, we were trying to produce a traditional Outward Bound school right there in the city and have it centered there," Armstrong said. "We never intended to use the city the way the New York center does." Today, in addition to running two- and three-week wilderness courses in the area, Baltimore offers a variety of other community-service and education-focused opportunities for the city's population, including one- and two-day teamwork courses for school groups; state-funded peer leadership courses; and SuperKids, a literacy and adventure course for third- and fourth-graders (and the only Outward Bound course in the United States that serves children so young).

Said Starnes about his job, "I can sit in my office and get frustrated with administrative stuff—management and budgeting and staffing—just like anyone on Wall Street, but then I walk out the door and there's a group of students whose lives we've touched. We can inspire them to make the world a positive, wonderful, light place."

In 1992, a spin-off of the Baltimore effort started up in Philadelphia at the behest of a handful of community businesspeople. Among them were Tim Greenwood, a Hurricane Island alumnus and its first board member from

Philadelphia; city councilman Michael Nutter; and Nancy Goldenberg, a volunteer in the Big Brothers and Sisters organization who took her Little Sister for a walk in Wissahickon Park and was sad to see that the inner-city teen was "petrified." Fueled by the desire to make urban youth feel at home in their city—ten percent of which is park land—Philadelphia Friends of Outward Bound began collecting funds to create a presence there. In the meantime, they also raised scholarship money to send students to Baltimore. Welcomed into the Hurricane Island fold, the group worked with four local schools to bus students south.

With the help of David Starnes and others, the ambitious founders eventually managed to secure downtown office space and build a high-ropes course in Fairmount Park. In 2000, the group created "Philadelphia: The Urban Expedition," which uses public transportation to explore places like Independence Hall, the Betsy Ross House, and the Schuylkill Center for Environmental Education. Expeditions might include rock climbing in the park and canoeing the Schuylkill River, and each concludes with a service project—cooking supper at a homeless shelter, sprucing up the park, or painting a mural. The Philadelphia group now works with students and teachers from twenty-one schools.

"We are offering young people the opportunity to learn through experience in their own city," said director Katie Newsom Pastuszek. She recalls a young girl, Xiu Hui, for whom English was a second language. The girl was quiet, shy, but a whiz at rock climbing, earning the nickname "Spiderwoman" from her peers. That confidence booster caused enough of a change in her bearing that, when she returned to school, the vice principal commented on it. "I do this work for the Xiu Huis," Pastuszek said. "Philadelphia is a wonderful city, as is New York, as is Boston, and kids who are not typical Outward Bound participants deserve as much of Kurt Hahn's educational philosophy as anyone else."

■ ■ ■

Boston became part of our urban efforts in 1987, when we started bringing kids to Thompson Island. It was a historical find: there had been an experiential school out there since 1833. I became a trustee of the Thompson Island Academy about 1960, after transferring a boy there from Phillips Academy at the dean's suggestion. It was fascinating to find such a place in the middle of Boston Harbor. We spent the next couple of decades trying to figure out what might fit that fantastic piece of real estate—it was an island looking for an excuse to exist. One hundred fifty acres, a mile offshore, the Boston skyline in one direction, Spain in the other.

We considered several ideas: Outward Bound national headquarters, a nautical training school for instructors, a post-baccalaureate program for people who intended to make a life's career of dealing with youth. In the mid-1980s, the school out there couldn't stay afloat, and the Thompson Academy Board asked for proposals. It seemed to be a great chance to place ourselves right in Boston and work with the city's youth. Stepping into the remarkable tradition of the already existing school, our version of Thompson Island would run adventure courses and keep the school going as well. The final decision came down to two ideas: a bird sanctuary and ours. The board was split, 6-6, with the chair standing to break the tie in our favor at 1:30 A.M.

The new Thompson Island center relied on already established arms of Outward Bound in the beginning, starting under the Hurricane Island umbrella and leasing the pulling boats built in Baltimore for its first year. It was chartered as the independent Thompson Island Outward Bound Education Center in 1992. George Armstrong, who arrived as director in 1996, pointed out that Thompson Island actually offers little programming in the city proper. "We serve an urban population, but we're more in a gray area," he said, "or even lean toward the wilderness-school side. The beauty of Thompson Island is we're serving kids in their own backyard."

"A lot of these kids from Boston haven't seen the city skyline," Armstrong said. "They stand out on our dock and say, 'I didn't realize it looked like that.' For most of them, to get on our boat and come out to the island is, in itself, a new experience." One group of boys takes that boat ride every day to attend the Willauer School, named after Hurricane Island founder Peter Willauer. The middle school—which is run according to the same principles that fuel the Expeditionary Learning initiative we started in the 1990s—serves fifty sixth- through eighth-grade boys, some of whom overnight on the island. They are a mix of students: some are exceptionally bright boys who would be bored in a traditional public school; others are there because they need a small teacher-student ratio. And all prepare for continuing their education in high school.

Thompson Island not only sends kids off to good high schools, but also boasts a high completion rate on its courses. These include programs such as Choices, a series of one- and five-day expeditions for sixth- and seventh-graders that serves sixteen hundred students a year; Environmental Expeditions, a fourteen-day sailing trip for thirty-two high school students; and Intercept, a twenty-two-day course for thirteen-to seventeen-year-olds who are in a pattern of bad decision-making. Thompson Island also offers custom-designed courses for schools and private groups, as well as Outward Bound professional courses for business groups, and hosts conferences and outings whose proceeds help support the youth programming. It's the daily challenges that keep him on his toes, Armstrong said, "but I love knowing we're making an impact on kids' lives, feeling the energy."

■ ■ ■

By the late 1980s, Outward Bound wilderness schools and urban centers had made an impact on the lives of ten thousand urban youth. We were working with hundreds of schools and agencies, and we were still growing. We were reaching students who came away feeling the same outlook expressed by one young woman in Baltimore: "I ain't gonna say 'can't' no more." The wilderness schools began increasing their efforts in the cities, running programs in or dedicating staff members to Chicago and Minneapolis/St. Paul (Voyageur), Denver and San Diego (Colorado), Los Angeles, San Francisco, and Portland (Pacific Crest), and Atlanta (North Carolina). In every case, there was an administrative presence; in some cases, the schools came to the city—with offerings such as "Career Beginnings," "City Quest," "Urban Survival Skills," and "Voyageurs in the Parks"—while in others, they recruited urban youth for programs back at the wilderness base.

During that time we also got together with the Harvard School of Education to establish the Harvard–Outward Bound Project on Experience-

Based Education. It seemed to us a wonderful way to introduce the school to some experiential learning in its curriculum, subject ourselves to scholarly inquiry, and move us closer to getting our ideas into the educational mainstream, results Expeditionary Learning would later develop (see next chapter). In 1990, we formally created our Urban/Education Initiative, based on what was happening at the New York center, to explore the potential of bringing more of Outward Bound's philosophies into school settings.

Through sustained work with teachers and students—work that would foster active learning, cooperation, and community service—we sought to create a "critical mass" of informed participants at involved schools. While the open-enrollment courses at our wilderness schools drew participants from across the country, we believed geographically focused efforts could have a real impact on the areas, and the school systems, where they took place. And though we had proved to ourselves that one-day workshops and short courses could get the Outward Bound message across, we wanted to build even stronger relationships with urban schools.

As we continued our work with students and institutions in the cities, the value of partnering with local agencies was reenforced for us. Thompson Island, for instance, had cooperative relationships not only with public schools, but, among others, the Unitarian Universalist Urban Ministry in Roxbury, Massachusetts, and Compass Inc., an agency that works with Boston's troubled youth. Perhaps most crucial, we learned that we could have an effect on American education—whether it came in the form of students in a New York City school dedicating a peace garden to a fallen comrade, teachers from Denver attending an experiential learning workshop in Colorado, conflict-resolution courses in Portland, Maine, or an outdoor-education class in San Francisco.

We were delighted to discover that we could measure this impact. Through Outward Bound programs, students' reading scores go up, dropout rates decrease, and attendance records improve. At Theodore Roosevelt High School in the Bronx, Outward Bound students had a ninety-four percent attendance rate in the 1999–2000 school year, compared to seventy-three percent schoolwide. Richard Stopol of New York City Outward Bound is pleased with these tangible results. "What was clearly an experiment when we started is now very solidly entrenched," he said. "And we have barely scratched the surface of our potential."

We continue to work to overcome Outward Bound's identification in the public mind as a wilderness-only organization, and to convince urban kids and their families and administrators that we have something to offer. And challenges abound. Except for Atlanta, the new urban efforts started by the wilderness schools around 1990 shut down within a year or two, due mainly to the competing financial strain of developing publicly funded programs in the cities while supporting their wilderness programs through recruitment and tuition. Another issue is that staff needs to be trained differently for urban work, which takes time and resources. As Stopol pointed out, "We're operating in the most diverse city in the world, and it's really important that our staff be diverse, be representative of the city where we're working, and be able to connect with different cultures and people of different backgrounds."

We've also asked ourselves—and are still asking ourselves—some hard questions: Can we run effective city- and school-based programs from a wilderness school? Should they all move toward the New York City model of a freestanding entity? Can we ensure that this "loose federation" of schools and instructors, who are all working toward the same goal, continues to learn from each other? Answers to the last question have come in the form of periodic systemwide meetings and informal staff exchange, but it is an issue that requires constant attention.

When it comes to the cities, we are still learning, still experimenting, still growing. Still, we have been pleased with our successes. As Bill Abelow put it so well, Outward Bound is "not about climbing, it's a process—and it can happen anywhere." Embarking on our urban efforts did not, by any stretch of the imagination, mean abandoning the vital and successful programs established in our wilderness schools, programs that defined Outward Bound USA for so long and are still at our core. But this new work would help us prove what Kurt Hahn believed, what many of us have long known, and what Tom James put into writing so well: "Adventure in wild and beautiful places hardly begins to describe the promise of Outward Bound."

EXPEDITIONARY LEARNING: OUTWARD BOUND AT THE CENTER OF EDUCATION, NOT THE PERIPHERY

✣

To start a school is to proclaim what it means to be a human being.

—From Outward Bound proposal to
New American Schools, 1992

I n its first thirty years in the United States, Outward Bound built a solid, respectable home on the foundation of the short-term relationship. Our existing contact with youth was powerful and memorable, but the brief, once-in-a-lifetime experiences didn't offer the repeated in-depth support and development that was needed. Some Outward Bounders were wondering if we couldn't do more. In the words of Arnie Shore, Outward Bound had become steeped in the very American notion that "short, shorter, shortest is the best way." By the late 1980s we had a strong presence in a handful of schools and immediate name recognition around the country. We were good at what we did—and we were in a position to get serious about our next phase. Paul Ylvisaker, dean of the Harvard Graduate School of Education (HGSE), gave us the kick we needed. His speech at the 1987 International Outward Bound Conference in Cooperstown, New York, became our call to arms:

What can we use more of, from Outward Bound? One, a more articulate and . . . aggressive participation in the educational dialogue.

The last ten years in America . . . have been full of the debate about where we ought to go in education. You have a tremendous amount to offer in that debate . . . We at the Graduate School of Education could use this voice, and I would like it from somebody who has a hands-on background and a capacity to articulate. Let's work together.

To be a greater voice in education, and urged on by this speech, the Harvard–Outward Bound Project was born in 1988. The project was designed to focus on applying experience-based education in mainstream and traditional schools using a mix of Outward Bound principles and the rigors of academic inquiry. Richard Holzman, superintendent of schools in Schenectady, New York, summed up the project by saying, "Today, young people . . . are drowned in information, but starved for experience."

For the few years previous, a forward-thinking community-activist-turned-educator named Meg Campbell had been working as special assistant to superintendent Diana Lam at the Chelsea (Massachusetts) Schools. She was also pursuing her Ph.D. at Harvard, drawn there by the work of Eleanor Duckworth and Harold "Doc" Howe II. Howe, who held a chair in the HGSE, had been U.S. commissioner of education under President Johnson and later received the Kurt Hahn Award, would be instrumental in the collaboration between Outward Bound and the university.

At Chelsea, and in her role at several nonprofit agencies before that, Campbell was a self-described "change agent," restructuring schools and organizations. Although she had taught high school, she considered her greater strengths to lie in early-childhood and elementary education. And she kept thinking about how to incorporate experience into mainstream education. From her desk at a Boston inner city school, she applied for the directorship of the Harvard–Outward Bound Project. It was the eve of the Gulf War, February 1991.

Attention to kids under the age of fourteen was something new—and very intriguing—to Outward Bound. Fueled by a $2.9 million DeWitt Wallace–Reader's Digest Foundation grant to support the Urban/Education Initiative, we gathered staff and board members together to spend several days at Thompson Island. Our task was to create five- and ten-year plans for reaching the mainstream by deepening our relationships with public schools. At the meeting, we came up with four guiding themes for Outward Bound's future:

1. *Create institutional change.*
2. *Have a central rather than peripheral role.*
3. *Hold on to a long-term perspective.*
4. *Focus on quality rather than quantity.*

Back when we started Outward Bound in the United States, the wilderness experiences looked to us like a natural way to break the ice so that we could get on to the real ends: to affect the mainstream of public education using the Hahn philosophy. Now we could put our money where our mouth was. The generous DeWitt Wallace grant allowed us to formalize our commitment to create effective, sustainable, and replicable school program models. One thing was sure: we had a huge potential audience. Before he left to head up Project Adventure, Bob Lentz had mused about weaving Outward Bound in with school programs. "When you get involved with it," he said, "you're relating to the country's ongoing educational system, where ninety-eight percent of kids spend a good bit of their time."

That year, 1991, fully one-third of the total Outward Bound budget in the United States—about $10.6 million—was spent on projects related to the Urban and Education Initiative. We focused our beam on the urban centers and their outreach into communities, teacher-development programs in six states, Summer Scholarship reading programs, and dozens of technical assistance and other programs we were running for schools and social agencies. Greg Farrell was busy increasing the quality and sustainability of activity in urban schools along with developing individual school contracts. He recalled the very fertile period: "People just kept coming up with ideas and communicating them." Though the board was in favor of looking beyond the wilderness courses to examine new applications for Hahn's values, he said, "It wasn't at all a matter of decisions coming down from the top."

Then came the proposal that changed everything. In the spring of 1991, a compelling "request for proposal" (RFP) from the New American Schools Development Corporation (NAS) came along. NAS had been established that year under President George H. W. Bush and was headed by Lamar Alexander and a host of corporate leaders from companies like IBM, Xerox, and the Rand Corporation. It was designed to jump-start education reform by gathering proposals for "break-the-mold" schools. President Bush issued this challenge: "To reinvent American Education . . . to design new American schools for the year 2000 and beyond." The schools would be funded with $150 million in grants from the Nabisco Foundation, the Pew Charitable Trust, the Ford Foundation, IBM, The Boeing Company, the Annenberg Foundation, and other major corporations and foundations. The initial request called for "plans for reorganizing an entire school around a common vision of high student achievement, replacing the traditional approach of piecemeal improvement programs," and had its roots in the idea, according to Farrell, that "American genius is not for small incremental change, but for big breakthrough ideas."

The unusual RFP fired the imaginations of many in the educational reform movement, including Meg Campbell. She had not yet heard back from Harvard, but she approached her friend Greg Farrell, RFP in hand. Together they set out to gather a group of thinkers to dig into the roots of Outward Bound and craft a proposal.

"Looking back, for me Trenton Action Bound was actually the first draft of Expeditionary Learning," said Farrell of the 1963 program that got him started with Outward Bound. But while that was more of a one-shot deal, we were determined to create a new program that could succeed and replicate—a program that would "grow trees," as Farrell had said more than a decade before. To do this, we pulled together experts from a variety of backgrounds who each added critical dimensions to the original vision.

"One of the impressive parts of the process," said Tom James, "was the willingness at Outward Bound—of Greg, the board, the directors of the various programs—to come into a very new context and talk with those who are very different from them. They had river guides, teachers, and a community organizer working together in catalyzing reactions. This took place hundreds of times in the creation of Expeditionary Learning."

The roster included soon-to-be Dubuque superintendent of schools Diana Lam, with whom Meg worked at Chelsea Schools and whom we hired, at Meg's suggestion, to head up the development of the proposal; Alexandra

Weinbaum from the Academy for Educational Development (AED); Rachel Poliner from Educators for Social Responsibility (ESR); Mark Skvirsky from Facing History and Ourselves; Steve Truitt from Harvard–Outward Bound; Richard Prouty from Project Adventure; Dr. Robert Tinker from TERC; Richard Ackerman of the Harvard Principals' Center; Patricia Anne Kelly, a Boston Public Schools principal; Mieko Kamii, professor at Wheelock College; Linda Nathan of Fenway Middle College High School; Jerry Pieh; Outward Bound's Lewis Glenn; Geraldine Robinson of the Boston Children's Museum; and Robert Snyder, Brookline High science teacher.

Together, the team assembled a proposal for a New American School called Expeditionary Learning (EL), rooted in the time-tested philosophies of Outward Bound. Hooked on the basic concept of "learning expeditions"—long-term intellectual investigations, culminating in projects and performances that take students and teachers out into the community—and using the guideposts of courage, intellect, and compassion, Expeditionary Learning also found inspiration in the powerful speech by Paul Ylvisaker, the philosophy of Duckworth, and the seven laws of Hahn's Salem School.[35]

As Farrell recounted about the RFP: "It sang to us and we sang back." Just responding to the RFP was an extremely useful exercise in focus, said Farrell. The team came up with ten "design principles" that they thought best reflected the philosophy and core values of Outward Bound as applied to education. In January 1992, the exhausted, exhilarated team sent off a thirty-page proposal organized around these principles:

1. *The primacy of self-discovery*
2. *The having of wonderful ideas*
3. *The responsibility for learning*

---

[35] The Seven Laws of Salem, which guided Hahn's school in Germany were:
1. Give children the opportunity for self-discovery.
2. Make the child meet with triumph and defeat.
3. Give children the opportunity of self-effacement in the common cause.
4. Provide periods of silence.
5. Train the imagination.
6. Make games important but not predominant.
7. Free the sons of the wealthy and powerful from the enervating sense of privilege.

4. *Intimacy and caring*
5. *Success and failure*
6. *Collaboration and competition*
7. *Diversity and inclusivity*
8. *The natural world*
9. *Solitude and reflection*
10. *Service and compassion*

Each of the principles resulted from intense, months-long dialogue. The team members Farrell and Campbell had pulled together each brought to the table very specific areas of expertise and passion. Campbell was concerned that we infuse an "intellectual tradition," which she felt was missing from traditional Outward Bound programs. Jerry Pieh, she recalls, "helped us see the bridge— how we could take Outward Bound's ideas and use them as an inspirational metaphor for schools." Linda Nathan was critical in pushing for the diversity and inclusiveness piece of the puzzle, and Ted Sizer's work in creating networks of schools was also a valuable guide. As Scott Hartl, principal of Boston's Harbor School, described them, "the elements of Expeditionary Learning weren't mountains and rivers, they were school designs and structures."

Meanwhile, in Washington, D.C., NAS staff assistant Liz Berry was busy opening mail. With a background in management and business, she'd been drawn to the organization by Saul Cooperman in its early stages, after deciding on a career move to the education field. She couldn't have picked a more exciting time. "We had seven hundred proposals come in. Boxes and boxes of them," she remembers. "But when I saw the one from Outward Bound, my heart started pumping faster."

Berry, who was promoted after a year to director of design team operations, said the Expeditionary Learning proposal stood out from the pack. "Many [of the proposals] were submitted by school districts working with think tanks and by established leaders in school reform. So selecting this one was definitely more of a stretch. It was more of an unknown, but it captured people's interest."

The whole process, said Berry, was "a lot of fun—a once-in-a-lifetime opportunity. We had a loose charge: to take an idea of what an ideal school might look like, but make it realistic enough to put in place around the country."

In the summer of 1992, while Farrell was out on a river and hadn't a clue what was happening, recalled Klingenstein, NAS decided to fund Expeditionary Learning Outward Bound (ELOB) as a five-year pilot program. Out of the 698 design proposals they received, their review panel narrowed the list to eleven models they would use, in a "Whitman's Sampler of designs," as Farrell called it.

"We never thought we'd be selected," he said. Indeed, in a report to the Hearst Foundation that February, he wrote: "If we are selected for a planning grant, the attendant spotlighting would do much to get our pedagogies and ideas into the educational drinking water. In the likelier event we are not, we intend to proceed anyway with the team we have put together to develop and test these ideas further, and find funding on a more organic and incremental basis elsewhere."

Once selected, the real work began. Farrell immediately hired Meg Campbell as executive director of Expeditionary Learning Outward Bound and they hit the ground running. "Among people in the Outward Bound family who knew the philosophy of Kurt Hahn," recalled Klingenstein, "Greg was our choice to introduce it into the classroom."

Looking back to the early 1990s, Lewis Glenn said, "Each time we do something like this, it causes us to reflect on who we are, on what Outward Bound is. That's never been clearly defined, which is both a problem and a saving grace. It's allowed us to interpret and apply [the philosophy] in new ways and with new people. . . . Darwin is always out there—but so is Murphy."

▪ ▪ ▪

Scott Hartl was starting to think about the future as he led an Outward Bound river-rafting trip on the Green River in 1990. It turned out to be a fateful journey. On his boat was Schenectady schools superintendent Richard Holzman, who'd heard about Outward Bound through Greg Farrell's urban work in New York. Hartl was already looking for more stability and community when, while sitting on a log and eating the traditional last-night dinner of pizoli pie, Holzman offered him a teaching job and a promise to subsidize his master's degree in education. Hartl packed his bags for Schenectady.

After a few years teaching in Schenectady, and with degree in hand, Hartl followed his girlfriend to Boston. He used the office of a few friends to do some job networking. It was another fateful move: His friends worked for the Harvard–Outward Bound Project, and Expeditionary Learning was just in its infancy.

"They were looking for amphibious people," Hartl recalled, referring to those with backgrounds in both wilderness programs and classrooms. He was hired as Expeditionary Learning's first school designer, a position he held for five years, working with most of the school districts involved across the country. Then came the day he saw the RFP for pilot Expeditionary Learning schools in Boston. "We applied—and we got it."

In 1997, "six hours after the birth of my daughter Mia," Hartl started the Harbor School in Dorchester. "That was a tough year," he said of his experience as principal of a pilot school. "We had no facilities at all. We clawed our way through." From sixty students that first year, the school grew to accommodate 264 sixth- through eighth-graders and occupy two former Catholic school buildings on a cheerful street, its classroom walls covered in bright art projects and posters with slogans like "My own self, my very best, all the time," and "Truth regardless of the consequences."

■ ■ ■

The ten original pilot schools were in Boston; Denver; Portland, Maine; Dubuque, Iowa; and New York City. All but Dubuque were schools in which Outward Bound had an influence or was part of the curriculum as a result of the work of the Urban Education Initiative. Dubuque was a lucky result of personal contacts—Diana Lam had gone right from helping to write the Expeditionary Learning proposal to her post as Dubuque schools superintendent, and had offered it to the schools there. "[As a magnet for other schools] it was so helpful to have a highly functional school system like Dubuque with competent teachers" on board, said Campbell. "If we hadn't had Dubuque, it would have ended up a very different design."

"Dubuque," said Farrell, "is the one place in the country where most everyone you might stop on the street would know what Expeditionary Learning is."

These schools had to really want to do it. This was "comprehensive" school reform, not the "faddish, Band-Aid approach" as NAS referred to previous models. "The change process is intense and time consuming," said Campbell. The commitment required at all levels—administration, faculty, community, students, parents—is enormous, as Expeditionary Learning calls for changes in the school structure, culture, and instructional practice."

"Some schools dropped out—they weren't taking it seriously," Farrell said. The pilot schools had a promise of two years of funding from NAS, and since everything was paid for there was a lot more interest. "But," he added, "it won't work at a school where at least eighty percent of the faculty hasn't taken it on."

The questions we would typically hear—and still do—at information sessions at potential Expeditionary Learning schools were "Is it rigorous? Do we have to be able to climb mountains? What if I'm not outdoorsy? Will the children actually learn to read? What does a typical day look like?"

Yes, we would answer, it is rigorous. Yes, you will climb many mountains, though they might not be outdoors. The children will, with hope, learn to read. And by all accounts, there will be no typical day. Like an Outward Bound expedition, you'll have to make up some of the rules as you go along. And it is very different from what you've known before. "EL gets hold of the whole school," said Tom James.

Expeditionary Learning, even with the assistance of NAS, was a giant step into the unknown, often with the teachers learning right along with the students. But it was important to remind our schools—and ourselves—that this wasn't a new philosophy that we were talking about; it was something very old. Hahn had thought along these lines five decades before. Rudolf Steiner had used the idea of multiyear student groups in creating Waldorf Schools in the early twentieth century. Plato had even outlined such methods of education in *The Republic.*

And it wasn't all on our shoulders alone; NAS took a very proactive role, developing school contracts along with monitoring and overseeing the work. The first year (1992–1993), said Berry, was the design year, and after that EL "showed enough promise to continue. In Phase 2, we [tested it] at ten schools, and in Phase 3, our goal was to open new schools in new markets, and to help the design team make a new animal called a 'school design,' and scale up that design to make it an ongoing business. Then we stepped in to help with marketing and pricing." The idea, she said, was for NAS to pay for everything through Phase 2, then the districts would need to pay in order to make Expeditionary Learning sustaining.

For a host of reasons, "that first year was very challenging," Campbell said, "because we went in with a paradigm that we'd be contracting for curriculum development and services from Outward Bound. Instead, what became clear was . . . the teachers would need to design it themselves."

Added Farrell, "In the RFP there was an assumption that we would deal with the curriculum, but then we soon realized that we couldn't do that. It would take experts and millions of dollars." Like teachers on an expedition, they had to change this aspect of the design midstream.

The speed of implementation, recalled Berry, was also a major issue. "We all learned it takes a long time for a school to implement change," she said. "We thought it would be much neater and cleaner than it was."

■ ■ ■

Getting clear on what makes an expedition was crucial. Dennis Udall described it in his book *Journeys Through Our Classrooms.*

> *[An expedition is] an apt metaphor for intellectual inquiry. A real-life expedition is a journey with purpose. . . . The deeper you are drawn into it, the more the terrain reveals itself. An expedition's mission is meaningful . . . because [students] must lend their hearts and minds to it. Through grappling with the problems, questions, and dilemmas that emerge along the way, they test their ideas and develop them further. . . . [They] have to acknowledge what they do not know without becoming paralyzed with fear. . . . and what they have to do about it.*

A successful expedition is made up of many pieces. One of them is that it allows room for mistakes, for self-correction, for revision, for true learning. This pedagogy of mistakes can be unnerving for some teachers. They have to let go of control, and many teachers have learned to teach by always maintaining control. Built in, as well, is time for reflection and understanding afterward. Time for, as Howard Gardner put it, the "crystal-lizing experience."

Another piece is setting an "impossible" goal, as participants do on a wilderness Outward Bound course. While it's harder to do in an academic setting than on a sheer rock face, "the best learning expeditions have this quality of doing the impossible. EL first-graders in Denver have put on a production of *Cats*, and third-graders have built a faithful replica of Thoreau's cabin. . . . Middle-school students in Portland, Maine, have designed a new wing for their school," Farrell wrote in *Roots: From Outward Bound to Expeditionary Learning*. At the Um'o'ho Nation Public School in Macy, Nebraska, the entire student body took part in a re-creation of their tribe's last buffalo hunts. Oregon kindergarten students published a book about insects.

But there is no proven recipe for designing expeditions, said school designer Steven Levy. "The experience comes first, then the concept. The experience creates a 'vessel' that the concept 'fills.' If we pour in concepts without having created vessels to fill them, they will run off the sides of understanding and be forgotten—if not before the test, then surely after."

Expeditions also teach the meaning of service and culminate in a perform-ance or presentation through which students share the highlights of their learning. "The real audience is powerful," said Pam Shelly, principal of the Metropolitan Learning Center, an Expeditionary Learning K–12 school in Portland, Oregon, who watched proudly as her high-school students reported their findings on Portland's endangered water supply to a rapt adult commu-nity audience.

Expeditions are designed with "rubrics," explicit criteria for what teachers and students have agreed they should master by the end. "The secret of a good rubric," said Farrell, "is that it shouldn't be a secret." To mark their progress, students create a portfolio, which may include many drafts of a writing project or drawing, photos, research, and so on. It is a major compo-nent of their grade and in some schools a requisite for promotion, reviewed often and accompanying students throughout their school years.

The most important part of expeditionary learning is the expedition guide—the teacher. "It's often said," said Farrell, "that you see the best teaching on an Outward Bound expedition." How do those skills translate to the classroom? Many Outward Bound instructors come to the wilderness program because they haven't done well in school; some are even anti-school because they have been made to feel less in school. "Mother Nature is a big help in teaching," Farrell said. "School doesn't provide that kind of discipline. You can't talk your way off the top of a mountain—Outward Bound instructors actually get lots of help from the mountain."

The goal of such teaching, said Arnie Shore, is to use "minimum adequate instruction and maximum immediate application." On an Outward Bound course, the instructor will set out the problem, let the participants dive in and start to solve it, then guide and help them as they become fully engaged in applying themselves. Can this model work in the public schools? Are there academic situations as compelling as the following: You've never rowed a boat before. Lunch is in two hours. How are you going to get this boat from this island to the dock in time for lunch? In this case, once a student *needs* to learn to row, he or she will learn to row.

So we set up a model in which teachers would design academic expeditions based on such questions, then use "what is available," as Duckworth described, to inspire and motivate students. What is available can mean just about anything. Ron Berger, a sixth-grade teacher in Shutesbury, Massachusetts, and an Expeditionary Learning consultant, chooses themes for expeditions that have some "intrinsic interest" to him. He then investigates to find out if other teachers have used the theme, notes what resources they found, and researches as much as he can. Anything can serve as resource material: "For geology, I use *Tom Sawyer* because we spend a big portion of geology on cave exploration," he notes. "It seems like an obscure fit, but it is a great piece of literature and a lot of it takes place in a cave. . . . A unit will sink or swim depending on the appropriateness and complexity of the projects you have picked to integrate into the theme."

Said Joe Zaremba, art teacher at Boston's Harbor School, as kids swarm around him, "You've got to reach each kid at their own entry point. If we go to Thompson Island and then don't talk about it, it's a lost teaching opportunity. This is key. We take the learning moments and tie a bow around the design principles."

Though the sky may be the limit for expedition topics, public-school teachers must still teach to state and district standards and prepare students for the increasingly more frequent tests that they have to take. To do this, some subjects, such as math and particular "science nuggets," as TERC's Robert Tinker called them, must be taught separately and traditionally. Though standards remain a fundamental big concern, Expeditionary Learning experts Melissa Rodgers and Mieko Kamii suggest teachers also use the guiding phrase "By the end of this expedition, I want the children to be able to _____."

Many teachers coming to Expeditionary Learning have been engrained with a very traditional mode of teaching. Even if they have been involved in alternative methods, they're often used to being fairly autonomous. They must adjust to "looping"—staying with "crews" of kids for more than one year. In other words, a teacher might teach first grade, then second grade, then third grade, then go back to teaching first grade. Schedules are radically altered. Gone are the forty-minute blocks of teaching time: most of the day is spent on the expedition, and at least three hours of group planning time is scheduled each week.

Expeditionary Learning asks a lot of teachers, but it offers them a lot, too. They work with colleagues in creative, inspiring ways that they never have before—meeting regularly to set up, prepare, reflect, and come up with plans for expeditions and fieldwork. They are supported with summer summits—learning expeditions for teachers—in subjects ranging from the human body to the Holocaust. Thirty days a year are devoted to teacher development with a school designer visit from ELOB. Schools engage in an annual school review to "assess their progress toward full implementation of the design, set priorities for improvement, and create an action plan for achieving those priorities." The teacher has as great a stake in the expedition as the student. As we predicted in our original NAS proposal:

Mr. Hill will no longer see himself as a fifth-grade teacher; he will be an expedition guide for the same group of students for three years. He will be held accountable for their effective learning. To draw the best from one's students, one must know them very well.

In the words of Meg Campbell, this kind of teaching results in an "in-your-bones knowing of the kids—a cross between parenting and being a country doctor. The teachers have dreams for the kids like a parent's dreams."

■ ■ ■

These dreams were vital to the growth of Expeditionary Learning. And while the design principles—the "ten commandments" of Expeditionary Learning, as Southeast field director Angela Jollife described them—were the belief system behind the dreams, something was missing. Fairly soon, we realized we needed to help schools with the structure first—reworking schedules and forty-two-minute periods, tracking kids, providing a common planning time for teachers, determining the use of worksheets, and so on. We articulated and refined a list of what we called the "five core practices" to help us pay attention to the structures in which Expeditionary Learning could best work. They are:

1. *Learning expeditions*
2. *Reflection and critique*
3. *School culture*
4. *School structures*
5. *School review*

"These are the pieces," said Jolliffe, "that provide the delivery system to implement the design. When you do them, you improve school culture. You can have the ten commandments in your life, but what good are they unless you live them? In the early days [when Jolliffe was a middle-school teacher] we focused on the design principles so much, but then I started to say, "I have kids who can't read! Help me with that.""

The core practices, she said, help to level the playing field at schools. In a classroom shared by readers and non-readers alike, the core practices actually create a model that can work for all kids. "What they help us do," she said, "is *pay attention* to what we're doing. Nobody can be complacent, but nobody can work any harder than they currently do, either. So we have to work smarter, not harder. The core practices actually help the design principles come alive and be visible; [otherwise] they're just words on paper. To me, Expeditionary Learning is a perfect mix of head and heart—with design principles being the heart and the core practices, the head."

■ ■ ■

In 1995, with a two-year track record, NAS began to scale up, introducing its nine education designs, including Expeditionary Learning, in more schools. At this point, said Allen Grossman, professor of management at Harvard Business School who served as Outward Bound president from 1991 to 1997, "we realized Expeditionary Learning could [someday] spin off from the organization."

Two years later, in 1997, according to NAS, "Congress took notice of the student achievement gains . . . and created a national demonstration program giving thousands of schools funding to support what they named 'comprehensive school reform' [CSR]."

Has there been a sense of competition with the other CSR designs that NAS is developing and supporting? "We're all pilgrims on the same path," said Farrell about the other NAS programs. "We treat each other like colleagues." And NAS doesn't appear to play favorites. "They have kept our feet to the fire," he said. "They used contracts, not grants, so like any business we had to have 'deliverables' to them every quarter. They had planned to go out of business in five years after these pilot programs started. Then they realized that five years is just the start." With this momentum, Grossman recalled, "we realized our objective was to have it financially self-sufficient. We'd underestimated the amount of investment capital we'd need to get it up and running."

"But [NAS] was a funder who was healthy and private sector," said Campbell. "Coming from the school and nonprofit world, it was hard for me at first. There was no check each quarter unless they got what was promised. It was a system of discipline and feedback. The Rand Corporation taught me that feedback keeps you improving. I've learned from the process that the minute you think you know what you're doing, you're dead."

CSR differs from traditional school reform in that it works with a common vision for the entire school, not a single program on top of existing programs, and it targets all students and teachers in the school. According to NAS, the three ingredients for successful CSR are a research-based design, assistance in implementing that design, and district and state support.

NAS's current role is to help with guidance and feedback and moving into new markets, and they provide low-interest loans and financial help. Starting in 1995, the schools were no longer assured of private dollars for their programs; they had to raise the money themselves. Principals with nonexistent working budgets learned how to be creative grant writers. In some schools, such as the Metropolitan Learning Center, teachers turned over their yearly professional development allowance to help keep Expeditionary Learning up and running.

■ ■ ■

"Educational experiments are doomed to success," said Ylvisaker in the Cooperstown speech. "You perfect the experiment, you encapsulate it, you dogmatize it, and it becomes doctrinaire, and this is patent medicine. It never communicates, because people feel more excluded than helped by what something essentially constructive represents." Have we created something that will be sustaining, fluid, communicative, and open? How long will it take to prove it? What if the educational climate changes drastically?

When Pam Shelly heard Greg Farrell speak at an AEE conference five years ago, she stood up and clapped. "I was so excited that this could happen in a public school setting. . . . It was getting harder to be alternative in the public schools. You had to fight staff, the district, the state."

"[Our teachers] chose it because there was a deep value system they already believed in," continued Shelly. "EL is about the whole, entire school culture. At a time of great change—schools being listed in priority of academic scores—and budget cuts, I saw my colleagues going back to what they knew. It made me want to leave public schools. It became very linear.

"I believe public education is part science and part art. . . . I don't like models that take away the ability for the teacher to be a good artist. Teachers never get the opportunity to share their work. The ELOB methodology sets it up for success. It's my dream to have a school that is deeply EL."

But how about the view from the outside? How does the education world view Expeditionary Learning, especially in today's intense world of school assessment, accountability, and high-stakes testing? "If a design like this is going to work," said Joliffe, "we have to *prove* it works."

Doug Kilmeister, Expeditionary Learning's director of research and evaluation, said that the "schools that implement the design are getting good results. If they had lower performance before, it goes up. If they had good performance, then things like attendance go up. There are so many variables to consider, but there have been a lot of good studies."

Indeed. In a 1999 report, *An Educators' Guide to Schoolwide Reform*, the American Institutes for Research concluded that

> *despite the fact that this is a relatively new approach . . . the research results indicate that Expeditionary Learning can help to improve student achievement. Students tend to perform well compared to state and district averages on standardized tests . . .*

They also found that the design provided "strong support," and noted that "the professional development provided by Expeditionary Learning was a particular strength."

And in her report, "Academic Achievement in Two Expeditionary Learning/Outward Bound Demonstration Schools, 2000," Dr. Polly Ulichny of Brown University evaluated students at the King Middle School in Portland, Maine, and the Rafael Hernandez School in Boston. Her findings on both were encouraging: "The academic achievement of Hernandez's students has not only matched or surpassed that of other schools in the district over the last several years, but it has steadily been on the rise since initial Expeditionary Learning implementation."

In Denver, the waiting list for slots at Denver's Rocky Mountain School of Expeditionary Learning regularly runs to hundreds of names. More than half the student body shows up for voluntary weekend programs at the Harbor School. By the end of the 2001–2002 school year, Farrell expects 117 active school contracts that are all meeting the district standards. Success can be measured in many ways.

For as Jolliffe goes on to say, "Schools can't just be about test scores. They also need to feel joyous." Reports from students, like this one from Dalles

Kalmes of Dubuque's Table Mound Elementary School, are heartening: "When you are done with the expedition, you go home and tell your mom and dad what you learned and they practically don't even know what you are talking about. It's like you wrote a new chapter in the encyclopedia."

So *is* Expeditionary Learning a working model? There are no proven models, said James. "I think that's an incorrect, empirical view. Building a school is more like building a family. It's about love and loyalty. The 'model' approach suggests something you can roll in on wheels—it's a biomedical way of looking at things. You can fail on one level in a school, but succeed beautifully in other ways."

In a very uncertain educational moment in our history, what does the future hold for Expeditionary Learning? Many other school reform movements have not taken root. "In these," said Tom James, "they'd been able to convert a few teachers, who'd then get suffocated by the culture of the school. They would either leave or adapt to the old patterns. Expeditionary Learning came in with the knowledge that you had to change the entire school to have success."

The trends working against EL, said James, are the acceleration of the testing and accountability culture and fiscal constraints that schools face, particularly in urban areas. In places like Memphis and New York City, he said, chancellors and superintendents have come in with radically different philosophies and a suspicious view of any school reform.

But in some schools, he continued, it seems like Expeditionary Learning has become deeply embedded. He describes an elementary school he's visited in Dubuque where the students created a prairie and tree break on school grounds. "It will probably stay there," he said.

Scott Hartl plans to leave the Harbor School at the end of the 2003 school year to live abroad while his children are young. "I'm confident," he said, "that the [Expeditionary Learning] culture will hold up. It's penetrated the school and staff enough. We didn't found this school on just getting through the start-up phase. These beliefs better not go away."

We can only hope that in these schools the paradigm has truly been altered and that teachers are working together, thinking about how to energize and release the motivation in kids. "Do teachers feel like they've moved to a new level?" James asked. If they do, then they have changed and if they think this way, they can work together to keep the culture in place.

"I think education will fall off the national political agenda," said James. "There is a new consciousness of scarcity. Reforms come in cycles, and we're not going to see national resources except for testing and accountability. The kind of money out there in the 1990s just won't be around."

Our initial strategy for Expeditionary Learning was to cultivate unique school designs that work with unique schools. "It was wise not to just offer a curriculum package," said James. "This isn't wares to peddle or something you can just sell. To me this strategy was a good decision and means Expeditionary Learning will be around longer. The philosophy will get into the schools' drinking water."

"Expeditionary Learning has come a long way," said Grossman. "And, wow, it's exciting, it understands itself, and it delivers a hell of an educational product. But right now there isn't a single education reform that's profitable. They'll have to go an even longer distance than they've traveled. That board charge to have a material impact on American education—that was naiveté and hubris at an astounding level. But this [design] has truly embraced the spirit of Hahn, of Outward Bound and the goals of leadership. Expeditionary Learning didn't fall far from the tree."

■ ■ ■

In a church basement across the street from the Harbor School, Scott Hartl leads a weekly sixth-graders' "crew" gathering. As a few kids distribute giant, sticky doughnuts to their fifteen classmates sitting in a circle, he throws out a question for discussion: "What does this sentence mean to you? 'The parrot does not remember the sound of his own voice.'"

The kids think for a moment before responding: "It means about copying other people," one shouts out.

Hartl replies, "Yes, go on."

More kids jump in: "So we all don't sound the same." "Because we all have different personalities." "It means you need to know your own voice."

AFTERWORD

❖

In these final pages we have a chance to touch on the stories of the individual schools subsequent to their founding—in particular, to present second- and third-generation school directors who have done so much to make Outward Bound what it is and what it is becoming.

DAN MEYER was the fourth director of the North Carolina School (NCOBS). He came to the school via the U.S. Forest Service and a demonstrated competence as a fine manager. He brought to the post a warm, friend-making personality and an innovative temperament balanced by a high regard for the Hahn tradition. The school grew steadily under his leadership.

What Dan remembers with the greatest satisfaction is that he changed the student assessment system that U.S. Outward Bound had adapted from the British. Because so many Outward Bound students in Britain were sent by their employers, the schools there followed the practice of sending an instructor's report on each student to his sponsor or, alternatively, to his parents or perhaps both. In the beginning the U.S. schools took over this practice, reporting on each student to parents and, in the case of those on scholarship, to his sponsor. Dan did not like what he called this "report-card approach." He decided to treat the student, rather than the parent or sponsor, as the client. The student was called on to evaluate his or her own performance in writing just before going home. The instructor in turn wrote to his students, evaluating the course without singling out individuals. The other schools largely adopted this practice, at first on a trial basis and eventually as standard procedure. Dan has remained a part of the Outward Bound family, and as of August 2002 continues as an active member of the NCOBS board of trustees.

GARY TEMPLIN, initially Joe Nold's number-one man, was director of the Colorado School (COBS) from 1974 to 1980. Gary became director, and Nold moved up to the new post of president of COBS. Gary, like many future Outward Bound leaders, came out of college and was feeling his way toward a career path when his life was influenced profoundly upon encountering Outward Bound. In the summer of 1961, just after graduating from Wheaton College, Gary worked for Jim Vaus in Jim's Youth Development project in New York's East Harlem. Vaus made him director of a summer camp facility that had just been given to Youth Development. Gary's Montana ranch upbringing had given him no idea of how a summer camp functioned, and he wrote, among others, to OBI for information. We sent a copy of his letter to Joe Nold, who looked up Gary on his next visit to New York and showed him the *Tall as the Mountains* film. Gary went home and told his wife, "If anything ever took me out of Harlem, it would be Outward Bound." The two men kept in touch over the next two years. In 1965 Joe hired Gary for a month as a consultant on the OEO project in Collbran. A month after he returned to New York, Gary got a letter offering him the job of assistant director of the Colorado Outward Bound School. He started in the spring of 1966.

Gary was one of the seminal builders of U.S. Outward Bound and can lay claim to an impressive list of initiatives. He played a major role in changing the solo-experience emphasis from survival to one of contemplation and fasting. He did pioneer work in integrating minority, inner-city, and delinquent youth into the standard course and likewise played a central role in the early adaptive programs that spoke to the needs of disadvantaged populations, such as Dare to Care, Urban Bound, and others. Gary wrote the first curriculum outline as a means of standardizing the experience students would receive. He developed a strong leadership cadre that moved on to top positions in Outward Bound and in other areas of the experiential education community. He formulated the first semester-long leadership development course as a vehicle for producing adaptive program leaders. As chairman of the Outward Bound Coordinating Committee, he led a productive reorganization of U.S. Outward Bound's structure and procedural policies. To this day, Gary continues to provide vital leadership to Outward Bound as a trustee and chairman of the Pacific Crest Outward Bound School's safety committee.

DEREK PRITCHARD was the third director of the Minnesota School (MOBS). Derek began his association with international Outward Bound as a student at Aberdovey in 1949. After a stint in the British Army, he became an instructor in British Outward Bound and at training centers in East Africa. He was made director of the Outward Bound Mountain School at Loitokitok, Kenya, in 1963, and served as director of the British school at Devon from 1968 to 1973. In 1972 Derek spent a summer visiting and instructing at the Colorado, Minnesota, and Hurricane Island schools. He had no inkling then that a year and a half hence he would come back as the MOBS's new director.

Derek was a consistent innovator in his Outward Bound leadership. In Kenya he started a course for the blind that culminated in guiding seven blind climbers to the snow-covered summit of Kilimanjaro. At Devon he initiated mobile courses, coed courses, and courses for school dropouts. At Minnesota, he introduced courses for the physically disabled and hearing-impaired, making MOBS a pioneering agency in this important aspect of adventure-based education. Within a few years these courses were included in the school's standard curriculum, with a mixed handicapped and non-handicapped enrollment.

In 1976 Derek established Project Center as an experimental arm of the school, reaching beyond the standard curriculum to innovative courses and consulting services, to make the school available as "an educational model dynamic and flexible enough to respond to changing educational and social needs by developing new uses of Outward Bound for new audiences." Project Center started a life/career renewal course in conjunction with the Human Renewal Association of Minneapolis, designed to assist individuals in making decisions and clarifying values in the context of midcareer change. It also created a contract course for adolescents sponsored by the British Children's Thalidomide Trust. The center also designed a youth leadership community project for the Fort Peck Indian Reservation, and an experimental program for the Minnesota Mental Health Association in which Outward Bound instructors worked with thirty therapists and their clients to strengthen client/therapist relationships for improved therapy goals. Derek's most recent service to Outward Bound resulted from his appointment as executive director of Outward Bound International, a post he held from 1996 to 1999.

JOHN HUIE, director of the North Carolina Outward Bound School (NCOBS) from 1977 to 1995, was Georgia-born and raised. He had done some independent school teaching and coaching and was a graduate student at Emory University when Bob Pieh offered him a teaching/coaching job at Anniston Academy in Alabama. Bob explained that he would not be coming back as headmaster. "I asked him where he was going," John remembers. "'To start an Outward Bound school in Minnesota,' he said. I asked him what an Outward Bound school was. Bob's answer—philosophical, even poetic— was beautiful. I told him Outward Bound sounded like the best thing I'd ever heard of. He said, 'Then why don't you come with me?' And so I did, that summer of 1965, starting at twenty-seven as an assistant instructor, and then full instructor in August, and program director the next two summers. Good years, in which I identified Outward Bound as a magnificent vehicle for stimulating and nurturing personal growth, for really making a difference in human relationships."

When the NCOBS trustees were looking for a successor to Dan Meyer, John was their man. By then a Ph.D. candidate at the University of California at Santa Barbara, he had a lot more teaching and headmastering under his belt. As instructor and dean of students at St. Mark's School in Dallas and as headmaster of Verde Valley School in Sedona, Arizona, he had instituted Outward Bound adaptive programs.

"The focus of the North Carolina School in the 1970s," John said, "was strongly on personal growth and human relations. The physical side of the Outward Bound experience is not allowed to dominate the tone of the course but is used to open up the mind, touch the spirit. If there is any tension in the Outward Bound movement between the Athenians and the Spartans, count us among the Athenians. The key to Outward Bound is how the stress is handled, what resources the instructor has to set a tone of reverence for the world, respect for human differences, compassion for people, desire to serve, and so on."

Huie is a staunch adherent of the service ethic in Outward Bound. An advantage of NCOBS, he points out, is its close access to institutions—a state mental hospital, a school for the deaf, a prison for youthful offenders, a center for handicapped children—that offer opportunity for service projects. "Our emphasis on service," he said, "is important to us—is, in fact, what Outward Bound should be all about. The philosophical assumption behind that statement is that being fully human means acting on the impulse to serve fellow man, to behave unselfishly." John remains a leader and advocate for wilderness experiential education in 2002, holding a senior teaching position at Warren Wilson College, directly adjacent to the school he directed for eighteen years.

VICTOR WALSH was the director of the Northwest School (NOBS) from 1977 to 1983 and a director at the Pacific Crest Outward Bound School from 1984 to 1990. He is currently director of the Professional Development Center in the School of Extended Studies at Portland State University.

Like other Britishers, Vic was pushed into a vocational stream by the English educational system. When the English system spit him out at fourteen, Vic chose to be an apprentice automobile mechanic, which led to a factory toolmaker apprenticeship. He escaped that track by enlisting in the Royal Air Force, where his proficiency as a mountain climber got him into the Air Force's mountain rescue unit, with which he trained all over Europe, taking part in some three hundred rescues.

Back in England in 1962, Vic became an instructor at the Eskdale Outward Bound School under Tom Price, a leader whose educational philosophy profoundly influenced him. In 1964 Vic was one of the British instructors who helped the Minnesota School get started. The next summer he was at the Colorado School, the Moray Sea School in Scotland, and German Outward Bound at Baad. He came back to Colorado in 1966. In the years that followed, Vic earned an A.B. degree at Fort Lewis College in Durango, Colorado, and a master of education degree at the University of Colorado. He also wrote, along with Jerry Golins, "The Exploration of the Outward Bound Process," a seminal paper on the Outward Bound dynamic that traces how the process works.

In Vic's first three years as director, enrollment in the NOBS year-round schedule of mountaineering, ski mountaineering, and river-running courses, conducted in six areas in Oregon, Washington, and Idaho, was up eighty percent. Growth was aided by the headquarters' move to Portland, the opening of a Seattle branch office, and a broadening of trustee representation. The most significant aspect of the enrollment increase was that a relatively small part of it was in the standard summer program. This reflects a considerable development of year-round operation and a substantial increase in special programs and contract courses.

The NOBS clientele for contract courses includes the American Stock Exchange staff, juveniles in corrections residences, a migrant workers' high-school equivalency class at the University of Oregon, the Seattle Girls Club, hearing-impaired persons, as well as physically and mentally handicapped young adults. "We are committed to the philosophy that Outward Bound experiences should be made available, with adaptations, to populations with special needs," Walsh said. In 1979 he appointed a full-time "special program" chief instructor, whose responsibilities included a continuing effort to refine the school's special-program capability.

GERALD GOLINS served as director of the Colorado Outward Bound School from 1980 to 1985. Jerry graduated from Claremont Men's College in 1968. Two years later, following an uneasy year of teaching social studies in a suburban high school—uneasy because of his feeling that the school and he were not addressing the central concerns of many of the youngsters—he took a teachers' practicum at COBS. "I found a vehicle that made sense to me," he said. "It addressed the issues an adolescent needs to face. . . . I said to myself, 'This is where the action is.' The following June I quit teaching."

Jerry enrolled at the University of Colorado's School of Education in a master's degree program with emphasis on outdoor education. After receiving his master's, Jerry instructed through the summer at COBS, and in the spring of 1973 Nold called him in and, handing him a check, informed him that he was being sent on a survey trip to find out all he could about Outward Bound and corrections. With that survey as a basis, he became COBS's corrections specialist. He negotiated a three-year contract with the state of Michigan, whereby COBS would set up and service a program called "Michigan Expeditions" for selected juvenile delinquents. A similar contract followed for a program dubbed "Osage Expeditions" at the Missouri Intermediate Reformatory in Jefferson City.

Jerry read intensively and experimented with courses for delinquents. "The Michigan people were testing us," he recalled. "We did a course for a homogeneous group of assaultive delinquent kids from some of the worst sections of Detroit. It turned out pretty well and taught us a lot. We did another for delinquents from Lansing. When they went back, their social workers were so amazed at the positive changes that they asked how come. So we went to Lansing and put the social workers through a course that was a revelation to them. We did a pre-release course for Colorado adult offenders that had some extraordinarily good results."

An Instructor and Course Director for COBS for five years prior to becoming the COBS director, Jerry is credited with having started OBP and advancing "adaptive" programming in Outward Bound. He is the author of "The Outward Bound Process," a guiding methodology for Outward Bound for many years to this day. Jerry left COBS to become an administrator for a large accounting firm, then moved to Vernal, Utah, to run an outfitting business and finally to become a county administrator there. Jerry developed Parkinson's disease at some point along the way, and battles that affliction to this day. He currently resides in Salt Lake City.

THE ASSOCIATION FOR EXPERIENTIAL EDUCATION. In 1971, Appalachian State University at Boone, North Carolina, began to give its summer-session students credit for taking an Outward Bound course at the North Carolina School—a first. Professor Keener Smathers, who had administrative charge, participated in a course himself and became a powerful convert. When a stream of inquiries generated by national publicity about the liaison between the university and NCOBS made him aware of a strong current of interest in outdoor adventure at the college level, he conceived of organizing a conference. In the fall of 1973 he wrote Hank Taft to solicit OBI's cooperation. Hank sent John Rhoades, program coordinator of OBI, to Boone, where he and Smathers wrote a plan for a "National Conference on Outdoor Pursuits in Higher Education." OBI also put its promotional machinery to work and, through the generosity of the Ingersoll-Rand Company, obtained funds to help defray costs. The conference took place at Boone in February 1974. Despite the short time that had been available for spreading the word, more than two hundred people attended, coming from as far away as Utah, Ontario, and Maine.

Hank Taft gave the keynote address. The conference was a success; the zeal evidenced there left no doubt that Smathers's hunch had probed a movement waiting to spring into existence. Before the year was out a follow-up conference was held at Estes Park, Colorado, under the joint sponsorship of COBS and the University of Colorado's School of Education, with the COBS's Bob Godfrey as chief organizer. Billed as a "National Conference on Experiential Education," it had a considerably broadened participant appeal, which included educators at all levels and representatives of youth and other social agencies. After the Estes Park meeting, Outward Bound continued to provide seed money, personnel, energy, and promotion for organizing subsequent conferences, but also sought to keep an ever-lower profile in anticipation of the annual ad hoc gathering eventually taking on an organizational life of its own.

In 1976 Bob Pieh and his wife, Margueritta Kluensch, had the organizing responsibility for the Fourth National Conference on Experiential Education held at Queens University in Kingston, Ontario. It was through machinery set up at Kingston that there finally came a formal organization: the Association for Experiential Education (AEE). When the newly identified AEE convened at Asilomar, California, in 1977, it was an association of individuals, schools, and other agencies sharing comparable interests and similar visions in support of a variety of experience-based teaching and learning methodologies. With each new conference there was a diminution in the careless use—understandably annoying to non–Outward Bounders—of "Outward Bound" as the generic term for the experiential. However, OB people continue to play important roles in the AEE's leadership.

From Outward Bound's viewpoint, the AEE serves an extremely valuable function as a cohering base for its loose network of numerous and multifaceted outreaches. At the same time the AEE has brought the Outward Bound movement into useful alliances with others who have kindred purposes. AEE's serving as a common home for OB spin-offs has greatly helped to solve the predicament that troubled the early Mainstream days—the need for giving leadership to the proliferating adaptive program complex when OB was neither staffed nor funded for the task. The association not only provided these varied OB-derived programs with channels for talking with each other, but it also served as a catalyst for the formation of a series of special interest and professional groups (SIGs) within the mother organization.Thus the college people who comprised the core of the conference at Boone in 1974 now have their own higher education SIG. Members whose concerns are with juvenile delinquents and other special populations have a SIG that calls itself "Adventure Activities in Corrections, Mental Health, and Special Education." Other SIGs embrace persons and agencies concerned with Outdoor leadership, classroom teachers, teacher training, the arts, the handicapped, urban programming, women's issues, and spiritual awareness, moral, and ethical issues.

OUTWARD BOUND AND HIGH SCHOOLS. An idea whose time has come reveals itself by popping up in different places at the same time: Trenton City High's Action Bound; the Dare to Care program of Adams City High School in Commerce City, Colorado; an adaptation by New York's Horace Mann School in its John Dorr Natural Laboratory in western Connecticut; Southern Illinois University's Underway program; and Phillips Academy's search-and-rescue course, all launched in the mid-1960s, were the first OB outreaches. As we have seen, the Dare to Care program led to Denver East High's involvement a year later. At about that time Atikokan High School in Ontario was obtaining inspiration and ideas from MOBS, across the border, for its Outers program. In the 1967–1970 school years every OB school was servicing public and private school adaptive programs, frequently in a formal consulting capacity. A representative (but not complete) list of schools that pioneered Outward Bound adaptions, along with those already mentioned, includes: Athenian School in Dauville and Thacher School in Ojai, California; Winston Churchill High in Eugene, Oregon; Minnetonka High in Excelsior, Minnesota; Webb–Bell Buckle School in Bell Buckle, Tennessee; Fort Worth Country Day in Fort Worth and St. Mark's School in Dallas, Texas; the Toledo, Ohio, public schools; Freedom 7 Elementary in Cocoa Beach, Florida; St. Alban's School and Cardozo High in Washington, D.C.; Sterling School in Craftsbury Common and Stowe School in Stowe, Vermont; Hyde School in Bath, Maine; Proctor Academy in Andover, New Hampshire; St. George's School in Newport, Rhode Island; Concord-Carlisle and Walpole high schools in Massachusetts, and also the Gifford School, for youngsters with perceptual handicaps, in Cambridge, Massachusetts.

Among these, the Athenian School was the first to integrate an OB course into its own learning plan. Athenian is a coeducational day and boarding school founded in 1965 by Dyke Brown, who as a Ford Foundation executive had made youth his special province. In 1931, Dyke was a student at Kurt Hahn's Salem Schule in Germany. He remembers: "Hahn made an indelible impression on me. He had a tremendous capacity to put his finger on the jugular of a young person's character. He ticked me off in a way I wasn't accustomed to. He was inspirational, through his beliefs in what one ought to do and how to do it. Before setting up the Athenian School, I wrote to him about my ideas. Soon came a call from New York: 'Brown? This is Hahn. I want to see you.' He made the Founding Day address the first year of the school."

In 1969 Athenian contracted with the Northwest School to conduct a compulsory three-week course for the junior class before the regular school opening in the fall. About the compulsory feature Brown said, "There were few things at the school that we were that rigid about, but I felt strongly that the very people who needed it most were those who, if it were optional, would drop out." In time the school developed its own staff to conduct the course. Subsequently it introduced an optional enriched version running an entire six-week term and earning credits in science and humanities. This was just one of a number of steps taken at Athenian to provide field experience in support of classroom learning. Athenian was among the first to discover that an on-campus OB-type facility tends to become a valued experiential learning vehicle.

In 1970–1971 Joe Schulze researched, and OBI published, his exploratory (and optimistic) monograph, "An Analysis of the Impact of Outward Bound on Twelve High Schools." At that time there were only a few more than twelve from which to choose: a few years later at least three hundred adaptive programs were spread across the country. Now the total is large and growing enough to be uncountable. What once was a trickle of Outward Bound influence in the educational mainstream has swollen to a strong, steady current.

Howard Greene, a leading educational consultant, has been a fascinated observer of the phenomenon. "The manner in which the Outward Bound movement—labeled and unlabeled—has impacted the schools in recent years is simply extraordinary," Greene said. "Whereas even a half dozen years ago Outward Bound adaptive programs were more the exception than the rule, today it would be difficult to put together a list of schools that have not instituted some form of outdoor pursuit activity as a highly acceptable, positive educational force. It's happening in both the independent and the public schools, and increasingly it's spreading downward from the senior to the junior high and the elementary levels. It is quite clear that Outward Bound is directly responsible for much of this, and that it is a principal catalyst in a movement that has considerable significance for education in the future."

As Greene indicated, there have been enough Outward Bound adaptations at the elementary and junior high levels to assure that the idea also worked for kids in those age brackets. What probably was the first of these—it remains a model for integrating classroom study with adventure-based learning—was Rafe Parker's Pioneers program for seventh- and eighth-graders at the Fenn School in Concord, Massachusetts.

Rafe discovered that a wild tract near the school, known as the Estabrook Woods after one of Concord's earliest settlers, offered an ideal outdoor classroom. The area, which is rich in Concord history and has reverted to wilderness, is much alluded to in Thoreau's journal. ("Shall we call it the Estabrook Country? It would make a princely estate in Europe. Yet it is owned by farmers who live by the labor of their hands and do not esteem it much.") In addition to regular Outward Bound–type activities on school days, the students explored the Estabrook Woods on weekend overnights as part of a classroom-related project that Rafe worked out with their English, math, history, and science teachers. He took the students to the Overlanders program at the Lyman School, to be instructed in rescue techniques by their incarcerated peers. Rafe involved them with the Fernald Institute, where they spent two afternoons a week helping retarded children.

"This was perhaps the most significant thing we did," Rafe said, "because our students were used to a very set, very insular, very comfortable way of life. Being confronted with a kid of their own age who wasn't even toilet trained, didn't know how to tie his shoes or button his coat, made them adjust. The experience pulled a tremendous amount out of them."

Bounders is a modified Outward Bound program for dyslexic youngsters at the Carroll School in Lincoln, Massachusetts. It was established in 1971 under the guidance of the Hurricane Island School (HIOBS), with instructor Mike "Strats" Stratton in charge. Headmaster Bill Adams observed the Stowe School's adaptive OB program while on the faculty there and saw Outward Bound as fitting eminently into the confidence-building structure that is one key to Carroll's success in helping students overcome their learning disabilities. A Bounder course runs for four weeks, after school plus weekend expeditions. Rocks I is rappelling off the school's third-story fire escape. The expeditions go as far afield as Hurricane Island, Dartmouth, and New Hampshire's Mount Moosilauke.

OUTWARD BOUND AND HIGHER EDUCATION. In 1973 Rick Medrick produced for COBS a survey of OB and the colleges. Like Schulze in his study at the secondary-school level, Rick did not then have a plethora of college programs to draw conclusions from. He selected seven—Prescott, Dartmouth, Colorado College, Wheaton, Boston University, Evergreen, and the University of North Carolina at Charlotte—for the variety of OB designs or services they utilized.

Colorado College, in conjunction with COBS, was employing Outward Bound courses for counselors in freshman dormitories, as a catalyst contributing to self-knowledge and decision-making ability, and prompting acquisition of new skills. Wheaton's Vanguard School was a pre-college course seeking to prepare freshmen for campus life, emphasizing personal development and enhancement of the ability to work with others in a Christian setting.

The program at Evergreen State College in Olympia, Washington, reflected the strong influence of faculty member Willi Unsoeld. In the institution's first year, five of the ten academic programs experimented with outdoor programs as part of their course designs. Subsequently Willi shepherded a student-designed course called "Wilderness and Consciousness." He continued each year, until his tragic death, to encourage students to conceive a wilderness-oriented course with Outward Bound elements, to design the curriculum, and to participate.

Some of the ways in which OB has influenced college outdoor pursuits include the following:

■ Keene State College Operation LIVE (Learning in Vigorous Environments), Keene, New Hampshire. Under the dynamic directorship of Keith King, alumnus and instructor of Dartmouth Center (DOBC) courses, this program offers the student body a highly varied week-to-week program of Outward Bound–type activities and a summer-school curriculum in experiential learning. LIVE also sponsors a Living-Learning Term, which includes an outdoor phase modeled on the standard Outward Bound course.

■ Bob Pieh and Margueritta Kluensch's comprehensive offering of courses in outdoor, affective, and experiential education, open country workshops, and others. They conduct the courses as members of the Faculty of Education, Queens University, at Kingston, Ontario; much of the curriculum is rooted in Bob's Outward Bound associations.

■ Murray State University's Project Apollo in the western Kentucky TVA country. Under commission from the U.S. Office of Education and shepherded by Professor Bill Holt, this project has provided an Outward Bound–type course to more than 2,500 Upward Bound students and their teachers from schools in forty-two states and Puerto Rico.

■ Mann Adventures at Kentfield, California, established by the College of Mann. Conceived and created by Dan Campbell in his COBS-sponsored master of experiential education internship at the University of Colorado, Mann Adventures is a splendid model for a year-round community recreational/educational curriculum, for people of all ages, utilizing nature and the outdoors in an extraordinary variety of ways. It serves more than three thousand people annually, operating "on the theory that direct experience is the best teacher and nature the best text," and in close coordination with the college's natural and physical sciences, social science, and physical education departments.

■ The St. Louis story, where Project STREAM (St. Louis Regional Experiential Adventure Movement), the city's remarkable Outward Bound spin-off, services a metropolis-wide experiential education network on a multifaceted basis, and integrates it with a number of higher education institutions, including St. Louis University, Webster College, Washington

University, Augustana College, Florissant Valley Community College, and the University of Missouri at St. Louis.

BOB VANDER WILT was dean of students at Mankato College (now University) in Minnesota when Ronald Barnes came there to develop the educational plan for the proposed Minnesota Experimental City. "I had heard Ron on the subject several times," Vander Wilt remembered, "when one day I thought, How come we aren't doing anything with Outward Bound when we have a school right here in the state with headquarters an hour and a half up the road?" Vander Wilt decided to launch an experimental three-week orientation course run by MOBS at the start of the 1970–1971 year for twenty students, two faculty members, and two residential advisers involved in Mankato's Experimental Studies program. That experiment was rated a success, especially by Dr. Charles Lofy, who headed up Experimental Studies.

Out of Lofy and Vander Wilt's enthusiasm came a proposal for a graduate program offering a master of science degree in "studies in experiential education." OBI was sufficiently persuaded by the proposal, and by Alan Hale's advocacy, to make a grant of $10,000 from the DeWitt Wallace Fund, a trust newly created by a second million-dollar gift from Mr. Wallace, the income designated for new programs of national significance.

Launched in 1971, Mankato's Experiential Studies, the first graduate program of its kind, has proved a valuable source of leadership for the experiential education movement. In addition to its master's program, Mankato operates a training center for outdoor educators at Bemidji State University's Bald Eagle Center.

In a paper entitled "Growth and Crisis in a Developing Organization: Outward Bound," published in 1976, Joe Nold presented a model for the organizational development of an Outward Bound–type undertaking. Explaining why he believed such a model was needed, Joe pointed out that of nine Outward Bound adaptive programs launched with promise and enthusiasm in the late 1960s, seven had failed—despite having been run by dedicated, energetic, and competent people, and even though they had been effective. Most of the failures, he observed, had resulted not from poor programs but rather from poor management.

Nold realized that "we simply had not come to grips with the whole infrastructure of rooting an adaptive program. What was lacking were people with organization and administrative and political skills and a commitment to stabilize and institutionalize essentially sound programs." Outward Bound itself had a vacuum in middle-management areas that made it difficult, for example, to fill a program director post. Nold had asked himself if there was a way to develop "a group of people with leadership ability who had not only the philosophic, emotional, educational commitments that we all identify with so very deeply and fully and readily in Outward Bound, but also could make a commitment to go beyond that—to deal with the hard nuts-and-bolts issues that are really essential to the success of any of these programs over any but the shortest of time frames." This had been Joe's motivation for the Master of Education (M.E.) in Experiential Education Degree program jointly established by COBS and the School of Education at the University of Colorado at Boulder in 1973

The program was launched with a grant from the General Services Foundation in St. Paul, Minnesota, to develop a leadership cadre "in the new professional area of education we have come to call experiential education," with focus primarily on those who would translate and transfer the ideas and concepts of Outward Bound into other institutional settings. Enrollment was limited to twelve candidates. Each year there were more than fifty applicants, making this the most sought after of the School of Education's graduate programs.

As it ultimately evolved, the Colorado M.E. curriculum started with an outdoor-based summer semester that included an Outward Bound–instructing internship and a mountain expedition seminar. In the fall the candidates combined an urban intercultural experience, "The City as Classroom," with formal on-campus studies, including Nold's core course in organization and planning. For the spring semester candidates were given the option of a field internship or an academic inquiry. Both as interns and graduates, the M.E. members initiated successful Outward Bound–adaptive projects.

The success of the M.E. program was persuasive to several members of the School of Education faculty. Aware that many well-qualified applicants were being turned down each year due only to the strict enrollment limit, the group initiated a School of Education version separate from the Outward Bound label and cosponsorship, starting with the 1977–1978 year. For a year the two versions coexisted and in some measure cross-fertilized each other.

Only the university program is now extant. With the phasing out of his successful experiment, Nold could look back with a satisfied sense of achievement. "We've given people deeper insights into the philosophic and sociological underpinnings of Outward Bound. We arrived at a fairly systematic way of how the adaptive art can be applied within institutions that were not initially set up to run programs of an Outward Bound nature. I think we've legitimized management as a worthy profession in Outward Bound— and that's been a problem in that we're highly adventurous and action-oriented and see being at a desk as an inferior way to fulfill one's life commitment. I think we broke through that syndrome."

■ ■ ■

Finally, as we prepare this book for publication, two of the five wilderness schools, Colorado and Pacific Crest, have announced their intention to merge. The formation of a single western school has the unanimous support of both boards of trustees and has prompted the other three schools to actively consider their own strategic alternatives, including the prospect of a single, national wilderness school.

However these discussions conclude, they reflect the vitality and commitment with which the current leadership of Outward Bound, at all levels, intends to carry the principles of Kurt Hahn and the mission of OBUSA into the twenty-first century.

ACKNOWLEDGMENTS

✳

J osh and the whole Miner family wish to thank the board and staff of OBUSA. We are deeply appreciative of the encouragement and help we have received in producing this new edition of Outward Bound USA. The chapters added in this edition were developed during Josh's illness, and though he did not put pen to paper, he enjoyed the prospect of having the new edition published. There are many ways to expose people to Outward Bound, this is just one. And Josh's mission has always been to find ways to get the word of Outward Bound spread as widely as possible. Nonetheless, we offer particular thanks to Madeleine Eno and Katharine Wroth for their incisive and thorough depiction of Outward Bound's new initiatives and to Christian Kallen for his able assistance in editing and coordination of the project. Finally, we are especially grateful to Greg Farrell and Frances Rubacha, Chairman of Outward Bound USA, for their leadership in seeing the project through to completion.

Outward Bound USA would like to acknowledge Phebe Miner; Robert L. Gable; Phillips Academy, Andover, Mass.; and the Reverend William Sloane Coffin.

INDEX